Harmer John

AN UNWORLDLY STORY

By
HUGH WALPOLE

First Published 1926

Republished 2023

CONTENTS

BOOK III: HOW HE LEFT US

CHAPTER I

HOW HE CAME TO OUR TOWN ON A STORMY NIGHT AND FOUND UNEXPECTEDLY A HOME

O<small>N</small> a December night in the year 1906 a ferocious storm swept across our town.

There was nothing unusual in this: in Southern Glebeshire the winter is so often mild that the sea (impatient at the lassitude of the air) seems suddenly to rise, and to wish to beat its way across the narrow peninsula, to sweep the fields and hedges with its salt water: it calls the heavens to its assistance, the skies open, water pours out in torrents, the wind screams, shrieks, bellows—suddenly it knows that all is vanity, shrugs its hoary shoulders, creeps back muttering, lifts its hand to the sky in a gesture of cynical farewell, and lies, heaving, hoping for a more victorious day.

In the weeks around Christmas there is often such a storm, and, when other parts of England are showing gratitude sentimentally for the traditional snow, we recover from our torrents of rain to find the air warm, our skies mildly blue, the tower of our Cathedral stretching pearl-grey to heaven, and the Pol rumpled, with sunshine sliding to the sea.

But the storm while it lasts seems to shake our town to its very roots; you can almost feel wild hands tearing at the stones beneath your feet, rocking, rocking, rocking, hoping that at least one house may tumble. . . .

On this especial evening, December 22, 1906, Mrs. Penethen, a well-known and respected widow, was sitting in front of her kitchen fire, her skirt drawn up to her knees, her toes resting on a wool-worked cushion, in her old old house in Canon's Yard. The houses in Canon's Yard are, as every one knows, the oldest in Polchester, and Mrs. Penethen's was possibly the oldest in Canon's Yard, so you can guess from that how old it was.

Mrs. Penethen had lived in that house for forty years: she had come into that same kitchen with the brown splashes on the ceiling and the two big warming-pans on the right of the oven when she was a blushing bride of twenty; she had borne two children in the four-poster upstairs, she had nursed her husband in the weeks of his fever, had seen him laid in his coffin, had seen the coffin carried down the crooked black oak staircase—and now there she sat with her feet upon the fender reading *Thelma*, by Miss Marie Corelli, and wondering whether she would hear the Cathedral clock strike ten through the storm.

She was not alone in the kitchen. There were also with her a cat, a dog and a sharp-eyed girl. The cat and the dog were asleep, one on either side of the fire; the girl was sitting staring straight before her. Her hands were clasped, not tightly, on her lap.

Mrs. Penethen was accustomed that her daughter Judy, who was now twenty-one and should know better, should sit for hours, saying nothing, doing nothing, only her eyes and her rising, falling breasts moving.

Through the icy cold and black waters of *Thelma's* theatrical lumber her mind moved searching for her children. She was always carried away by anything that she read—that was why she liked novels, especially did they lead her into loves and countries that were strange to her. So she had, during the last two hours, been wandering with Thelma; her daughter's eyes now dragged her back. Fifteen years of married life and no child! All thought of one abandoned—and then Maude. Four more years and then Judy. One more year and the sudden fever, and poor old John with his brown eyes, his side-whiskers and the slight hunch on his left shoulder, shoved down into the ground!

The book slipped on to her lap. She stared into the crimson crystal coals. John! . . . His hand was on her arm, his soft voice like a lazy cat's begging her pardon for one of his so many infidelities. He always confessed to her. At first she had been unhappy; once she had run away for two nights, but he always told her that he loved her far the best, that she would outlast all the others. And she did. He was her lover to the very end, and kind and tender. . . . His brown eyes and the slight hunch on his shoulder.

He had been so sorry always for his infidelities, but he had never promised that there would not be another. He knew that he could not resist. . . . Here, in Polchester, there had never been a scandal because of him. Women loved him and kept their mouths shut. Not as she had loved him. Not as she had kept her mouth shut. Shut for forty years. That was why they called her a bitter old woman. She put up her hand to her hair. Perhaps she was bitter. Indifferent. She did not believe in people. Cats and monkeys, she had read somewhere. . . . Only in novels were they fine and noble.

She picked up *Thelma* again, saying as she did so:

"Do you think the Cathedral's struck ten, Judy?"

"Maybe," said the girl.

"It's time Maude was home!"

The girl said nothing.

"Mr. Fletch is bringing her back."

The girl said nothing.

She read half a page, and the storm forced her to put the book down again. She looked up, listening, rather like a dog sniffing, with her grey hair parted, her fine sharp nose, her cool chin, her long shapely neck wrinkled a little now above the white collar of her grey dress, her hands long and thin, one like a spread fan before the fire. The storm! One of the worst for years. Every window-pane and door in the old house was whining and shivering. The gusts of wind came down the chimney, bringing with them flurries of rain that spluttered upon the coals. She heard a door banging somewhere above in the house. She got up, the book falling on the floor. She listened. Dimly through all the noise she heard the Cathedral chimes strike ten. Strange how dim when the Cathedral was almost next to their own house-wall! She stood listening. Was there not another sound? Some one knocking? She turned back to the room:

"Did you hear anything, Judy?"

The girl shook her head impatiently. Mrs. Penethen took the lamp from the table, went to the kitchen door and opened it. She stood in the little dark space between the two doors, listening, the lamp raised. The storm had suddenly died down, running now like an animal whimpering about the room.

Now unmistakably there was a knock on the outer door—a pause, and then two more. "With her free hand she pulled back a bolt, turned a key and opened the door a little way. A man was standing there. She always afterwards remembered that he had seemed there in the darkness, lit only by gleams from the blowing street lamp, gigantic.

"Who is it?" she asked.

There was no answer. The figure stepped forward.

"What do you want?" she asked more sharply, drawing back. The scurrying rain was keen against her face, and the wind, rising once more, blew her clothes against her legs.

"I want some supper and a bed." He drew nearer to her, and she saw that he was carrying a bag. She realised instantly that his voice was a foreigner's.

"I have nothing here," she answered sharply.

"There is a card," he said, raising one arm, "in your window. It says 'Spare room for gentleman.'"

The storm was now shouting at them, trying to drive them in. "There is no room," she screamed against the storm. "Engaged."

Then she saw his face as he stepped back beneath the street lamp. It was the face of a boy. She had expected some foreigner, some hulking tramp threatening her. She was not afraid; she had only once or twice in all her life known fear. She knew how to protect herself. But now suddenly she realised that there was no need for protection—no need at all. Then she remembered that the voice had been soft, foreign, but an educated voice.

She moved back carefully into the house. "You had better come in for a moment out of this," she said, raising the lamp.

"Thank you," he said, and followed her in.

In the kitchen there was the light of the fire and the steady flame of the lamp set now on the table. She looked at him sharply, keenly, as she always looked at every one.

She saw now that he was not gigantic but tall indeed, well over six foot. Broad with it. Very broad in the oilskins that he was wearing, the collar turned up high and a seaman's oilskin cap on his head low down over his brow. The first thing that she noticed seriously was the child-like face shining with the rain through the oilskin. It was as though a boy had dressed in his father's clothes. But he was not a boy. Thirty, perhaps, or more. The mouth which turned up at the corners now, smiling, was a boy's mouth. The eyes were bright blue and clear. A lock of damp black hair straggled down beneath the cap, touching his eyebrow.

He made a movement with his hand to push it back.

"You'd better take that oilskin off," she said severely. "You're dripping."

"I don't hope," he said in a voice rather husky, with a foreign accent that puzzled her because it was strangely familiar, "that you'll think me rude for coming at this hour. My heartliest thanks for your courtesy."

He suddenly clicked his heels and bowed stiffly from the waist up in what she supposed was German fashion, in what at any rate was not English. Then he took off his oilskins, piling them on a chair. He was dressed in a decent dark-blue suit. He was certainly a very large man, as broad as he was tall. He was not fat, but his face was chubby, rosy and plump, his blue eyes staring with a little blinking bewilderment as though he were in truth a small boy suddenly wakened from sleep. He was a man though. He stood like a man, a little on the defensive, balanced stoutly on his legs, ready for any one. Perhaps he *was* a German, with his bow and his chubby cheeks, his blue eyes and his thick body. She didn't like Germans.

"You can rest here a minute or two if you care to," she said, "but you'd better be getting on soon if you're wanting a bed to-night." She looked at him, then added: "There's a hotel down in the town. In the market-place. Down the hill."

"Yes," he said, smiling at her, "I were there and all was engaged." He smiled so that she was compelled to smile too. She did not wish to. She was compelled. Then suddenly he saw Judy.

"My daughter," Mrs. Penethen said. "My name is Penethen."

He bowed, then said: "Hjalmar Johanson."

"I beg your pardon."

"Hjalmar Johanson. Svedish. Wait—I have a card."

He delved into his clothes and produced a very large pocket-book, then, after searching, a card. She read:

HJALMAR JOHANSON,
Gymnastic Instructor,
Certified Professor of Gymnastics, Stockholm.
Address: Amager Faelledvej II/5,
Kobenhavn.

"Kobenhavn?" she repeated.

"Yes. Copenhagen. That's what you call it in England. But I'm a Swede. Half—and half English."

"Half English?"

"Yes, my mother were English."

Having gone so far, accidentally as it were, without intending it, she felt that she must offer him some food and drink. Afterwards when, as she so often did, she looked back to the events of this evening, she wondered at her own actions.

Unlike her to admit a strange man into her house without a question! But it seemed to her that she was caught by some force stronger than herself, and before she realised it he had drawn up his chair to the table and was eating the cold ham and bread and butter and drinking the beer, talking, laughing, jolly as though he had known them a hundred years. And had he not? It seemed to her that in no time at all he was completely familiar to her. She recognised a dozen little tricks—the foreign accent, the fling back of the head, the sudden dramatic gesture (this so un-English and yet so known to her), the smile that had in some way a touching childish crookedness, the corners of the mouth turning up so that it was saucer-shaped, clown-like, or rather a child laughing so eagerly that the whole face must share. Through it all the clear, steady blue eyes were the most familiar of any. Her own steady, earnest gaze seemed to be returned to her by his, so that their eyes held separate converse, gravely, honestly, apart from the rest of his tale, like two old friends who meet happily in a crowded inn.

As he talked Judy too was caught, Judy who never thought of a man. She turned in her chair to look at him, fixing upon him that same incredulous questioning glance that she had for all humankind. She said nothing, she did not move; she might have been a figure painted in pale blue and grey against her dark chair.

Yes, he was half English, half Swede. His mother was English, a Glebeshire woman indeed—family Polruan, Annie Polruan.

She had gone out when quite a girl with some English people to service in Stockholm. There she had met his father. He was a farmer—not a good man, no. He had been thrown from a horse and killed when he, the boy, was sixteen. The only child. He had had to work for his mother then. Had been all sorts of things in Stockholm, barber's boy, waiter, sold newspapers, door-boy at a hotel, then because he was tall and strong he had been for some years an artist's model. He liked that. Oh yes, he loved pictures—never could see enough of them, would go to Italy one day, Florence, yes, and Rome. Then an artist had been good to him and advised him because of his strength to go in for gymnasium, to be a physical instructor, or a masseur. Yes, there were many in Stockholm. He had gone through the course in Stockholm, doing it well. In the middle of it his mother had died. Yes, he had missed her terribly. It was his first great loneliness. He was so lonely, although he had many friends, that so soon as he had finished his course he went to Christiania. He was there for a year teaching gymnastics and doing a special medical course. Then he went to Copenhagen. Yes, the capital of Denmark. A very nice town. He did very well there, teaching exercises, making fat gentlemen and ladies thin, instructing schools. He made some money too—quite a bit. He was restless. His great ambition was to go to England and see where his mother had lived, and afterwards, perhaps Italy . . . Donatello. . . .

Mrs. Penethen asked whether that was a place.

No, it was a man. A sculptor. Who made statues. Not the greatest, perhaps, but the kindest, the most human, the one to be loved most. . . .

He pulled himself up. He was talking too long. But now he was here. In the town that his mother had always spoken of, with the Cathedral. He would perhaps live here. Make fat ladies thin, teach the children to be strong—and he had wonderful exercises. . . . He stopped again. After all, if he were to find a bed in the town. . . .

It was at this moment that Mrs. Penethen said that after all she *had* a spare room. She had been speaking the truth when she had said that she had no bed. This room she did not let save to some one who would take it for a period, several months. But on such a night—and it was late—She was conscious of Judy's sharp gaze. Yes, she was being impulsive, she who always acted so cautiously, but this man was honest, she would wager her life on it. And his boy's face. She *could* not turn him out into that rain. She had the room. It would not take five minutes to make it ready. But some consciousness, perhaps, of her unusual impetuosity made her voice grim as she said to him:

"You had better come and see it: you may not like it."

She picked up the lamp, raised it and walked ahead of him. He got up, pulling his big body together.

"It will have to be a bad bed not to be right enough for such a night," he said, laughing. He went with his bag after her up the dark stairs, having to bend his head beneath the door-post.

When they had gone the girl rose from her chair and stood in the middle of the room, listening. Her stare as she waited, one hand on her hip, was ironical, and at the same time rather pathetic, as though she had lost her way, wondered of whom she should ask her direction, but would have no real belief in the security of the answer.

"Perhaps it's Miss Midgeley," she said aloud. But it was not Miss Midgeley. There were the sounds of a key fitting in the lock, of the door swinging back, of voices, and then three persons came into the room, two men and a girl.

The girl was at once the most noticeable, being quite remarkably beautiful. Her beauty shone through the ugly waterproof that reached to her heels, and in spite of the common cartwheel of a hat burdened with a multitude of cheap pink roses. She did not know how to dress, that was evident, but at once with her very entrance into the room she had taken the pins out of the hat and the hat off her head and was shaking the shabby roses in front of the fire, and so revealed her beautiful fair hair, masses of it, piled and crowned on the top of her tiny head. She was small and slight, perfectly proportioned, and giving the effect of being for ever "on tiptoe for a flight," as though at any moment she might be discovered to have wings and float out into the air, vanishing, a speck of white and gold, into the blue sky. As she turned from the fire to speak to her companions it could be seen that she was happy, excited, pleased. Her ulster had been thrown off and she stood there in her rather common pink dress, her bosom heaving, her eyes dancing, her feet still moving to some enchanting strain.

"Oh, Judy, it was heaven!" she cried. "You should have been there!"

The two men were watching her each in his own way. The one was a big man, fat and fleshy, his face naturally red, turning in the veins around the nose to purple, the eyes small, the eyebrows so lightly marked as scarcely to be seen. He was jauntily dressed in a suit of light grey, and he wore a purple tie with a big horse-shoe pin. He had fat hands with short stumpy fingers. His air was genial but, for some reason to-night, a little uneasy—his age anything between fifty-five and sixty. His clothes fitted his stout limbs too tightly, just as the flower in his coat and the pin in his tie were too large. His companion was a pale, rather ascetic man, with a gentle smile and a courteous manner; nearly obsequious, he nevertheless gave the impression that he had his own private power. His name was Reuben Fletch. He wore a black tie and a neat pair of black shoes.

He was of a well-known Polchester family, had been born and bred in Polchester and had lived there all his life. He had lodged now at Mrs. Penethen's for a number of years, was a solicitor by profession and a miser above all. He was said to be extremely able, to know neither conscience nor morals, and to have much power over important individuals in our town. He was forty-five years of age and unmarried.

The two men looked at the girl, the eyes of the stout man narrowing until they had almost vanished, and a very faint smile hovering about his lips. Fletch stared, his face immobile.

The girls as they stood together offered an interesting contrast. It was plain that they were sisters, and that they were Mrs. Penethen's daughters; they had, both of them, something of her refinement in the sharp-pointed noses, the delicate ears and the white shapely necks; but all the life and colour seemed to have been stolen by the one girl from the other—stolen because Maude, the elder, had the air of a victorious captor, and in her lovely shining hair, her gleaming eyes, the soft colour of her cheeks, the grace and movement of her body, she seemed to proclaim her contempt for, her superiority over, the thin little lustreless girl at her side. Lustreless was what poor Judy was, her complexion pale, her mouth frowning, her whole body uneasy and awkward in its pose. A plain girl, even were Maude not there—plainer by far in contrast and from the power of some secret resentment and anger that she was feeling.

Maude turned round to the men. "Make yourself comfortable, Mr. Hogg, do. You know my sister Judy? . . . Where's mother?"

"Upstairs," Judy said, staring at the two men as though she hated them.

"She's not gone to bed? I want my cocoa. You know where the whisky is, Mr. Fletch. I'm sure Mr. Hogg would like a glass."

"Mother will be down in a moment," Judy said. "She's showing a new lodger his room."

"A new lodger!" Maude cried. "At this time of night!—And mother said she wasn't going to let the red room anyway. As though we hadn't enough with Miss Midgeley as it is—"

"I know. She didn't mean to let it. But he came in out of the rain, and mother took a fancy to him. He's a foreigner—"

"A foreigner!"

"Yes. A Norwegian or Swede or something. And he's about eight feet tall."

Judy threw all this out scornfully as though she had contempt for them all but wished to see what effect this news would have upon them.

Not very much apparently. The two men were seated at the table helping themselves to the whisky, and Maude broke out:

"Oh well, bother it all anyway. I want my cocoa. It was a *lovely* dance, wasn't it, Mr. Hogg? Didn't you *love* every minute of it?"

She danced a few steps and then stopped abruptly as the door opened and her mother came in, followed by the stranger.

It was strange to observe the effect that at once he made upon all of them. Perhaps Judy alone of all that group observed it. His height had something to do with the challenge that he always presented to any company that he confronted, but it was not only his height. No one, save possibly Miss Midgeley, quite defined it during all that time that he was in Polchester. Mrs. Penethen had *her* version, Mary Longstaffe had *hers*, Fletch certainly had his, Ronder his, Cole his—all of them different. Why, to this very moment, so many years afterwards, when it is all a legend, his arrival, his deeds, the after effects, that exact impression of his personality is still hotly debated. "All I know is," Mrs. Penethen herself used to say (she died in 1917), "you couldn't be the same as you were before he came in, none of you. You fell in love with him at once or you couldn't bear him. And I fell in love with him. Yes, that very first wet night when he was sitting at my table eating my bread and ham.

" 'I've got a room,' I said, just as though it were some one else speaking the words behind me, for I assure you I had had no more intention of letting that room that night than I had of sailing through the ceiling on wings. But there it was, from the first I couldn't resist him!"

On this present occasion Mrs. Penethen saw the new arrivals and said shortly, "Oh, so you've got back. Why, Mr. Hogg, good evening!" He got up and she shook hands with him, not overpleased at his presence it seemed. "Pray make yourself at home" (here just a touch of irony perhaps). "Oh, let me introduce. This is Mr. Johnson from Copenhagen. My daughter Maude, Mr. Johnson. Mr. Fletch, Mr. Hogg. Have a drop of whisky, Mr. Johnson, I'm sure you need it."

Johanson shook hands with every one, clicking his heels and bending from the waist. That little habit may seem unimportant in itself, but it had its later seriousness, as it led certain people in our town to speak of him as "that German" at a time when Germans were not very popular with us because of Hoffmann's proposed Town Hall.

He sat down very comfortably at the table next to Samuel Hogg, and was very soon telling that gentleman all about himself, his mother and father, Stockholm and Copenhagen, his hopes and his ambitions, it being always his simple way to believe that every one must be interested in hearing about himself just as he was interested in everything that they had to tell *him*. And Hogg sat with a smile, drinking his whisky.

From the first moment, however, eagerly though he talked, Johanson was conscious of Maude Penethen. He could not but be conscious of her with her wonderful hair, her perpetual movement about the room, her cries and laughter, her little coquetries and brazenries. And she also was conscious of him.

"Mother, I want my cocoa. Never mind the men, mother, they can look after themselves. Ladies first. Oh, mother, it was heavenly. I danced *every* dance. Such a shame it had to be over so early. Lady St. Leath looked in for a moment, mother. Yes, she did. She spoke to Miss Cardigan and asked how the Club was getting on. She made us a little speech and said how glad she was we were all enjoying ourselves. Oh, she looked all right, but a little *dowdy*, you know, like she always is. She doesn't know how to dress a bit, and they say her husband would give her anything she'd ask for. Oh yes, and Canon Ronder came, just for ten minutes, and danced with Miss Cardigan. Oh, mother, you *would* have laughed! He's like a tub and she's so skinny. He spoke to me, too, and asked how you were. And I was much the prettiest girl there. I'm sure I was. Wasn't I, Mr. Hogg?"

"Indeed you were, Miss Penethen," he answered, smiling at her.

"Well, you shouldn't say so even though you thought it, and you shouldn't think it even though you were it," said her mother. "It's not for you to say."

Maude laughed, drinking her cocoa, balancing on the edge of her chair and stealing glances at Johanson. Suddenly he looked directly at her. Their eyes met. She sprang up from her chair and danced about, flinging her arms around her mother, then rushing at Judy and kissing her, then pausing near Mr. Fletch.

"You never danced with me once," she said.

He looked at her full with his round black eyes. "You never asked me," he said.

"Oh, I did! I'm sure I did! Hundreds of times. Never mind! There's another on Tuesday—"

Samuel Hogg got up. "I must be going, Mrs. Penethen. It's late. Thank you for your hospitality."

She did not try to prevent him, but said good night to him gravely. Maude saw him to the door, and there was some giggling and laughter, some low-voiced words before the outer door closed.

"I'm sure it's bed-time for everybody," said Mrs. Penethen.

But even then the evening was not concluded. The farther door opened, and a little woman with a wrinkled face looked in:

"Oh, I beg your pardon, but could I have another candle, Mrs. Penethen? Mine's about done."

She stepped into the kitchen. Her face was a map of wrinkles, she wore a red woollen jacket and a grey skirt. She was just like a robin. Johanson happened to be near the door. She looked up and saw him.

"Good heavens!" she cried.

Maude burst into laughter. "Oh, I can't help it. . . . I beg your pardon. . . . But the difference in height. . . . Oh dear. . . . Mr. Johnson so tall and Miss Midgeley—!"

It *was* amusing! Mrs. Penethen herself smiled as she said:

"Miss Midgeley, this is Mr. Johnson. He has taken a room here."

She looked up at him whimsically. "It will never do for us to go about together," she said drily. "The whole town will laugh."

He smiled. "They was always saying when I were a boy that I'd be a giant. I were as big when I were fourteen as I am now. There are plenty taller than me in Denmark."

No one had anything to say to this, so they all prepared to go to bed. Only Maude at the last, as he stood aside for her to pass, said, smiling up at him:

"Good night, Mr. Johnson. I do hope the bed will be long enough!"

CHAPTER II

THE REVEREND TOM AT HOME AND ABROAD

THE steepest street in our town, and one of the steepest in Southern England, is Orange Street, and nearly at the top of Orange Street, just below the Monument, is St. Paul's Church. The Rector of St. Paul's at this time was the Reverend Thomas Longstaffe. He had been Rector of St. Paul's for ten years now, coming to Polchester in 1897, Jubilee Year, the very week that Archdeacon Brandon died so tragically.

He was a widower, about fifty years old when he arrived, and with him a daughter of eighteen, Mary, a very pretty girl, the adored of his heart, his only child.

When he had been four years in Polchester a terribly tragic thing occurred. Mary Longstaffe was a very bright, clever girl, modern in her ideas, knowing many things that were entirely beyond the average Polchester young lady of that time. She even talked of going up to Oxford, which was thought very daring of her by Mrs. Sampson, Mrs. Preston and other ladies in the Precincts. The Precincts ladies in fact did not like her, called her fast, and did not invite her to their houses. In any case, the Cathedral set always kept to itself in our town, and Tom Longstaffe, being only Rector of St. Paul's and not even a Minor Canon, would be, of course, outside it. A certain Major Waring, a retired Indian officer, lived in our town and had an only son who was at Oxford. Lance Waring fell violently in love with Mary Longstaffe, and throughout one summer they were always together, riding, playing tennis, walking, and dancing. Early in the September of that year he was thrown from his horse and killed. In October it was known that Mary Longstaffe was going to have a baby, and that Lance Waring was its father.

What horrified every one so terribly was that she stayed calmly on in our town for several months after this was known. She seemed to have no shame at all, and walked up and down the High Street and took her usual seat in the Cathedral just as though she were like every one else. Of course every one cut her, every one except old Mrs. Combermere, who was eccentric and just did things to show her eccentricity, and young Lady St. Leath, whose brother had married the daughter of Samuel Hogg the publican, once owner of a low public-house down in Seatown, who was "queer," therefore, in any case, and the perpetual sorrow and cross of the old Dowager's life.

Mary Longstaffe had stayed in Polchester until Christmas of that year, and after that she vanished. It was rumoured vaguely from time to time that she lived in London, that she had a son, that she lived by writing for the newspapers; in any case she was not seen again in Polchester.

On the whole there had been considerable sympathy felt for poor Tom Longstaffe. He had always been a popular man: she was his only child, and he must be very lonely now without her. It all came of the girl having no mother and picking up all these advanced ideas. It was as likely as not that she had become one of these Suffragettes about whom now in London every one was talking.

Yes, the Reverend Tom was lonely, very lonely indeed. He was now, in 1907, sixty years of age, and for the five last years he had lived quite alone save for an old family servant. He was a short, thick-set man with a face red-brown, the colour of a pippin apple, grey hair, and a good strong chin. He was a man who adored sport of every kind and was never indoors when he could be out of it. This was the man known to most of the Polcastrians, a jolly, red-faced, kind-hearted sportsman with not too much of the parson about him.

Within this man there was another, a man deeply religious and passionately affectionate. He was never much of a reader, his sermons were so simple as to be called by many people childish, and he never spoke of his religion unless it were his duty to do so; it was, nevertheless, at the root of his whole life.

He was also, outwardly, nothing of a sentimentalist—nevertheless he had had in earlier years two friendships, and afterwards his love for his wife and his daughter, and these few relationships had been passionate in their hidden intensity. Of his two friends one had died and the other had married; his wife had endured two years of agony from cancer before her death; his daughter's tragedy was common knowledge to every one. What he had suffered through these things no one save his daughter knew—nevertheless here he was, the cheeriest and merriest clergyman in Polchester.

The Rectory was a square grey-roofed building standing back from Orange Street and having a lawn and two old trees in front of it. To the left of it and almost touching it was the church, and to the right of it Hay Street, where was the famous Polchester High School for Girls.

It was a jolly old Rectory with solid, square rooms, plenty of space and light, and a fine view over Polchester from the attic windows.

On a certain day in January 1907 Tom Longstaffe suffered from an agonising temptation, and alone in his study on that grey January morning he wrestled with this temptation, knowing in his heart that he would be beaten by it.

He had that morning found on his breakfast table the following letter from his daughter:

11 GOWER STREET, LONDON, W.C.,
January 3, 1907.

DARLING FATHER—I am coming home. Podge and I can endure being away from you no longer. I think I could have held out a while more but for your last letter, which, for all its pretended cheeriness, gave the whole show away. If you miss me so much and I miss you so much, aren't we sillies, when life is so short, to keep away from one another? And all for what? All for a lot of chattering old women about whose opinion we neither of us care a scrap. More serious than that is the one that if I come back to live with you I may damage your congregation. They may stay away because of me. Well, if they do I can but go away again. But why should they? It isn't as though they didn't know all about it and haven't known for the last five years. And it isn't as though I were going to make myself prominent in any way. They'll never see either Podge or myself if they don't want to. You shall give them their tea and listen to their outpourings just as you have always done. I shan't expect to be asked to any of their houses, and you must go to them just as you have always done. I shall make that quite plain as soon as I arrive. They'll be used to me in no time, and only pity you and love you the more because you have such a heavy burden to bear! (Isn't that the phrase?) And meanwhile, oh *meanwhile*, darling Daddy, we shall have one another! Just think of that! Morning, noon and night we shall be together and shall be wondering all the time what we have been doing to have wasted five precious years of our lives away from one another!

It is true that I have Podge, and that he is everything a mother can want in a son, but he isn't you—and I need you both. I do indeed. And so it shall be.

As to finances, we shall manage quite well. I'm becoming quite an authority on Housing questions, the Way the Poor Live (or Don't Live), Women's Suffrage and anything else you like. My articles are the astonishment of economic London!

After all this you will expect to see your daughter with ink (instead of vine-leaves) in her hair and holes in her cotton frocks. Wait! Only you wait! And you shan't wait very long either. Whether you like it or no, I am coming—so Prepare! Your always loving

MARY.

This was the letter that caused him to pace up and down his study, his head a little forward, his hands closed behind his back, his short, rather stumpy body being moved forward in jerks as though by the action of some secret spring within him. As he moved, all his past life seemed to swing around him, up and down through the bare study, bare save for his untidy table with its crucifix, its piles of letters and papers, his arm-chair, a worn sofa—bare and grey in the ugly January light.

All his life, which seemed to him now in retrospect to have consisted only of one brief moment, had been engaged in this same war between his affections and his duty. There had been that first friendship made by him at Oxford—and he saw instantly a succession of pictures of English summers and bathes and cricket-matches and long walks in dusky evenings, an Italian holiday, a trip to Egypt—and how surprised they had both been by the emotion that after a while rushed in and filled their hearts, and how he, with his English public-school training, had been afraid of sentiment and feeling and had felt that his love for his friend was stepping in front of his love for God, and how he had gradually withdrawn . . . and his friend had married and that had been the end. Then came his meeting with the woman whom he married, his passionate adoration of her, her quieter affection for him, some aloofness that she had, something that he never quite touched. And then in the very middle of this, when his married life and his religious life seemed so utterly to absorb him body and soul, the sudden upspringing of that strange friendship with Charles Upcott, a man of over forty, learned, a scholar, grave, an indoor man, nothing in common—and yet this sudden friendship that flamed up in a day and burnt with a steady fire until Upcott's death, a year after their first meeting, from pleurisy. Christina, his wife, had seemed to understand this friendship and fostered it in every way. She said that it was what he needed, smiling at him in that quiet, strange, aloof way that removed her sometimes so far from him. . . .

Here, too, he had doubted and felt that he was in the wrong. It was not only the emotional quality, felt both by Upcott and himself, that his training told him was weak and sentimental between men (although his soul told him that it was not), it was also that Upcott was a declared and convinced atheist, gentle towards Longstaffe's beliefs because he loved him, but showing with every word and movement that he held them to be childish and incredible. So once again Longstaffe's heart was in the way of his duty, but the matter was abruptly settled for him by Upcott's sudden death.

He recalled now as he paced his study the grief and agony that that death had meant to him. Had he before or afterwards known such pain and loneliness? No, he must confess to himself that even his wife's death had not afflicted himself so intolerably. There had never been a day, perhaps, when he had not thought of Upcott, seeing his hatchet-jawed face, his dreaming student's eyes, his long shambling body, heard the echo of his little stammer, felt the warm touch of his hand. . . .

And then he passed to his wife's agony and death—her patience, her courage, her wonderful, wonderful courage! He could see her lying, her eyes lost in distance, assuring him that she was not in any pain, asking him about the trivial things of the day. . . . Christina! Christina! Christina! He said that name aloud as though by the whisper of it he might bring her for a moment back to him. But in vain, in vain, as it had always been in vain. She had always eluded him, loving him as a traveller loves a town in which he likes to stay for a moment before passing on—her eyes had been fixed on other destinies.

And so there had been left to him only Mary. Mary had been everything to him, mother, daughter, brother, sister, friend. From the very first, long before she could speak, she had seemed to understand him exactly. They had been such companions as never were! He had taught her to run, to swim, to bowl quite a decent fast ball, to ride, to shoot. She had been clever, too, far cleverer than he had ever been, and was soon reading books that were far beyond him. He had sent her to a splendid school for girls in the Midlands; the wrench of her departures had been terrible, but then their meetings, the holidays, the fun, the walks, the games, the companionship.

And then—the awful tragedy. Just as she was growing into perfect womanhood. Once again his heart had confronted his duty. He learnt in one fierce, blinding flash that did you love enough nothing mattered—God Himself must turn and bow His head before human love at its most intense. He fought for her like a tiger, he would have gone with her to the end of the world. She would not have it, seeing truly that his Polchester work was the only thing to keep him sane.

His love of God saved him. In his faith there were no complexities, no doubts, no fears. God was there and loved His children. God was sorry for Mary's sin, but had forgiven her and was caring for her. Again and again he felt that he must leave Polchester and go to her; he did, of course, go up to London and visit her whenever it was possible, but the loneliness as the years passed grew harder and harder to bear. And yet he knew that he must not leave Polchester. His duty was there, the only work that his older years were likely to have for him. Oh! how he longed to have her back! How every room in the house called for her; how old Hephzibah, who had nursed her from her birth, longed for her; how at night he would rise from his bed and pace his room fighting his desire to ask her to return.

And yet he must not. He could not ask her to face the ostracism and social banning that there would be. He did not know, too, how he himself could endure it, what his own anger might not be. Her name was never mentioned by any one in Polchester save by Mrs. Combermere, a rather eccentric widow who lived with her dogs in an old house in the Precincts, but outside the Precincts life and social code. She seemed to be Mary's only friend. And yet it might not be so. When they saw Mary and realised her sweetness and goodness they would surely forgive that earlier fault. How could they help it? he said, looking up at her photograph on the mantelpiece.

And at that look he yielded. She shall come back. For a little while at any rate. At the very thought of having her again in that house his heart leapt with joy and his eyes filled with tears.

He sat down at the table and then again paused. There was another side to her return, a side involving wider and more public issues.

I have said already that the Rector of St. Paul's, unless he were a man of very exceptional talent and intellect, would be by necessity outside the Cathedral politics.

Tom Longstaffe was neither in talent nor intellect an exceptional man, and during all his ten years in Polchester he had never on one occasion been asked to dine with the Dean, nor had any of the Cathedral ladies called on his daughter after their arrival. Old Bishop Purcell had indeed invited him to luncheon at Carpledon and he had gone and had spent a most happy afternoon, but within six months Bishop Purcell was dead and Bishop Franklin reigned in his stead. Bishop Franklin had not the personality of his predecessor, who was a saint of God if ever one walked this sinful earth. Bishop Franklin was a good man, but not too good, and his thoughts were for ever with the Kings of Israel, whose slightest habits and most abstruse customs were more real to him than were his wife (an invalid) and two dried-up, pigeon-breasted daughters.

As to the Archdeacons, Witheram was growing an old man now and was nearly always out of Polchester busied with visitations throughout Glebeshire;

the other Archdeacon, Brodribb, who had succeeded Brandon in '97, was a man without any colour of personality, agreeable, negligible, interested in Shakespeare Texts and Elizabethan dramatists, a man who did his duty, was easily influenced, and was something of a hypochondriac.

No, it was not these men who directed the Cathedral politics of our town. These were directed by two others, one the Rev. Ambrose Wistons, Vicar of the church of Pybus St. Anthony, a village a few miles out of Polchester, one the Rev. Frederick Ronder, Canon of the Cathedral. It may seem strange that some of the Cathedral policy should have been directed from a small village outside our town, but this was not the first occasion on which Pybus St. Anthony had played an important part in the affairs of the Cathedral.

It had been the custom for a number of years past that the Vicar of Pybus St. Anthony should be a man of mark, and promotion to positions of great importance had often arisen out of that humble appointment. Ambrose Wistons had been asked to come to Pybus with the quite definite understanding that he would play a large part in the Cathedral's affairs, the larger perhaps because he was not actually one of the Cathedral staff.

Wistons had been at Pybus now for ten years, and he had made his personality felt throughout the whole of Southern England. He had on several occasions refused advancement; he was a man who kept his counsel, had few intimate friends, and was feared as much as he was loved. Himself was fearless, as every one knew, and was utterly single-minded.

He was perhaps the greatest preacher in the whole of England at that time, and Polcastrians crowded his village church on Sunday evenings. On the three or four occasions during the year when he preached in the Cathedral, the Cathedral nave was packed. People went perhaps as much for sensation as for eloquence. He seemed to love to shock the orthodox; he was a modern of the moderns, as his books showed, and to simple minds like Tom Longstaffe's many of his utterances were treason.

"He seems to hate the Cathedral," Tom Longstaffe said, pacing his study. "He would pull it down if he could. He says that it stands in the way of Christ. And yet there are times when he seems to hate Christ too, or at least His Divinity. Surely we are not meant to destroy the Bible utterly, as Wistons would have us do. He is a terrible danger here!" And yet the man's courage drew him and attracted him as nothing else in Polchester did. But Wistons never noticed him, although they had met at many ecclesiastical gatherings. Wistons never did more than nod to him sternly. He never stopped to speak to him as did Ryle, or Bentinck-Major, or Martin. He did not want, it seemed, to know him. He went with his dry, wizened, almost sarcastic, spare face up and down the city intent on his own affairs, wanting nothing for himself, not even the love and affection of his fellow-men.

Very different was this other, Canon Ronder. Ronder was now a man of some fifty years of age, fat like a tub, with a red, jolly face, smart and even elegant in appearance (a difficult thing for a stout clergyman to be), and living with an elderly aunt in a comfortable house in the Precincts. Ronder was certainly at this time in 1907 the most important man in Polchester. There was no pie whatever, lay or ecclesiastical, in which he had not some finger.

"He is surely," said Longstaffe to himself, "the most popular human being in Polchester, and quite naturally so. He is hail-fellow with every one. He brings the Cathedral really into contact with the town, and you will see Shandon the Mayor and Sharpe the Town-clerk as often there as Bentinck-Major or Brodribb—more often perhaps. Every one must like him—he is so genial and kindly and remembers every one, and is ready to listen to anybody's story."

And yet every one did not like him. Although no open breach had come it was quite certain that the town was divided into two parties, the Wistons party and the Ronder party, and the Wistons party did not hesitate to say terrible things about Ronder—that he was false, money-grabbing, sycophantic, would sell his mother, if he had one, to increase his personal comfort. On the other hand, the Ronder party said that Wistons was an atheist, a socialist, propagator of immoral opinions, a scientist before he was a Christian, an iconoclast, and so on.

The Ronder party were all for the development of the town. They wanted a better railway station, a new town hall, a golf links, a racecourse, a theatre, two more hotels—heaven knows what! Their argument was that our town with its Cathedral should be the most important in Glebeshire, that it *could* be if only the Polcastrians would wake up and realise that we were in a new world now, the Victorian era was, thank God, over and the Boer War had shaken us all up.

And the Wistons party retorted that we were forgetting God altogether, that the Cathedral was becoming a temple of Mammon, that the very Canons were concerned in shady money transactions that no honest man would touch, that officials in the position of Ronder and Bentinck-Major ought not even to know such men as Samuel Hogg and Jim Curtis.

To which the Ronder party retorted that the clergymen of the town ought to know every one, that the fortunes of the town and the Cathedral were intimately connected, that the Cathedral was badly in need of funds, that restoration of one of the Towers was necessary, that there were many other things to be done, that it was all very well to have fine ideas about the Four Gospels and be a professor of the very latest Higher Criticism, but where was Higher Criticism if one of the Western Towers fell down?

And so on. And so on.

Of all this Tom Longstaffe had been, until the last two months, only a spectator. Then suddenly, only a month or so ago, Miss Ronder had asked him to dinner, and he had found there the old Dean and his wife, the Bentinck-Majors and the Ryles—all the Cathedral set. Shortly after that Ronder had called upon him about tea-time, had been very jolly, had played on his piano, had admired a little bronze that he had picked up once in Rome, and had finally said that they did not see enough of one another, and that they must all pull together now for the good of the town and the Cathedral. This surprising visit had been followed by an invitation to dine at Bentinck-Major's (every one knew that Bentinck-Major was a tool of Ronder), and then, most amazing of all, he had received an invitation to join the Shakespeare Reading Society, that society that had for its members only the most exclusive part of the Cathedral set.

The Cathedral had just discovered Tom Longstaffe—that was clear: or at any rate that section of Cathedral society that claimed Ronder for its leader. It would be idle to pretend that Longstaffe was not pleased. He had had a very lonely five years; he wished, as do most of us, to be liked by his fellows; above all, he adored the Cathedral. He had always felt that he was kept away from the Cathedral, not so much by a set of social snobs as rather by some force in the Cathedral itself. He had seen no way by which he might come closer to it. There was, it is true, a third party in the town who would have welcomed him to its arms, the party headed years ago triumphantly by old Archdeacon Brandon, the old-fashioned party who wanted everything to be as it always had been, who hated any change whether in town or Cathedral; but that party was dying, if it were not already dead, and consisted only of a few old men and women who may have had some rightful place in the world before the Boer War, but certainly had none anywhere now.

No, Tom Longstaffe was touched and pleased. He would rather, it is true, that it had been Wistons who had made some advance to him. He was not sure of Ronder, there was something about the man that he did not trust. . . . Nevertheless . . .

He at once accepted the invitation to join the Shakespeare Reading Society and received by return the notice that on January 18 the play of *Hamlet* would be read at the Precentor's house at 8.15 sharp, and that he had been cast for the part of Guildenstern.

And if Mary returned? Well, good-bye to the Cathedral set. Not that it mattered. For himself he did not care at all, and if he had Mary with him the whole world might cut him dead for all that he minded. But if God intended him to play a greater part in the town, to take more share in the Cathedral's affairs? Well, if God intended that, He certainly also intended that he should love his own dear daughter—and, at the thought of her, at the mere glimpse of her smiling down at him from the mantelpiece, he sat at his table once again and wrote to her saying that she was right, that he could not bear to be apart from her any longer, that she must come as soon as possible. . . .

Early in the afternoon of that dank day the mists came up from the Pol and wreathed themselves about the town. Longstaffe lit the gas in his study soon after he had finished his solitary luncheon and sat down and tried to work. He had much to do, and had not intended to go outside the house that day. But the thoughts needed for the prefatory letter to next month's parish magazine would not come. This was never in any case an easy task for him; he certainly had not, of all men, the pen of a ready writer; and to-day the face of his daughter slipped in between himself and the paper and danced bewitchingly before him. And something else too. He did not know, he could not say. Perhaps he was not well. In any case, this fog disturbed him, filling the room with a strange brown, smoky light, and if he looked across at the window the bare-armed trees beyond were hidden and then revealed, suddenly peering in at him like skinny witches.

It was as though the whole world were smouldering in a cold, billowy, smoky fire, and then, as though at the word of a mysterious command beyond the window, it cleared and there was a cold blue sky and the limbs of the trees were stark grey; only in his room the brown mist still smouldered.

He would go out. He had done enough for to-day—enough, that is nothing, only that letter to his daughter which as he posted it in the Orange Street letter-box surely changed his life for him.

He went slowly up the High Street through a ghostly town in which doors closed, bells rang, voices murmured, walls slid forward and back again, colours in windows flamed and were veiled, houses leapt from the mist like centaurs and plunged then into a lake of grey.

Almost at one time he thought he had lost his way, and then the Arden Gate was before him and the Cathedral hung like a gigantic ship sailing through opalescent mist. Near to the Arden Gate, on the very edge of the Cathedral Green, a man was standing. Longstaffe ran into him, apologised, stopped and looked up. The man was like a statue, and, in that mist, gigantic. A hand was laid on Longstaffe's shoulder and a voice, kindly, foreign, said, "My carelessness. But it is difficult in this mist. I have heard of your terrible English fogs, and now I see one. Could you tell me kindly if one may go into the Cathedral at this time?"

"Yes," said Longstaffe, "certainly. Evensong is at half-past three. You have nearly an hour before that."

"My heartliest thanks."

Something kept Longstaffe there. "You are a stranger? Can I help you in any way?"

"Oh, I have been in your town two weeks and into your Cathedral every day. But there are hours—once they wouldn't let me go in and another time I must leave before I wished!"

It came into Longstaffe's mind then that he had heard something; some one had told him about a Scandinavian, a Dane or a Swede, who had come to the town, and intended to start a gymnasium or something of the sort. This might be he.

He liked the man's kindly face, and something husky and boy-like in the voice. But it was not his business. "Nobody will disturb you in the Cathedral for at least an hour," he said. "It will be too dark for you to see much, I'm afraid."

"You are very kind," the stranger bowed. "My heartliest thanks."

But he did not move, and stood beaming down at Longstaffe as though he expected him to speak.

"Are you staying long in Polchester?" Longstaffe asked, feeling foolish.

"For a long time as I hope. I am half English, you know. My mother was from this county." He felt in his pocket and produced a card. "I am intending to start some gymnasia here. There are none in your town. I like this town. I like your people. I have already many friends. I am very happy here."

"I am delighted to hear it," said Longstaffe. "It's a very good idea, a gymnasium. Just what we want."

"Ah, you think so. I am so glad. I think so. Mrs. Penethen think so and her daughters, and Miss Midgeley and all my friends. I have some money that I have saved, and I have seen two rooms that is very cheap, and an old sailor who will help, and his son who is very strong. Exercises is very good for everybody—for the muscles, for the heart, for the brain. It clears up everything and makes every one happy."

This was a subject close to Longstaffe's heart. "You are right, Mr.—Mr.—" he consulted the card—"Mr. Johanson. I wish you very good fortune." He found a card of his own. "If I can be of any help to you—" His hand was gripped.

"Very kind indeed. My heartliest thanks." The man bowed and strode off into the mist.

Longstaffe stood there for a moment, then turned up the Precincts.

CHAPTER III

FROM GABRIELLE MIDGELEY'S DIARY—I

*F*EB. *7, 11.30 P.M.*—. . . which isn't what I meant to say to her in the least, but she aggravates me so intensely sometimes that I say what I don't mean at all. The truth is that, unless I'm very careful, I shall be in another year or two nothing but a cross, sour old woman. It was because of my fear of this, I suppose, that I stopped this Diary six months back. What's the use of recording the thoughts, fears, likes and dislikes of a bad-tempered old maid whom nobody wants and who, thank God, herself wants nobody. I meant never to open this shabby old book again. But I have a new reason—not a bad one either. At any rate it isn't myself this time.

The strange thing is that I'm getting back some of the hot temper and nasty liveliness of fifteen years ago. Who ever would have supposed it? Fifteen years' superb indifference and now suddenly I want to wring Maude's beautiful neck until her head's round the other way! And the difference isn't in Maude. She's always been a pig. The difference is in myself. Yes, and in Ma Penethen and in Judy. All of us widows or virgins. Us women—and all because there's a man in the house.

Not altogether that either. Our dear friend Reuben with his yellow poll has been with us for years, and we weren't excited. But this new man is something special. It's certainly because of him that I've opened this book again. There is to be in these pages as little of myself as I can manage. One creeps in all the same, of course, but I have some of my old novel-writing instinct back again. After the schoolgirl's pap that I've been serving out for the last ten years—what a relief! Perhaps—who knows—some of my poor lost talent will come whistling back, the talent that Ruff once said was going to burn the Thames dry! Poor Ruff, if he could only see me now!

The house is so quiet that it isn't difficult to bring those years back again. I haven't thought of them for ages. Haven't I? No, I truly have not. But this man brings them back whether I will or no. There is something in common between us there. The belief in things that I had then—the belief that he has now. That belief that he has irritates me, of course. When he was talking to me the other night I turned on him like a savage. I told him that he might as well know once for all that I hated sentimentality above all things. All this talk about changing the world! As though you could ever change anybody! And he just smiled and said that that was the last thing that he wanted to do, that he didn't want to change anything or anybody. He just had his ideas, and if two or three other people thought as he did it would be nice to try a few things. I told him that he was deceived in people, they weren't as nice as he thought them, or loyal or true or anything—they were all rotten somewhere, and that one only made a fool of oneself by believing in people.

He laughed and said that he was sure he'd met more rotten people than I had, but he'd found most of them good somewhere—all this with his funny accent and his singulars and plurals and pronouns all wrong, and his large blue eyes that are like a baby's or a hero of one of Crockett's novels. I said he was romantic and idealistic and sentimental, all things that I loathed, and that we'd never get on. And then he laughed and I laughed, and Maude came in and was angry at his wasting his time even with an old woman like me covered with wrinkles, and I liked that. I'd do anything to spite Maude.

Then there's no doubt that he's kind and polite—both things that I like and see little enough of here. He asked me whether there had never been a time when I'd believed in things, and I said yes, there had been. And I saw myself that day Harland took my first story for *The Yellow Book*, and asked me to go and see him, and how rosy the world looked, and what a darling Harland was, and how I loved every one! And the night Ruff told me he loved me, that night at Chris's party when Oscar Wilde came, and Ada Leverson was there, and Max, and I seemed to be sitting with my hand on the very wheel that turned the world round! And that first month that I had with Ruff when we went up to that little inn by Ullswater, the nights and the days! . . . Yes, yes, there *was* a time when I too believed!

As I sit here the rain has begun, the only sound save for the clock on the stairs in all the world, and although it's pattering on my window-pane, it's from behind my Cathedral wall that it seems to come. As always! Everything comes from inside the Cathedral, the carts, the horses, the errand-boys, the bicycles, the old ladies—a whole ghostly world—so that as I sit here for so many long hours together in this room I have grown to imagine that building peopled with ghosts—all the trade and traffic of a ghostly hemisphere.

And now to-night the rain is the ghostliest of the lot, footstep after footstep pattering down that long dark nave, figures grey and shadowy staring from behind every tomb and from under every brass. For years I have been sitting here thinking that my life was over, and now suddenly the stream seems to be trickling down from the hills again, the dry bed beginning to be moistened. The very energy of that man downstairs seems to have touched me, laugh at him though I may.

Feb. 15.—Our friend the Swede is getting on. He is making acquaintances everywhere. People take to him, which is strange enough in a conservative little place like this where the very word "foreigner" frightens every one. He has started his gymnasium or whatever he calls it. He has taken three rooms over the market-place—where Bassett the dentist was—has hired an old sailor and his son as assistants and already has some clients.

Little Longstaffe of St. Paul's has taken him up warmly, old Bently of the Bank goes to him to get his stomach down, and they say that the Choir School is going to have him for some hours a week, and that even THE School itself may condescend to give him work.

It might easily develop into a craze here. During the last few years every one has been after any new thing, and what with Mrs. Sheringham and the Pageant last year, and the Regatta, and doing "Elijah" in the Cathedral, and the Benson Company coming to the Assembly Rooms, there's no knowing where we may end. I'm sure I wish Johnson or Johanson, or whatever his name is, all the luck. They can't manage his name here, and every one calls him Harmer John, and that will stick, I should think.

Personally and privately he isn't as tiresome as I at first expected. He hasn't impressed upon me any more of his views about the goodness of humanity; he is, in fact, a great deal more practical than I had fancied him, but if I were responsible for him (which, thank God, I'm not), two things would worry me.

One is that he got the rooms, or did the business of getting them, through Fletch. Now Fletch hates him—hated him on sight—and is of course a perfect devil in anything to do with money. I tried to warn him about Fletch, but he only laughed and said that he had been kind to him and made him special terms, and that he was sure that he was honest. Fletch honest!

The second thing is our dear little friend Maude. The man is fascinated by her, and in that, to do him justice, there's nothing very remarkable. She has fascinated plenty before him. She's the prettiest girl in the place, and she has ways ... ! Moreover, she herself is really taken with him, his physique, I suppose, his laugh and the rest. Then he's really something new for her. She has never been farther than a trip to Drymouth, and the men of this town are not Adonises. She is determined to catch him, and dances round him like a puppy round a juicy bone.

There is something good in the girl, I daresay. I have never been able to be fair to her. She's so young that her character can't be formed yet, and he may form it for her. They go for walks together; she's been several times to his gymnasium. The trouble is that she's bone selfish. He'll please her until she's tired of him. I don't know. As I say, this may change her. She's become more serious in the last fortnight than I've ever before known her.

She is nicer to me, too—quite polite, and when I went to bed with one of my headaches the other night, brought me some tea herself. We had a funny little conversation on that occasion. I was lying there like an old scarecrow, sallow as a fog, and she was looking lovely, all youth and life and colour.

"You don't like me, Miss Midgeley, do you?" she said. "You never have. Why don't you?"

"Don't bother me with your questions," I said, "my head's too bad."

"I'm not so silly as you think," she said. "I want to get away from here and improve myself. What chance has a girl got in a stuffy old town like this?"

"Oh, I don't know," I answered, "there are plenty of ways of improving yourself here if you like."

"I want to see foreign countries," she said. "Mr. Johnson's been telling me wonderful things."

So he's been playing Othello to her Desdemona? But Desdemona is not her type. Cressida, perhaps? And if Othello had married Cressida? . . .

Feb. 24.—The man's mad. Eaten up with idealism and fantastic desires. He's been here a little over two months and he wants to strip every Polcastrian naked, pull down the town, beat drums in the Cathedral, anything impossible you like. We were a funny lot the other night gathered in the kitchen (one of the finest old rooms in Polchester, yes, or in England for that matter). The wind was curling down the chimney, Ma Penethen and Judy were playing patience, Fletch reading the paper, Maude making eyes at Johnson.

Suddenly he comes out with it, speaking to the air—what he wanted to do. WHAT he wanted to do! To have a wonderful town, a town of craftsmen, modern Donatellos; to pull down the slums, Seatown and the rest; to build magnificent streets up from the river with statues and towers; to have the most splendid architects, the most wonderful sculptors to come down to us and start a school here; for every one in the town who cared for beauty to work to make the town beautiful, to work not for gain but for love of art and your country; even a little—one street, a statue or two—and other towns would see, admire, and imitate; to pay some great architect to design new buildings instead of the Seatown slums; to develop our own school of craftsmen, nineteenth and twentieth-century craftsmen, who would work with their hands as they did in the Florence of the Renaissance—no machinery, no ceaseless reproduction of beautiful things, but the beautiful things themselves, each one made by the loving hands of the loving craftsman. And with this we Polcastrians are to have beautiful bodies, not too fat and not too scraggy, and we are to have beautiful children, and to lead beautiful lives—jolly lives, he explained, all of us in good health and loving one another and speaking the truth and being jolly. Oh dear! Shades of William Morris! The idiot! . . .

I burst forth. I couldn't see Fletch looking at him over the top of his paper with those cold glass eyes without wanting to protect him as though he had been a baby in a perambulator playing with a snake. And yet I had to attack him. I did, too. I asked him whether he knew our town, whether he knew the parsons and the old women. I reminded him that only the other day he had told me that he didn't want to change anybody, and that here he was, propaganding with all the silly old-woman business that cranks had tried over and over again—and always failed. He looked at me as though he had been lost in sleep and I had jerked him awake. He said, as he had said the other day, that he didn't want to change anybody, but he thought people weren't as happy as they might be or as beautiful as they ought to be, and that if a few saw things as he did they could band together and do a little, and that then others perhaps would join them. He said that he had always thought that it would be nice to have a few men and women working together as they used to in Florence. He knew that many others had tried it, but they hadn't altogether failed if they had worked hard. That there was the most wonderful Cathedral here, and that he loved the town because his mother had lived near to it. But that he didn't want to alter anybody. . . . He only dreamt sometimes . . .

Then Maude broke out, jumping up and banging on the table. She thought Mr. Johnson's ideas were beautiful and that I was always down on everything, and then to every one's amazement she burst into tears and rushed out of the room. Johnson got up and stood staring after her, his eyes shining. All Fletch said was, slowly, "Pull down Seatown! Why, Mr. Johnson, you don't understand things here!"

And all the shadows in the Cathedral pressed close and listened with their ears up against the wall, and a little titter went down the nave, the echo of an echo! I heard it behind the rustle of Fletch's paper.

Johnson stood there looking at the door through which Maude had flung herself, as though carved in stone. Then he turned round to me.

"You was talking sense, I'm sure, Miss Midgeley," he said. "I dream sometimes, and it's foolish to dream aloud. I don't hope Miss Penethen's really upset."

That brought out from Judy a ferocious, "Oh, Maude's all right. Don't you worry."

Then he sighed as a dog does just before it settles to sleep, and sat down at the table again.

Am I a little queer, I wonder, living in this funny old house so long? Am I being drawn back into life again? Is it against my own will? I like him. How can I help it? He would drag the maternal out of any woman—yes, even out of me. And on the other side of the wall they titter, I am sure, long after I am asleep.

CHAPTER IV

PORTRAIT OF THE HERO

"**Y**OUR hot water, Mr. Johnson."

He almost slipped on the white stone, turning back for a moment to catch the reflection of the light on the green sloping lawn as it ran like bright water down the sharp hill. The house was extraordinarily quiet around him—not a sound. He turned from the steps, opened the door on his right and stared, as though drunk with the delight of it, at the long high room with the white walls, the bare gleaming floor flooded now with sun. What would he have here? Only two pictures. And two statues. The Donatello "Amourette"—the boy with his foot on the snake at the farther end, and there in that corner by the door the "David," the David with the helmet. . . . Nothing else.

"Your hot water, Mr. Johnson."

He turned reluctantly from the room and, standing still, sniffed the sharp morning air, heard suddenly the birds beyond the door at the bottom of the white steps, heard the trees knocking, ever so softly, their heads together, saw through that gap in the branches that was so wonderfully right that he never *could* believe that it was accidental, the faint line of the dim plum-coloured hills. The voice of one bird rose in a thin flute-like cry above the others, and the peace of the house rose beautifully, nobly to meet it. The purple shadow of the trees in their spring dress seemed to slip very faintly across the sunny hall. A clock struck.

Then—knock, Knock, KNOCK.

"Mr. Johnson, your hot water—half-past seven."

Slowly he opened his eyes, rubbed his hand across them, then scratched and ruffled his tangled hair. The little dark room met his gaze. He could hear the rain drizzling against the window. In the centre of the room on the oil-cloth stood the tin bath filled with water the night before. A large square patch of grey sky, like a sheet sagging with moisture, stretched beyond the window. There was the faded green wall-paper with the pink roses, and the mottle-coloured wardrobe, and the chest of drawers with the looking-glass that was for ever suddenly jerking forward and striking you.

In another moment he was out of bed, had gone to the door and brought in the hot water, had crossed to the open window, looked out on rain-scarred Canon's Yard and the grey butting end of the Cathedral. A moment after that his pyjamas were on the floor and he was in his bath, then, naked before the window, was doing his exercises, his mind utterly concentrated upon them, although for how many years now had he done them without missing a day? But he could only think of one thing at a time, and that thing must be whatever he was at the moment doing. One—two—three. Right, left, left, right. Down to the toes. Up again. Above the head . . .

He stopped and looked in the glass. Every morning there was this same anxiety. Was he out of condition, becoming fat anywhere? Any signs of a belly? His chest, his thighs, his buttocks? No, his face was the fattest part of him. The chubbiness of his cheeks was his old enemy. But that had always been so. He passed his hands down his thighs, hard like iron, touched his toes, then fell to on the exercises again furiously. He counted. Thirty-two, thirty-three, thirty-four—enough for to-day.

Rubbing himself he began to hum; then slowly, mysteriously the scene that he had left on opening his eyes began to steal back to him, the high white staircase, the gentle sunlight, the empty white room, the plum-coloured hills . . .

He stopped whistling, stared in front of him, lost, gone away, his eyes seeming to film with some dim shadow. The Cathedral struck the quarter. With a jerk he was back, in his shirt, shaving, cursing the razor-blade, finding a collar, pulling on the blue trousers, brushing his hair with a kind of windmill movement, singing now, fastening up his boots—then, just once again before he left the room, staring at his bed as though he might recover. . . .

He was well accustomed now to that scene in the old kitchen, but never came down the little staircase without pausing before he pushed back the door, because he hoped—what did he hope?

He looked in through the door, lowering his head, and saw them all there, Mrs. Penethen, Judy, Miss Midgeley, Fletch, all at their breakfast, that extraordinary habit of these English to stuff themselves with food early in the morning before the day has properly begun!

He adored the kitchen with its huge fire-place, its immense beams, its uneven brick floor, its whitewashed walls, its heavy oak door. "The finest kitchen in Polchester," he said to himself, "and here am I living in it. I find it first shot." The room had, too, some of the happiness and warmth that comes from continuous habitation. The whole life of Mrs. Penethen's household hung about it. The sitting-room on the next floor with its stuffed birds behind glass, its feathery everlastings, its green plush table-cloth, was dead as a coffin. All the life was here and the kitchen knew it.

They seemed a silent breakfast party. Somebody was missing. Maude, of course. Down at eight o'clock in the morning she never could manage to be. She always so intended. "See you at breakfast, Mr. Fletch," she would say, and now, to Johanson, "You'll see me on your way through in the morning, Mr. Johnson"—but of course he did not—no, he never did. He could imagine her curled up in bed like a little cat, her cheek on her hand, her lovely hair scattered over the pillow. . . .

They seemed a dull enough party without her. Not one of them—Mrs. Penethen, Miss Midgeley, Judy, Fletch—could be called talkative. But as he passed through they all, save Judy, smiled. Fletch said, raising his yellow pate, "Wet morning, Mr. Johnson." Mrs. Penethen said something, and that funny cross-patch of an old maid something sharp, and he replied with a laugh and a joke, turned once towards the door to see whether it would not open, then shouldered his way out into the rain.

Already, during the few weeks that he had been in the place, he had made numbers of friends on his way down to the market. In Canon's Yard there was the old cobbler who, like Hans Sachs, chose to sit in his doorway from morning to night hammering at his shoes; there was the butcher at the very end of the Yard; then the stationer's assistant in Bodger's Street, pimply and sallow-faced; then the old barber with a black patch over one eye, who stood in his doorway chatting during so great a part of the day that it was difficult to see when he did any work; after these, who were all now accustomed to see the tall, smiling, broad-shouldered man striding past, there were the birds and the trees of green flame; then at the top of Orange Street the Monument, whose frock-coated hero seemed to bend forward and give Johanson a special gracious bow; then down Orange Street there were the maids scrubbing the steps of the neat little houses (all lawyers and doctors surely), and on the right St. Paul's and the house, where his friend Tom Longstaffe lived, already so great a friend of his that it was difficult not to step in across the lawn and look in through the bow window and greet him at his breakfast; then, at the bottom of Orange Street, the shops beginning, the really smart shops, shops as smart as any in the High Street—Polrudden's, the hairdresser's, Crack's, the confectioner's (Mrs. Crack, orange hair, often in the doorway and always ready with a smile for Mr. Johanson); and so into the market-place, where already the day was in full bustle and the old apple-woman was arranged under her green umbrella, and the cabs were drawn up in a row along the cobbles, and the stalls in the dark cloister market were opening. So, with smiles to Mr. Fletcher, the cabman, and more smiles to Beckit, another cabman (shabbier than Fletcher), and a nod to Mr. Green in his doorway (the smartest hairdresser in Polchester); so, a step aside into Pinner Street, through the door, up the broad stone staircase, past the first floor (W. Quid, Solicitor, left side—Mund & Son, Provision Merchants, right side), on to the second floor. One moment to look with pride at the brass plate:

HJALMAR JOHANSON,

Gymnastic Instructor.

Hours, 9-6.

Saturday, 9-1.

and so into the home of health and vigour and physical beauty, THE sacred dwelling-place whence all the future strength and glory of Polchester life was to issue.

The sacred dwelling consisted of three rooms—a little room first, and that was the office; a large one second, and that was the room for exercise and drill; and a little room third, and that was the room for private examination and consultation.

The little first room was furnished with some things that Johanson had bought from the last tenant, the dentist: a decent red carpet, a solid office table, four chairs—and a portrait of the King and Queen of Sweden over the fire-place (these brought from Copenhagen). At the table there was seated a boy of about eighteen. He had yellow untidy hair, freckles, a thin, pointed face and a very high white collar. He looked up when Johanson came in and smiled with the whole of his large mouth.

This was Fred Trenant, only son of Billy Trenant, Johanson's assistant. Fred was a clever boy with a real head for figures. He had been in a bank two months ago, hating it, and when his father went to Johanson he had insisted on going too, "to manage his affairs for him." His duties were:

1. To manage the accounts.
2. To deal with correspondence.
3. To interview strangers.

Of these three duties he loved most the last, having a glib tongue, an engaging manner, and adoring his master so passionately that it was not difficult to put a special urgency into his voice when persuading hesitators. His faults were:

1. A passion for the worst and cheapest of cigarettes.
2. A tendency to magnify the achievements, virtues and appearance of those whom he admired.
3. Untidiness.

Johanson smiled at him, hung his coat on a peg and went through into the farther room. This room was bare and white. Its furniture consisted in a pair of parallel-bars (second-hand from Drymouth), a rather faded, battered "horse," a spring-board, half-a-dozen pairs of dumb-bells, and around the whitewashed walls a series of large photographs displaying Johanson in a series of exercises. There were twenty of these.

When Johanson came in Billy Trenant was rubbing up the parallel-bars, whistling through his teeth as though he were scrubbing a horse. He was a short, square man with a very large head thatched with stiff, wiry grey hair. His legs were short, thick and sturdy, his back broad, his face red. He had a scar across his forehead, and two fingers of the right hand had lost their tips. These accidents had befallen him during his service in Her Majesty's Navy, where he had been a gymnastic instructor for twenty years.

Shortly after his arrival in Polchester Johanson had been told of this man; it had seemed to him the very thing that he needed. Billy lived in a very shabby pair of rooms with his son in Seatown. He had a small pension and was a widower. Both father and son lost their hearts to Johanson at first sight. Billy adored physical strength and cleanliness; he also adored himself, his comfort and his two shabby rooms; for no one else would he have left them. He was an obstinate man, thought that he knew everything about physical culture, was garrulous about himself and his achievements; his brain was slow and his outlook upon life immature. These things might mean trouble in the future, but for the moment all was well.

Johanson, no dreamer now, but moving, the sure captain on his accustomed deck, greeted Billy and went into the question of the parallel-bars.

"They'm not as handsome as I'd like to have 'em," said Billy, shaking his head. "In point of fact, they'm not handsome at all."

"They'll do for the time," said Johanson. "We shall afford better ones soon."

Billy shook his head. "The prettier to start with, the richer to end with," he said. "When folks come along and see it all shabby-like they'll be thinking the instructor's the same—not worth their money."

Johanson was looking out of the window into the market-place, coloured now with figures, the sun shining on the cobbles bright like jewels after the rain. He turned round and put his hands on Billy's shoulders, looking down on him.

"If you don't believe in me, Billy," he said, "we shall part and be friends."

"I believe in 'ee," said Billy, looking up at him. "Fust foreigner I ever took to. I ain't saying nothing agin they bars—only that they ain't as fresh as I'd like 'em."

He shook his head rather like a dog out of the water. "You'm powerful strong," he said. "You could pretty well throw me out o' that there winder. . . . Well, well, I'm not so young as I was."

Johanson moved off into the other room. "Now, Fred," he said, "we shall look at the morning's letters."

Quite a number. One from a gentleman who was always dizzy when he awoke in the morning, had tried every medicine and many doctors, and now wondered whether exercises might not be what he needed. One from a lady who had two children with perpetual colds—would exercises be good for them? One from a firm of sports providers in Drymouth; one from a vegetarian who would like to join forces "for the good of humanity"—to preach vegetables and exercises hand-in-hand—and one letter that shall be given in full:

3 Pepper Lane, Polchester.

Dear Sir—Last night at the meeting of the Glebeshire Antiquarian Society I had the great pleasure of a conversation with the Reverend Thomas Longstaffe, Rector of St. Paul's Church in this town. Before I go any further, I should say that I am an Art Instructor, Teacher of Painting (oils and water-colours), Drawing, Modelling in Wax, etc., etc. For twenty years now I have instructed the Young Ladies of the High School of this town. Thirty years ago I worked in the Art Schools of Paris and London, my dear Father and Mother sacrificing their All that I might benefit. I had in those far-gone days Great Ambitions, now, alas, long quenched by the Waters of Disappointment. The Reverend Thomas Longstaffe last night informed me of your arrival in this town and of your desire to improve the Bodies of our Fellow-Citizens. He informed me further of your enthusiasm and Love for the Great Artists of the Italian Renaissance—for the mighty Michael Angelo, the graceful Verrocchio, the tender Mino da Fiesole, the beloved Donatello—and that, inspired by their

Glorious Masterpieces, you would revive in our town some of the lost Arts and Handicrafts.

What a draught of nectar was this news to your humble servant who more than thirty years back lit the fires of his Soul at the Altars of Divine Art in Florence, in Rome and in Naples! May I not come and call upon you? I know that your time must be precious indeed, but I will not detain you for long, and, by your courtesy, you will be blessing the lonely hours of your faithful servant,

BENJAMIN SHORTT.

Johanson turned to the boy. "Know any one called Benjamin Shortt, Fred?" he asked.

"What! Old feller with long hair below his collar—looks as though 'e never washed—teaches droring?"

"That sounds like it!"

"I know—used to go to the High School to teach the girls. Hard luck on the girls!"

They started on the day's engagements. "Nobody this mornin', sir," said Fred. "Mr. Barnstaple, 3 to 4, Major Comstock, 4.15 to 5.15. To-morrer mornin's the Choir School, 10 to 11. The Band of Hope's comin' along to see you this afternoon, sir, leastways the head man, Mr. Tittmuss."

"And what does he want?"

"Exercisin' the bodies of the Band of Hope, I shouldn't wonder," said Fred, "and they need it. But he won't pay much. Mean as mustard."

Johanson got up, stretching his long arms. "It's this hanging about is the hardest," he said, talking to Fred as though he were his equal in age, experience, size and authority. "I'm impatient. I want to be forward with this. When I look out through this window I would wish to go down into the market and bring them all up here. They all of them wants something done to them. It's a shame all men doesn't realise how strong they might be!"

"Most of 'em haven't got time, sir, I expect," said Fred. He looked up with intense admiration at Johanson's size and strength. "If you'd been born small and crooked," he said, "you wouldn't *know* you were small and crooked. Leastways you'd be proud of yourself for *being* small and crooked, think it made you more interestin' or something."

Johanson laughed. "They are coming in all right, though, aren't they, Fred? New ones every day."

Fred beamed. "Why, we're doing something wonderful, sir," he said. "All the town's talking of us. We'll be famous right through Glebeshire in a week or two!" The door-bell rang. Johanson went through into the inner room. The door opened. Three clergymen appeared.

"Mr. Johanson in?"

"Yes, sir."

"Could he see me for a moment?"

"I'm sure he'd see *you*, sir, at any time." Fred's face was beaming. This was Mr. Longstaffe, friend and chief supporter of the establishment. With him the

Reverend Canon Ronder, the Reverend Canon Bentinck-Major, dignitaries of the Cathedral. An important visit for the establishment.

Fred disappeared—reappeared.

"Will you come through, gentlemen? Mr. Johanson will see you."

They went through to the inner room, the little one where important interviews (this was the first the establishment had encountered) were held.

Of the four men Tom Longstaffe was the most nervous and self-conscious. That little man had the virtue or the defect (whichever way this modern cynical world may see it) of greeting a new friendship with terrific enthusiasm and of working in every possible direction for that new friend like a little Mercury. He had taken to this man quite enormously, taken to him for himself, taken to him for the work that he wanted to do. There was nothing this town needed so much as new physical vigour, something to brace everybody up and send the citizens skidding along in fresh, healthy directions.

Here was the very man, a man also who was himself after Longstaffe's own heart in sincerity, honesty, courage. So far so good, but the next step was difficult. Johanson and his little gymnasium would never get anywhere without the patronage of Polchester's Upper Ten, and Longstaffe had not himself penetrated so deeply into the sacred circle that he was thoroughly at home in there.

Everything was a little more difficult because of Johanson's simplicity. Longstaffe was simple, but not so simple as Johanson. Johanson, eager though he was for his venture to succeed, confessing indeed to Longstaffe that he had put every penny of his savings into it and that therefore succeed it must, nevertheless seemed to fail to understand the real importance of Ronder, of Wistons, of Mrs. Sampson, of Lady St. Leath. He was convinced, it appeared, that all reasonable people would realise at once the advantage of good health, the splendour of physical fitness, and that the rest would follow. They were all, it appeared, good and wise and intelligent. That there should be cliques and rivalries and jealousies seemed never to occur to him at all, and that he should go out and solicit favours was an obvious impossibility. It was true that people were coming in just now thick and fast, but when the novelty was over only the patronage of the Cathedral, the School, the Cathedral set would keep it going. Johanson was so simple about people that Longstaffe could only wonder where, then, he had lived all his days. Were they all angels in Scandinavia? Was no one false, jealous, mean, spiteful, dishonest in Copenhagen?

Oh yes, there were such, Johanson did not doubt, but he had been very fortunate. And he would be still more fortunate here. Were not all Englishmen honest, and was not he, Johanson, a wonderful reader of character? He could tell at a glance, he was never deceived. And nine out of ten human beings were honest and true. After all, he had seen the world. His father had been a bad one. *There* was a bad man if you like, but he had never had a proper chance, and when he was sober he was not so bad after all. . . .

"But don't you understand," Longstaffe had broken in desperately, "that in a little town like this there are dozens of intrigues and sets within sets? It's always so in a small town. You must choose your friends and stick by them—but you can't be friends with every one."

Johanson had clapped Longstaffe on the shoulder with a mighty smack. "Well, I shall stick by you," he said, "for ever"—which finally had nothing to do with the real question. So, when Longstaffe had met Ronder and Bentinck-Major in the High Street and Ronder had stopped to talk and, soon afterwards, had mentioned Johanson's name, and Longstaffe, on impulse, had asked them to come with him to see him, he had wondered as he walked with them through the market-place whether he had been wise. Johanson was a queer fellow. These were important men, and Johanson might not realise it in the least . . .

It appeared that he did not. He was completely at his ease. He asked them to sit down, and then stood opposite them leaning against the wall, smiling upon them as though they were his long-lost brothers.

Little Bentinck-Major was at once uneasy. As he explained afterwards to his wife, "The fellow leaning against the wall looked tall enough to go through the ceiling and broad enough to break the window and door at the same moment without stirring. I was sitting down, my dear, and although I am not exactly a dwarf, never felt, physically, so small in my life." So he sat there fingering his gold watch-chain, looking at his neat, shining boots, touching, once and again, his neat, shining hair.

Ronder, on the other hand, was at his best. He liked this man at first sight.

Ronder always liked men better than women, liked them better and trusted them more. In the furthering of his many little schemes and plans (schemes and plans never malevolent in their intention) he found that women were easier to use and adapt, and therefore he liked men better. He despised always his agents, and when a man became soft and pliable in his hands he always noticed that he had much in his character that was feminine. Here, he saw at once, was a proper man. Himself was now growing much too fat, and some exercises, some massage, perhaps, would be an admirable thing. And upon that instant seizure on an opportunity for his own increased personal comfort there began to work in him a little moving pattern of possible combinations and developments. This man might have his place in larger issues than the reduction of Ronder's figure. You cannot be the most important man in Polchester for ten years without much manipulation of human beings, and the manipulation of human beings (always with good intentions) was the very breath of Ronder's nostrils.

Yes, but Johanson was of course entirely unaware of all this. What, at first, he was mainly aware of (as he told Longstaffe afterwards) was Ronder's figure. He had not for a long time seen anything so fat and round and also so neat and shining. Fat men, he had often noticed, were as a rule untidy, creased as to their garments, unbrushed and spotted. But Ronder was a miracle of smartness from the tips of his boots to the splendour of his admirably parted hair. His face (that of a blooming cherub) was kindly indeed, his expression clever and animated. In three minutes Johanson liked him very much indeed.

Ronder, in fact, took trouble to be his most charming, and how charming that could be every one in Polchester by this time well knew. So genuine, too. When his heart wanted to burst through his waistcoat he allowed it to burst through; the pleasantest sensation he knew—like a thorough and hearty sneeze. He loved to be moved warmly towards people—he was moved warmly towards Johanson now.

The little meeting ended by being a great success. Johanson did not say very much. Ronder talked for everybody. This was exactly, in his opinion, what Polchester needed. He knew that it was what he, Ronder, needed. Johanson might count on his hearty co-operation. It was not much that he could do, but he had his little influence in the place, and, such as it was, it should be all at Johanson's service. Then there was the School—THE School. Would Johanson have time for some work up there? He thought that a word from him in that direction . . . He had some slight influence. . . .

Longstaffe, watching his friend, was immensely relieved. Johanson took Ronder's advances just as they should be taken—with friendliness but no sycophancy, thanking him but with no effusiveness, looking him straight between the eyes, and shaking hands so heartily at the last that the Canon's bones must have remembered for a good hour afterwards.

"I don't hope," Johanson said at the last with his courteous bow, "that you shall think that what we have here is as it will be. Everything begins. I mean that the continuation shall be very good."

He suddenly turned on Bentinck-Major, who was picking his way delicately like a hen round the parallel-bars.

"I do hope you like it," he said rather as a child might who has built a castle of bricks and turns to his father for approval.

"Oh yes, yes," Bentinck-Major stammered nervously—"Delightful! Delightful! Charming!"

Johanson tossed his head. "It shall be better," he said as though Bentinck-Major had criticised him, "much, much better."

In the outer room they saw as they came through an old man waiting there. Not so old in years, perhaps, but shabby with that hopelessness that can only come to a human being when he has abandoned altogether even the semblance of a struggle.

He presented at first sight the image of a decayed actor in the familiar Irving pattern—hooked nose, long wispy hair falling over a greasy velvet collar, tightly buttoned long faded black coat, thin bony frame, large patent-leather boots with a crack across the toe. His face was anxious, submissive, a little furtive.

Seeing Ronder and Bentinck-Major, who were, it appeared, sufficiently well known to him to call a faint flush into his sallow features, he bowed low. Ronder gave him a sharp glance. It was as though he realised that now that he had taken

Johanson under his protection, had drawn him into the world of his manœuvres, he must attend to every detail of his circumstances, to his visitors above all. They had become of great significance to him.

He bowed to the shabby old man, repeated his assurances to Johanson and departed, followed by Bentinck-Major.

Longstaffe for a moment remained. He knew this shabby figure well enough, and felt impatient at his appearance there.

Were the charlatans and the beggars of the place already gathering round his friend? He had himself a tender heart, but no good could come from association with old back-me-downs like this old Benjamin Shortt—right on the back of Ronder, too.

But Johanson apparently realised nothing of the kind. Fred superciliously had given the old man's name—"You had a letter from him this morning, sir"—and Johanson had at once gripped the shabby one's dingy hand as heartily as before he had gripped Ronder's plump one, and in his eyes shone a light of kindliness and compassion. He turned to Longstaffe.

"You'll excuse me? I must talk to my friend here. He has written to me. Heartily thanks for your goodness in bringing your friends to see me. One day I will show you how I am grateful."

He put his hands on Longstaffe's shoulders, shaking him a little. "Good-bye," he said. He burst out laughing. "That's a fat clergyman," he said, "if he wants massage he will have it. And it shall hurt too!"

Then he turned back and led the way into the other room, followed apprehensively by Mr. Shortt. He sat the man down in the chair but now occupied by Canon Ronder, then himself sat down close to him, balanced on the end of the table, his long legs swinging.

"Mr. Shortt, half an hour ago I read your letter. Thank you for writing it. It was good of you."

The man's eyes filled with tears, filled too readily, a cynical observer might have fancied. "Oh, Mr. Johnson, when our friend Mr. Longstaffe—he seemed in something of a hurry this morning I fancied—told me the other night of your projects and ambitions for our town, my heart swelled with gladness, and I said to myself, 'I will not delay, I will go at once and put myself at the feet of this stranger who is realising at last dreams—dreams—'"

He paused. He pulled out a very grimy handkerchief and wiped his eyes. "Forgive me, sir," he said, "I have not been well of late. . . . It is too much. . . ."

"You're hungry, that's what you are," said Johanson, "wait a moment." He swung off the table and went out. Soon he returned. "You will have some sandwiches in a minute. I've sent the boy out. You can eat them in here where you shan't be interrupted."

Mr. Shortt blinked his eyes. "Your goodness—coming after these hard years. . . . Since my wife died five years ago I have had nothing but tribulation. I must tell you," he hesitated, "in my letter there was something that was untrue. It is two years now since I last instructed the young ladies of the High School. It was a foolish lie, because you would discover it so quickly. I have here some drawings—" He fumbled with a dirty roll of paper.

He produced something for Johanson's inspection. Johanson took them in his hands. They were drawings, rather faded now, copies—Michael Angelo's "Moses," Verrocchio's "Madonna and Child" from the Bargello, a baby from one of Mino da Fiesole's tombs, and here his beloved Donatello, two of them, the David with the helmet and the St. George.

They had never been very good drawings, and now they were faded and smudged, but Johanson's heart beat excitedly as he looked at them.

"Oh, you're in luck to have been there," he said. "Soon, when, this is successful, I too will go. We shall go together and then return and have a school for sculptors and artists and painters and make this town beautiful, keeping the old lovely things and making new things in tune with them, and the Cathedral above all ... and fine men and women all working for the love of their town...."

He began to stride about the room.

The man watched him with blurred eyes which occasionally he rubbed. Fred came in with a pile of sandwiches on a plate and a bottle of Bass. Mr. Shortt gave him a sharp look to see whether he were laughing or sneering at him, then between gulps and bites he murmured, "Oh yes, indeed, ... glor-i-ous ... glor-i-ous! Our beautiful town.... My dreams coming true, Mr. Johnson, indeed they are. What is life but the pursuit of beauty? And all these years I have been labouring in the wilderness alone—and now at last when I had almost given up hope." A tear welled into his eye and slowly trickled down his cheek, to mingle with the crumbs of sandwich on his chin.

Johanson turned round abruptly and stood over him. He was tremendously excited. He raised his arms. That already when he had been in the place only a month or two men and women should be springing from the very stones of the city as it were to join him with their enthusiasm!

"We can found our school here, we can make it perhaps famous throughout the country—a new life, simpler, kinder, a new town rising out of the beautiful old one, every one happier!"

He wrung Mr. Shortt's hand again. "All your life you have worked here and not seen your dreams realised, now at last they may come true...."

Mr. Shortt looked at the plate to see whether the sandwiches were finished. They were. He rose slowly from the chair wiping the crumbs from his mouth with a very dirty handkerchief.

"Indeed, indeed, Mr. Johnson, this is a very great moment in my life. You can be assured now and always of my cordial co-operation. This is truly a happy day for me." He paused, looking anxiously about him. "There is one little matter," he glanced down at his boots; "coming this morning I was compelled to miss a possible engagement. Five shillings would, I imagine, cover the loss. I quite understand, of course, if you find it impossible—"

Johanson had not heard him. He was staring towards the window. "Five shillings would cover—" repeated Mr. Shortt anxiously.

Johanson wheeled round. "What's that? Five shillings? Why, of course. . . ." From his trouser-pocket he produced some silver. "There, Mr. Shortt. Come and see me soon again, remember. We shall have much to discuss. . . ."

Fred appeared in the doorway. "Two ladies to see you, sir," he said. Mr. Shortt started apprehensively. "Well, well, I must hasten back to my work. I have found a friend, Mr. Johnson. I shall never forget that to-day I have found a friend. . . ."

He shuffled off. In the outer room he almost shuffled into Mrs. Penethen and her daughter Maude. He bowed and, his head bent, disappeared through the door.

Miraculous morning! Johanson in his happiness could have kissed Mrs. Penethen, who greeted him with her customary severe smile.

"I have no right to intrude, Mr. Johnson," she said, "I can see that you are very busy, but we are passing and I have a little matter that will take me only a minute to discuss with you."

"Certainly," he said, smiling at Maude, "I am delighted to see you."

They moved, the three of them, into the little room, and all stood together looking out of the window on to the market-place, now soaked with sun under a faint pigeon-blue sky. What Mrs. Penethen wanted to say was that March 13 was Maude's birthday and she intended to give a little party. Would Mr. Johnson honour them with his presence? Only perhaps a dozen people—Mr. Ben Squires, her brother-in-law, Mrs. Boultewood (a friend from girlhood) and her daughter, Miss Midgeley and Mr. Fletch, and one or two more? In the kitchen, of course, supper and then a dance. They would have old Mr. Harty, who played the fiddle like a two-year-old. Now, what Mrs. Penethen wanted to ask was not only would Mr. Johnson come, but would he ask his friend Mr. Longstaffe? Did he think that he dared? It would be so nice to have a clergyman, and Mr. Longstaffe was so popular. It would just give a finish to the evening. Mrs. Penethen didn't dare herself . . . but perhaps Mr. Johnson wouldn't mind. . . .

"Why, of course I'll ask him!" Johanson cried, "and I'm sure he'll come unless he have some other engagement. I'll ask him, that's certain."

Mrs. Penethen's stern features relaxed as she thanked him. What a charming place he had here. It really was charming. She moved into the other room to examine everything and began one of her dignified polite conversations with Billy. The other two remained beside the window.

They spoke no word. Johanson, staring down into the market-place, saw nothing. Slowly, as though a thin paper sheet had been held before his eyes and was suddenly split by some strong hand, he beheld the scene of his now so familiar dream. He heard the fountain. The long white staircase came into view, the cool of the dark sheltered garden, the long, high, empty room with the shining floor, utter peace, the voice of the birds.

He had never known such happiness. In another moment he would be shown the secret of life, some secret so simple that it would be amazing that for so long every one could have been so blind—

He turned to the girl. Almost on his lips were the words, "Come and see my garden. It is so quiet there and no one will interrupt us. . . ." The girl's hand touched the back of his. "Well, Mr. Johnson, we must be getting along," she said almost as though she had been waiting for something that had not happened, and was disappointed. "We've got ever so much to do this morning."

She waited yet a moment looking up at him. She knew that she was bewitching when she looked up at some one, her chin tilted ever so slightly. Then, as he did not move, she turned with a little shrug of her shoulders and walked out of the room.

CHAPTER V

FRIENDSHIP: MARCH WEATHER

HOWEVER tightly I stretch out the quivering elastic of my memories, I can summon up no vision of a time when I was not conscious of our Cathedral.

When I was very small it came to me with two quite separate personalities, the distant, magical, mysterious one, an animal with grey ears, a ship with silver masts, a box ruby-coloured, a net salmon-tinted, always above the town, separated from it, swinging with its own life in space—the other the long shining distending nave with its slippery floor, down which our family, always late, would self-consciously clatter, the heads on either side turning as we moved, the verger undoing the cord for us, the pause, the choir slipping past, the cold clear voice of the Precentor.

It was not until I was much older that the inside of the church approached me—and that on a never-forgotten day when, having nothing to do, urged by the lovely evening to wait a moment before going home, I slipped in, was caught by the grey cloud of the dusky walls and pillars, and then saw, suddenly flaming, the windows near the King's Chapel, all six of them, the windows known as "the Virgin and the Children." These were, with the exception of the great Rose window at the East end, the oldest in the Cathedral. In one of them the Virgin Mary, in a purple gown, bent down over a field of lilies to watch the baby Christ at play; in another the Christ and St. John paddled in a stream while Mary watched them from the windows of a crooked house set in a cup of hills; in another children were running in a crowd after a white kid and Mary held back her Son, who stretched out his arms after his playmates; in another Joseph was in the workshop, Jesus was sitting on the floor looking up, and the Virgin, in a dress of vivid green, stood over him, guarding him; in another they were walking, Father, Mother and Child, up the steps of the Temple, watched by a group of grave old men; in another Jesus was playing at his Mother's feet, while an ox, an ass and three strange dogs with large black eyes seemed to be protecting them.

On this late afternoon the sun lit the windows with a rage of colour, and every detail of colour was visible to me. More than the central figures the detail of the backgrounds fascinated me, the little roads winding into purple hills, the stiff trees so vividly green, the white castles like toys on craggy rocks, little boys with networks of shipping, and then suddenly the colour was so intense—the purple, the green, the crimson, the pale silver white, the dark ruby red—that I lost the detail and seemed to swim through the dusk of the darkening church on a jewelled carpet to heaven.

From that day the Cathedral was mine; I seemed to know it all, from the Black Bishop's tomb with its wonderful green stone to the smallest babyest cherub hiding in the right-hand corner of the monument to Henry, eighth Marquis of Brytte.

The history of that monument was a strange one. Henry, eighth Marquis of Brytte, the last of his family, the oldest perhaps of all Glebeshire's great families, spent the last years of his long life at Brytte Court, ten miles from Polchester, and died in 1735. He had done many things during his lifetime for our town, which he loved, and, of course, we gave him a monument. A curious thing happened. A local artist was discovered, a young man Simon Petre, a protégé of the old Marquis, who, learning of the boy's talent, had sent him to London, Paris and finally to Italy. He came back a sculptor of fine promise. His benefactor's monument was his first public commission. He worked at it for a year and a half and died of some queer fever a week or two after finishing it. He was a poet too, young Simon Petre, and a writer of no mean prose. After his death a little memoir with some poems and an Italian diary were published. The book has vanished now, but I have a copy, *The Life and Remains of Simon Petre*, London, 1739—a small brown book stamped in thin gold. There are some curious things in that Italian diary and one little section—"A Florentine Adventure"—that may one day be republished—curious and unusual at least, saturated with the decadent colour of that place at that period.

I, of course, had never been to Italy when I decided that for myself the "Virgin and Children" windows and the Brytte Monument were the loveliest things in our Cathedral. It is certain, though, that Mino da Fiesole himself would not disdain the babies crowding at the head and feet of the recumbent figure—the loveliest babies, some laughing, some grave, one with his finger on his lips, one looking back, calling to his friend, two bending forward, their chubby fingers on one another's shoulders—adorable, adorable babies making perfect the delicacy of the lace-like background, the strength and dignity of the simple figure, the symmetry and pattern of the wings of the guarding Angel.

In this thing at least Johanson and I were one—it was this monument that at once won his heart.

One of the most mysterious elements in the whole of his story is his connection with the Cathedral. After tradition had set to work and had piled absurdity on absurdity it became the habit to acclaim him a kind of St. George defending the Cathedral from its many foes. I believe the truth to be exactly the opposite. His religion was Protestant of the plainest, simplest kind; he repeatedly exclaimed against what seemed to him the falseness and flummery of the Cathedral life, but what caught him, I fancy, was its Past, its beautiful, romantic, fighting, poignant Past.

He found here, as he had found nowhere in his own Scandinavia, the work of the craftsman, striving with his hands to make Beauty for the World that he loved. He found it in the floor, in the roof, in the pillars, in the windows, in the Cloisters, in the Bishop's tomb, in the Brytte Monument—in the Brytte Monument above all. That must have been, at his first vision of it, as though it had stepped straight out of his beloved "Donatello" book (*Donatello*, by Lord

Balcarres, Duckworth, 1903). And then when behind the sight of it he learnt the history of young Simon Petre, it must have seemed to him as though here, right before his eyes, was the very example of native craftsmanship for which he had been longing ever since he set foot in our town. A boy of the town, born and bred here, returning to it, doing his first work in the heart of it and for very love of it, and doing it so beautifully too! I believe that from the moment when he heard the history of young Simon Petre he felt that that same boy was at his side, caring for him, encouraging him, urging him on. . . . Something that he said afterwards, just before the end, to Mary Longstaffe . . . but that is a later story.

On a certain day he lunched with the Rev. Thomas at St. Paul's Rectory and went with him afterwards to a football match—a day that they were never, either of them, to forget.

Leaving the Choir School, where he had been drilling the choir boys for a most strenuous hour, he looked into the Cathedral for one moment before going on to the Rectory.

The nave was deserted save for three visitors, who were being conducted by Cobbett, the Verger, seventy years of age now, as brisk as a young bee, but with some of the pomposity proper to his office.

He knew Johanson by this time and greeted him with fitting dignity. He liked Johanson. The fellow made no fuss, was always cheery and respected Cobbett's office. Moreover, Cobbett's youngest was at the Choir School and was already ecstatic over Johanson's physical prowess.

"This," he said to the three visitors, a burly man, a timid woman and a little girl with creaking shoes, "is known as the Brytte Monument. A work in commemoration of Henry, eighth Marquis of Brytte. . . ."

They gaped, gasped, and moved on. Soon the only sound was the creaking shoes of the little girl. A faint, very faint, breeze seemed to whisper round the dim corners of the distant pillars. The floor was like a lake, the colours from the "Virgin" windows faintly staining it. Johanson held his breath, staring up at the clustering babies until they seemed to move, to turn towards him, smiling, inviting him.

Oh! if only things turned out as he hoped, what would he not do here, for the town, for the Cathedral, perchance for England! It had all begun so marvellously, he coming as a stranger, swept into the town, as it were, by a torrent of rain—

He drew himself up and a prayer formed in his heart, a prayer without words, and he felt again an ecstatic vision, of worship towards the beauty that he felt in the world, of humility in the face of his own capacities, of happiness because every one was so good to him. He liked to be liked, he liked to have friends, he liked to be moving in tune with the life around him; he felt an intense gratitude because of the love in the world.

"I'll do my best," the words formed in his heart. "I'll work as I have never worked before—I'll spare nothing—I'll give myself utterly. I have found at last the work that I was put into the world to do."

And before he turned away he seemed to hear the friendly voice in his ear of that strange young man, and to see at his side the thin face, the burning eyes. . . .

He left the Cathedral and went through Bodger's Street and Green Lane to St. Paul's.

Old Hephzibah looked after Tom Longstaffe like a cat after her only kitten. She was a short stout woman with the coal-black hair that one so often finds in Glebeshire people, an inheritance from those ancestors who once invaded the Glebeshire shores in their pirate ships and put the Glebeshire wastes to fire and sword and then settled there and begat children of the women they spared.

Warm of heart, irascible, impetuous and untidy, Hephzibah made of the Rectory a haystack. Nothing was in its right place, and Tom was too busy to care. The two men sat down to a meal that was dumped down on the table anyhow. They didn't notice. They had other things to think about. Tom was in tremendous spirits and very soon he gave his friend the reason.

"My girl's coming home next week," he said. He paused, suddenly looking sharply at Johanson. This was the first time that he had mentioned his girl to his friend. Johanson must have heard some gossip. This thing was nearer to his heart than anything else in the world. What would Johanson say?

Johanson had heard nothing. His face lit up.

"You have a daughter? You never told me."

"I was waiting until we had a time really alone. My girl is more to me than all the rest of the world put together. She's been living in London for seven years. She's very clever. She's a journalist and makes a good income."

"She's all alone in London?"

"She has a boy of six."

"What does her husband do?"

"She's not married."

The colour rose in Longstaffe's face. "I'm prouder of her, Johanson, than I can ever say. Don't you make any mistake about that. She lived here with me, of course. We were splendid together, never a cross word, perfect confidence, love such as father and daughter can seldom have had. She met a young fellow, son of an Army officer here. She told me something about it. I was pleased because I liked the boy. But his father had great ambitions for him, and wouldn't consent to an engagement. I should have stopped her then perhaps seeing him, but I couldn't. She loved him so, and I thought the old man was coming round. He was, I think. No one could resist Mary once they knew her. Then the boy was killed in an accident. A month later Mary told me that she was going to have a baby."

"Poor girl, poor girl!" said Johanson.

"Then we had our first difference—the first in all our lives together. Mary was happy. She stayed on here, not caring what any one said or thought. She said she was glad that he had left something of himself that she could keep. That he would always be with her through the child. . . . The people here, of course, were very hostile. I had my own struggle. She had committed, by my own lights of everything in which I had been taught to believe, a great sin. I tried to speak to her of that, but I broke down. She seemed suddenly to know so much more of life than I. And if you love some one truly, how can you change, especially if they are in trouble and disgrace?

"But she felt after a time that she was doing me harm here, my church and my congregation. So she went away. Her baby was born, a boy. She lived in London and began to write, and, as I say, has been very successful. I needn't tell you, Johanson, how I've missed her—it's been an agony sometimes—but I wouldn't press her to come back. I couldn't, when I knew of the way they might treat her here. But at last she has insisted. She is coming back with the boy next week."

The look that the two men exchanged settled their friendship. It had its birth in that first moment of meeting, that misty day in the Cathedral Precincts, it had had its growth through their happy and easy comradeship of the last few weeks, now it was certain. No separation of time or place could change it.

"My heartliest thanks for telling me," Johanson said. "It will be fine to know her."

After the meal Longstaffe took his friend over the house. It was one of those old rambling spidery houses that are so especially English, and then still more especially Glebeshire. In the upper rooms there was a smell of apples and candle-grease. In the attics there were torn wall-papers and supplements from the Christmas numbers tacked on to the walls, and out of the attic windows there were views of Polchester, smoky orange in the spring weather, with the Cathedral sailing through the air. The house was a mess. Fine though Hephzibah was, the house was a mess. Longstaffe's bedroom was sad to see—drawers were half opened, ties like tongues, collars like yawns hanging from them. Over the back of the chair clothes were tumbled, shaving things, the brush soapy, the razor gaping for a fresh victim, were lying loosely on the dressing-table.

"I beg your pardon," said Tom Longstaffe, "I oughtn't to have brought you in here."

Instantly Johanson was busy. The drawers were closed, the clothes were folded and put away, the shaving things were in their case.

He stopped in the middle of the room, his face flushed. "I do beg your pardon. I had no right to do that. I could not bear to see that confusion. It hurts. How can you live like that?"

Longstaffe looked rather like a scolded school-boy. Then suddenly he roared with laughter.

"Fancy you," he cried, "a man of your size putting those things away. You're right, of course. I've lived in the most awful mess here for years. I've never thought about it. But it's the last thing I expected you to do."

Johanson suddenly came across to Longstaffe and putting his hands under his shoulders lifted him into the air.

"You're getting fat," he said. He put him down. "You're having stomach."

Longstaffe shook himself. "By Jove, you're strong—and yet you put those clothes away like a fussy old bachelor."

"No, I'm not fussy. But untidiness, I hate it. It makes dirt. This house, I should wash it all down with soap and water." He suddenly looked anxiously at Longstaffe. "You aren't angry? I don't think first. I do something and then I think afterwards. I will be in trouble one day for that." He put his hands on Longstaffe's shoulders: "You're not angry?"

"Angry?" said Longstaffe. "Why, I think you're the best fellow I ever met."

They started off for the football match. Johanson and Tom Longstaffe were both very simple men. Longstaffe had that simplicity that is often to be met with in clergymen who have lived good and pure lives, and who are not mentally very subtle, who believe utterly in the dogmas of their religion, who have lived for a long period in a rather remote place. They are moved by feeling rather than thought, and their feelings are direct, honest, and, as a rule, uncomplicated.

The problems that Longstaffe had hitherto in his life been compelled to face, his problems of love, friendship and belief, would have soon been constructed into complicated shapes had a subtle brain worked on them, but Longstaffe's brain was not subtle. He had that confidence in God which a small child feels for his mother, and so all his earthly life was simplified.

Johanson was like Longstaffe in many ways, the reason perhaps of the beginning of their friendship, and was unlike him in many more, the reason undoubtedly of its continuance. In some things he had not developed since he was a boy of fifteen, in his faith in human nature, in his naïve pleasure in his physical strength, in his sudden angers and instant after-forgetfulness of any grudge, in his impetuous enthusiasms, in his generosity, in his sudden distresses and equally sudden joys—in all these things he was a boy. But he had a nature capable of far deeper complications than his friend's. He had the soul of the artist, and therefore would know suffering, failure, strange longing, deep loneliness, passionate regret, exquisite happiness as Longstaffe would never know them. He had in him the artist's complex of woman and man, masculine absolutely in his physical self and its nature, feminine often in comprehension, sympathy, and the longing for something that he would never attain. His mixed blood, too, had flooded him with an imagination that Longstaffe's English blood would never know. There were also his dreams.

The two men moved up the hill, past the Monument, out on to the road above the town. The day was one of a little group that marked the end of winter and the beginning of spring. The trees were yet bare, but from their heart there seemed to steal a faint pink flush as though the sap that throbbed in their veins prompted them already to some timid expression of their approaching beauty. They stretched out their arms to a sky of blue washed with water, and in this lake of thin colour shapes of cloud-like swans floated gently, aimlessly, now in concert, now singly, now fading, with an almost audible whisper of farewell, into some farther silence. The fields and the grass and moss in the hedges were of a bright sharp colour, not yet fully green, but accentuated as though painted on china. Here and there a primrose, a yellow eye, peeped out, wondering whether the world were yet ready for its full approach. The road was hard and rang beneath the men's feet, but here, too, there was promise of warmth and running sap beneath the yielding frost.

When they reached the turn of the road both men instinctively looked back. Polchester, like a child's collection of coloured bricks huddled into a green basket, lay below them; from its heart, a pennon of blue, the Pol streamed out to the hills and the Cathedral rode over all.

"You wouldn't believe," said Longstaffe, "how I love that place! After Mary, it is everything in this world to me. And you wouldn't believe either," he added, "the intrigues and plots and cabals that are going on there."

"You see it too close," Johanson said. "Look at it from above and get your real picture. You must not be too near to a man, you see only his waistcoat buttons. How beautiful that place is! I am a man in luck to have found my home at last."

"And do you really feel this town in which you have been only a few weeks to be your home more than the country in which you have spent all your life?"

"I do so. We have all of us a dream-town, and my one was to be always in England. You see, I loved my mother, and she, because she were an exile, would always talk of England as of Paradise, and it was *this* England that she talked about, the high deep hedges, the grey cottages hanging with their toes to the sliding hills, the sea on both sides, so narrow that one big wave could sweep the country, the salt smell in the breeze, the women with their black hair. . . . And my father was a bad man, so that his country seemed unkind to me and unfriendly. He were bad because he could not help himself; his lusts was so strong. He must have a woman every minute, and always a new one, never the same one twice. He did not care what he did to them, and yet my mother loved him, always, to the very last of his life. She said she liked him bad better than other men good. It were well, she said sometimes, that he was so bad, because if he were good she would die at once of such happiness. She said he was good, an angel, just for two weeks after their marriage—wonderful—and those two weeks was enough to have made living worth while. English-women, I am sure, are very patient."

They were moving now between thick, high hedges that hid all the world from them.

"Tell me," said Longstaffe, "did you always, since you were very small, mean to come to England?"

"Yes, always. I cannot remember the time when I did not dream of it. I used to lead always two lives: the one that had my father in it and earning my living, and all the daily Stockholm life—that was fun, especially when we went out to the Islands, and in the summer when we was all day in the water . . . and the other when I would try to draw and paint and make things out of coloured paper and ask my mother questions, and then at night I'd dream!"

"So you're a painter too?" Longstaffe asked.

"No. I hadn't any gift. It was because I had not that I determined to do what I might with my body. My strength seemed the best thing I had. First, I was a model for artists, and then a painter took interest in me and paid for my lessons in massage and gymnastics. But it was not until I went to Copenhagen that I saw really what I wanted."

"Don't the Danes hate the Swedes?" asked Longstaffe.

"Oh, hate! No. That's too much of a thing. But you know what it is when people lives close to one another—they see the spots. But they was kind to me in Copenhagen. Very kind. The Danes are jolly people—they drink and laugh and make love all the time. I soon had plenty of work—much as I could do. And good work. The doctors they liked me and sent me their patients. And I had work with the schools, too. And many friends. I was very happy."

"And, if it isn't impertinent, how was it you didn't marry?" Longstaffe asked.

"I was too busy. Always I wanted to make enough to come to England and see the place where mother was born. I hadn't time to be in love. There was the beginnings, yes, of course. The Danish women are very jolly, and they understand love, but when it came to something serious—I had no time. I had a nice flat out in Amager, and I worked from six in the morning until eleven at night. I can tell you I was tired sometimes.

"Then one day a strange thing occurred. One day I was walking by the shops and I saw a blue plate—one of those deep blues like the sea. I thought it was the most beautiful colour I'd ever seen. It wasn't glass, it were some sort of clay. I bought it and took it home.

"I put it on the mantelpiece of my sitting-room, and before it had been there half an hour the mantelpiece looked shabby, so I went out and bought two pictures—prints of Copenhagen. In the evening I was looking up at that plate, and the rug in front of the fire were so faded I was properly ashamed of it. So in the morning I went out and bought a new rug, a good one, purple colour to go with the plate. Then I had a terrible time. Everything in the room looked wrong by that rug—old shabby things, no sort of use. I cleared them all out. The room was bare. I whitewashed the walls. I put my money together and bought a Zorn etching. It was like a fever, then. It spread to my other rooms, then my clothes, then the view out of my windows. My flat looked on to a blank wall. I changed the flat and got another that looked over the water and the trees. Then one day in a bookshop window I saw a book open, and one page had Donatello's 'David,' and the other one of his prophets for the Florence

Cathedral. I couldn't forget that prophet all day. I went back the next morning and bought the book. That morning my life changed. I said, why shouldn't it be now once again in the world as it was then—why shouldn't we build towns in which everything was beautiful, lovely streets, wonderful statues?

"And I thought of England and that town my mother had talked about with the Cathedral, and I swore that one day I would go there and would live there and work there, and—and—here I am!"

He stretched out his arms. "And I'm happy. I've found my work and my life, and every one are kind to me, and already I make a living. Oh! how fortunate I have been!"

"And you don't feel," Longstaffe asked, "any sense of exile? You're not home-sick?"

"No; how can I be? Is not this my home? Was not my mother born here? And for that is not the world my home? Will I not go afterwards to Italy and China and Spain and see all the wonderful things men before me have made? All the world is my home."

Once again Longstaffe felt as he had done when first he had heard his friend talking to Ronder—a wish to warn him that this place into which he had come was not so simple and that these people with whom he had chosen to live were neither so straightforward nor so unsophisticated. But he could not. He could say nothing. It might be that after all Johanson was seeing them more truly than he. He had lived in the place so long. He had his prejudices; especially he had them since Mary's disgrace. What if Johanson after all did make the place different, the place and every one in it? Did not people become what you thought them? And might not some one as genuine and sincere as this man . . . ?

But Ronder. And Bentinck-Major. And the Bishop. And men in the town like that rogue Hogg. He would wait. At least Johanson had made a good beginning. The Town, conservative to its core about foreigners, nevertheless liked him. He heard nothing but good reports of him. Every one seemed to be glad that he had come. He would leave it alone and wait.

They had walked on a little while in silence when Johanson said:

"Do you ever dream?"

"Dream?" Longstaffe laughed. "Too busy."

"No, but I mean at night. Do you ever have the same dream again and again?"

"Why, I have a nightmare sometimes if I've been working too late or eating something."

"No, not a nightmare. A happy dream. The vision of a place—a house, a garden. Always the same house, very quiet, very beautiful. Somewhere that is yours more than anything in real life is, something so quiet and so still—"

Their road suddenly joined the other road from the town, the St. Mary's Road, and they were caught in a throng of men and boys who were going up to the football. Some one spoke to Longstaffe. They were no longer alone.

They arrived at the field where the game was, passed through the gate, paid their sixpences and walked forward.

Along the centre of one side there was a rough-and-ready stand, but most of the company were lining up beside the ropes and Johanson and Longstaffe did the same. They had scarcely taken their places when the teams ran out on to the field.

"It's South *versus* North Glebeshire," Longstaffe explained. "A very important game. It's the last of the season, a return match. The North won in the game before Christmas, but only just, twelve points to nine, so we're bent on winning this time."

Johanson had never seen a game of Rugby football before. They played plenty of Association in Scandinavia, and he was himself a good player. At once, when the Southern forwards had kicked off and charged down the field, he sniffed the air, his heart began to pound and his fingers to twitch. It was always so when he watched any game. It was the same, too, with Longstaffe, and it was as though the one electric current ran through the bodies of the two men, eagerly hanging forward over the rope, pressed shoulder to shoulder.

Johanson very quickly picked up the main points of the game, helped by Longstaffe. The principle was the same as in all the other games in the world. At first the frequent blowing of the referee's whistle and the many ensuing "scrums" troubled him, but from the moment, about ten minutes after the start, when the Southern three-quarters started down the field slinging the ball from man to man, his excitement knew no bounds. He stamped with his feet and shouted, crying, "Splendid! Splendid! Good! Very good! Bravo!"

Longstaffe too was shouting like a man possessed, his little twisted face purple: "Go on! Run yourself! Don't pass, Coppy! Keep it! Keep it, you fool ..." and then his voice suddenly dropping, "What *did* he pass for? He'd have got in if he'd held on!"

"Yes, damned fool," said a youth next to Longstaffe, sucking a straw. "It was young Coppy let us down the last blasted time. Got a match, mister?"

"That was fine," Johanson cried, his face flushed, his feet still tapping the ground.

"We ought to get over now," Longstaffe said excitedly, "we're right on their line."

Johanson felt, as he had felt so often before in his life, that surge of vitality that almost forbade him to stand where he was.

As he stared at the straining backs and thighs of the pushing, struggling scrums he wanted to rush into the field and shove too. Several boys and young men were running up to the far end of the field to see better what was occurring, and his impulse was to run with them. But he held on to the ropes, leaning forward, the men on either side of him yelling, "Shove them over! Shove the b——s over! You've got them! You've got them, by G——!"

But the South had not got them. The Northern back ran in and relieved by a long kick into touch, and the men came streaming down the field.

As the players came towards mid-field Johanson noticed in the Northern team one of the three-quarters—the merest boy—and suddenly he was deeply sympathetic to him. He looked younger and slighter than any other man on the ground, and in his face was a look of eager, almost bitter, determination which Johanson understood exactly.

This was perhaps his first important game, it meant almost everything to him, and so far not a chance had come his way. It might be that he had been put into the team at the last moment as a substitute and was being watched and criticised by the men behind the rope and knew that it was so. He was outside wing on the far side of the field and the ball *would* not come his way. Then suddenly it was swinging in his direction. The inside wing, getting it, seemed to hesitate as to whether he would go on himself, then, a Southern three-quarter coming for him, at the last moment, before he fell, slung it out to the boy.

The young fellow was off. He had slipped his opposing "three" and now had a clear course, running like slipping water, just inside the touch line. Oh, he could run! and Johanson was glad. Five minutes before he had been shouting for the Southerners, but now, although it was a Northern three-quarter who had the ball, once again, crimson in the face, he was shouting, "Well done! Bravo! Splendid! Splendid!"

The Southern full-back was after him, made a dash for his knees, missed them, went sprawling. The boy was over and, unopposed, touched the ball down between the posts.

There was a roar from the Northern supporters. Johanson roared too.

"Well, you're a nice one," said Longstaffe. "You're a Southerner. What are you shouting North for?"

"I'm very sorry," said Johanson, "I couldn't help it. He wanted his chance and he *could* run. Oh, he could! Bravo! Bravo!"

The kick for goal failed: the game went on for a while in the middle of the field, the whistle blew and it was halftime. The teams moved about sucking lemons, lying on their backs, kicking the lemon-peel. . . .

There was a hush, and the sun, and the pale sky, and a March wind blowing across the ground suddenly seemed to enter the field like new spectators.

Longstaffe put his hand through Johanson's arm:

"Enjoying yourself?"

"Should just think so."

"That's right. We'll come to lots more games together. I am glad you've come to this town. It's not that I've been lonely exactly these last years. Oh, well I have, if you want to know. It's strange, but I can talk to you more easily than to most of my own countrymen."

"Yes. I can to you."

"It's as though we had known one another all our lives."

Johanson pressed Longstaffe's arm. "We'll stick together always—just like this. It don't matter *what* shall happen. I have always thought it should be the finest thing in the whole world to have a man friend whom nothing can alter.

Love—that is something different. It comes—it goes. Now it is up, now it is down. But friendship is a steady thing. It is always there. You must not for ever be looking to see whether it grows or dies. I have never had a real man friend before."

It seemed to him as he looked across the field that everything had suddenly been given to him. Home, ambition, work, friendship—and love? At that he caught his breath. The figures, talking their places for the second half, were blurred. Was that the true reason for all his happiness to-day? Was he at last, after all these years, in love? He saw the girl moving before him with that tantalising glance, that eye suddenly soft and appealing, the yellow hair. . . . His happiness was suddenly confused. He did not know that he wanted to be in love. Work and friendship, those were straightforward things that he understood. But this—there was some hint of danger in it. It seemed suddenly to thicken the pure austerity of the work that he had before him. But could he deny it? If it came to him, could he refuse it? And why should he? Would not a home and children be the best thing for him?

His happiness was changed. His eyes were no longer on the game. He did not notice that, as is the way with March weather, a little wind had come up and with it a flurry of thin rain driving in thin silver lines about the field. A cloud reached out and caught the sun. Men on every side were turning up their coat collars.

He realised that some one was speaking to Longstaffe, and, turning, saw that it was that stout, red-faced fellow who had come in on that first evening at Mrs. Penethen's. He was smiling. He stretched out his hand.

"Good-day, Mr. Johnson. You won't remember me. We met some weeks ago. Seen you about the streets occasionally."

"How do you do?" Johanson shook his hand, which was soft and warm.

"Fine game!"

"Yes, it is."

"Ever seen our Rugby before?"

"No, never."

"Ah! must be interesting for you?"

"Yes, very."

"Glad to hear you're doing so well. Must come in one day and 'ave some exercises. Take down some of my fat."

Johanson said nothing. The man nodded and moved on.

Johanson said to Longstaffe, "That man came into Mrs. Penethen's the first night I arrived. What's his name?"

"Hogg—Samuel Hogg."

"I don't like him."

Longstaffe dropped his voice. "No, he's a bad lot. Was a publican once. Now he owns most of the Polchester slums. He's behind most of the rotten things in the town. He's a bad hat."

"He's a friend of a man at Mrs. Penethen's who helped me about getting my rooms."

"I'm sorry to hear that," Longstaffe said. "Have as little to do with him as you can."

They turned back to the game. The misty rain made it difficult to see. There was no more scoring, however, and just as the whistle blew for "time" the storm drove across the field in torrents.

CHAPTER VI

THE SISTERS

Maude Penethen had known, ever since she was conscious of anything at all that she was beautiful to look upon. Almost as swiftly had come the further discovery that others were, for the most part, ugly, or if not ugly, plain, undistinguished.

She had WONDERFUL HAIR—gold, auburn, butter-cups, sunset, amber, but for the most part GOLDEN—"liquid gold" an old fat friend of her mother's had once called it, running the strands through his podgy fingers when she was quite a little girl.

This hair, this delicate, slight body, these tiny hands and feet, these red lips and large "laughing eyes"—that also from the little podgy man—she realised, very early indeed, that these were the things that she had, and that because of these people would pay her more attention than they did to other girls.

She naturally centred in more and more upon herself.

As she grew she became, in certain directions, frank about herself. She knew that she was not what people called "clever"—that is, not clever at books and sums and things like geography and history. But she could see, very quickly indeed, what people were after, especially boys—and then, in a year or two, especially men. She could hold her own with any man. She knew, or thought that she knew, from a very early time everything about "Love." As a matter of honest record she knew nothing about "Love" at all.

She was vain, violent-tempered and selfish, but with those things went a most attaching streak of naïveté, simplicity, purity. She never listened to the other girls when they whispered stories to one another at the High School. Just as she would spend hours, were she permitted, in attending to her body, washing it, beautifying it in every way that she knew, so also she kept her mind clean. She fussed about her bedroom seeing that it was spotlessly neat. Her linen, a tremendous preoccupation with her, was bright and fresh like clear water.

Her violent temper was considered by herself rather an asset. She could "turn it on" when it would be useful to her. She was afraid of one person in the world—her mother—but only of one. Upon her mother her tempers had no effect whatever.

With the mind and vision, of a grown woman she knew that she was beautiful and that men would always desire her. Behind that knowledge was the heart and ignorance of a little child. She thought that she was astonishingly unusual. She saw no one in her world in the least like her. They said in the town that young Lady St. Leath was beautiful. Maude liked to look at Lady St. Leath, and then indulge in one of her triumphant exultations. That girl, riding in her carriage, opening a bazaar, walking with her husband—that girl with the simple face and the simple clothes and the timid smile—she might have her castle and her fat husband, her old cockatoo of a mother-in-law and her little baby boy—have them and welcome—she couldn't hold a candle to Maude Penethen!

And in her heart Maude knew that Lady St. Leath had something that she had not but would adore to have!

Sometimes, after she had gone up to bed, she would strip and sit naked on her bed looking out at the moon, and let her red-gold hair down and dip her shoulders luxuriously into it, putting her hands round the small firm cups of her breasts, and so sit, hunched up, breathing with deep luxurious pleasure, staring through the window, then glancing down at her tiny feet, then through the window again as though she were inviting some one to come in.

And once in his calm, unblinking fashion Reuben Fletch had placed his arm round her waist and tried to kiss her. How she had slapped his cheeks! Her rage! How terrible! How magnificent! And Reuben Fletch had seemed to like her anger.

She had a plain sister. She had never *quite* accustomed herself to Judy's plainness. And there was something more than that—the fact that Judy seemed to be proud of her plainness. Had she, Maude, been as plain as Judy she would not have known how to lift her head in company. But Judy had a pride, the sort of pride that baffled Maude just as something in Lady St. Leath baffled her. She could not understand why people who should surely have baffled her much more—old Canon Ronder, for instance, and Reuben Fletch and Samuel Hogg, did not baffle her at all, whereas Judy and Lady St. Leath had something . . .

She did not know Judy's feelings towards her. She herself did not dislike Judy. She pitied her. And she was honest enough not to pretend to herself that Judy was jealous of her. No, with all her plainness, Judy envied no one in the world. She wanted to be only herself.

And Maude was more honest than that. She knew that she was selfish and that Judy, were her affection moved, was not. She, Maude, gloried in her selfishness. She didn't care. She wanted to live—to have Everything! As Reuben Fletch in his room upstairs was greedy of money, so was she greedy of life and success and admiration.

She wanted to be the first in this house, and then the first in the town, and then the first in England, and then—the first in the world. Well, why not? Was there any one like her anywhere? Any one so lovely?

She stood up naked before her glass, her hands rippling through her hair, seeing the faint thin shadows lie, as though they were painted, under her breasts, on her thighs.

She sighed. She laughed. Yes, she was lovely. And the Swede, the Dane, whatever he was, the child, the simpleton, was in love with her.

She thought of that. Saw him standing above her, around her. She saw herself, a little ball. He picked her up with his great arms and held her close to his breast. She shivered with delight. At least she would be engaged to him. Just to annoy Judy. Just to feel his lips upon hers. Just to see that childish look of wonder lighten his eyes. To know that she could do that—do that with any man!

But marriage? She began to put on her clothes. Well, marriage was a long way off.

She was downstairs in the big kitchen-living-room, alone in the house. She was sitting in the old rocking-chair, creaking backwards and forwards, reading the serial story in *The Golden Penny*. The round, moon-faced clock clattered the hour—four o'clock. There was a knock on the door. She went across, opened it and looked into the darkening street. An old woman stood there.

"I beg your pardon," said Maude.

"Oh, isn't this Mrs. Penethen's?"

"Yes, it is. But she's out."

"Oh! I wanted to speak to a Mr. Johnson, a foreign gentleman, who lodges here."

"Yes, he does. But he's out too."

"Oh . . . Oh yes. Thank you, I'm sure. I wonder if I might leave a message for him?"

"Certainly. Won't you come in? It's growing dark outside."

"Oh, thank you, I will."

Maude was nice to every one until she had conquered them and won them to her side. Then she didn't care. She knew at once who this old woman was when she saw her standing there under the light of the kitchen lamp. It was poor old Miss Eldred.

Poor Miss Eldred. As Maude emphasised to herself that happy adjective she felt an increased tenderness for her visitor. Seen there under the mellow light of the lamp she was indeed a poor old creature with her black bonnet and its faded strings, her crinkled, anxious pink face, her worn black mantle, her thin black cotton gloves. Some wisps of grey hair straggled untidily beneath the bonnet. At the tip of her pinched, inquisitive nose was a dew-drop of emotion. She had the faded air of a print exposed too long to every kind of weather. She was mottled and anxious and obsequious.

"I am sure, Miss Penethen, it is too, too good of you to have me in like this. And your time so valuable too, I'm sure. It is merely—if I might entrust a message—if I am not too—"

She came to a sudden pause as though her agitation—which she had been expressing with every kind of movement of the gloved hands, pushing them now at her throat, now at her watery eyes, now to cover her thin and hard lips—was too strong for her.

"Oh dear, oh dear," she murmured at last, gazing about the room with an eye that was both despairing and inquisitive. "I *know* that I'm taking up your time—"

"Of course you're not," said Maude, gazing on her with kindness. The poor old thing! And to think that when Maude had been a little girl Miss Eldred had been a Power. Well, if not exactly a Power, at any rate some one held up to admiration with her class for Modelling in Wax, her "Bead-work" Courses and her "Talks on British Painters." Why had it all come so suddenly to an end? Maude did not know. She did not greatly care. And suddenly her patience was over. She wished to return to her *Golden Penny*. Her eyes hardened. Miss Eldred perceived it. She was suddenly quite brisk.

"Yes, dear Miss Penethen. It is only that your lodger, Mr. Johnson, expressed a wish to a friend of mine that he might meet me. It seems that he is interested in the Arts. He heard that there we had a common bond. . . . Quite, quite. I thought that I would leave my address—and a word to say that if I can be, in my poor, humble way, of any use—"

She pressed a soiled card into Maude's hand and turned to the door.

Her voice was suddenly sharp and acid:

"You won't forget to give it to him, I beg?"

"No," said Maude, startled at the new tone.

"Good night, then," and the old figure was gone.

The clock ticked on, the coal slipped and stuttered in the grate and Maude read on. The serial story, "A Princess of Vascovy," was exciting, the pictures enchanting, but—but—

What was he about to have an old wretch like that in his company? What could that old thing do for him but make him ridiculous? What kind of a man must he be to seem so simple about other people? The paper slipped to the floor. The man rose in front of her, standing with his stature and strength between her and the fire, and as she gazed at her picture of him there rose in her breast a strange mingling of pity and contempt—contempt that he, so mature and so strong, could be such a fool, pity because he needed some one to look after him, to advise him. She jumped up and began to move about the room and soon, as they so often did, her steps turned into a dancing measure. She was turning, twisting, twirling, turning . . .

The street door opened. Some one paused to hang up a coat. Maude turned expectant, then sighed—it was only Judy!

Judy was the last person she wanted just then. But Judy was always the last person she wanted. She wondered—as she had so often wondered before—how Judy could be her sister! That straight, thin creature, like a stick, without a curve in her, so black and so frowning and disapproving! Judy disapproved of everything she did, of everything she said, of everything that she thought! Well, so much the worse for Judy, then—stupid, stuck-up thing! *She* didn't care! Let her disapprove! And yet well she knew how pleasant it would be to win Judy's approval, to win it only for a moment and then to show her how little she cared whether she had it or no!

Judy, as was her custom, said nothing. She came forward, bent upon the fire her dark, far-seeing eyes, then quietly sat down on a little stiff-backed chair. And, as had happened on many thousand occasions before, Maude was irritated by her silence, was uncomfortable indeed at anybody's silence, fearing it as something dangerous and threatening.

"Old Miss Eldred's been here," she said half truculently, half expectantly. Judy said nothing.

"She was asking for Mr. Johnson." Judy slowly raised her eyes.

"Mr. Johnson? What did she want with him?"

Maude continued to dance, moving in and out, up and down across the old floor.

"Oh, I don't know. He wanted to see her."

"To see her? To see Miss Eldred?"

"Yes. . . . You heard, stupid."

"To see Miss Eldred? Mr. Johnson?"

Maude stopped and came over to the fire. "Yes. . . . Oh please, Miss Penethen. . . ." She imitated Miss Eldred's obsequious voice and nervous movements. "I know I'm taking up your time, but that nice Mr. Johnson—"

"She didn't say that nice Mr. Johnson," Judy interrupted indignantly.

"All right, have it your own way. I ought to know, oughtn't I?" Continuing Miss Eldred: "He wants some one to help him make Polchester beautiful, and he's asked me to help him, and here I am—"

"I don't believe a word of it," Judy answered. "Why, Miss Eldred's awful! She drinks and steals and does everything dreadful."

"The man's a simpleton," said Maude. "That's the truth about Mr. Harmer John. He's been having old Benjie Shortt in his office. He's going to give him work to do and pay him a regular salary. He's potty."

"How dare you," Judy flared up. "What do you know about it? You're the laziest and most ignorant girl in Polchester. What do you know about his reasons or his work or anything else? If he thinks Mr. Shortt can help him he probably can. It's just his kindness, anyway."

Maude's beautiful eyes gleamed with malicious pleasure.

"So that's it, is it?" she said, laughing. "You're in love with him, are you, like Miss Midgeley and mother? Like every one in this house except Mr. Fletch and myself."

Judy sprang up.

"Now, don't you say that, Maude Penethen. You're always making mischief wherever you can. I'm not in love with any man, I hate them all."

"Well, you're jealous of me, then. You know you are. You know he's in love with me and has been from the first moment he set eyes on me. And you hate me having any fun. You always do and you always have."

"He's too good for you," Judy answered fiercely, "a thousand times too good for you. You're playing with him as you've played with lots of others. When you're tired of it you'll just break his heart, and it's a shame, a wicked shame!"

Maude did not resent this. She took it as a tribute.

"How do you know it's just like the others?" she said slowly. "Perhaps it isn't. *He* isn't like the others. Not a bit like any one else. Maybe you're wrong this time, Miss Know-All. You're not always right, with all your cleverness."

"I know this, anyway," said Judy, "that there couldn't be anything more unhappy for him in the world than his marrying you. He isn't your sort. He doesn't begin to understand a girl like you. He *is* simple in a kind of a way. He hasn't met many women, I should think—not *really* met them. Oh, leave him alone, Maude! You wouldn't be happy if you *were* married to him! He would take it so seriously. And you couldn't be faithful to any one, not if you tried ever so!"

"Oh, couldn't I?" Maude began to dance again. "You know an awful lot, don't you? But I tell you this," she came dancing round until she stood over her sister: "If you try and interfere with me in this, I—I—I'll pull your hair out! And you haven't such a lot that you can afford to miss any."

Their mother came in. Mrs. Penethen, although she was only a daughter of a small Glebeshire farmer, had a very fine air. She had got it, perhaps, from the Castle, where she had been, as a girl, under-housemaid. Or she had it from one of those old Glebeshire raiders who had been kings in their day. Or she had got it . . . but never mind. She had it. She was a distinguished woman, and "what I like about Mrs. Penethen," Mrs. Sampson, the Dean's wife, had said, "is that she always keeps her place." In 1907 in Polchester it was still important that places should be kept.

Never mind. Mrs. Penethen was passive about this, as she was about everything else. Every mother must learn passivity, must develop that internal security and peace whence no eccentricity or selfishness of husband or children can drive them.

Years of married life with her John had begun to teach her, years of motherhood of Maude and Judy had completed the lesson. She was serene whatever occurred, the serenest woman in Polchester. To her boarders, her children, her friends, to them all alike she was, if not indifferent (that would imply a cold heart, and she had a warm one), remote. She lived her own secret life.

But, just at this time, for the first occasion for many a while, her remoteness was threatened. It was threatened because of her feeling for her lodger, Mr. Johnson. She had never recovered from that strange sense of intimacy with which she had recognised him on that evening of his sudden arrival, and that intimacy was the stranger because she never liked foreigners; but he had not been a foreigner, in spite of his accent, his broken English and the rest.

He was almost like a son of her own; he drew from her the maternal, and the maternal was the strongest passion in her. She had been maternal to her John in spite of, perchance because of, his many infidelities, and she would have been maternal to Maude and Judy had they allowed her. They had not allowed her, and therefore she had taken refuge in her own dignified serenity.

But now once again, after so many years, there was some one who needed her. And he was in love with her Maude. It was this that threatened her serenity, because she was not sure of Maude. She was not sure, although she was her own mother, whether the girl were good or bad. Not all good, of course, nor all bad. She knew the girl's faults, her vanity, her selfishness, her obstinacy, her bad temper, but she knew also something childlike and touching that was there, something innocent and wondering and naïve.

A real love, a true love, might be the making of the girl, but did she care for him? Was it only vanity or his strangeness that touched her? And meanwhile if he, Harmer John, as the whole town now called him, was to be hurt and wounded by her own child, she would never forgive herself. No, she would never forgive herself.

As she came into the kitchen she looked at her two daughters and saw that they had been quarrelling again. They were always quarrelling. She stood before the fire warming her thin hands and gazing into the crimson glow very much as Judy had done a little while before.

"Oh, mother," Maude burst out, "who do you think has been here? That old Miss Eldred. And what do you think she wanted? To see Mr. Johnson. To help him in his Art, if you please. She said he wanted her to help him. What can he be thinking of?"

"More than you understand, I've no doubt, dear," said Mrs. Penethen.

"Oh, of course, I don't understand anything," said Maude, tossing her head, "*I* never do," and wondering for the thousandth time, as many a girl before her has wondered and many a time since, why they were all so stupid in her family (yes, and old Miss Midgeley too) not to see how charming and amusing and attractive she was, a fact most patent to all the outside world.

"You don't understand much, and that's a fact," said Mrs. Penethen placidly, "and I won't have you going about with Samuel Hogg. For one thing, he's nearly old enough to be your grandfather, and for another he's no gentleman."

"I don't go about with him," said Maude, suddenly sulking. "If he speaks to me, I can't prevent him, can I?"

"Now, I mean this, Maude. You've got no father, and I'm the only one to look after you. You know he's a bad man, and all the town knows it, so that's enough."

"Who says I go about with him?"

"Never mind who. It's a fact and I've told you. He's not coming inside this house again if I know it."

"Well, I don't like him," said Maude with one of those sudden submissions of hers that were so charming, "so you needn't bother your head, mother."

"That's a good girl," said Mrs. Penethen.

Upon the tranquil scene there suddenly ventured Miss Midgeley, coming in, as she always did, with a sarcastic expression on her twisted countenance. Miss Midgeley was a lady, a lady born and a lady bred, and all the Penethens were aware of that. Mrs. Penethen and Judy liked her, liked her both because she was a lady and because she was sarcastic, and those were precisely the reasons why Maude disliked her but wished to be liked *by* her.

Miss Midgeley was carrying various small parcels and was looking rather pleased with herself. She dressed mannishly, a brown waistcoat with brass buttons, a hard white collar and a short brown skirt. Her iron-grey hair was brushed back sharply under her hat. Her little puckered face, strawberry colour, was alert and cynical.

She leaned on the table and looked at the three women.

"Well," she said, "now you'll ask me where I've been and what I've been doing, and I'll tell you. I've been shopping and talking to Society. You'll ask, 'What Society?' and I'll reply, 'The very best.' None other than our dear Mrs. Bond, who met me in the High Street and said, 'Why, Miss Midgeley, what an age it is since we've met!' Smiling so sweetly too, and I said, 'Yes'; and she said, 'Working at anything just now?' and I said, 'Yes'; and she said, 'One of your delightful girl stories, I suppose?' and I said, 'Yes,' and she said, 'I do so wonder how you can write. It *must* be so difficult. I remember once I met Olive Schreiner in South Africa and said the same thing to her.' I said, 'Yes' again, and here I am just as though nothing had happened!"

Maude never knew how to take Miss Midgeley when she talked in this fashion. Had she met Mrs. Bond in the High Street and Mrs. Bond had stopped and spoken to her, she would have alluded to it carelessly afterwards as though she didn't care in the least, but Miss Midgeley really seemed *not* to care! Maude would have cared very much.

"Well, I don't like that Mrs. Bond," said Mrs. Penethen. "She talks too much and says things about people she shouldn't."

"Which reminds me," said Miss Midgeley suddenly, "she had something else to say to me. She understood that this gymnastic instructor Mr.—what was his name?—was living in the same house as myself. She had heard that he was a delightful man—what was my opinion? Well, my opinion was not for her basket, and so I just said 'Yes' again and left her staring; but you'll all be glad to hear that she's sending both her younger boys to his gymnasium class, so our Mr. Johnson is in luck."

She paused, raised her head sharply, whistled a few notes of a little tune (a favourite habit of hers) and said:

"Judy, suppose you come up to my room a minute and arrange these odds and ends—and very odds and ends they are, too. I've got some flowers here that want water."

"She never asks me to her room," said Maude discontentedly, as she watched them vanish through the door, "and I'm much more amusing than Judy."

"Perhaps that's why," said Mrs. Penethen placidly.

Maude suddenly burst out, "Mother, I'm sick of this! I'm going to find some work and get away from this town."

"Yes, dear," said her mother, "what kind of work?"

"Oh, anything! All sorts of girls are working nowadays—nobody stays at home any more."

"Yes, dear. But what direction exactly were you thinking of?"

"Oh, I don't know. There are lots of things. I know you think I can't do anything. You all do in this house. You and Miss Midgeley and Judy. And Judy's jealous because Mr. Johnson's in love with me."

For once Mrs. Penethen was indignant. "I just won't have you saying that, Maude. For one thing, it isn't true, and then it's a nasty thought to have of your sister. You don't seem to have any natural feelings."

"Well, she is, then," retorted Maude. "You should have seen her flare up just now when I said he was a fool to have people like old Shortt and Miss Eldred round. And so he *is* a fool. I'd tell him to his face."

Mrs. Penethen put out her hand and drew Maude towards her. The girl came reluctantly.

"Be more loving, Maude. Don't be hating everybody so. Hating never did any one any good that I ever heard of. Yes, wriggle away from your old mother. She won't try to keep you. I've learnt my lesson. You can't keep any one in this world if they don't want to stay—no, not though you break your heart trying. But your mother's your friend—the best friend you'll ever have, maybe. I seem dried-up and old, but I've had my tempers in my time and have got 'em still, if all were known; but life's so short and men so everlastingly childish that it isn't worth fashing yourself. You're pretty, Maude, and men will run after your body from all sides of the town, but a good man will ask questions about your soul, and that's the only way you'll hold him."

"Oh, the soul!" Maude broke in impatiently. She had been standing close at her mother's side, her head cocked a little like a bird on the alarm. "That's all right, mother, when you're old, but I'm young and I want to have some fun. I know I'm the prettiest girl in the town, and every one else knows it. I won't be pretty always. I know that. No one ever is. And I want to dance, and have men look at me as though they could eat me, and then tell them I don't like them. I'm all right, mother. I can look after myself. There isn't a man in the place can touch me if I don't want him to."

"Well, that's bad talk, Maude," Mrs. Penethen answered, "that's what it is. You and your prettiness! So you *are* pretty in a sort of way, but you haven't done half for yourself that you might have done. When have you ever learnt anything? Haven't I tried again and again to get you to make yourself useful? What man will want to marry you when he knows you can't cook nor sew nor look after a house to keep it clean and decent? And the way you talk as though any man who saw you would fall at your feet! There's many of them would think you too stupid to spend five minutes with. No, if a good man comes along and likes you, think yourself lucky and take your chance. And consider others a little—Selfish! Why, I never met such selfishness!"

Maude was so often unexpected. Now she smiled, bent down and kissed her mother's cheek.

"Mother, dear, I know who you're thinking of. He does like me, doesn't he? And I like him. He's so strong and he's such a baby. I can do anything with him—*anything*. And he's going to have a good position here, too. Every one likes him. He goes to Canon Ronder's house three times a week to bring his fat down. Do you think he'll ask me to marry him, mother?"

Mrs. Penethen looked past her daughter into space.

"If he does," she said slowly, "and you accept him, it will be more than you deserve, Maude Penethen. And if after that you treat him badly, don't look to me for sympathy. I would never forgive you."

The kitchen door opened, and the man of whom they were speaking came in.

The thing that Mrs. Penethen noticed about him now—and it was the first thing always that she noticed about him—was his cleanliness. No men with whom she had been concerned—not her husband nor his friends nor the men about the house, not Fletch nor, if you carried it farther, any of the townsmen of the place, had *his* kind of cleanliness! Of course the gentry—Bentinck-Major, Ronder, Ryle and *their* world—with them you expected a superior neatness, although some of them were shabby enough. But with Harmer John—she had fallen, as they all had, into the town's diminutive—it was something much more than neatness—he wasn't neat at all—something more than cleanliness even: a radiant physical health that came from his contentment of mind as well as from fitness of body.

He hung up his hat and his coat, then came across to them, ruffling his hand through his hair. He stood over them, looking down upon them, his legs wide. But it was not true that he was looking down upon them; he was staring at Maude as though he saw her for the first time.

She, looking up at him, was aware, as though she had slipped from one room into another, of a new experience. Was it love? She had never felt like this before. Call it rather physical consciousness. She was aware, as she had never been, of his black rumpled hair, his blue eyes, his round face crooked a little because he was smiling, his immense breadth, rocking himself so slightly on his heels. She had a consciousness that his arms were moving out towards her (although she knew that they stayed motionless at his side), and for the very first time in her life she was confused, tranced in a hot mist of arrested feeling, so that her heart was not beating, her eyes not stirring and she could think of nothing—only of those advancing arms that yet did not advance.

It seemed to be long after that she moved her head and saw that her mother had left them and was attending to something in a cupboard at a far part of the room.

Their conversation then was absurd, meaningless, a scattering out on the floor of little coloured counters, nothing in themselves, but standing for a game of great import.

"Well, how's to-day been? Any new customers?"

"Yes . . . and I've been to Ronder's and given him a rub."

"Is he nice when you're rubbing him?"

"Yes—if he wouldn't be I could soon make him. He don't like to be hurt, that's certain. But he's a kind gentleman, speaking well of everybody."

"Oh, I expect he's all right. And what else have you done to-day?"

"I don't hope it could interest you telling you all about the class from the Boys' School, Miss Maude. But they'll be fine all the same when I've finished with them."

"Do you like boys better to drill, or men—or girls, perhaps?"

"Oh, it's much in a muchness. What I want is work, don't you see. Oh! I can't have too much of it . . . work . . . and love . . . only love . . ." His voice dropped. He was standing very close to her. She had sat down in the chair that her mother had vacated.

She had not heard anything that he had said. She felt his body above her; it was standing, it seemed to her, on every side of her. His eyes—so childlike and simple and unquestioning—embraced her. It was as though already he had held her in his arms, although in reality he had not touched her.

"Yes," she said, "go on, Mr. Johnson, it is so interesting."

"And so—and so—" he went on. But his voice broke. He could say nothing. His hand moved and touched the arm of the chair and the sleeve of her dress. "Now I must go—I must go—"

She said nothing. The kitchen was silent save for the ticking of the old round-faced clock. Mrs. Penethen was sitting at the table working at something in a black book.

"I must go—I must go—" She touched his hand lightly for a moment with hers. Then she sprang from her chair.

He moved carefully, as though he feared lest with an awkward movement he should break something, out to the stairs that led up to his room.

CHAPTER VII

THE BIRTHDAY PARTY

ALTHOUGH the year 1907 is not, as years go, so very distant, yet immense differences of thought and of actual living separate it from the life of our own day. One great difference—in our English country towns at any rate—is that we still in those pre-war years found much of our entertainment under the shadow of our own roof, beside the warmth of our own hearthstone. For the Polcastrian at any rate the cinema was not, the theatre *almost* was not, the circus twice a year only, the ball likewise. But in our own homes we had our own fun. It would seem simple enough, that fun, I have no doubt, to the dancers and theatre-goers of 1926, just as the dancers of 1926 will show a kind of barnyard air to the chickens of 1970, but happiness is happiness wherever and whenever it may come—and perhaps the simpler pleasures are, the happier they are. I don't know; I merely offer it as a possible suggestion.

In any case the Penethen kitchen was famous for its festivities. From the very earliest days of the Penethen married life parties—rollicking, rolling, riotous parties—had been given there, and even when Mr. Penethen had been at his most unfaithful, and the family coffer most nearly bankrupt, the parties had continued, nor had any observer detected at the heart of their splendour fainter fires.

For they *were* splendid, and they were splendid because Mrs. Penethen intended them to be so. Dry, austere, ironic as she might appear, at her heart she adored a party. Nothing pleased her more than to be asked to one—save in truth to give one herself.

She had the gift for a party. She knew precisely the ingredients of one. She could *bake* a party with the best—a little salt here, a little sugar there, so many raisins, some ginger and candied peel. . . . She had the lightest hand for a party in the four kingdoms. Christmas, Easter, and Maude's and Judy's birthdays, these were the occasions—and an out-of-doors picnic in the summer. She never invited too many guests. A dozen was enough for that kitchen. She knew her mind and held to it, and no agonised appeals on Maude's part to add one, two or three could change her.

"But it's *my* party, mother. It's *my* birthday."

"So it is, child."

"Then why can't I . . ."

And this year there was no begging for additions. Maude seemed satisfied. And every one knew why.

Maude was in time for breakfast *this* morning. Oh yes, certainly. And she timed her arrival with a charming appropriate gesture—every one there save

Reuben Fletch, but *only* just there, still gazing at the breakfast table and wondering whether it was eggs and bacon or sausages.

A moment later—just behind her in fact—Harmer John arrived on his way, as usual, to his office. He was carrying a pot of flowers in his hand. Wrapped in tissue paper. Maude, with a cry of delight, tore off the paper before looking at the other things on her plate. Very early daffodils.

"Oh, thank you, Mr. Johnson. Aren't they sweet?" But she was disappointed. She had expected that he would give her something better than mere flowers. He did not know that. He was blushing and staring straight into her eyes.

"Many happy birthdays!" he said. "I don't hope that you'll grow old—ever!" Which was so odd that they all laughed and while they were laughing he was gone.

There followed for Maude a slight sense of reaction. She had thought that he would stay "just this once." Not as though she had a birthday every day. Always his silly old business. What did ten minutes matter? And flowers? After all any one could give her flowers, and with all his talk of beautiful things. . . .

Nevertheless it was her intention to-day to be charming, and in a moment charming she was. It was not difficult. She loved to be given presents, she *adored* to be liked, to be the centre of attraction, to make people around her happy if to do so was easy, and did not make herself unhappy, and here they were, even Judy and Miss Midgeley looking at her kindly without that nasty "I-know-your-game" look in their eyes.

Herself looked bewitching. She knew that she did. She was never prettier than when she was in her simplest dress, to-day a pale blue frock, and an airy gentle poise about her as though at an instant she might be off through the window dancing through the light spring-whispering March air.

Her mother gave her a bead necklace, Judy a pair of gloves, old Midgeley some handkerchiefs. Fletch gave her nothing, of course. He had never been known to give anybody anything, but so gentle was his air, so amiable his smile as he wished her "Many happy returns," that it was as good as a present. And then the street bell rang. She danced herself to the door. A boy with a parcel. She was back among them, her face alight with excitement. What could it be? Something unusual. A box? No. A cage! And in the cage a nightingale. A card tied to the cage: "For Miss Maude Penethen, with the respectful compliments of Samuel Hogg."

"Samuel Hogg! But how did he know? How—?"

Her mother's voice interrupted her. "You must send it back. I won't have you taking presents from that man."

Her face clouded. Such a pretty cage! With gilt bars. And the nightingale was singing already.

Mrs. Penethen saw the frowning face. After all it was the child's birthday. Afterwards. . . . To-morrow. . . .

"Well, Maude, leave it. Only you've got to make it plain to him he's not to be giving you presents."

"Why, it's the first thing he's ever given me! And after all it'll be Judy's as much as mine."

"Yes," said Judy, "I'll have the looking after it. If it were left to you it would be dead in a day." Already she had gone to the cage and was talking to the bird. She loved animals passionately. The fox-terrier, Caesar, was hers. Maude hated dogs—rough messy things. But she liked cats—when they purred and nestled in your arms.

So every one was happy, and they settled down to the merriest breakfast ever.

Later there was peace in the kitchen. Only Mrs. Penethen was there, seated at the table peeling potatoes. They were all away busy about their own affairs, Fletch at his office, Maude shopping in the town, Judy upstairs doing the rooms, assisted by Mary-Thomasine, the maid-of-all-work, who was stupid but willing, Miss Midgeley in *her* room writing perhaps, reading perhaps—who knows? A funny old maid with her own ideas. And Mrs. Penethen as she peeled her potatoes (just as Miss Midgeley upstairs was peeling her ideas) was thinking deeply.

On the preceding evening Harmer John had spoken to her. They had been alone in the kitchen and he had sat down beside her and asked her whether he had her permission to propose marriage to her daughter. She had heard him out in her silent determined way. What he had said had been very simple. He loved her daughter, Maude, with all his heart and soul. He had loved her from the first moment he had seen her. Of course he was a foreigner and she might not wish that her daughter should marry a foreigner. But he was half English, the stronger half of himself, he thought. He had saved a little money, not much but something. He was doing very well here. His business was increasing every day. In the last month he had made a profit. It might become a very large business, and in any case he was not a boy to lose his head and be extravagant. He would be faithful to Maude. He was not a man who ran after women. He did not drink nor gamble.

He was strong and would work for her with every muscle in his body. He had never loved a woman before. He thought that perhaps she cared for him.

Mrs. Penethen heard him out and then she said that if Maude was willing she also was willing, and upon that he turned and had his arms around her and hugged the breath out of her body. No one had ever hugged her before. Her husband had never hugged her in his most loving moments. His way had been different, looking at her with his brown eyes and his strange pleading smile. But this man had hugged her as her son might have hugged her had she had one. Now as she sat there peeling her potatoes the memory of that embrace touched her heart, so lonely for so long a time, most deeply. She had tried, after that, to be her sensible self, telling him that Maude was very young and knew nothing about life at all; that his position was still uncertain, and that even if Maude were willing to marry him they must be engaged for a while and see how everything went.

He agreed to that: it was what he himself would wish. Looking back, his triumphant unquestioning happiness frightened her. How little he knew Maude! He thought her an angel! Maude an angel!

But then love might change Maude, might give her all that at present she lacked. She sighed over her potatoes. Had she done right? Right for him, she meant.

It occurred to her as she sat there how strange it was that all her anxiety should be for *him*! Here was she, about to accomplish the thing that had been for years to her a harrowing and constant anxiety—Maude's engagement to a good man (it had always been so possible with her looks that she would marry a bad one), and now it was about the *man's* happiness that she was thinking, the man whom, a few weeks ago, she had neither seen nor considered. And with that she was aware, sharply, of her deep affection for this man. Affection! Nay, love—love as though he had been truly her son. It was all the maternal in her that he had touched. He would appeal chiefly perhaps to rather elderly lonely women, women who had lost their husbands or sons, or had better have lost them, women who had longed for children and been denied, women who had loved and not been loved in return. There was something simple, trusting and ignorant about him that made her for ever want to call out to him: "Look out! Take care! There's danger that way!" Not that the man was a fool or unpractical—his ability at his job showed that he was not that—but he did not know enough about people, he trusted them too readily, he—And with that she was aware with a second stab of sharpness that it was against her very own girl, Maude, that she was moving forward now to warn him—"Look out! Take care! She's not like that! I know her!"

For shame! Her own daughter! A good girl at heart. Love for a good man was what she needed. This was the very thing. . . . But as she peeled her potatoes she shook her head and sighed. If any harm came to him through her daughter! But what harm could come? He was a man. He could fend for himself. He was a boy too, a child—and as she thought of that she smiled. And she was in no kind of way whatever a sentimental woman.

By seven o'clock that evening everything was ready. The carpet was up, the old board floor waxed and shining, and the trestles and boards (a hundred years old at least) in the place of the familiar table.

It was a chill March evening, the sky palely green beyond the window at the setting of the sun, little aguish winds creeping round the Cathedral corners, the few primroses in the lanes above the town shivering before they slept, but in the great oven the fire was so hot that the warming-pans, blue plates, the copper pots and the picture of Queen Victoria receiving news of her Accession, all smiled in the heat. Down the long table, causing the sturdy trestles to do their full duty, were the "Eatables." "Eatables" sanctioned by a strange Penethen tradition that had persisted now for twenty years at least without the shadow of a change—a huge Glebeshire-cured ham, two vast veal and ham pies, two great dishes of Cornish pasties, loaves of bread mountain high, moons of butter so handsome that the face of the great Alderney cow stamped upon them was triumphant in its arrogance, honeycombs dripping with amber sweetness, and Glebeshire cream with a crust as richly thick as a parchment missal. And this Gargantuan feast for twelve persons only! Well, there—were others—Mrs. Penethen made her Feasts the excuse for After-Feast charities, and the pensioners on her bounty would be calling to-morrow morning and mornings again after that.

I have said nothing of the drinks because the guests, for the chief part, would drink—tea! Yes, and tea of no ordinary quality, so strong and so black that Glebeshire women boasted that one cup of it would slaughter strangers from "Up-Along" by the myriad; even "Quality" from the town, though they had lived in Polchester all their days, had been known to faint before it.

But there was beer and cider for the men—and a large jug of water for Fletch, who had never been known to drink anything else. In the centre of the table—the table-cloth was pink with large staring red roses marked upon it—was a great brown jug of Glebeshire pottery, and this was filled with daffodils sent all the way from the Scillies by a cousin flower-farmer.

The chairs, with thick black arms to them, were a hundred years old at least, and a "silly old fule" from London had once offered enough money for them to give both the girls princess's dowries. His offer had been rejected with mockery and scorn.

The Boultewood family arrived, as it always did when it was invited anywhere, before the fitting time. Luckily Mrs. Penethen, in her grey silk and her cameo brooch, was there to receive them, knowing from olden time "Fanny Boultewood's little ways."

Her affection for Fanny Boultewood was sustained rather by tradition and the memory of "ancient days" than by heart-felt love and admiration. Mrs. Boultewood had one overwhelming quality that, as the years had advanced, had like the lean kine in the old story eaten up all the others—she was "terrible mean." You could see it in her spare nervous figure, in her restless inquisitive eyes that noticed everything and its positive value in lightning strokes of appraisal. Not a bad woman but a widow, who, having, while her husband lived, to "make both ends meet," and finding, on his death, "that he had ever so much more" than she had fancied, had continued the paring practice out of habit and then had made it her only friend. Her only daughter, Aggie Boultewood, was a silly giggling girl, plain, over-dressed and coquettish, but an heiress. Many a young man, hoping to make her wealth his own, had approached, summoned up courage, and then on further examination of her faded away.

She had indeed been engaged for a whole year to a young farmer from St. Mary's Moor, but at last, after much suffering from Mrs. Boultewood's many economies, he had fled.

Young Isaac Boultewood, thin and pallid and liable to "sweats," was said to be as mean as his mother, but of this no one was sure because he spoke so seldom and did in general so little with his young life save to eat and to sleep.

His mother loved him dearly, and sometimes a Homeric struggle might be observed between her maternal feelings and her habits of economy. If she was generous to any one it was towards her Isaac. Finally about Mrs. Boultewood it may be said that she admired Reuben Fletch beyond any one in the world; his ability to create shillings out of nothing and then to keep them for ever chained to his side was the cause of her admiration.

Soon after the Boultewoods arrived Mr. Ben Squires, a stout jolly roaring widower, half-brother to John Penethen but ten years younger than he. He kept an excellent haberdashery establishment—No. 10 High Street—and was known everywhere for his jolly ways, his genius for billiards and his merry laughing evasion of all the Polchester young women, who had endeavoured to marry him and had not yet abandoned hope. He was stout, square and red-faced; he had lost most of his hair, but all that remained to him was tended so carefully, watered so frequently and parted so handsomely that it was still one of his most engaging features. He was a kindly good-natured creature, with a great affection for his sister-in-law and his two nieces. On occasion he drank too freely, and his stories gained what they lost by their repetition in their energy and air of excitement. He wore gay waistcoats and laughed at everything.

One of the remaining guests from the outside world was Mr. Longstaffe, and about him, although she would confess it to nobody, Mrs. Penethen was anxiously nervous. Of course clergymen went everywhere and were no respecters of class. Mrs. Penethen had been to his church on many occasions, and he had always spoken in the friendliest way to her and her daughters when he met them in the town, but she would never have ventured to invite him had it not been for his great friendship with Mr. Johanson. He was a little different too from the others because of that story about his daughter. Of course the girl had left the town years ago, but the affair had made him "less of the quality," more like "anybody else." Mrs. Penethen had been divided in her judgement over that story. Her natural humanity had caused her to pity both the girl and her father, but her traditional morality had led her to judge with the rest of the world. Girls "who went astray"—there could be only one verdict. She pitied and she condemned. But that was so long ago; there wasn't a better man in the world; and while the girl had the decency to stay away from the town the matter must surely be forgotten.

Nevertheless he was a "foreigner"—not one of their kind—would he spoil their jollity and merriment? Would every one be shy and awkward and silent? She wondered whether she had been wise.

But her questions were soon answered. As soon as he came in she was reassured. So smart in his black silk waistcoat and yet so healthy with his red-brown, pippin apple face, and yet again so easy with his handshake and his boyish laugh as he saw the bright, loaded table. Oh! a nice little man! And he started with surprise when he saw Maude, hadn't expected that she would be so beautiful, in white, radiant, so beautiful, so beautiful.—And Mrs. Boultewood? No, he didn't know Mrs. Boultewood, nor Miss Boultewood, nor Mr. Boultewood. He was greatly pleased to have the honour. . . . But Squires! You here! Now that is excellent. Excellent. Upon my word, excellent. And Mr. Fletch. Of course he knows Mr. Fletch. Who in Polchester doesn't? How do you do, Mr. Fletch? A nasty March evening with a nip in the . . . but his gaze continually returned to Maude. He hadn't expected her to be like that. And to-night she was wonderful. . . . Wonderful was the word. Her birthday of course. Her party. She would be excited, and excitement always lends . . . Miss Midgeley? Why, of course, he knew Miss Midgeley! How do you do, Miss Midgeley? Isn't this a delightful gathering? Yes, a cold evening but it's warm enough in . . . And where's my friend Harmer John? A most punctual man as a rule. Oh yes, every one calls him that now. He seems to have become a regular town favourite, which is odd because the town's conservative. Oh, conservative undoubtedly. None the worse for that, perhaps, but for a foreigner to have made so emphatic a mark in so short a time is remarkable, nothing short of remarkable. What's that? A bird-cage? Under that green cloth? A nightingale? A present for Miss Maude? Why, how charming! Birds are such pleasant . . . ! Does he know Mr. Harty? No, he hasn't that pleasure. Mr. Harty plays the violin. Will give them some dance music after supper. First rate.

First rate. Nice old gentleman with long white hair, knee-breeches and large buckles to his shoes.

Every one was present save Johanson, and in another moment he was there too. He came down the stairs and through the door with a rush as he always did, having very little time, it seemed, to waste. He was fine to-night, splendidly washed and brushed and handsome. "Never seen him look so well," thought Longstaffe—and then for the first time considered the two—Harmer John and Maude Penethen. Maude Penethen and Harmer John. He had not considered it. His friend had said nothing. But now when he looked at them—how could either help it? She so lovely and he so jolly. What woman would not love him, not in every mood perhaps, but as he stood there laughing, so good-humoured, so boyish, so honest and true? Sentimental? But no. Why was it sentimental to admire good-humour and courage and honesty, qualities quite as interesting in their way as cynicism, irony and disbelief, and easier, far easier, to live with? But as he looked at his friend he was unexpectedly irritated. He did not want him to marry that girl. Why? He did not know. He knew nothing against her. She looked good-nature and amiability itself as she stood there laughing with her uncle. He did not know why, but he did not want it.

Then Harmer John's hand was on his shoulder, his voice in his ear: "It's jolly, no? You was thinking I was dead? Yes, not to-night, thank you."

Then they all sat down with a great deal of laughter and confusion and barking from Caesar the dog, who had a blue ribbon tied through his collar and looked foolish accordingly.

This was the way they sat down:

Rev. T.
Longstaff
e

| Mrs. Pen ethe n | Mis s Bou ltew ood |

| Mr. Squi res | Har mer Joh n |

| Judy | Mau de |

| Mr. Har ty | Isaa c Bou ltew ood |

| Mrs. Bou ltew ood | Mis s Mid gele y |

Mr.
Fletch

That was exactly what the table looked like except that, as I have said, it was all in the gayest colours. In the background was Mary-Thomasine, crimson in the face, breathing hard through the nostrils, and in fact like any serving-maid in any novel of English country life.

She was as happy as any one of them. In any case she adored a party, but her special devotion was for Mr. Squires. Whenever he came to the house she was in ecstasies. To look at him was enough for her in any ordinary way, but to have an opportunity of serving him, of handing him potatoes in their jackets, and beer and fruit in its season—was not that enough good fortune to last her for a week of Sundays? Last of all there was Prudence the cat, who, motionless with closed eyes, lay in patient unswerving hopefulness beneath the nightingale's cage.

They were soon all jolly enough. At first there had been a little stiffness, and Mrs. Penethen and the girls were busied with attending to different appetites, but Ben Squires was not one to remain quiet for long and he had scarcely taken a mouthful before he was leaning broadside across the table shouting out to Harmer John his famous story of Ma Appletree and the Ghost of the Butcher—a story so well known to every one else at the table that the mere sound of the accustomed words put the company at ease.

Mrs. Boultewood was exceedingly well pleased. To have Mr. Fletch at her side for a whole meal with only that old crooked-faced Miss Midgeley on the other side of him was wonderful indeed. She pecked at her food like a hungry but nervous bird, and examined every mouthful very carefully as though she were enquiring its price.

"Why, Mr. Fletch," she said, "it's a long time since I've had the chance of having a word with you. I've always wanted to thank you for telling me about that sale at Rosemeath Farm. There were one or two things there that were real bargains, I assure you."

Reuben Fletch, who, in his party black (shiny and faded, but scrupulously clean) and his over-long locks, resembled to-night more than ever a poet whose works were superior to the vulgar demand, turned upon her the gentlest of smiles and said that he was glad to help his friends. "Well, yes, I'm sure you are, Mr. Fletch. No one could call me mean whatever else they might say of me, but if there's a bargain or two about I don't see why I shouldn't be there with the rest. As I've many a time said to Aggie: Look after the shillings and the pounds will look after themselves—talking of which," dropping her voice, "that ham's cost Fanny Penethen a pretty penny, I'll be bound. However, if she likes to fling her money about—she's a good soul. I've known her all my life and if I were at my last gasp I couldn't say better than that—she's a good soul if foolish." Then, raising her voice again, "I suppose you've not been letting the grass grow under your feet since I saw you last, Mr. Fletch?"

Reuben looked at her with the mildness of a cow contemplating its next dandelion: "I beg your pardon?"

"In the money way, I mean. You've brought off one or two pretty little things, I'll be bound."

"I wish I had, Mrs. Boultewood," he said, sighing gently into his plate. "I grub along. That's about all there is to it."

"Oh, come now. We're too old friends for that, you know. You can talk safely to me, Mr. Fletch, old friends as we are."

But Mr. Fletch still sighed. "A solicitor in a small way in a little town like this, Mrs. Boultewood, stands no chance of becoming a millionaire, I fear.

Appreciative though I am of my hostess's good qualities, I should not be living here, Mrs. Boultewood, could I afford a little place of my own. And that's the truth."

Mrs. Boultewood knew well that it was far from the truth, but for the moment she abandoned the attack. Indeed she had on this particular evening other preoccupations—family cares. Her beloved Isaac had, for more than a year, been, engrossed with the beauty of Maude Penethen and, so far as he was capable of any passion, loved her to distraction. Mrs. Boultewood did not like Maude; she was, she thought, a stuck-up, self-opinionated little minx, but she adored her boy and for his sake she would suffer such a daughter-in-law. She thought, too, that she could train Maude into a very pretty little piece of subjection before she had finished with her.

On the other hand there was this strange large foreigner about whom all the town had, apparently, gone crazy, and Maude, it was said, went with the town. At the mere thought that he might interfere with her dear Isaac's happiness, her maternal protective feelings were aroused.

She disliked the great big baby-faced man, who behaved as though the whole kitchen belonged to him, at sight. She was prepared in any case to dislike him, because during the last six months her Isaac had walked considerably in the company of Samuel Hogg, had gone with him to local race meetings and football matches. This friendship had at first alarmed the anxious mother because Hogg's reputation in the town was queer enough; on the other hand the man was a kind of uncle-in-law to young Lady St. Leath and owned about half the town; he was, she had no doubt, not half what he was painted, and, at least, he was clever enough at making money—and Isaac thought the world of him. Isaac had, in fact, on one or two occasions brought him back to the house, and he had been very polite. On the last of these visits he had spoken of this foreigner and had given the worst possible account of him, saying that he was nothing better than an adventurer, here to plunder the town, as the town would find out one day.

Well, well. . . . Dear, dear. . . . To think that every one should be so taken in. Great, fat, noisy creature! And to make your living by rubbing people's stomachs! It was scarcely decent.

So she had plenty to do, with her good food and her admiration for Reuben Fletch and her anxiety about her family. Plenty to do. She was as busy as a hen in a neighbour's garden.

Like mother was not, in the Boultewood family, like daughter. Aggie Boultewood frequently differed from her mother. She did so on this occasion, falling in love with Mr. Johnson at sight. This was nothing new for her. She was always falling in love with men and then hating them when they abandoned her. She always saw it as wicked abandonment, although, often enough, all the advance movements were made by herself. But to-night it seemed that she received real encouragement. To her tittering and giggling remarks Harmer John made the most generous replies, turning round to her, giving her his full attention and looking into her eyes in a way that, surely, every one at the table must be remarking. Of course, she was an heiress. And he was a foreigner—and foreigners were always laying traps for heiresses; she must be careful. She did think him the most beautiful man she had ever seen, and banished entirely from her heart and memory Mr. Ned Poinder, clerk to the solicitors Kenworthy and Frost, who had, until this evening, occupied that position.

"Mr. Johnson—I do want—you'll think me too silly—but might I ask . . . ?"

"Yes, of course. Anything you please."

"Do you—you'll think it too silly of me—do you have exercises for ladies too?"

"Too? Too what, Miss Boulteware?"

"No. Too—as well, I mean. Oh! how silly I am not to explain. But what I mean is, can you, can I, I mean, have exercises in your school? or office is it? Where you work, I mean."

"But, of course, Miss Boulteware. Any day you wish. There was two ladies this morning, and I made them work, I can tell you. You come along any morning. It will do you plenty of good, truly it will. You bring your mother, too. Do her good. I shall be very pleased to welcome you."

"Oh dear. That *is* kind. I'm sure mother would. And will you really give me them yourself—the exercises, I mean—and not leave me to some assistant?"

"If we appoint a time I shall give them you all myself, but the day now are getting full, and I thank God for it too. I don't hope I'll ever be idle another minute, I can tell you, Miss Boulteware."

But by this time the whole table was in an uproar. Every one was so jolly and so noisy and so merry that Mary-Thomasine, bringing the jam tarts from the oven, thought that there had never before been such a party. Even Miss Midgeley was happy, practising some innocent sarcasms on the helpless Isaac, who could but gaze on her, open his mouth and shut it again as though he were pretending to guess the answer to some riddle far too difficult for him.

The festival was now so triumphant that no one need notice the demureness of Maude. It *was* noticed. Her mother and her sister and Reuben Fletch noticed it—no one else. Unless it were Prudence under the bird-cage who, absorbed in the bird as she was, nevertheless remembered her mistress.

Never before at her birthday party had Maude Penethen been so quiet. From the moment when Mr. Longstaffe said his beautiful Grace, wishing for a blessing on all God's bountiful gifts here provided, to the moment of Ben Squires' birthday speech, Maude sat like a little nun, helping at first to make sure that every one was happily started, then eating a little, talking a little, smiling a little, and turning upon Isaac Boultewood so rich and lustrous a gaze that that poor young man, harassed already by Miss Midgeley's incomprehensibilities, could only plunge ever deeper into the mire of his adoration and feel himself to be sinking, sinking, sinking. . . .

She did not rouse herself even at the boisterous birthday greetings showered down upon her by her uncle. What compliments he paid her! To what flowers he compared her, to what dawns and stars and moons, to what goddesses and Peris and Naiads, to what virtues and estimabilities and heavenly qualities! He reached that stage so customary in after-dinner speaking, when he had said everything that he had to say, but could not wind up and conclude; in a desperation bred of amiability and cider he leaned forward across the table and mentioned "our foreign guest" whom we were all so pleased to see, whom the town of Polchester was proud to honour, whom we were all so thankful to have the chance of knowing, whom we were all so pleased to see, whom the town, etc.: and then quite unexpectedly sat down, to his own surprise as much as to any one else's.

Harmer John rose and said that he thanked them all very much; that he didn't know English well, so that perhaps they would excuse the way he spoke it. That he knew what an honour it was that a foreigner like himself, who had been in the town but a short time, should be invited to so intimate a gathering, but that he was so proud to be a friend of Miss Maude Penethen and of Mrs. Penethen and of all his other friends here that he sometimes forgot, perhaps too easily, how lucky he was. That was their fault for being so kind to him. He felt that this town was his home, and he would like to do something for this town in return for its being good to him. But he didn't want to talk about himself. It was Miss Maude Penethen's birthday. He would not pay her compliments. The gentleman opposite him had already done that so beautifully. They had a story in Sweden about a dwarf who lived in a hole in an island near Stockholm, and he was very miserable and very lonely and very bitter. And one day the young Princess went by in her beautiful golden boat, and the dwarf looked out from his hole and hated the Princess because she was beautiful and he was so ugly. And the Princess was so good and so pure that she always felt in her spirit when some one near her was unhappy. "Some one is unhappy near me," she cried. And the Court Magician who was at her side said, "Yes, there is some one ugly and unhappy near you. If you throw what you treasure most into the water, that will make him happy and beautiful again." She hesitated a moment because she knew what it was that she loved most; it was her gold box that held the crystal ball. But it was only for a moment that she hesitated. She picked it up and threw it into the water. At the same moment the dwarf was changed into a beautiful Prince. A week later he came to the Court, bringing with him the gold box which had been washed on to his island by the kindly waves. A little metal polish and it was bright as ever. The moment the Princess saw him she loved him and *of course* he loved her. So they were married and lived happily ever after. "You must see," he ended, bowing a little to Maude, "what power beauty when it are joined to great goodness of heart can be able of. I will drink Miss Maude Penethen's health."

How they applauded! What a beautiful story! Only Maude had not a word. She blushed, rose for a moment, said something that was the ghost of "Thank you," and sat down again. It was then that Tom Longstaffe knew how correct his suspicions had been.

The tables were cleared, the chairs ranged against the wall. Then old Mr. Harty was seen in his full glory. He had been a little overwhelmed at supper with all the noise and heartiness, and his teeth behaved erratically, and his digestion was uncertain so that he must be careful about his food, but now behold him in his glory perched upon a chair with his beloved fiddle tucked under his chin! Before this he had been a rather decrepit old gentleman who had the obscene and derelict habit of taking snuff; now, in a moment of time, he had his rightful place in the world, his eyes shining, his nose twitching, his buckled shoe tapping, and his fingers moving like loving spirits about the violin. No one in Polchester was better than he at this; none of your modern bands and ridiculous pianists. He had the music in his blood, and his fiddle had it too. He was in it for love, for love of Mrs. Penethen, whom he greatly admired, for love of that pretty little "piece," her daughter, but best of all for love of his divine mistress, music. Was he bachelor and childless? Was he poor, and had he only a small bed-sitting-room off Orange Street? Was he considered mad by his relations, and a dotard by his contemporaries? Ask his mistress why this was so. And did he regret an instant of his faithful service? Look at him, perched up there, with his white hair flying and you had your answer. They were all dancing—Mrs. Penethen and Tom Longstaffe, Miss Midgeley and Mr. Squires, young Boultewood and Maude; Judy and Harmer John, Miss Boultewood and Mr. Fletch; only Mrs. Boultewood sat bolt upright in her chair counting the cost of the shoe leather, and Mary-Thomasine, standing in the doorway sucking the corner of her apron and imagining the arrival of a fairy godmother who would throw her straight into the glorious arms of Mr. Squires.

Dance followed dance; the world was ever gayer and more gay; midnight had struck and beyond the windows the moon was cold like a cheese-paring, and the stars through the wisps of fog gleamed like fire-flies in a scatter of hay. The lights of the streets were dead, and the Cathedral was humped, black, its paws out, gripping the town; a cold wind nipped round the corners and sighed away into the woods and the tufted hills; but in the Penethen kitchen it was hotter and hotter and hotter.

"Come up, Miss Maude," a voice was in her ear, "up the staircase."

They stayed side by side on the landing by the little window that looked out to the faintly shining sky. They stood side by side. She was trembling. He put his arm around her, and drew her close to him. She trembled yet more, put out her hand, and timidly rested it on his broad back. His other hand caught hers and drew her arm around him—"I love you, Maude. I ever loved you from the first moment I saw your sweet face. You've took me your prisoner, and now, whichever way you think of me, I can't ever escape again. It wouldn't be much to say I'd be good to you—any man would be that—but what other could I say? I don't suppose you can love me yet. I'm a stranger here and foreign—any ways half of me—but you have the beginnings of liking me, and I'll make it grow like a flower. Will you marry me? I don't hope—oh! I don't hope you'll say no."

He sighed with his anxiety. If she looked up she could just see his round face and black hair untidy with the dancing. He seemed immense to her just then; immense in his height and breadth, in his strength and force. She had no thought of anything save his physical proximity. This was what she had desired, thought of for weeks and weeks; of no more than this and of nothing further than this. That she should be held by him and pressed close by his arms and feel his heart beating beneath her cheek; that with the physical power that he had she should feel on her side also power, that she so small and weak could force him to such subjection that he would do all that she should ask.

She murmured something. He did not hear what it was, but her gesture towards him, her hand moving up to his neck above his collar, her head resting against his heart, told him everything.

They stayed in the dim shadow of that wall, the music coming up to them utterly unheeded, the little sad breeze teasing at the window with restless fingers, then, wandering off into the dark, knowing that its time would come.

CHAPTER VIII

FOUR MEN

So swiftly do superstition and legend climb mountain-high that although we are now but some seventeen or eighteen years from the period with which this history is concerned, nevertheless the facts of Johanson's first connection with the Cathedral authorities are hard accurately to discover. Nor is that discovery of great importance. In so small a town as Polchester the settling there of any stranger would have, at least, its gossipy consequences. Afterwards when it was discovered that he was a man of unusual character who intended to take some place in the town's affairs, it followed naturally that the leaders of the town's parties in local politics would consider him and his possibilities. And at about the time of Johanson's engagement to Maude Penethen, four men, entirely opposed to one another in training, temperament and purpose, did so consider him. Upon the lives of all those men he was to have a deep and lasting effect. And he himself was not to know, even at the very end, that he had affected them at all.

One of these men he hated. With all his amiable and friendly qualities he could be an excellent hater. He was not mean nor sly in his hatred, but a streak of obstinacy ran through it, obstinacy that came from his simplicity of view and inability for subtleties; did he once convince himself that a man was, from his position, really bad, it was hard to shake him in that.

Now bad men in this world of ours are exceedingly rare—rarer than anything else to be found here; weak and stupid men on every side, but bad—no. There is insanity in absolute badness, something motiveless, or something that reaches out, with a longing arrogance, beyond the motive: Iago lusted after Desdemona a little and hated Othello a great deal, but beyond those tiny passions was a lust to possess the evil deed as a thing worth having in itself, a flower, a jewel of the mind, a trophy of the intellect.

In this same fashion Samuel Hogg, who is perhaps the true protagonist in Harmer John's battle, lusted after vanity and cruelty and lies not as things in any way valuable in themselves, but rather as paying fine tribute to his ever hungry arrogance. He was indeed no Iago; mentally sluggish, ignorant, loutish, without any vision, but vanity clothed him with all the robes of glory.

He had at this time an odd position in our town. It was significant of the social change that had enveloped us that such as he should hold it. Born the son of an itinerant pedlar, kicked up through the mire and filth of Seatown, the Polchester slums, into the position of bottle-boy in a Seatown public-house, keeping always one of his little eyes open to the main chance, betting successfully here, stealing triumphantly there, winning at last the heart of the publican's meek white-faced daughter, he succeeded to those pot-house splendours. And there, in all probability, he would for ever have stayed, in spite of mean little conspiracies and unsuccessful little blackmails, had not his only child, a handsome independent girl, hating her father and longing for any escape, eloped to London with the son of our Archdeacon Brandon, the lord at that time of our ecclesiastical country. This had been swiftly followed by the death of Brandon and the marriage of his only daughter to young Lord St. Leath, owner of most of Glebeshire and the king of the castle above Polchester. By the strangest sequence of events, therefore, Sam Hogg, proprietor of "The Dog and Pilchard," became cousin-of-a-sort to lords, ladies and "all the clergy." Not that his daughter ever set eyes on him again (although he did what he could to force claims upon her), nor, naturally enough, did Johnny St. Leath greet him as a brother; that mattered little enough; sufficient for him that he could boast and rant to all his vanity's desire, and boast and rant he did. It happened also that from this time things went well with him. Perchance his wits were sharpened; maybe men dealt with him more readily now that he was related to the "Quality." He made money; he bought property; soon most of Seatown was his. He found an ally in Reuben Fletch, and through him formed some loose connection in small business affairs with some of the better people of the town, with some of the clergy and even with our great Canon Ronder himself who, advised by Fletch, bought a little Seatown property from Hogg. He mended his manners, wore quieter clothes, took a little house in Orange Street, and was cared for by an elderly and most respectable widow. His principal danger was liquor; he had been a drunkard in his Seatown days, and the evidence was yet in the little purple veins that ran across his puffy cheeks, but had you seen him walking slowly up the High Street in decent broadcloth, his bowler hat smartly brushed, a fine cane held behind his stout back, you would have thought him a prosperous and respectable farmer. There was indeed something remarkable in the way that he threaded the whole life of our town, having relations of one sort or another with almost every one from the Bishop and Ryle and Ronder at the top down to the strange animals that moved hither and thither in the dark obscurity of the Seatown mists.

Socially he did not press his claims upon the town. Dark things were said of his sensual passions, queer reports peered up once and again out of the darkness, tales hinted at and mysteriously whispered—but nothing was positively known.

"A useful man, Hogg. Wouldn't wonder if he's Mayor one day."

If no one exactly liked him, no one exactly hated him either—no one until Harmer John came along. And Hogg was useful. He was useful especially to those men—Croppet and Harrow, Barnaby and Summers—who wanted to popularise our town, to make it a sort of perpetual Fair with hurdy-gurdies and roundabouts, to make the Cathedral a peep-show and the market-place a railway centre, to run excursions to the seaside and from the seaside to the town. He was the kind of man they needed. He would do their dirty work and would be fool enough to be tricked by them at the end when his services had been rendered.

Meanwhile his vanity mounted and mounted and mounted. That was his true vice, the hidden creature biting at his breast. And it must be fed and protected and cared for. Any slight to it, something far short of insult, and his anger was roused with all the force and strength that only the vanity of small and mean and cruel men can summon.

And that was why *he* hated Harmer John. On that first evening in Mrs. Penethen's kitchen his vanity had been wounded by the attention paid to this stranger. Soon there were many other fine reasons.

On an afternoon late in March Sam Hogg stood in Reuben Fletch's small office that was second floor in 19 Winnery's Lane to the back of the market-place and just under St. James's Church. An obscure little cul-de-sac that grew grass between its cobbles, and a poor little room with oleographs of their Majesties the King and the Queen on the walls, an American roll-top desk and precious little else. Where Fletch kept all his papers, papers that involved most of the town in one way or another, was always a mystery.

Hogg leant back against the mantelpiece, his stout body covering the empty fire-place, his arms akimbo and his hat on the back of his head. His flushed cheeks, his bulging waistcoat, formed a well-fed contrast with the thin poetic features of Fletch seated at his desk. Hogg to-day, as on many a past occasion, was trying to discover both what Fletch thought and what he intended to do, and for once in a way Fletch told him. He doubtless had his own good reasons.

"You're much too impetuous, Sam," Fletch said, raising his mild eyes to the faded ceiling. "Wait and see how things turn out. There's plenty of time."

"That's just what I'm not so sure there is," said Hogg, impatiently moving his shoulders and kicking one leg forward, "he's getting so damned popular, blarst him. I went in the other afternoon, pretending I wanted some exercises, just to look around a bit, and the place was fair humming. 'Is 'Ighness couldn't see me just at the moment. Would I wait? Well, no, I wouldn't. I'd have kicked his whole bloody place to pieces if I'd stayed another five seconds."

"That's you all over," said Fletch quietly. "Why get so excited about it? The man hasn't done you any harm as yet, beyond getting engaged to a girl whom you couldn't marry however hard you wanted to. We've got a hold over him with those rooms of his. He's as simple and unsuspicious as a puppy. Leave him alone and watch the way things turn out. Either he'll be a real success and very useful to us, or he'll make a mess of it and cook his own goose, so to speak."

"You're so detached, Reuben," said Hogg, quite plaintively. "And yet you've got your passions—as far as money goes, anyway. If he stole five pounds from your till you'd be excited enough."

"I don't know that I'd show it if I were," said Fletch. "You always get more by keeping quiet. Besides, I quite like the fellow. There's something rather taking about him."

"Taking! That's just the word!" said Hogg, with an oath. "He's taken the only pretty girl in the place as it is, although he hasn't got her yet, by God. But I fair hate the man. I did from the first moment I set eyes on him, and when I hate a man I want to do him an injury. That's the sort of man I am."

"You've been drinking, Sam," said Fletch. "That's foolish of you. You know you can't stand liquor nowadays, and you've been drinking much too often lately. You always go and do something foolish when you're this way. What do you do it for?"

"What do I do it for? What does any man do it for? Isn't a man what is a man to have any bloody pleasure?"

"Yes, but you can't stand it as another man can. You know how well things have gone with you lately, and it's only because you've kept off drink. Why go and spoil everything?"

"By God, you're right, Reuben!" Hogg moved away from the fire-place and stood, his fat legs straddling. "There isn't a man in the place that has risen as I've done. And who's there been to help me? No one. Who's ever held me out a helping finger? No one. I'm the most remarkable man in this town, and most of them knows it. And I haven't stopped growing neither. No, by God, I haven't."

Fletch looked at him as though surrendering to a mild and pleasant admiration. "Well, then," he said, "don't ruin it all by taking to drink again."

"Paugh!" said Hogg, "what's a drop now and then? The thought of that foreign bastard pawing that girl all over's enough to make any decent man drink. Damn 'im! With 'is baby face and 'is foreign words and 'is Almighty manners! I'll have him on his knees before the year's out or my name's not Sam Hogg."

He moved about the room, lurching ever so slightly, then, as though at some sudden thought, steadied himself and moved across to Fletch's table. "But you're right, Reuben. You're right. Quiet and patient's the word. If Ronder and those other bugs are going to take to him we can work a thing or two. I see that as clearly as you can."

A door of an inner room opened, and a long thin boy with spectacles and a haggard expression brought Fletch some papers, then, without a word, but sighing deeply, retired into the inner room again.

"Well, I can see you're busy," said Hogg, who had long ago learnt his friend's signals. "I'll be off. I'll make up to that swine and see if I can get something out of him. But he'd better not come up against me. He'd better look out. He'll be sorry before he's finished with me. So long, old cock." He swaggered out, banging the door behind him. He had been drinking a little, but not very much, and the cool March air soon sobered him completely.

As he turned the corner out of the shabby little street and came abruptly into the noise and bustle that eddied, like a pool stirred by wind, at the bottom of the High Street, he thought what a good fellow he was. A good sort. A kindly man. A credit to any town. And because it had always been the way with him that he could only think of one thing at a time, he saw himself a glorious figure, just above the flight of steps that led down to the river, the town a quaint huddled background to his splendour, and the world compressed into one bending figure murmuring, "And all this he has done for himself, no one helping him! He has made himself what he is! From small beginnings he has come to this!'' Clever too! He could see as far as Fletch with all his cunning and secrecy! A trifle more impetuous, perhaps, more red blood in his body, not a bag of grasping bones like—He was interrupted, called from his glorious self-contemplation, and the thing that called him was the vision of his friend, Canon Ronder, on the very point of beginning his ascent of the High Street.

He smiled, a little sly, self-congratulatory smile. He had drunk just enough and was self-flattered just enough to receive his opportunity with open arms. He saw two things with a swiftness a little above his everyday perception. He saw that it would add greatly to his own self-esteem to walk up the High Street with the Canon, and that it would be a kind of demonstration in the face of all the world as to how friendly with the Canon he was.

His self-esteem prevented him from perceiving a third point in its favour—namely, that it would annoy the Canon very greatly.

It *did* annoy him when, feeling a tap on his shoulder, he turned and saw Hogg's red face and sly, confidential smile. It was true that he had been forced of late, for the good of the town, to see something of the man. For the good of the town he had thought it right to take an interest in civic things and even to buy a little town property, but all this was very far from being seen prominently in close companionship.

Only ten years ago Hogg had been concerned with the death of one of the town's most prominent Churchmen in a fashion that was more than suspicious; he had been a drunkard and a wastrel, thief and even blackmailer, it was said. It was true that he was now a greatly reformed character, and that such men as Croppet and Harrow took him into their civic confidences and even suggested him as a possible future Town Councillor: all this was far from the open demonstration of acquaintanceship that an intimate walk up the High Street admitted. And yet how difficult! It seemed that if you took one step, a thoroughly justified step, in a certain direction it led you inevitably to a future step not quite so justified. He disliked the man cordially, but he could not, as things now were, afford to make an enemy of him. The man was at his side. He must endure his company. With every step, however, his discomfort grew. The ten years that he had spent at Polchester had not made him less sensitive to public opinion. He had won success and popularity in the very first six months of his life there, won them with exceeding ease. Circumstances had helped him, of course, but once those pleasant things were his, once the comfort and even luxury of his life cushioned him round, ease, popularity and high position became important to him as they had never been before. He had always liked them, of course, but now they were absolute necessities, and clutching them to himself he heard, more and more clearly as the years passed, voices, whispers, shadows of whispers threatening to take them away. He could not put his finger on his detractors; that was the trouble; he would have said that he had no enemies in the place. And yet—and yet—Ambrose Wistons, whom he had himself helped to bring into the diocese; it was not true to say that he was more respected, nevertheless his name was for ever to be heard, now an article in a paper, now a sermon in his village church, now a discussion at some gathering over something that Wistons had said, now some comment on his strange, ascetic life—and all this although Wistons held himself apart from all men, made no friends, went socially almost nowhere, interested himself not at all in the life of the town, paid no man compliments, was of the rude and brusque in his manner. And yet—and yet—Would Sam Hogg have tapped Wistons on the shoulder and said in that thick, confidential voice, "Well, Canon. A bit nippy this air—more rain before night"?

No, Ronder, behind that rosy, cheery face, behind those round, shining glasses, was not comfortable, nor was his happiness increased when, as he advanced up the street with his unwelcome companion, he seemed to pass every one whom he least wished to see: there was that gossipy Mrs. Bond with her eldest boy, there was that simpering Mrs. Ryle, there Julia Preston and Mrs. Bentinck-Major—all the chattering women of the town!

"About those bits of houses of yours, Canon," Hogg was saying (odious figure with his rolling, swaggering gait, stick fixed between his arms behind his back, hat tilted slightly to one side), "there's another nice little lot likely to come into the market pretty soon—a bit higher up than your two or three—towards Roston's Mill. They should come in for a mere song, I should say, and nothing wants doing to them; least when I say *nothing*, what I mean is they can go on very well for a year or two without anything doing. The tenants that's there now seems contented enough."

"Which reminds me, Mr. Hogg," said Ronder, speaking nervously and looking about him left and right, "some one was saying the other night that the whole of Seatown wants pulling down, that conditions there are a disgrace. I haven't gone into it myself, and I believe the Town Council's very well satisfied. Of course there was all that trouble in Nineteen Two and things should be all right now. Nevertheless, I shouldn't like to be owning property that's a disgrace to the town. I must go down myself and have a look."

"*Was* somebody saying?" broke in Hogg bitterly. "That's just the sort of gentleman who wants ducking in the Pol, if you ask *me*! Just the sort of nosing round into somebody else's business that you'd expect from a foreigner, a dirty German or a Dutchman like that booby-face who's going to teach us all gymnastics. Beg pardon, Canon, if I'm speaking too strong, but I can't abide these nosey-parkers with their meddling round other folks' business. It's true enough that there ain't any marble-tiled bathrooms in Seatown, but what would they do with 'em if you gave 'em them? Fill them with a month's coal, of course. Who knows if I don't? Who's lived there if I haven't? And mighty comfortable I was, too, for donkey's years. Why, I'd never have moved if it hadn't been the thought of my daughter who used to make it homelike for me, and her deserting me as she did sort of made me take against the place. No, Canon, don't you pay no attention to those gas-bags. Go down for yourself, Canon, and see. There isn't a brighter or a 'appier spot in Polchester than Seatown."

After which long speech, Samuel Hogg brought his stick to the ground with a bang and looked about him with a triumphant smirk.

They were half-way up the High Street by now. The street was filled with people and on every side of him Ronder fancied that he detected glances of surprise at his company. Detected falsely, no doubt! There was a time when he was wise enough to know that every man is concerned first with himself, and only afterwards, and at a great distance, with the behaviours and eccentricities of his fellow human beings. We are safer than we know. But his nervousness made him speak more sharply than he intended. "Well, Mr. Hogg, you can take it as settled that I buy no more property in that direction. I would not have done what I did had I not thought it for the town's good that some of the Cathedral Chapter should take a closer interest in the town's progress. I must go more nearly into this question of conditions down in Seatown. If all I hear is true, something must be done."

So that was the way of it, was it? Hogg's little eyes narrowed. This fat, sleek parson was going to make trouble, was he? He'd better look out! Hogg knew a thing or two, Hogg did. He'd better look out. But who was this who'd been talking about Seatown? Devilish awkward if people began poking their noses in that direction again. What about this Harmer John with his gymnastics and the rest, improving the body and all that my-eye? Why not? Just the kind of rotten foreigner to go interfering with other people's business!

"Beg your pardon, Canon," Hogg said confidentially (how odious his confidence to Ronder's sensitive soul!), "but it wasn't this new gymnastic fellow what's been talking to you about Seatown, was it?"

"Gymnastic fellow?" said Ronder, bowing to Mrs. Preston and looking about him for some avenue of escape. "Gymnastic fellow?"

"Yes, him they call Harmer John. Great tall fellow who's opened a gymnasium. I know you're acquainted with him, and I thought—"

"Dear me, no," said Ronder, hurriedly; "an excellent man. Quite an asset to the town. Oh no, he knows nothing about Seatown. Why should he? Ah, I go in here—if you'll excuse me, Mr. Hogg. Good afternoon. *Good* afternoon." He turned into Bennett's bookshop, that same doorway in which his old dead rival had once also sought refuge, and left Hogg standing there. Left him also in no amiable state of mind, left him in that unhappy state of wounded pride and creeping suspicion that can only mean danger when men of Hogg's half-human mentality see their security threatened.

Stepping hurriedly into the dim bookishness of the old shop, he saw, as on a similar occasion Brandon himself had once seen, that Wistons was there. Wistons was, just then, exactly the man whom he did not wish to see. But it was too late to retreat. He nodded friendlily, his spectacles catching the gaslight so that he seemed all shining with amiability. Then he sat down in the old arm-chair near the books, the arm-chair that had held so many a worthy book-lover before him, and gazed pleasantly about him, at the framed letter of

Walter Scott's, the two holograph verses from *Don Juan*, a Dickens scribble with lines like a staircase under the signature; pleasantly, but in his heart he was irritated to-day by that tall, lean, ascetic body as perhaps he had never been before. How it towered above him and how quiet and aloof and reserved it was! He looked down at his own stout thighs, spotless trousers, shining boots, and wished, how fervently he wished, that he had avoided this meeting.

One never knew how Wistons would take anything: on a day he would scarcely be aware of his surroundings, on another he would be friendly and agreeable. To-day little Mr. Carter, the new shopman (from London with new ideas, new authors, new prophecies), came rolling forward and asked what it was that he could do for Canon Ronder. Canon Ronder wanted Trelawny's *Recollections of Shelley and Byron*, and Mr. Carter went to search among the second-hand shelves in the rear of the shop.

Wistons, whose nose had been buried in a number of the *Hibbert Journal*, looked up and said:

"Ronder, do you know anything of a man I am about to visit, a Swede, I think, Johanson by name, a gymnast or a masseur?"

Ronder looked up smiling:

"Why, yes, I know him quite well. He has been coming during the last fortnight and giving me massage. A good fellow, I think. I like him. But *you* don't look as though you needed massage."

He laughed in that friendly, easy, natural manner of his that had become by now so natural to him that it had ceased to be natural at all; only nobody knew that. Wistons seldom laughed. "No," he answered gravely, "it isn't for that I'm going. I'm interested in what I've heard about him. You know little Longstaffe?"

"Yes, of course."

"He has been talking about him to me. Longstaffe's a loyal little fellow and all his geese are swans, but this man does seem something out of the common. I promised Longstaffe I'd go, so I wrote and made an appointment. He *is* a Swede, isn't he?"

"A Swede or a Dane. I can never tell them apart. His English might belong to either. He seems to mean to settle down here. He has got himself engaged to a girl of the place."

"Oh, I didn't know that!" Wistons' nose was deep in *Hibbert* again. Ronder said: "Did you know that Longstaffe's daughter is coming back here to live?"

And in his heart he was saying, "You pig! I'll make you attend to me. Who brought you to this place if I didn't, and now you are as remote from me as though I lived in another world. Not good enough for yours, I suppose! But I'll smash your remoteness. I'll make you come down from your pedestal!" A strange little wind of anger blew up in his soul, strange because he was seldom angry. But he seemed to feel a crisis between himself and Wistons as though months and months of action had been preparing for this meeting in the bookshop, a crisis the stronger because Wistons was himself so completely unaware of it. His anger needed physical expression and he jumped to his feet.

They stood close together under the gaslight, one round and shining, the other brown and spare.

"Isn't it a pity, don't you think, that Longstaffe should have his daughter back here?" His voice was peremptory and so unlike his accustomed suavity that Wistons' attention was caught. He stood, twisting his lips in a way that he had, his eyes staring into the bookshelves.

"No. It all happened long ago. It should be forgotten now. Poor girl, she has paid in sorrow and grief."

"Yes," said Ronder irritably. "But that is just what some of the women in this place will not remember. They have long memories for the scandalous part of it, though."

"How long is it since it happened?"

"Some seven or eight years, I fancy."

"And she's bringing the child with her?"

"Of course." Then Ronder went on. "It's for Longstaffe's sake I'm sorry. He's a fine fellow and doing a fine work here. He'll have trouble, I'm afraid."

"Well, what if he does?" Wistons turned on Ronder. "You're too much afraid of trouble. Why not trouble and difficulty and sorrow? Why not? Why not? Good for us. Good for us all," and, turning, dropping the *Hibbert Journal* on the chair as he passed, he had left the shop.

Ronder stared about him, hoping that no one had witnessed that abruptness. But really! To treat him, Ronder, in that fashion! Things were going too far. They were indeed. As good as though he had told Ronder to his face that he was too comfortable. After Ronder's own courtesy and kindness. He did hope that nobody had witnessed that strange outburst. For Wistons' own sake it would never do. Mr. Carter came forward washing his hands and grievously saying that there was no "Trelawny" just now.

"Never mind. Never mind." Ronder was nervously brushing his hat. "Try and get it for me from London. Good day. Good day."

He passed under the Arden Gate, angry as though some one had rolled him in the dust. The thing was going too far! He would let Wistons know.

But Wistons had already forgotten that Ronder existed. He was suffering just now, as he often suffered, from a mood of intense depression. God had veiled Himself from him, and He had veiled Himself rightly, because he, Ambrose Wistons, had so terribly failed in his task. That task, given to him ten years ago, had been to bring these people nearer to God. And he had not brought them. He had done nothing. It was as though he had never existed.

When he had spoken those words to Render he had intended them for himself. It seemed to him to-day that his life during these last ten years had been spent in the very apron of luxury. His little country vicarage with its small tangled garden, its few bare rooms, its old cook-housekeeper, appeared to him extravagant splendour. Everything had gone well with him there; he had been tended and watched over like a woman; he had grown soft and flabby. And as he strode down the hill people looked after him, at his long bony body, his fierce protesting gaze, his thin swinging arms, and saw the ascetic, the man who lived only for God, and felt, too, for a brief instant a strange rending in the clouds, a glimpse of another journey, a more distant kingdom. . . .

He liked Johanson's rooms as soon as he crossed the threshold. A class of boys from the School had just finished their exercises and were pouring through the doorways, jolly little boys like dogs, Sealyhams and Scotch terriers and cockers, pugs and poodles. A man taller and broader than Wistons had expected stood in the middle of them, himself a collie or Newfoundland. They had to be pushed out of the room, and old Billy Trenant shouted at them and pretended terrible rage and enjoyed it hugely. Then they all saw Wistons, whom they knew well by sight, and in a moment they were transformed, touching their school caps, decorous, slipping away in quiet restraint.

Johanson had seen Wistons before although he had never spoken to him. He came forward holding out his hand.

"How do you do, sir?" he said. "Will you not come in?"

The two men looked at one another as fearless men estimate a newcomer in the first glance, and at once a firm relationship was established—not at all one of friendship as it had been immediately between Johanson and Longstaffe, but of something quite different. Wistons, as he felt the strong, warm grasp of the other man's hand, knew that in that moment some of his trouble and depression slipped away from him. Here was a man whom he could trust: whatever else might appear, that was certain. He was not a man who made friendships or desired them. He had an ascetic mind, he had no atom of sentiment in him. He only knew as he looked at that other honest, open face that he was reassured and rested as though he had come to a room where there was a comfortable chair.

And Johanson knew instantly that he was face to face with the most remarkable human being whom he had yet in his life encountered. With him also it was not friendship he felt, but subservience, discipleship. He was eager to hear everything that this man might say. He would drink in every word, and he had a curious sense of haste and urgency, as though he knew that he would not see this man many times but that every meeting would be of extreme importance to him.

So it was that when they were seated in the little inner room, close to one another and searching one another's faces, they dropped all preliminaries, all fencing, all hesitations, and began at once about themselves, talking eagerly like men to whom this time is very precious.

The room was small. Wistons sat in the only armchair, his long thin legs stretched out in front of him. Harmer John, leaning against the wall, spread out his broad back, looking at his visitor with eagerness, with a sort of hunger of interest. "Longstaffe," Wistons began, "is a friend of yours, I know, Mr. Johanson, and it was he the other day who was speaking of you. Of course I've heard of you from many people here—you can quickly become famous in this little town, you know—but Longstaffe told me that in his opinion you were going to do a great work here, and therefore—I'll be perfectly frank with you—I was inquisitive to see the kind of man you are."

Johanson laughed. "I am very happy. I will tell you anything and perhaps you would help me. This grows so quickly that it is very difficult to make the foundations steady. So many people have been writing how it would be possible to make it perfect in two minutes. I don't hope for that, but I have my own thoughts, you know, as to how it will all be." Wistons, looking at the man, liked with every moment increasingly the honest gaze and fearless mouth. The man was happy with some inner impetus: it might be merely physical well-being or pleasure at his immediate success, but with a sort of envy Wistons fancied that it was something deeper, something for which he had himself long been searching.

"And what is it exactly, this 'IT' that you are after?" Wistons asked. Johanson needed no encouragement. He never did. He was always eager to pour out all his story to any one who would care to listen, touchingly confident that what seemed to himself so true and amusing would seem so to others. At the first hint of weariness, however, on the side of the listener he would cease, blaming himself for his stupidity or carelessness or selfishness, but he never learnt from these checks. And it was from no egotism that he poured out his story: he would have told any other story as eagerly, only this one happened to be true—he would vouch for it—and so it *must* perforce, because of that truth, have an appeal!

Wistons was far from any boredom. He heard it all—the youth in Stockholm, the bad father, the good mother, half-English, the artists and their models, the gymnastic training, Copenhagen; and then the little story of the blue plate, the carpet and Donatello, the desire for England, the journey, the arrival, the Penethens, the start of the venture, the money borrowed, some of it, from that kind, generous man, Mr. Fletch; the success, then the dream of the new town, the artists coming to Polchester to make it beautiful, the wonderful world with everything beautiful, all starting from a *little* thing—one beautiful stone and so the beautiful building, one beautiful building and so the beautiful street, one beautiful street and so the beautiful town, one beautiful town and so the beautiful country, one beautiful country and so the beautiful world . . .

"And here is the place with the Cathedral standing in the middle. Don't you see, sir, that because that monument that the young man made who was in Italy is so lovely everything in the town can surely be, in its own way, its own style, and we think of beautiful things and there are no room in our brain for other things. The brain have only so much room—fill it up, then, with what is fine—"

He stopped abruptly. "You will think, sir, that I want to make people better. No, sir, I would have them only to see my idea and then perhaps of themselves they say: 'This is fine. It is fun to do this.' But not to change them against their wish. That is so tiresome to interfere in other people's business, don't you think so, sir? But a few will come who like to be strong in body and happy in their minds and look out of the window on fine sights and always to be occupied with kindly feelings."

"Your idea is not a new one, Mr. Johanson. Many men have thought as you do and wished passionately to clear some of the mess away: it has seemed so simple to get a few to think as they do and then all to work together—and it has been so difficult—and they have died, most of them, defeated men."

"Oh, indeed I know, sir," said Johanson eagerly, "I am not clever. I have had no education, you understand. I have not seen the world. But it may be because I am an ignorant man and only know some true things about the body, and have only *one* idea, I can do a little and then wiser men come afterwards and do more.

"We have a clever lady at our house, Miss Midgeley, and she have read everything, and she lends me books and talks. She has told me of an Italian gentleman, Garibaldi, who went to Sicily with only a few friends and one old gun and he conquered everybody. Yes, he did!" Johanson cried, waxing as enthusiastic as though Wistons must be hearing of Garibaldi for the first time in his life. "Indeed he did, sir! and when it were all over and the King came along and finished it with a big army, Garibaldi took off his hat and bowed and went home to his farm. Oh, that were great. I would have liked to have been one of his men and fought with him—or only just to have seen him . . ." His eyes stared beyond the walls of the little room. "There isn't time. I know nothing, I had no education, no books, no clever friends," he brought his gaze back, "but I am strong and young and every one is good to me here."

Wistons, no mean judge of his fellow human beings, gave this man a penetrating, searching stare. Was he a charlatan? Was he one of those windy gas-bags who appeared once and again covering some mean little selfish, mercenary project with fine cheap phrases and the patter of a tub-thumping park orator? Could any one in these sophisticated, semi-educated, journalistic days be so naïve, so platitudinous in idea and yet genuine? One glance was enough to assure him, once for all and for ever, that this man *was* genuine, complete, authentic. And who knew but that out of the mouths of babes and sucklings . . . ?

He was stirred beyond anything that he had expected, but he did not surrender himself. He was in himself so selfless, so ascetic in his abnegations that if, for a moment, the thought came to him that here was a man with whom he could work, into whom he could pour his own beliefs and creeds, he withdrew at once. There were to be for him (he knew it absolutely) no human contacts; he would be alone always; his search for Christ, his passionate thirst for *that* intimacy, precluded all others. Nevertheless, he was touched by this man as he had never before been touched by any human being.

"I understand," he said slowly. "All my life the beauty of holiness has been to me perhaps too exclusively the first thing in all our existence, but I know that there is also a holiness of beauty, only another door through which we pass to the same temple." He sighed. "There are other things, though, Mr. Johanson. Practical things. There is that difficulty you mentioned—how to spread your idea, your belief, without interfering with other people's lives. If you build you must destroy and you must destroy things that other people care for. You must preach. People, most people—and this little town is not unlike other towns in this—resent it when you touch what they care for. They hate your interference with their private lives. They think you dangerous or foolish. Or they think you can serve their purpose and would drag you in to fulfil *their* plans, not your own. They have their own affairs, money, love, ambition, and only care for their own projects. To build castles in the air is one thing, but to pull down castles that other people have built to make room for your own—then the difficulty begins. I wouldn't discourage you. I know that what you say is true. But the people here are like the people elsewhere, no better, no worse, human. A time may come for you when you will have to choose—to choose perhaps between a fine business and profit and success and your Idea, persecution, loneliness, apparent failure. It has happened many times before; the seeming failure has been the final success, but the man himself sees no results. They remain when he has gone."

Johanson nodded his head. "I know something of what you say. I have felt it myself—but, sir, if such a moment would come I would try to remember what you tell me. I know, as well, that there are very many people in the world who will never think the things beautiful I think—that is natural; but there is some things *so* beautiful that every one must be keen at them, and some things so ugly that every one must wish to destroy them. I don't hope I'm so conceited as to want to do more than to get a few friends together and all of us, together, make something. Shall I show you first what we are doing here and how it goes at present? Will you come along?"

Wistons readily came with him and was at once astonished at the other side of the man now revealed to him. Here, at the business end of the affair, was no dreamer but a very practical man of business.

It was about human nature, apparently, that the man was sentimental and idealistic, seeing men and women at a complete remove from reality, but now in the arrangement of his gymnastic concern he was as sharp and acute as a "two-thimble lawyer." First he introduced old Billy Trenant and the boy, who knew Wistons well enough, but snatched delightedly at an entirely fresh introduction in honour of the place and occasion.

Their pride and pleasure in their master was very pleasant to witness. Then he showed Wistons the instruments of torture, the spring-boards and the horse, the dumb-bells and the rings, the ropes and the boxing-gloves. Then he showed him his books, all the engagements he had, and the classes he was starting and the letters of advice and instruction he was sending into the country.

He made Billy and the boy do some exercises, and then, tearing off his collar and coat and waistcoat, he swung himself up to the rings and did some marvellous evolutions, convolutions, and what Charles Lamb, speaking of the Elizabethan dramatists, calls "extraditions."

Wistons, who had never before seen such grace and beauty of movement in a man, nor a body so strong and magnificently formed, felt as though he were listening to a piece of very fine music and was moved accordingly.

Then they went back and sat in the little room again. After a short silence he said:

"I told you I'd be frank, Mr. Johanson, and so I will be. I know by now that it is what you would like me to be. I believe you will have here a very difficult time. I can see that your gymnasium and your work in connection with it is going to be a great success. Our town is just ready for such a thing. Ten years ago, when I first came here, it was shut up inside itself; it had changed very little, I fancy, in the last hundred years. But of late many outside influences have attacked it, and there are many people here who would push it and make it commercially profitable, and there are others who would have it more gay and up-to-date. They will all seize on such a man as you. You are just the man for their purpose, and they will use you if they can to their advantage. There is nothing wrong in that. This gymnasium will be very good for them. But when it comes to the other half of your project—your spiritual beauty, if that phrase isn't offensive to you—then I fancy you are in for trouble.

"We are not bad people here, but, like people everywhere else, we are lazy and selfish. The two hardest things in the world to find are true altruism and honest clear thinking. If we all thought more of the good of others than of ourselves, and if we thought *straight* without allowing sentiment and self-interest to confuse us, this world would be your beautiful country to-morrow. But we are all afraid—you and I like the rest—afraid of our safety, afraid that some one will rob us, or laugh at us, or hurt us physically, or make us feel small. We are not—most of us—cowards about big crises, but it is the little things that destroy us. You have been given your vision clearly at this moment. But later on—when you have built up a fine business and discover that people will like you while you are successful and don't interfere with their lives, but will hate you if you try to change their comfort, their profit, their moral code, their safety—will you see as clearly then?"

Johanson was gazing out of the window on to the market-place. "I don't know, sir," he answered gravely, "I have had a happy life. I don't know how I would do when people did not like me. I like them to like me. I want to be happy, and for them to be happy. But I must see what I see," he cried, jumping up from his chair, "I can see no other. I see the wide street and the noble houses and the fine bodies of the people, and kind thoughts one of another. Every one would wish that, sir." He turned to Wistons pleadingly. "Seat any one in that chair and say to him, 'Do you wish that?' and I don't hope he would say no. I must go on and follow it as it comes to me."

"Wistons stood up and held out his hand to him.

"I wish you good luck," he said. "If I can help you I will, but I shall not be able to help you much. I fancy that you will have to work alone. And if you are alone, think of Christ Who was the loneliest of all. And on my side I shall like to think of you. You will help me, give me courage. Well . . . good night. Good night. Thank you. Thank you. Good night."

He turned, leaving the room abruptly, hurrying away with his head bent, his long arms swinging. He looked back once, timidly smiling, and was gone. Johanson stood at the window looking down at the darkening Square but not seeing it.

He was wrapt in the future. It was as though the trumpets had sounded for battle, afar off from the other side of the river, but clear, challenging. He stood up, bracing his shoulders, waiting for the attack.

CHAPTER IX

MARY'S RETURN

Every one in the house was astonished at the change in Maude Penethen—every one save Reuben Fletch, and what he thought no one save himself knew.

Maude was another creature.

She had no asperities, no conceits, no sudden tempers. She was neither vain nor noisy. She thought of others. She was in love with some one other than herself.

Even Miss Midgeley, who considered that she understood human nature, was surprised. Still she did not trust Maude, but she was compelled to admit that "if the girl remained like this very long she would be forced to change her mind." Maude's beauty shone through all the house. It had needed to be softened. Kindliness had been missing in it, that it might shine like a lamp through the texture of it. The lamp was lighted now and shone steadily.

No one was more astonished than Mrs. Penethen. She had thought that she knew her Maude. The best that she had hoped was that in time, after constant companionship with that kindly, simple creature, she would herself soften a little. But this instant transformation! Something not put on—a sort of spring-cleaning polish—but rather something that came from the girl's very heart so that she was herself surprised by it, taken by an emotion so new and overwhelming that she could only submit to it.

She did not "show off" her Harmer John as Mrs. Penethen had expected that she would do, did not ask people in that they might see what a capture she had made of this big clumsy giant, she so small and delicate and he in her hands to be ordered whither she pleased. She did not order him anywhere, but rather waited for him. She was passive, expectant, altogether transformed by this submission to another personality.

Only Harmer John was not astonished. As he had from the first thought her very perfection, it was not odd to him that she should be kind and unselfish and gentle. It was only odd to him—astonishing indeed—that she, so beautiful and so perfect, should care for him.

They did not see one another very often during the daytime. Business was now coming to him in full flood, and she agreed absolutely with him that he must neglect his work for nobody. She was intensely ambitious for him, and the only impatience she ever showed was in connection with his job. She was down in the morning to see him off, she went sometimes with her mother to fetch him in the afternoon. When the spring evenings with their pale primrose light began to steal upon the town she walked with him, strolling up the lanes above Orange Street.

But after supper was the best time. She sat very quietly in the kitchen close to him, her hand in his, saying very little, looking at him sometimes, meeting his eyes and holding them. She busied herself about his clothes, mending his socks, sewing buttons on his shirts. She liked best of all to be quiet, very close to him, her body touching his, feeling his body through his clothes, feeling the pulse beat in his hand against hers. It was as though she were holding this moment like Joshua bidding the sun stand still in its course, as though she had some forewarning that just this moment was the best that she would ever have.

He loved her so terribly that it frightened Mrs. Penethen sometimes to see the way that he looked at her, as though he drew her in and in and in to himself, and then fiercely held her against all possible challenge. But as yet there was no challenge.

He was for ever buying her things, and such strange things, not at all like the things that any one else would buy. Where on earth did he find them? Maude liked what he bought for her because she was in love with him, but had she not been in love she would have preferred more ordinary things like necklaces of pink coral or bright ribbons or pieces of lace. His engagement ring for her was a funny old one of twisted silver, with a small blue stone. He found her little silver boxes and old porcelain figures, and an amber seal, and a silver dish and a print of a ship in full sail, and a string of glass green beads, and a shawl with roses. Where did he find them? Little old shops. They were beautiful things, but people would think them odd. Now, because Maude was in love, she did not mind that; had she not been in love she would have thought them rather shabby.

He was extremely gentle with her, and she liked it best when he put his arms around her and held her close to him; she could feel his heart beating in the struggle that he was making not to hold her closer to him and crush her. She would be crushed one day; that was in the future.

She liked to put her hand up and stroke the back of his neck. His skin was warm and smooth, and then just below the neck it was cold and smoother yet, like marble. She laid her hand gently against his cheek, and then she knew that he closed his eyes and she could feel his hand clench around her.

He talked to her a great deal, but she did not listen very much. She had never listened to what other people said, and she could not, all in a moment, acquire that habit.

She sat, dreaming, beside him, hearing his voice very far away beating through the beating of her own heart; it was her own heart to which she was listening. She soon trained herself to say "Yes" and "No" at the right places, and "Yes, that she agreed," or "Wasn't that interesting?" and "Just fancy!" Curiously, although she was so ambitious for him and wanted him to be a thunderous success, and that every one should be proud, yet she was not interested to hear about his hopes, his dreams, his schemes for the future. When he mentioned names, important names, Canon Ronder, Wistons, Mrs. Bond, Ryle, Mrs.

Combermere—she listened greedily. When it was Tom Longstaffe or old Miss Eldred she sank back into her trance-like lethargy.

And he poured out everything to her—to Mrs. Penethen and Judy also. To Caesar the dog and also the cat. These were happy evenings in the old high kitchen: the two lovers close, side by side, Mrs. Penethen sewing at the table, Judy a book on her lap but not reading, and sometimes Miss Midgeley.

He felt now that he was a member of the family, and so he might tell them what he meant to do. But it was all in reality for Maude; everything was for her. Only when he was caught into the very heart of his dream, when he saw Polchester rising about him, the Cathedral in its midst, beautiful streets with avenues of trees spreading to the central Square, and there a wonderful fountain, its waters sparkling in the blue air, happy people, wonderful children . . . for the moment Maude was forgotten. No dirt, no squalor, no unkindness. . . . Foolish words Maude thought them when she caught a few, but she loved him, she loved him. He would be a great man, the greatest man in the town. Even Lady St. Leath . . . and she also had her dreams. . . .

They had in those first days only one quarrel, and that was a little one.

One evening before supper Johanson, looking up at the gilt cage and the nightingale drooping, said:

"I will let that bird go, Maude; you don't want it to be unhappy. Birds in cages is like wrongly-married people. Maude, let it go."

For a moment she was like the old Maude. "It was a present," she said quite fiercely.

Laughing, he went up to the cage. She sprang forward and stopped him. "It's mine. Don't you touch it."

He saw that she was angry. The light left his eyes. He turned away. "Well, if you like it. It's cruel, you know. How would you wish it—to beat your hands again and again against the wire? Always the same prison. But if you like it . . ."

Mrs. Penethen, watching him, thought: "Ah, he can be sulky—like an angry child."

Maude then was wonderful. She went up to him, pulled his head down and kissed him.

"Of course you're right. It's horrid; I didn't see it that way before." They went to the door together with the cage.

Hardly a quarrel.

He loved to tell them about his earlier life, days in Stockholm and the Islands, Copenhagen and the long sea-shore.

He had a great gift for word-painting through his broken English, English that now became with every week of his stay less broken. He had imagination, and, through it, he could awaken theirs.

The waters of Stockholm, the canals, the bridges, the sea; the lights as they swim in a long amber chain over the dark water; the ripples that the steamers

97

made as they slipped like secret messengers from landing to landing; the sudden avenues of dark trees with the band playing; the light on the white walls and the green trees and the blue water—no light and no water like that anywhere else, except in Venice, maybe. He had heard that in Venice . . .

And Stockholm drew near to his vision of his ideal town. They were doing things there, men of our own time, beautiful things.

But he had not been happy in Stockholm. He told them terrible stories of how, when he had been a small boy, his mother and he had waited in terror for the return of his father, waited in a little grey flat right up in an immense grey building, and the flat was so small and had so little air that it seemed like a cage. They had heard the fumbling at the door, had seen, the handle turn, and then the big man with the black beard would come in quite sober. That made it worse. He beat them out of cruelty. He beat the small boy until the blood ran down his naked body, while the mother, tied to the bed-post, hid her face in her hands.

And then Harmer John grew too big to be beaten any longer. That was a fine day when at last he defied his father and liberated his mother. "Father and I was sort of friends after that—friendly enemies; watching one the other like dogs. There were an understanding between us."

The odd thing was that he, Harmer John, was happy through all of that—some happiness deep inside that nothing could touch. Life was too interesting for one to be unhappy.

"I can understand that," Mrs. Penethen remarked, biting off a thread. "That's true what you say, Mr. Johnson. However deeply you're touched, however sick in body you are, something remains interested. I could read Marie Corelli if the house was on fire."

Oh, novels! He didn't think much of novels. But pictures and music, and the forest outside Stockholm and men unloading barges, and little fruit and flower shops, and a funeral going into a church with the door open and the lights over the altar, and two strong men wrestling.

Then Maude, drawing him back, made him forget all these things. It was one of his troubles that he had so much work to do, but when he looked at her he forgot it, he forgot it all. He had not known that love burnt like a fire. The heat, the heat and then the chill, like fear!

One evening he was back earlier than usual, and washing his hands in his room he heard a knock on the door. He said, "Come in," and there was Maude. She had never before been in his room while he was there. She stepped back. "Oh! I didn't know . . ." she said.

"Come," he said, holding out his arms.

She came, and he held her to his breast. He sat down on the bed, and she, on his knees, had her arms around his neck and her cheek against his.

"Dear, I have wanted you so all day. All through my work you was there, standing beside me, waiting for me. Oh, Maude, I have never known that love was like this, never dreamt of it."

She was trembling and he held her closer as though defying some enemy. The spring light, orange behind the window square, made the chimneys and roofs black, and the sky was so pale that it might not have existed had not one silver star given it life. The room was dusk. Maude whispered, "I love you. I love you. I love you. You are so strong that I don't think of myself any more. Oh, why can't it always be like this?" she broke out passionately, turning a little away from him. "It won't be! It won't be! I won't be always like this, and I want to be. I'm better so."

"But it shall always be like this," he answered her gently, "I don't hope that we will ever change. I love you so that I can never be another man. I know it, I have always known it. When there was other women in Copenhagen I always shook my head because something were missing. 'It isn't this time,' I said. 'Not yet. But it will come, and I will be patient and wait for it.' And that first evening when you came in at once I knew—in one moment for ever."

"You knew the first second you saw me?"

"I knew the first second I saw you. As I came in at the door I saw you, the fire behind your hair. I don't hope there'll be another moment in my life like that."

Maude sighed, nestling close to him again, her eyes closed.

"And there won't be another moment like that," she murmured sleepily. "Oh, why does love start at the top and then it can only go down? Now there'll be marriage and children and it will all be common like other people. I'm selfish. I'll want my way later when you are less wonderful." She had a vision of herself. She shrank from it, creeping closer to him.

But he had no fear. "It shall grow more wonderful and more wonderful as we know each other better and better, and our children shall be beautiful, and when we are old we shall be so happy looking back—"

But she closed his mouth with her hand. "Don't let us talk of the future. It's now, now, now I want. Love me. Love me."

Their lips met. They had not kissed like that before. They lost individual consciousness, all sense of time and place. They were still, motionless, mouth pressed to mouth, as the light faded and all the stars came out.

From an immense distance she heard his voice as though he were conscious of some danger.

"Come down with me. The others—it is time."

But she held to him, her body quivering.

"No. Let us stay. A little longer."

"We must go down." He almost pushed her from him, then, picking her up, carried her out of the room, his mouth buried in her hair.

But his love did not cause him to forget his friends. Something very important now was about to happen to Tom Longstaffe—the return of his daughter and his grandson.

Now he could say to himself, "I have been given everything—health, work, love and a friend." He trusted Longstaffe absolutely, told him everything, would share with him everything, would defend him anywhere, laughed with him, argued with him, wanted him continually at his side, was always wondering what he was doing, thought often how he might make him happy, and all this he had in return. They were true friends.

On a certain day Mary with her boy would return to Polchester. At first Johanson did not understand all that that would mean, then he realised that Longstaffe was deeply apprehensive. Why? What could there be to fear? They would be rude to her, perhaps insulting, and then he, her father, would not be able to stand by and see. . . . Rude to her? But why? Because she had had a child out of wedlock. It was audacious of her to return. But that old story? It had happened years ago. Every one had forgotten. Forgotten? Wait and see, my friend. But Johanson in his fresh enthusiasm about everything that had to do with Polchester could not believe that any one in the place could be so narrow and so cruel.

He reassured his friend, laughing at him, encouraging him. Nevertheless some doubt crept into his own heart. There was even perhaps something selfish in his feeling. Why was this girl returning to disturb their friendship? She was very clever and very learned, he had heard. He was terrified of clever women. Or he thought so. It was true that he was not terrified of Miss Midgeley, but then he *knew* her. Was he to lose all those jolly times with Longstaffe, the evenings when he ran in on his way from his work, the half-holidays when they walked their feet off, the Sundays when they talked, their feet up on the fender? There would always be this girl now. He shook his head, then abused himself for a selfish brute. How happy Tom would be to have his girl back again, to see his grandson tumbling about the house, to hear the old rooms wake up and laugh and sing. He, Johanson, with his own marvellous love-story, how could he resent this piece of luck for his friend? Resent it? No. He was delighted.

Nevertheless as the day approached he caught much of Tom Longstaffe's nervousness. It was arranged that he should come along about six o'clock. She was to arrive at the station about five-thirty. Her father would meet her and bring her home.

That was an afternoon of pouring rain, and as Johanson turned up Orange Street he thought to himself: "There's something wrong about this. I feel badly about it. I believe something bad's going to come of it." He opened the gate and crossed the sodden lawn as though he were passing into some foreign country. Behind him Orange Street was dimmed with drizzle; in front of him the windows of the Rectory were blurred with rain.

He rang the bell, and when the door was opened he could see at once that the old housekeeper was in a quiver of excitement. She glittered with her starched apron and cap, and whispered in a voice hoarse with emotion, "She's here, Mr. Johanson, sir. Lizzie's up taking the tea now."

He felt as though the house was new to him: he did not bound up the stairs two steps at a time as was his usual habit, but hung up his waterproof and cap, carefully straightened his tie in the glass, passed his hand over the rebellious tuft at the back of his head that would never lie down, and then slowly mounted. At the turn of the stairs he almost crossed to the left, where was the study, the accustomed den in the evening of the two friends. But now it would be the drawing-room, that dim, yellow, chilly room haunted by ghosts of old water-colours and faded photographs. And with every step shyness gained upon him.

But when he opened the door he was at once surprised. The room was bright and almost gay. A large fire was burning; there were flowers in the vases, primroses and daffodils, and the tea-table, with its silver and hissing urn, was alive and friendly.

Seated there was a woman, Tom's daughter; standing in front of the fire was Tom himself, and at the window, looking out at the rain, was a small slight boy with a round head of jet-black hair.

Mary Longstaffe had her back to Johanson, but at the sound of the opening door she turned and then, seeing a stranger, rose.

Tom came forward.

"Old man, this is my daughter. Mary, this is my friend, Mr. Johanson, of whom I've told you."

She held out her hand and smiled. "How do you do? Father has written about you so often in his letters that I feel as though I know you quite well."

Her voice was soft and musical, and the grip of her hand strong and honest, but at first he felt that he did not like her. She was unlike her father in that she was largely built, broad, Scandinavian in her very fair colouring, her round open face and blue eyes; her hair was brushed back from her forehead and parted down the middle. She was not handsome, but pleasant, frank, friendly, a little masculine in her lack of subtlety and coquetry, meeting him almost as man to man. He could admire her health and strength, her fine colour, her honest sincere gaze, but, dominated as he was just then by a type so opposite from this in grace and delicacy and beauty, she seemed to him like one of the women in his own country, a kind that he had known all his life, women of the countryside, unsexual, uninteresting, plain.

When the boy came forward it scarcely seemed possible that he could be her son. He was dark and fragile, with close-cropped hair, large black eyes and a small obstinate mouth. He was proper boy, though, sturdy in spite of his delicate build, graceful in spite of his sturdiness; he was quite self-possessed, giving his hand, saying, "How do you do?" and making a funny little bob with his head.

Johanson was uncomfortable, ill at ease; so also was Tom Longstaffe. The girl and her son were perfectly possessed.

"I hope you've had a good journey," Johanson said, standing in the middle of the room, which he seemed to fill.

"Oh yes, thank you," she answered, smiling up at him. "How do you like your tea? Strong? Weak? Milk?"

"Oh, tea," he answered in a voice of disgust. "Oh, not for me, Miss Longstaffe. I'm not keen at it, thank you. I've never tasted any in all my life."

They all laughed.

She began to talk, telling him about the little adventures in the train—the old lady who would not have the windows open, and the country-woman with the hen in a basket, and that wonderful crossing of the river after Drymouth that must always bring a lump into the throat of every Glebeshire native returning home. This last might, in the especial circumstances of her return, have hinted at awkwardness, but she showed no hesitation or confusion. After a while she got up and put her hand through her father's arm, and the two of them stood there together facing the room.

That action roused in Johanson the oddest feeling of jealousy. It was so, then. He was to lose his friend; no longer the two of them together, but always this third. Nay, he would be the third. He would not be needed any longer, and he would come there less and less, and at last not at all.

Conversation flagged, and would perhaps have died, when the boy turned round from the window and said, looking up at Johanson:

"I've got a parrot!"

"Have you?" Johanson turned towards him, laughing. He would go anywhere, do anything, for children and animals. "Where is she?"

"It's not a she. It's a he. Mother, may I show this man my parrot?"

"No, dear. Not just now. And you mustn't say 'this man,' Billy. This is Mr. Johanson."

But he was paying no attention to his mother. He was gazing up at Johanson with eager excitement, as though he were seeing him now for the first time.

"Why, you're the highest man I've ever seen," he cried. "How high are you?"

Johanson laughed. "How high do you think I am?" he asked.

"Oh, I don't know," Billy answered, with a little swagger of the body. "About eight feet."

"No, I'm not so much. And how high are you yourself?"

"Oh, I don't know"—dismissing himself before this superior interest. "Do you think you could lift me with one hand?"

"I expect so."

He bent down, very gently caught Billy by the slack of his sailor trousers, then raised him slowly from the floor. He held him high in air, then lowered him again. Billy, whose face while this had been proceeding had been one of deep solemnity, was now in a state of wild excitement.

"Mother!" he cried, stamping with his feet on the ground. "Did you see that? He lifted me with one hand. He's terribly strong, I expect. Can you lie down and have a cart and a horse on your stomach?"

"I've never tried," answered Johanson gravely. "It needs practice, I should think."

"Oh, you could! you could!" cried Billy, dancing about the floor. "I'm sure you could. Will you take your things off and show me your muscles?"

"Not just now," Johanson answered, laughing. "Sometime I will."

"And I'll show you all my things. I've got a train and an engine and a whole railway and a cricket-bat and a parrot. Will you come now? They're all upstairs."

"Hush, Billy," his mother interrupted, "you mustn't bother Mr. Johanson now. Sometime he will, I'm sure. Besides, they're not unpacked yet."

"Perhaps they are," Billy cried, tugging at Johanson's hand. "Let's come and see! Oh, do let's!"

But they were prevented. The door opened and some one came in.

Johanson knew at once who it was. It was Mrs. Bond. There is something afterwards to be said of Mrs. Bond, who was at this time a very important person in our town; for the moment there is only her appearance as she stood there pausing in the doorway, so pretty, so fragile, egg-shell china, her cheeks pink with comfort, good living, and interest in her neighbours, her hair steely-black and dress silver-grey, smart as we in our town reckoned smartness, of the wider world, travelled, cosmopolitan, eagerly friendly in the way of one who is being constantly a friend to people to whom she is at heart indifferent.

She moved forward, not seeing Mary Longstaffe, and shook hands with Tom.

"I came in only for a moment—" She had the prettiest voice, and her eyes swam up to you as she spoke. Then she realised the company. "This is my daughter Mary, Mrs. Bond. She has just arrived. You know Mr. Johanson, don't you? And this is my grandson Billy."

She broke into rippling smiles. Then in a friendly, almost beseeching movement, as she laid her hand on Mary's arm, looking up at her:

"My dear, I'm so glad you've come. What happiness for your father! . . . And this is your little boy? Mr. Johanson, how do you do?"

They all sat down, and Mrs. Bond took the field. She had a gift of conversation as no one in our town had ever had before she came—something so accomplished, so widely travelled, so informing without patronage, so gentle and yet so bold. She seemed to the natives of Polchester to have been, everywhere; she was a widow and so a little sad, a mother of three boys and so a little mature, and yet so gay and so young that her widowhood and maturity were fantasies. She had seen all the world, and yet preferred to live and die in Polchester which was flattering to us. She had known French Presidents, had had tea with D'Annunzio, and called on Bernhardt, and yet took an interest—a very keen and active interest—in our little local affairs. She had charm and tact, and smiled and laughed and declared that she loved everybody and everything.

Nevertheless this was not one of her successful afternoons. Billy was sent upstairs. Johanson sat there and said nothing. Mary Longstaffe was not easy. At first, bathed by the cascades of Mrs. Bond's laughing chatter, she passively accepted the shower. Then, when she spoke, she was so quiet and gave so little assistance that Mrs. Bond seemed, in a moment, to be left deserted, naked and helpless beneath her own fountain of words.

Tom tried to help, but he was embarrassed to-day, uneasy, shy. Johanson tried to help. He began a long Copenhagen anecdote, but his English was so slow, and every one knew what must be the conclusions of his sentences long before they were reached.

Silence fell.

Mrs. Bond's eyes, blue like very pale butterflies, danced all over Mary Longstaffe. Up, down! Here, there! Then she rose.

"Well, this has been *delightful*," she said. "Tactless as I always am, I came right in on your domestic scene. I don't suppose you'll ever forgive me. Will you forgive me, you wicked man?" She put her little hand on Tom Longstaffe's arm. He was confused, murmured something. She turned to Mary. "I love your father. He is the only good man I know. The only one. In Spain once there was another. But he, alas . . ." She shook her head, then brightened with a brave triumphant effort.

"Will you forgive me for loving your father, dear? You will have to share him with a good many now, you know. I am so glad you have come to make him happy. Good-bye, Mr. Johanson. You are turning my boys into marvels of physical fitness. I am so grateful. Good-bye. Good-bye. No, no, you are not to bother. I can find my way perfectly."

But Tom Longstaffe did bother. Johanson and Mary were left alone.

Mary smiled.

"She didn't ask me to go and see her," she said. "They won't, you know."

"Do you mind?" he asked.

It seemed as though in a second they had become friends.

"For father's sake, yes. I want things to be easy for him. He'll be hurt if they are rude to me. But I mean to stay, to make my own life whatever they do. I won't slink away. This is Billy's home where his father was, and this is *my* home where my father is. I love every stick and stone here, Mr. Johanson. I've dreamt about the river and the fields and the Cathedral for years. They will like me to be back here if no one else will. Does that sound sentimental to you?"

"No" Johanson answered. "I oft have such thoughts."

He was troubled. He saw that his town that he loved and believed in would perhaps behave badly in this affair and so lose some of its beauty. He did not want that to be. And he did not want the girl to be hurt, nor Tom, nor the little boy. They must not be hurt. He would protect them. But if his town was against them, and then, because he protected them, was against him too?

He moved across the floor towards her as though already the attack were beginning.

CHAPTER X

SEATOWN CAVES

Looney One-Two-Three, no older now than he was forty years ago, sat on the old green bench in the corner of the market-place and frizzled in the sun. He was saying to himself, as he had been saying now for forty years, "Something Strange and New is coming," and his object was, as it had been for forty years, to catch that Something. To catch it and then to do what with it? He did not know. Like any wise man he would tell you when he caught it.

He was a fine man, very thick and broad, with hair snow-white (he had not worn a hat for forty years; he would make his catch all the better without it). He was dressed as a fisherman in a blue jersey and broad blue trousers, and he was dressed as a fisherman because he was one. Before he had given up his life to this catch of his he had been a very good fisherman at Propperty Zezan-Tolooth. Then one night a storm had come crackling down from the heavens, and ever since then he had given up catching pilchard and such poor trash, and lain in wait for this other. He had tried many a spot, but the best of all was just here, under the wall of the Free Library, whence you could see right across the shore to the line of breakers, and it was there that the sea came pounding up from above the Seatown Caves.

It amused him greatly (people often asked him why he smiled so much to himself) to see all the queer traffic that crossed that shore—not the sort of traffic that you would see on most seashores, but sheep and oxen, carts and barrows, shining bits of furniture and plates and flower-pots, all spread out there on the shore with the line of water held, gleaming, just under the ridge of high cliff that stupid idiots said were houses. Houses! As though he didn't know better! Houses! As though he couldn't hear the sea pounding down below in Seatown Caves; as though he couldn't see the glittering shine of the sea, held taut like a string. But one day it would not be taut. It would come roaring right across the shore, carrying the farmers' legs and the booths and the cattle in a fine confusion with it—and then, on that happy day, it would carry right to his feet that Something New and Strange for which he was waiting. And wouldn't he collar it then? It would be his, his own, his very own. No one else had waited as he had done, day after day. That was why he smiled to himself. Because he knew what was what.

He knew very well what the others would do if they found this new thing. They would play with it and praise it and show it to their friends, and be proud of it so long as it kept its proper place and didn't put their other things out: if it did they would throw it away. He would behave very differently. It should do what it liked with him. He knew its value well enough. Everything else should go—his seaman's chest, his baccy jar, his stuffed parrot, his copper coins, his compass and his Bible. Yes, his Bible too. He wouldn't want one when he had his treasure.

He felt as though to-day might be the day. There was something in the air, a kind of smell, a kind of shine. The sun was so powerful hot. He could feel it upon the smooth wall of his chest; it crawled up his trouser legs, it patted his arms. He would watch carefully to-day. This afternoon (the Cathedral had sounded three o'clock) the market-place was deserted. He could see right across to the line of thin white foam. At any moment the sea might lurch forward and cast the thing, round, glittering, golden, at his feet. He stroked his strong legs. He would watch . . . He would watch . . . And so he fell asleep.

Not very far above his old white head, in a little room on the first floor of the building that held the Free Library (given to us in 1900), Cooper's Art Gallery and Dennison's Stores, Mr. Temperly, the hairdresser's assistant, was also asleep, his pale hands crossed over his thin chest and his shiny black hair falling over his eyes. He too was dreaming of Something New and Strange, and his Strangeness was a woman all thighs and kindliness. There were no customers just then. Mr. Broadbent, his master, was still at his dinner. He would be angry if he returned and found Temperly sleeping: meanwhile the young man smiled and raised one hand. But One-Two-Three was right. Did he catch his Strangeness he would insist instantly on converting her into Temperly, and if she would not be converted he would break her and throw her away. But as yet he had not caught her.

To the right of him again, and on a floor yet higher, Mrs. Brodribb, the wife of the dentist, was nodding over her novel. The novel was entitled *Her Lover's Pride*, and between its pages Mrs. Brodribb was finding *her* Strangeness, a Strangeness to which Brodribb had not as yet introduced her. Her fingers clutched at the vision. Lord Hartopp bent towards her, his face all smiles. She turned to make him proper Brodribb—the book fell with a clatter to the floor. She woke, and the vision was departed.

Far to the right, again, Harmer John was holding his first class of middle-aged men. The dark-blue blinds were half way down the windows to keep away the sun, but patterns of colour lay across the boards of the floor, and lozenges of light slipped up the legs of the horse and fastened like leeches on to the parallel bars. Above the patterns of light six men, four fat and two lean, in their vests and trousers, bent and raised, grunted and groaned.

It had been the idea of Mr. Cassidy, our leading grocer, only a week ago. He had caught it from his boy, who, a day-boy at the School, was a member of Johanson's gymnastic class, and was so deeply enthusiastic that he had broken the washing jug in his bedroom. Mr. Cassidy, a large, jolly, red-faced man, as all grocers having to deal with delightful things like honey, dried plums, figs, seed-cake and orange marmalade ought to be, caught his son's enthusiasm, forgave the washing jug, and said to Mildmay the auctioneer that very evening, "Why shouldn't we? Good for us. I'm too fat and you're too fat. Puff and blow going upstairs. He's a good fellow, that Swede. I'll speak to him." He did, and here is the first class all puffing, bubbling, blowing and happy with self-righteous approval.

Harmer John, in singlet and trousers, his neck and half his chest and his arms bare, cracks out his commands, "One Two Three. To the right. To the left. Now forward. Up again. To the left. To the right. One Two Three."

He loved them as he looked at them. Not precisely as human beings, but as fat to be reduced, knees to be straightened, muscles to be developed, cheeks to be browned. Look at that Cassidy with his belly! How was his heart going to stand all that fat? And little Massing of the Post Office with legs like matchwood, no chest, no shoulders, no anything but a wispy moustache and an eager pathetic eye! And Carlyon the nurseryman—a giant of a man and brown, healthy, clear-eyed! What was he doing with that paunch and that double chin? The devil of it was that he had so little time with them. As it was they had squeezed this hour together with great difficulty! So busy they were! And yet what did they do? With the exception of Carlyon, spending their days behind counters, hiding in little rabbit-holes totting up their money, hurrying home at night to stuffy meals, stuffy rooms, stuffy beds. (This business of sleeping two in a bed, how disgusting and insanitary!) If only he could arouse them to the enthusiasm of five minutes in the morning before the open window! But looking at them, at their middle-aged solidities, he knew that it would be no easy task. He must put some fire into them, some beautiful, cleansing, golden fire that would burn away the dross, the fat, the sweat, the accumulated laziness of years!

His face glowed, his body moved in beautiful rhythmic time with his orders, "One Two Three. One Two Three. Forward. Now down. Up again . . . And now at rest! Mr. Cassidy, you breathe only with your nose. Open your mouth. So. Breathe! Breathe, man! So. That's better!"

The room was filled with friendliness and kindliness. As they rested they felt their pleasure with themselves and with him. They were stiff, they were hot, they were fatigued, but they were alive. He was a good fellow, although a foreigner. And really only half a foreigner. His mother had been an Englishwoman, and he was engaged to a proper English girl. They looked on him with approval. They admired the muscles of his arms and his great chest. The strongest man they had ever seen and modest with it. Liking the town. Best town he'd ever known, he said, although he'd seen plenty of those foreign places. New ideas were good for Polchester so long as you didn't upset everybody. And the "Quality" liked him. The Cathedral people. For a foreigner he was a remarkable man.

The hour was over. They put on the collars and coats. Better, he told them, if they could bring special vest and trousers for these exercises. Best of all to follow the exercises with a cold shower. And then in the morning five minutes at the open window, stripped. . . .

But they were not listening. They had done enough. They were pleased with themselves and did not wish to feel that they had any farther to go. But they had thoughts of forming a Club, a Town Gymnastic Club. What did he think of the idea? Drill in the evenings. Thirty, forty, fifty of them. He thought it a fine idea, and that led him on to the expansion of his own premises. He had thought of taking two much bigger rooms behind St. James's Church in West Street. Mr. Fletch knew about them and thought he could secure them. Not room enough here for the way things were going. Well, good day, good day! Next Tuesday. Same time. Just try five minutes before the open window . . .

He threw up the blind and the window and stood, looking on to the sun-bathed Square. He was free for the remainder of the afternoon. The Square was yet deserted save for old Looney One-Two-Three staring there in front of him. Poor old Looney! And yet not perhaps to be pitied! Always expecting something and happy in his expectation. Was there any better state? But happiness? Was there any one in the world so happy as he, Harmer John? Maude, his work and the beauty there was in the world. And this physical fitness running through him like some mysterious stream of beatitude and comfort. He doubted nothing this afternoon, neither his love nor his work nor his luck. This blessed town and these blessed people. Their kindness and generosity and simplicity. He was moving them all and yet without preaching at them or trying to change them. Simply showing them this good idea of theirs. And when he was married to Maude and they had their little house and a baby or two. . . . What had he done to deserve such happiness and such love? Wasn't it unfair that he should have all the luck and the work that he liked and the girl that he adored? He would make it up for the others, for the less fortunate.

At the very thought, as though he had evoked her, one of the less fortunate entered his vision. She was crossing the Square, moving into the sunlight slowly, mournfully, with a dreary purposelessness. Old Miss Eldred. He was conscious of a momentary irritation, a tiny pebble of annoyance breaking the shining surface of his pool of content. She moved across the Square trailing an umbrella after her. She looked up at the sky as though asking whether it were going to rain, the kind of thing that on a beautiful stainless blue day like this she would do. Then she trailed on, turning in melancholy fashion towards his building. He moved, on an impulse too sharp to be resisted, into the next room where Billy Trenant was scratching his round head over some accounts.

"Billy, if Miss Eldred calls I'm not in, see?"

Billy grinned. "Thought t'would come to that," he said.

"No, it hasn't come to nothing. It's just that I'm busy."

He went back, closing the door behind him. In his imagination he could see Miss Eldred, her old bonnet a little askew, her thin lips tightly set, umbrella clutched in her hand, pausing at the door downstairs, opening it, then slowly trailing upstairs. . . . Why was he avoiding her? It was his first piece of cowardice. Back at the window again he faced it. He knew that he had two jobs on hand and that one of these was prospering marvellously and the other was not prospering at all. The one that was prospering was the practical one: for this he had, he saw quite clearly, a positive genius. His arrangement of the different classes, his organisation of his different publics, the School, the Cathedral set, the town officials, the tradesmen, the beginnings of his outside correspondence (exercises sent by post, directions for fat reduction and so on), his individual cases for massage like Ronder, all this work was successful beyond his most ambitious hopes, and successful because his natural talent stretched out into that direction so that he worked in that field by intuition, by native instinct.

But behind this work lay another and strangely, obstinately, almost against his will, of far greater importance than the first. With the second work were embraced all his dreams, his visions, his longings. Those dreams of his at night that were of his very soul, those visions that sprang into full glory when he stood beside the Brytte Monument in the Cathedral, those longings that were all his inner life, his love for Maude, his worship of beauty; a ladder that stretched from the blue plate in his Copenhagen lodging to the full glory of Heaven.

It was this second work that was not progressing at all. Both Shortt and Miss Eldred were failures. He had asked Shortt to draw some pictures for him, his ideal street, his town with the beautiful buildings, the avenues of noble trees, the fountains and the Squares, and Shortt had produced mussy scribbles.

Moreover Shortt was always drunk.

He had suggested to Miss Eldred that she should, with his help, start a small class of girls, a class to discuss the Arts, to consider Italian painting and sculpture, but Miss Eldred had done nothing at all. She only complained and protested. He suspected that she also drank.

He knew that many people laughed at him for making any advance towards such failures as Shortt and Miss Eldred, and he was conscious that when his dreams moved him he became blinded about people and judged them badly. He thought perhaps that he would always be like that and would make the same mistakes in the future, choosing the Eldreds and the Shortts all over again.

He saw, too, very clearly that in this second business of his he would, as Wistons had warned him, have to pull down before he could build up, and that, in pulling down, he would offend people and would run into a new stream of contacts, many of them hostile.

And yet, although he saw this too clearly, his Dream was, with every new day, becoming more important to him than his Business.

He did not, no indeed he did not, wish to improve people or change them, but his fingers were itching to do things that would prove to them, even on a tiny scale, how beautiful life might be. It was not that people were lazy or wicked or selfish, but that they simply had not *seen*! Their eyes were closed. He was no better than they, but he had been given an opportunity of *seeing*. He was sure that it was all so simple. A little co-operation, a little comradeship with fun and goodwill, a little throwing aside of personal interests, animosities, rivalries and the thing was done. But where to begin? He could not with his own hands pull down the hideous brewery at the corner of Market Street, he could not go down to Seatown and . . .

At the thought of Seatown be turned back from the window. During all these months he had intended to go down to Seatown, but every moment had been occupied. Now he had two clear hours. He got his hat, called to Billy to close the place up and stamped down the stairs.

The market-place was busier now. Old Looney One-Two-Three still sat there staring before him. People moved in and out from the dim arcades that were filled with plum-coloured shadows. Two or three farmers, their stout legs apart, their hats tilted back on their heads, discussed together. A nurse and a child dragging a toy cart passed along. The warm day played on the dark surfaces of the sleepy buildings.

Harmer John, moving slowly forward across the Square, could not rid his mind of Miss Eldred. Anything more amateur than he had been in his dealings with her and with Shortt too. (He did not acknowledge to himself that Maude was influencing him.) Who had ever heard of engaging a besotted drawing-master to make plans of an ideal city! He should have engaged some capable efficient architect. Capable efficient architect! The very words cut his dreams into ribbons of air. It was because Shortt was *not* efficient, because he had also his dreams and visions, that Johanson had chosen him. Yes, Shortt had had his dreams once, but now so sodden, shiftless, mean had his life become that his dreams, in sorrowful regret, had spread their wings and left him. Dreams would not stay for ever.

He was thus thinking, looking neither to left nor right, when, close beside St. James's Church, he ran into somebody. He stopped abruptly, looked up, raised his hat. It was Mary Longstaffe. They were in the shadow here, and the end of the houses beyond the church ran forward, shutting them away from the market-place. During these last days he had had so much upon his hands that he had not thought of her. He had a sense of shame now because of that. As he looked at her he again felt as though she were a woman of his own country, flaxen, big-boned, upright, clear-eyed, brave and—unromantic, unstirring.

She smiled, without shyness, honestly, as one man might greet another.

"Good afternoon, Mr. Johanson," she said. "Isn't it lovely weather?"

"Yes." He felt again that he liked her because she was tranquil, calm, honest. She would give good advice, would be wise and temperate in council. "How is the boy? I must come one day and see his treasures."

"Oh, Billy!" She laughed. "You made a great effect on him the other day. He is always speaking of you. He calls you the Giant. Do come and see us one afternoon. We are both always in at tea-time."

"Yes, I will." He still held his hat in his hand. He looked straight into her eyes, and she had a deep impression of his honesty, just as he had had of hers. "I'm very busy and I like to be that. I can't have too much work. I'm so keen at it that I *never* can have enough to do. All the same," he looked at her with a little perplexity, rubbing one hand through his hair, "I want things to happen too quickly. Miss Longstaffe, why is it you can't make people see what you see, at

110

once—hey, crack crack—just like that. We had in Stockholm an old clown at the circus when I was a boy, and he went Hey, crack crack! like that with his fingers and in a moment the girl on the white horse was a princess in gold and silver. I'd like to do it too with a snap of the fingers! Hey, crack crack! And all is beautiful and people isn't fat any more, and no one—" He broke off. "I'm getting preachy like a parson. And I hate preaching, but I've gone so far I want to go farther, and it's the next step is so difficult."

"Yes," she answered. "But perhaps it wouldn't be good for you if the next step were too easy. You'd get conceited. I'm getting preachy too. How easy it is to be preachy if you have an idea that obsesses you. Perhaps you shouldn't be afraid of being preachy, but just go ahead. Risk everything. I'm all for risking! We're all so afraid of everything! Why, before I came down here I was afraid sometimes of whether the women would cut me. And now I don't care—I don't care a little bit."

"But they're not cutting you?" he asked almost fiercely.

"Oh no. Of course not!" She looked at him as though she dared him to doubt her, then with a smile left him and went on her way.

As he too went forward he thought of Mary Longstaffe, and considered her with his own Maude. Strange that one woman should move him not at all, and that the other with every glance should so fire his senses! His senses! Yes, he was aware that with every passing hour his love for Maude was growing. He must marry her soon. She, too, was aware of that. Their contact now, were it only the touch of hands, stirred with danger. He was unsteady with the physical sense of her, and that physical sense seemed to hang like a curtain of flame and smoke between his real spirit and hers. It was her spirit that he loved, but, oh! he loved her body too and he was afraid always now lest some movement, some accident of privacy and juxtaposition, should be too strong for them. A year ago he would have said that his control over his body was such that no earthly power or temptation could shake it. But now he was not sure. He had been so ignorant then of what that blinding, deafening, all-consuming physical need could be.

Old Miss Midgeley knew about this. She was his great confidant now. He told her everything, and she understood marvellously. She knew Maude too. He was not altogether blinded by his love. There were things in Maude that seemed very odd to him, English things he supposed them. Pruderies, conventions, superstitions, prejudices. Pruderies in the very heart of her love, so that she would astound him by her eager anxiety as to what neighbours would say or think. She had little jealousies and rancours that seemed to him altogether unworthy of her, and she had, apparently, a positive hatred for her sister Judy. That strange girl he did not pretend to fathom. She never said anything, only looked oddly and cynically at them both, went about her household work as though she scorned them all. He must confess that he did not himself like her very much.

In fine, complications were beginning to arise around Harmer John.

He was plunging down now into Bridge Street. This was a lovely afternoon, and if ever Seatown were to look its prettiest it would be now. But it was impossible for Seatown to be pretty. Once, perhaps, when, a few cottages had nestled together at the foot of the wooded hill and the Cathedral and Castle had towered into air above them, when the Pol had run full flood and birds had sung in the forest on the opposite hill. These days were long departed, nor would they ever return.

Seatown had been for many a day the place of outlaws, nor were these outlaws of the picturesque and romantic kind. Rather were they the off-scourings of the district, loafers, idlers, thieves and prostitutes. In 1902 a disturbance had been made, and it seemed for a moment as though the whole place would be uprooted, but other influences had prevailed, a few cottages at the far end of Pennicent Street had been pulled down, and that was all.

Disturb Seatown and you stirred a nest of wasps. The foreign strain always prevalent in Glebeshire blood was here paramount. During that 1902 disturbance a mob of wild creatures had penetrated the decent quarters of the town, threatening fire and brimstone, swearing that they would burn down the Cathedral were they not left alone, pulsing up to the very windows of Lord St. Leath himself. And left alone they were. At once they settled down to their old customs. To do them full justice, they did not interfere with the rest of the town. They despised and scorned their neighbours, kept their outlawry proudly before them, called themselves descendants of kings and Vikings, and hummed busily in their own hive. They are gone now, and their abiding-place with them, and the man at this moment descending Bridge Street was the prophet of their destruction.

The fine afternoon could do nothing for Bridge Street but make its dirt and disorder the more apparent. The very fashion in which the street tilted down to the river as though it had not intended to go as far but had been too backbone-less to stay its impulse, gave a slipshod air to the uneven and awkward buildings. Once there had been fine houses here—the doors and porticos showed that—but now windows were broken, washing fluttered in the sunny air, dirty unwashed children tumbled about the steps, mongrels sniffed the gutters. As he proceeded Johanson's wonder grew. He was entering into a new world, and a world for which he was not prepared. He had on two occasions been half-way down Bridge Street in search of somebody, but he had not realised anything of this present degradation. He had seen, of course, slums bad enough both in Stockholm and Copenhagen, and Nexö has painted for all the world pictures of that jungle civilisation. But those were big towns, marts for the world. The whole of the present world must change before that wild garden of despair and ruin could be uprooted. Here was another question. Here was his own little town, the little place that he had taken to his heart. Here, too, was something that *could* be altered. The occupied space was so small, the souls concerned comparatively so few. . . .

As he descended he had an odd sense that, like Wotan and Loge, he was penetrating into some Nibelungen world. The air thickened, life became furtive and mysterious, faces peered at him from behind dark windows, dogs slipped by busy on furtive errands, images leaning with waxen figures against the walls were inhuman—of some other race than man. The bright blue air fell as though through the opening of a vast encircling well. The sky was brilliant overhead, but the sunlight shadowed and thickened as it fell. He paused for a moment to gain some sense of the district that he was reaching. Above him on the left an old Georgian house with a carved doorway and two bow windows on its first floor stretched heavenwards. Charming that house must once have been; now it had fallen into slatternly and shabby habit. No sign of life there. He looked up to two attic windows on the top floor. High up. A superb view there. He did not know why he looked at them, or why, having gazed, he earnestly read the number of the house. One hundred and three, Bridge Street.

What told him that that house was to take its place so prominently in later events? Enough that he knew.

But the silence! He would not have believed, had he not witnessed, that so close to the market-place, St. James's Church, the High Street, life could thus change its character.

Above his head they were standing in the sun on the market cobbles discussing happily the world's affairs. Up the High Street the Cathedral folk were passing to their tea, soon the Cathedral bells would happily ring for Evensong, but here, as he stood, the strange purple light enfolded him as though it were a disease cloud descending from the heavens, as in some story that he had somewhere read, to slay the world.

He passed onward and downward. Bridge Street fell into Pennicent Street, the main thoroughfare of Seatown. This more than Bridge Street had, in eighteenth-century days, known a gay and polished life. The street ran beside the Pol and was bounded from it only by a thin grey wall. The waters of the Pol ran sluggishly, and with a strange blue iridescence. The houses were reflected in that water, dark, at odd angles with strange marks of personality, living and sinister things like the buildings in a Meryon etching. Here were ruin and destruction indeed. Once, maybe, these houses had had their gardens running to the river's edge gay with flowers. Grubby remnants of gardens truncated by the intersecting street remained, and in one there were even the ruins of a sundial. Little alley-ways ran through the houses and behind them. Beyond the open doorways dark passages gaped and shaky wooden staircases could be discerned. Here, along Pennicent Street, there was more life than in Bridge Street. The fine afternoon called the people out, and, like figures painted on some screen, they hung motionless against the stealthy background, sitting on the river wall, on steps, leaning against doors, or slipping in and out of passages. They stared at Harmer John as he passed. Because of his height and breadth and swinging walk he always commanded interest wherever he went. He turned round once and smiled at two children, and they ran silently into the house behind them. He spoke to a man leaning against a wall: "A splendid day," he said, but the man gave him no answer, only stared.

As he went anger rose in his heart, a strange confused anger new to his experience. He hated and loathed this place, and he hated and loathed the indifference of the people above them who made this place possible. Those sleek overfed Canons and their superior patronising women! Then he remembered that only an hour or two before he had been loving these people and praising them for their kindness; so then his anger swung round upon himself. How was he better than they? he busied about his little selfish money-making schemes, and he had been here for months and had not even bothered to come near the place. As he smelt the smells, saw the tattered rags that stuffed the windows, saw the filthy children tumbling in the puddles with the mongrel dogs, there was a great pain at his heart, a pain that in some way, instinctively he knew, would never let him go again.

He had stopped, without definite consciousness, in front of a building rather more tottery and damp-scarred than its neighbours. Some impulse moved him to penetrate the black passage, and then, scarcely conscious of his own movement, he started to climb the rickety staircase. Here silence indeed engulfed him. Almost frightened at the sound of his own footfall, he paused. As he stayed there in that gathering dark it seemed to him that if he moved higher he was taking a step that would change all his future life. Should he go up or should he go down? A fantastic fear held him; it was even as though some one laid a hand on his coat and bade him descend.

So soon as he recognised this as fear, the choice was settled. He moved forward, but, even as he moved, he knew that he had taken some decisive step.

Reaching a landing, he found on his left a closed door. After a moment's pause, moving still as though he were under the direction of an outside power, he pushed it open and entered. A room with some of the panes of the window broken, with a large dirty bed covered with sacking and one thin torn sheet, a smaller bed by the side of it in which a little girl was lying, some broken chairs, some bottles, some dirty plates on a table that had only three legs, a tall thin woman with a long pale face standing by the end of the bed, her hand to her throat, her eyes wide but not startled, all this he at once realised.

"I beg pardon," he said, taking off his hat. "I don't hope—" Then he paused. What had he to say? For what reason was he there?

The woman said nothing. She made no movement at all. He stood beside the door, smiling. The room smelt musty, of unwashed flesh, stale beer, cabbage, sickness, medicine, bad breath. The sight of the child touched him instantly. He forgot the room, the woman. He adored children always, one as another, good or wicked, weak or strong, noisy or quiet. He went over to the small bed. The little girl was perhaps five or six years of age. Her hair, jet black, scattered the pillow; her face, tiny for her age, like the face of a doll, was peaked with weariness and pain. She was not asleep: her eyes moved drearily from, right to left, from left to right. He bent forward and picked her up, then, with almost the same movement, wrapped the blanket about her, sat down on one of the chairs and held her close to him, feeling the hot little body through the thin nightdress. The child laid her head quite naturally against his breast and her hand moved forward and caught his. She thought perhaps that he was the doctor.

"What's the matter?" he asked the woman.

"It's 'er 'ead," the woman answered. "Terrible ache in 'er 'ead. The doctor can't do nothing. Says we came to 'im too late. . . . She's dying. Poor worm too." The woman burst into low passionate sobs. She still stared in front of her, but the tears trickled down her face as though she were powerless to stop them and did not care. She showed no surprise at his presence, nor at his holding the child. It was as though she had known him always.

Very gently he stroked the girl's forehead. Ever since he could remember there had lain special power in the touch of his hands. How many he had cured ere now of headache, neuralgia and such ills! His hands were strong and gentle, but also something emanated from him, something of his own strength and fortitude and tenderness. The little girl moved at first restlessly; once she looked up and stared into his face as though asking him a question, then, with a deep sigh, she settled down in his arms. His hand moved backwards and forwards across her forehead. He did not speak, nor did the woman. She did not move. Over all the house there stood silence. For a long time his hand moved, then, the child deeply sleeping, he took her and laid her gently in the bed.

The woman drew a deep breath. "She ain't slept, not to call it sleeping, for days and days," she whispered, gazing down at the child. She looked up at him, wonderingly.

He did not want to embarrass her. He would like to give her money, but thought that she might be proud, so he only said:

"I shall look in to-morrow, shan't I?" He gave her a bow, walked to the door, turned back once to look at the child and went out.

The little episode had relieved him for the moment of some of his anger. He must have been in that room a long while; when he was again in the street the sun had vanished behind the houses and long amber shadows engulfed the distance.

Then, once more, looking about him his anger came full tide. The dirt, the misery, the degradation! He stood, his legs apart, his arms moving as though, like Samson, he would pull the whole place about his ears, even, though himself were crushed in the ruins.

"Good evening, Mr. Johanson," a voice said in his ear. "Who would expect to find you down here?"

It was Samuel Hogg. Not strange that it should be. Johanson had had an odd sense for the last month or so that the man had an eye on him, watched his movements, followed him, insisted on some strange relationship with him. The very fact that this was the only man in all the world whom he, Harmer John, hated gave their relation some queer extra twist. A tie of melodrama, so that he always saw Hogg as some one unreal, out of drawing. This meeting now jerked his passion to a heat unusual to him. This man owned most of these houses. It was due to him rather than to any other that they were as they were.

"You've got a nice place down here," he said, turning round upon him. "Charming place—healthy and with every modern improvement. I congratulate you."

Hogg stood quite close to him, his hat tilted back on his head, smiling friendlily and gently.

"Now, come," he said, "it isn't all mine, you know."

"Oh, aren't it?" Johanson was shaking with anger. "You've had plenty to do with it though, with this dirt and ugliness and smell. You're proud with it, are you not? You look at it and smile and say: I'm a fine man, I! I make plenty of money from their sores and sickness and tears. I'm a clever man, am I not? I blind and deafen them up there in the Town Council so that they don't enquire too much and too often, and I find a Canon or two to buy a house or two, and then it all looks respectable. I have the finest slum in all England, I have! the dirtiest and smelliest and most dangerous, with disease so that all the children dies and the dogs feed in the gutters. I are a splendid man. Every one's keen at me. I will be decorated one day for the fine things I do."

But Hogg was not at all annoyed. He looked at Johanson in the friendliest fashion.

"Now, see here, Mr. Johanson, don't get all worked up. And take a word of advice from me. You've been abusing me, haven't you, so you've given me the right in a kind of way to give you some warning. You're a foreigner. You've been in this country only a few months. Every one's been nice to you and likes what you're doing for the town. Well and good. Well *and* good. So long as you're dealing with what you understand, it's all very handsome. You're good at the massage business. You understand about it, which no one else in this place does, and it's good for the town that you've come here. I'll grant you that. But you don't understand everything, and my advice to you is to keep your nose out of what don't concern you. You begin messing round here and you're asking for trouble—"

"Trouble! Trouble!" Johanson broke in. "You dare to talk to me of trouble and you let this go on, you make money of it, you—"

"Very well—very well," interrupted Hogg patiently. "Grant that I'm a scoundrel. By your beautiful lights I daresay I may be. But I'm not talking about myself. I'm talking of *yourself*. I'm in no danger that I need to worry about, but *you* are. You start fussing round in places that aren't your business and you see the sort of trouble you raise for yourself! Lord! what do you know of English social conditions or the way people live here or want to live? And you've got no poor in your own beautiful country, I suppose? All Paradise there, ain't it? I *don't* think."

Johanson answered more quietly. "You think you can frighten me. You can't. You think I'm talking of things I don't know. It's true I'm a foreigner, and it's true I don't know English social conditions, but I know enough with my eyes to see this are wicked and I'm going to make other people see too. And I say you are a dirty scoundrel, because you see how filthy this is and encourage it being filthy so you make more money out from it. That is the foulest thing a man can do. Any man would feel the same as me if he could see what I see, and so he *shall* see!"

Hogg stepped backwards. He stood, feet apart, his hands deep in his trouser pockets.

"So you're going to down me, are you?" he said. "Well, Mr. Preaching Parson, try it and see."

With a nod not unfriendly he strode off down the street.

BOOK II

OF HOW HE STAYED WITH US
<hr size=2 width="100%" align=center>

CHAPTER I

IN THE UPPER AIR—POPULARITY

T HE brotherhood of man might quickly be a realised happiness were it not for the soil that divides us. In spite of the timorous flatteries poured down upon the unbending head of Mother Earth by apprehensive worshippers, the soil divides. We are standing together, shoulder by shoulder, the view before us superb, the sentiment in our hearts warm and comforting, when—a sudden fissure at our feet, one of us tumbles in, the other hurries to safety.

Who knows but that Looney himself and Mrs. Bond might have been, years ago, twin brother and sister, had it not been for that hissing whisper from the sky that made all the Mrs. Bonds in the world in an instant meaningless? Other fish to fry. Meanwhile she, unaware of any friendship averted by nature, deserves a further word.

When she came to live in our town she came with the most amiable intentions. She was a most amiable woman, amiable to herself, amiable to others. With the double object of being kind to herself and very friendly to every one else, she settled down among us. She chose her home wisely. Her means were small. She was a widow and had three sons, Horace, Wellesley and Joseph, to educate.

In a larger town she might have slipped out of general notice; in the country she would not have seen enough of her fellow human beings whom she adored; she must be in some place where Horace, Wellesley and Joseph could be educated adequately but economically.

It shows, I think, how swiftly our town was advancing that Mrs. Bond should so easily and with so many smiles of welcome from her neighbours occupy the place taken only a few years before by Ellen Stiles and a few others. When Archdeacon Brandon was alive we were, socially, very small beer indeed. At the little tea-parties and dinners given by our upper ten, when scandal was talked at all it was scandal of a very local kind. We scarcely glanced beyond the Polchester walls, and if London were mentioned it was spoken of as a place remote and foreign. How swiftly Mrs. Bond altered all that! She had travelled so much, knew Europe so thoroughly and the East so charmingly that with one turn of her beautiful hand she swung Polchester into the centre of the Universe. "Pompeii!" she cried to timid Mrs. Ryle at the very first tea-party that she attended. "You should see Timgad!" (She was afterwards christened Timgad by her enemies. Who in this censorious world has not a few?)

Consciously or unconsciously we all assisted in this splendid attempt to push Polchester into the middle of Europe. One shove, all together, one more, together again, and we had done it. There Polchester is, somewhere nicely situated between Madrid and Paris. But, once landed there, she had to be kept there, and the only one of us who knew enough to carry *that* job through sufficiently was, of course, Mrs. Bond.

It followed then, "as the night the day," that in no time at all Mrs. Bond was the social leader of our town. She recognised the position and most graciously accepted it. Her house (near the bottom of Orange Street, just before you come to the river) was tiny, and her means of course ridiculously small. (Had she not three growing sons to educate, and were not investments always descending, and could you have expected Mr. Bond, who had had money in oil, to leave very much?) We never anticipated more than a cup of tea or a sandwich in the evening as entertainment; nevertheless her little dinner-parties were charming, and it was she who introduced into our town the fashion of reducing dinners to three courses, so much healthier for all of us. (As every one knows, the custom is now universal.)

The most wonderful thing about Mrs. Bond was the way in which, so swiftly, she had the whole of our town at her finger-ends, the people, I mean, and what they were all about, who loved whom, and hated whom too, why so-and-so was offended with so-and-so, and why, if you didn't take care, you'd have so-and-so at so-and-so's throat. . . . All about so-and-so, in fact.

Another wonderful thing was that she realised with astonishing rapidity all our social grades and differences, recognised them indeed a great deal more clearly than most of us ourselves had hitherto done. In Brandon's time there had not been many social differences: there was the Cathedral set, the Tradespeople, and what Mrs. Combermere used to call the "Huggermuggers," she of course declaring in her funny independent way that she liked the Huggermuggers best.

But now, developing as we were, every kind of social difference began to appear: Mrs. Bond had her little finger on them all. Which of us, for instance, had clearly perceived in the old days that Mrs. Ryle the Precentor's wife wasn't "quite quite," and had indeed in her earliest time been, for a short period, a governess? Mrs. Bond discovered this when she had only been in our town a fortnight. Not that she disliked Mrs. Ryle. She liked her immensely. She thought it a wicked shame that the fact that she had once been a governess should influence anybody. But there it was. Mrs. Bond wasn't going to allow it to influence *her*. That it influenced certain other people less high-minded than Mrs. Bond was, I am afraid, undeniable.

Then there was the question of the St. Leaths. Every one knew, of course, that young Lady St. Leath didn't get on very well with the old Dowager Countess. There was something to be said for both of them. You couldn't expect the Dowager to be glad that her only son had married the daughter of a man who had died in disgrace, and the sister of a man who had married Samuel Hogg's daughter, could you? On the other hand, it was scarcely the fault of dear little Lady St. Leath, who was so modest and kind and sweet-natured, that her family had behaved so badly.

But none of us had ever thought for a moment of interfering or taking sides in the St. Leath affair until Mrs. Bond came along and showed us that we really couldn't be indifferent to it all. For her part she liked them both so much—the old Dowager and the young Countess—that she was going to do her very best *not* to take sides. Nevertheless . . .

I think that the Dowager and young Lady St. Leath were just beginning to settle down together when Mrs. Bond came with her European standards and showed them that it was impossible that they should.

In a surprisingly short time Mrs. Bond knew every one in our town and the private circumstances of every one. This last was made easier for her by the willing co-operation and help of her three sons. Horace was sixteen years of age, Wellesley thirteen, and Joseph eleven. They were fat, pale-faced boys, curiously like one another, and not very popular at the School, I believe. But they were day-boys, and it is always difficult for day-boys to be popular at a school that consists mainly of boarders. Undoubtedly they were very useful in bringing home social news to their mother, whom they loved dearly. They picked up so much that was interesting from the other day-boys, and if they didn't actually pick things up they invented them, which was almost as good. They had very polite manners, and would sit for hours in a room quietly just noticing things—so quietly indeed that you forgot altogether they were there, which forgetfulness was sometimes unfortunate in its results. Mrs. Bond adored her boys. She called them her three jewels. They were all, she said, that she had now to live for.

If you wished, at any time, to discover just what it was that was occupying the Polchester mind, all that you had to do was to drop in at one of Mrs. Bond's delicious little tea-parties. Here you were most truly breathing "the Upper Air." Mrs. Bond was careful whom she had to these intimacies—she chose her generals, captains, lieutenants, with the greatest tact. Did you look in you would be almost certain to find Julia Preston, a pretty but not very intelligent lady, there. Then there would be, as likely as not, Canon Bentinck-Major, smart, shining and worshipful; Mrs. Hammersley, wife of our most prominent banker, one of the Callender girls, and Colonel Cartwright, our leading Conservative. These were Mrs. Bond's principal friends and supporters. She had no enemies. "At least," she would say, "I refuse to recognise any. If certain people don't like me it isn't my fault, is it? I like every one in this town. I do indeed. Why waste time and temper over hostilities? Yesterday some one told me that Ellen Stiles couldn't abide me. 'My dear,' I answered, 'is that my fault?' I think Ellen is a perfect dear. Only the other day I was defending her when Aggie Templar said that she wouldn't have any more to do with her because she wouldn't pay her card debts. Why, even if that were true . . ."

As I have said before, and as after events showed, it was a thousand pities that we hadn't, all of us, Mrs. Bond's spirit of charity and forgiving understanding.

Had you dropped in just now at one of Mrs. Bond's tea-parties you would have discovered at once that Harmer John was the centre of the town's observation. And you would have discovered another thing—that every one loved him.

He had taken the town's fancy, and when any one takes our town's fancy we are generous indeed.

He took our fancy the more securely because he took it gradually. At first there had been the sight of him—his tall, strong figure; his jolly, friendly countenance; then rumours of his personality, his kindliness, simplicity, love for our town; then a gradual interest in the work that he was doing. Gymnastics, health, vigour and strength; then the recognition of his social acceptance, giving Ronder massage, taken up by the School; then real knowledge of the man himself; almost every one met him. Because he was a foreigner and "different," room could be made for him socially in every kind of way; then his engagement to a girl of our town, his happiness at that, and *our* happiness at seeing *him* happy (because truly at heart we wanted nothing but to see every one happy). And then, finally, the creation of this Legend, the first of the Harmer John Legends. (It will be seen afterwards how many there have been, and even until this day . . .)

This was the Viking Legend. Straight from the icy North he had come, clean and straight and strong like a sapling from the northern frost. . . . And so on. And so on. The point was that he should not be seen by any of us any longer as a human being, but as a romantic illustration to some almost forgotten fairy tale. Not *quite* forgotten. He brought back with him our childhood again, those delightful days when, at our mother's knee, we sat before a roaring fire. . . .

In Mrs. Bond's little orange drawing-room, Julia Preston, gazing in front of her, balancing her tea-cup on the thinnest bone of her very thin knee, whispered in reminiscent murmur:

"There was that story of Hans Andersen's, that *lovely* story, about the forest and the man who cut down the trees. . . . Oh, don't you remember, Beatrice (to Mrs. Hammersley)? I can't remember it precisely, but I know there was a forest and that splendid man. . . . When I saw him coming up the High Street this morning swinging along in that fine way—"

"You're too romantic for anything, Julia dear," Mrs. Bond interrupted. "The point really is that he is exactly what the town wants. So long as he doesn't interfere with anything that any one else is doing—"

"Is it true," asked Beatrice Hammersley, "that he's a close friend of Mary Longstaffe's? That's a pity if it's true. I haven't heard it on any good authority, only somebody said . . ."

"There," broke in Mrs. Bond, standing up in her indignation and addressing them all, "isn't that exactly like this place? If there's one thing that I detest it's scandal. Why need we be for ever running others down and speaking of them uncharitably? Oh, I don't mean you, Beatrice dear. I'm sure a warmer-hearted woman never existed. But this is just another instance. Why, Mr. Longstaffe was the first friend he made in the place! It's most natural he should know the daughter. *I* don't think it odd that he should have been there to meet her the first afternoon she arrived."

"Was there when she arrived?" Julia Preston and Mrs. Hammersley cried in chorus.

"Yes, I was there myself," Mrs. Bond rather reluctantly admitted. "I'd no idea the girl was arriving just then. Went in quite by chance—and who should be there but the girl, her small boy, her father and Johanson. All most domestic. There are many people who would think from that that he was being admitted much too closely into the bosom of the family. It doesn't seem so to me. He's engaged to that nice pretty girl at the place where he lodges, and any one who says to me that there's anything between him and Mary Longstaffe . . ."

"All the same," Mrs. Hammersley broke in, "it does seem a pity. That nasty girl and that splendid man, especially as he's engaged. I think that some one ought to say something to him."

Mrs. Hammersley did not really *mean* that Mary Longstaffe was a "nasty" girl. She was a large red-faced woman brimming over with good nature, but she admired Mrs. Bond immensely, was happy to be there in that intimate circle drinking tea, and wished to take her part, to fit into the atmosphere, to say something that would seem striking and pleasant. Mary Longstaffe and Harmer John were both dim shadowy figures to her. They did not cross her actual intimate world. She would have faced the most fearful ostracism or deadliest isolation in defence of her lean, bald-headed husband, her two bespectacled little girls, or her old mother in Drymouth. But these distant figures, why should she not toss them about a little if to do so made her position more pleasant and assured round this charming tea-table?

Canon Render was announced. Every one was delighted. The moment that his friendly, beaming spectacles were seen, a cosiness was added to the cosiness already present. He was given the best chair. He smiled upon them all. He liked to be there. They adored to have him.

"We are talking of your protégé, Canon Ronder," Julia Preston said. "The Great Dane. The Viking. Harmer John, you know."

Ronder was pleased. He wished that Harmer John should be considered his protégé. He had heard that Wistons was taking him up. Just the way to ruin the fellow. Who had given him his first private job? Who was always first in looking after the town's real interests?

"Well, I can tell you something about that," he said, beaming round upon them all. "What do you say to a lecture from this hero, or even two or three? A demonstration, you know, with some of his ablest pupils. The suggestion has been made to him, and I think something will come of it. He's such a modest fellow that he needed some persuading, but when he was shown what a help such a thing would be to the cause that he had at heart he gave in. The affair is practically arranged. In the Town Hall about three weeks from now, and I am to take the chair."

Now wasn't that splendid? Wasn't that the very thing? How clever of Canon Ronder to have thought of it! A general sense of the progressiveness of our town stole through the tea-scented air. Who could say that we were not moving? Might not this man be the talk of the County before long, and then, beyond the County, of London, of England, of Europe? A general movement was made towards Mrs. Bond, naturally able to estimate Europe's trend of thought better than the rest of us.

"In Odessa I remember once when my husband and I were passing through ..." she contributed. Where exactly was Odessa? But it did not matter. Odessa and Polchester met, hands clasped.

"He must be a remarkable sort of man," old Colonel Cartwright said, stepping forward in his slow, cautious way. "Have you heard the way they're talking about him down in Seatown? I'm told he wandered down there the other day and into some rooms or other and found a child dying there. Just put his hands on the child's forehead and cured it. The women down there say he's a saint, they tell me, and when he goes down, bring their babies and their ailments, and one thing and another, just as though he were Christ Himself."

"Ah! that's a pity," said Ronder gravely. "He must stick to his job. He's just a fine young fellow who knows his work and is full of enthusiasm for it. If they begin spoiling him and making him theatrical it will be a thousand pities. I must speak to him about it."

There was general agreement about this. We don't want him spoilt, and we don't want him putting his nose into something that he can't possibly understand. That's the worst of it; if you're not an Englishman you never know where to stop. However, he's young and unspoilt. A word from Canon Ronder. And *what* a fine fellow! Straight from those northern mists, those virgin forests, those untrodden snows. . . . The figure rises, gigantic, God-like, higher and higher, above the tea-cups, out over the house-tops, towering titanic above the Cathedral roofs themselves.

At that very moment Johanson, in his shirt sleeves, was leaning over the table in the outer office of his gymnasium, reading from a book. He was bending down upon his straightened arms as though he had been arrested by the sight of the open book on the table as he was crossing to pick up his coat. His hair was tousled, his face flushed. He had just ceased work. He was about to close the place and go home. Old Billy Trenant was standing there, looking up at him with exactly the expression of a dog waiting for his master. With his short thick body, his stumpy legs, his impertinent mouth and affectionate eyes, he resembled precisely a Sealyham.

Johanson was reading:

When Levin reloaded his gun and moved on, the sun had already risen, although it was still invisible behind the clouds. The moon had lost all its splendour and looked faint and pale; not a single star could be seen. The puddles, that a short time ago had looked silvery in the dew, were now golden.

The grass too, that had appeared bluish before, now assumed a yellow-green tint. The swamp birds were chirping about in the bushes sparkling with dew and casting long shadows. A hawk was sitting on a rick wagging its head from side to side and looking discontentedly over the marsh. Jackdaws were flying about in the meadow; a bare-footed boy was leading the horses up to the old man, who raised himself from under his coat and began scratching different parts of his body. The smoke from the shot lay like a white mist on the green grass. A boy came running towards Levin.

"There were wild ducks here yesterday!" he shouted from a distance as he tried to catch him up.

Johanson was savouring a moment of exquisite pleasure. He drew a deep breath through his nostrils, raising his head, expanding his chest. The book was open there by chance—*Anna Karenina*, by Tolstoi. Miss Midgeley had lent it him. He had not begun to read it yet; the volume had been lying on the table there in the outside office and some one had opened it at that place. He had caught sight of the open page as he was passing through to get his coat, and he had stopped. He was caught instantly away into that world that during the last two or three months he had in some way lost. There again was the house, the open rooms bathed in light, the silver birch, the faintly purple sky, the Donatello "David" seen at the top of the gleaming staircase . . . and with it all this Tolstoi country blended, the bushes sparkling with dew, the bare-footed boy, the horses, the smoke lying like a white mist. . . .

He straightened himself, looking about the room like a man in a dream. "Ah, that's good!" he thought. "That life is mine. That is very true life." And again, as so often before, he understood that funny strawberry-faced old Miss Midgeley was always leading him back into his true life, either by a book or a word or a glance, as though she understood better than any one else in the world what his life was. There were people like that, not at all your most intimate friends, almost strangers to you perhaps, who yet understood better than any one else what your life ought to be and were always leading you back to it.

But, stretching his arms, feeling through all his body the magnificent weariness of a well-spent day, above all scenting ahead of him the exquisite joy that was in store for him (a joy freshly renewed every day, kept suspended in front of him and approached ever more closely as the afternoon advanced), his evening meeting with Maude, he went up to Trenant, took him by the shoulders and gently shook him. "I'm happy, Billy, terribly happy. Is it dangerous, do you think?"

"You deserve to be happy," Billy answered, looking at him with eyes full of pride. "You're a good man."

"Will you stick by me, Billy, whatever happens?"

"I'll never leave you," the old man answered, " 'less you ask me to. I've got terrible fond of you."

"You're an obstinate old devil," Johanson answered, "but I was lucky to find you. Well, good night."

"Good night, sir," Billy answered, and turned about to put the room straight before locking up.

Coming out of the building and into the market-place he sniffed the evening air, loving its freshness, its scents of the country town where, the business of the day over, the smell of the fields, the woods, the hill, comes stepping lightly into the streets, pressing up the stairway, threading through the windows. How small and simple this place, but how lovable and friendly with the greetings at the doorways, old Looney there on his faded green bench, and the Cathedral bells singing the time through the air as though especially for Harmer John going home from his work.

He felt, as so often before, that he would yet further postpone the glorious instant of that meeting with Maude; that sight of her that always told him with a rush of sensuous triumph that she was more wonderful than all his imagination of the afternoon, stretching like a gorgeous tapestry behind his hard and concentrated work, had assured him.

"I will go in for a moment to Tom's. The boy will just be going to bed. He misses me if I don't come." He climbed Orange Street, loving the English decorum of the old eighteenth-century doors, the shining knockers, the neat propriety of the little stone steps, the smiling pride of the gleaming professional plates, doctors and lawyers and architects. "No streets like these anywhere else in the world, and they are mine. Although I am half a foreigner, England is mine. I belong to it and trust it. It has given me my love and my work, and in return I will give it everything I have and am."

He opened the creaking gate and walked up the path. Soon he was in the old house smelling the old smells of varnish and books and geraniums and tobacco that seemed to speak to him with a personal voice.

"Hullo!" he called.

"Hullo!" came Mary Longstaffe's voice from upstairs.

Tom Longstaffe, puffing at his pipe, appeared at the doorway of the study.

"Mary's upstairs bathing the kid," he cried, "I'll join you in a minute."

He went up. He knew the way to the bathroom. The door was open; Billy was in the bath sailing his boat; his mother, her sleeves rolled up over her arms, was soaping his back. At sight of his friend he jumped up, scattering the water, pushing his mother back with his hand, standing waving his arms: "Mr. Johnson! Mr. Johnson! I've got to ride you to bed, haven't I? I've nearly finished. Oh, mother, that's soap enough. I'm clean, as clean. Mr. Johnson, I've got a dog. He's a Sealyham. Grandfather's got him. He's down in the kitchen."

His voice, in his excitement, broke into a funny squeak: his body shining in the light, the water running down his legs, his black hair sticking up in little points made him seem a little animal caught in the woods somewhere, quivering now with life.

"Good evening, Miss Longstaffe," Johanson said, "I don't hope you mind my coming a moment."

She smiled as though they were very old friends. "Oh no," she said, straightening herself, seeming very large in the little room; "Billy would have been terribly disappointed if you hadn't come. He always seems to expect you on bath nights." She sat down, a towel on her lap, another over her arm. Billy climbed out and stood between her knees.

He talked all the while as his mother dried him: "Mr. Johnson! Mr. Johnson! the puppy's got a black eye. That's why grandfather bought him, because of his black eye. Sealyhams oughtn't to, the man said, and he isn't a proper Sealyham, but he's nearer that than anything else. I'm going to teach him to walk and hunt and everything, only the awful thing is," here his voice dropped to great gravity, "that he likes the kitchen better than anywhere and he hasn't got to. Mother says it's because he picks up scraps, but I'm going to tie him to the leg of the dining-room table when I'm not there. That's enough, mother. I'm dry now. Yes, I really am. I'll do my ears myself. Mr. Johnson, I'm not fat, am I? I haven't a bit of fat on my body, have I?"

He said it with so grown-up an air that they both laughed. He turned round to Johanson, stretched out his arms, stood on his toes, his face pursed up, anxiously, for approval. So he stood, his perfect little naked body like a flower in its first bloom, the skin rosy from his bath, the eyes of absolute innocence and honesty, the head royally posed, the little muscles showing beneath the soft skin. So he stood before life had written its narrative upon him.

His mother threw his night-gown over his head; he wriggled into it as a butterfly might waggle back into his chrysalis after a moment's release.

"Now!" he cried, clapping his hands. Johanson bent down, touching the floor with his fingers. Billy climbed on to his back, fixing his arms around the thick, strong neck. Johanson slowly rose and the ride upstairs began. Billy sat, his face lit with a serious ecstasy, surveying the world from that great height. All the world was now different to him—the tops of the pictures, the corners under the ceiling, the funny sudden ending of the wall-paper when its pattern was only half finished, the great distance of the floor and the strange different pattern that the carpet now made, the foreshortened furniture with dumpy legs, but above all the pride, the adventure, the triumph at being so high, at taking such risks, at the companionship with the man whom already he admired more than any one else in the world—all this was happiness and all this was the first promise of that same spirit that was afterwards to lead him to such splendid adventure and so glorious a death.

Up the narrow stairs they went, brushing the Caldecott pictures as they went, along the passages lit now with the evening sun; soon he was sinking, sinking; strong hands were about his body holding him so firmly and yet so tenderly; he was between the sheets gazing in silence at the ceiling.

In silence because it had been so great an experience. Then he put up his arms, pulled down Johanson's head and kissed him. Then he turned to the wall, sighed with happiness and almost at once, like the animal that he was, was asleep.

They stood watching him for a moment, then went out into the passage. "What do you think?" Johanson said as they walked downstairs, "I'm to give a lecture, perhaps two or three. Canon Ronder made the suggestion. He says people want it. I don't know myself—what do you think?"

He was already feeling that this girl had more common sense than any one else he knew. No, not more than old Miss Midgeley, but common sense of a different sort, knowledge of the world. He felt that she had suffered in the way that he would suffer if Maude died or left him—suffer so that the wound would always be there, not to make him misanthropic or cynical, but to change him forever. So she was changed.

"I think it's a very good idea," she said, smiling up at her father, who had joined them. "What will you do? Read them a paper or just talk? Talking's better."

"Ah, that's one trouble," he said, "my English is so bad. I'm shy to expose it. But I thought I would speak a little, and then have some drilling exercises—four or five of us—and then speak some more. What do you say?"

"I think it's fine!" Tom Longstaffe cried eagerly. "Why, you're becoming the most important man in the place, Johnnie. And then you'll be so important that you'll be deserting us and going up to London, and we'll never see you again."

"No, but you do think it's good, wise?" he asked earnestly, turning round to her, his hand on her father's shoulder. "Not too conceited, not too bold?"

"Not a bit," she answered him confidently. "And you'll have the great satisfaction of being sure that no one else in the place knows anything about it. That's a great help, I'm sure, when you're lecturing."

As he walked to his house he thought of the two of them standing together in their doorway waving him good-bye. They were wonderful friends. They would stand by him for ever whatever happened. But why this eternal "whatever happened"? Into his happiness for a moment a little chill foreboding fell. It was because everything was prospering so that he feared. Not entirely. He stopped for an instant under the monument of that funny old frock-coated townsman to be honest with himself. It was because he was keeping things away from himself, because he would not face everything, Seatown and other things. He had been to Seatown a number of times during the last weeks seeing that sick child and—No, he would not! He gazed up at the evening sky with almost passionate entreaty. This day must be splendid. He would not make it miserable with thought of wrongs that he could not cure. No, that he could not cure. Not now. Afterwards. Later. Later. Later. Later. The sibilant trees seemed to whisper after him down the lane.

Outside the door of the house, as once before on that stormy night, he stopped, waiting, with a beating heart, as though he were afraid of the joy that was to come. What if Maude were ill or had been hurt in some accident, or were angry with him and would not see him or—Laughing aloud at his own folly, he turned the handle of the door and went in.

In the kitchen there was only Judy laying the table, gravely, silently as always. She did not like him, he could tell that; but to-night every one must like him, and, conscious that for another moment he was extending that gorgeous heart-throbbing anticipation of Maude, hanging up his coat he said to her:

"Well, Judy, how is it? All well although I'm away the whole day? Bearing up?"

"You mean is Maude well?" she said, not looking at him.

"No, I don't. I mean you—everybody. I love all of you."

"Yes, so you say."

"But I do." He went up to her, caught her head back and kissed her. Her cheeks flamed, but she replied nothing until, standing on the other side of the table, she said quietly:

"You shouldn't have done that, Mr. Johanson. It wasn't kind."

He was distressed. In Denmark you kissed every girl, you thought nothing about it at all; and she was Maude's sister. And now he had made her unhappy.

"Ah, Judy," he said, "I'm to be your brother. We're brother and sister almost already. I want you to be happy as I are happy."

"Keep your kisses for Maude," she answered fiercely, "I don't want them. And we're not brother and sister. You haven't married Maude yet."

He looked at her with so kindly and friendly an expression that she dropped her eyes as though she didn't wish to realise that he could look at her so.

"No," he said, "that's true. I've not married Maude yet. I'm terribly sorry I've hurt your feelings, Judy. Why is it I'm always wrong with you? If I'm keen at anybody or anything I don't stop to think enough. People think longer in England than in most countries. I'll be the same when I've been here a while."

Her hand trembled as she arranged some knives and forks. She only said, looking up at him quickly:

"Here's Maude."

She came towards him wearing her hat and coat. "Let's go out," she said to him quickly. "There's twenty minutes before supper. It's so close in here."

He took down his hat and they went out. They often did that now—privacy was difficult in the house; but on such a purple silver evening as this they could cut away, along the lane and then through the wicket-gate to the left down the slope of the field, through the hedge and up the hill on the other side, over the very ground, had they but known it, once trodden so disastrously by Brandon.

They had a favourite tree, old, thick, of multitudinous branches, and under it on a warm evening they could sit, close together, seeing the lights of the town come out, smelling the evening scents of grass and flower, sometimes facing the orange glow of sunset as it whirled across the sky.

To-night he knew, by the way that she clung to him, kissing him again and again, stroking slowly his hair, thrusting her hand in between his waistcoat and thin shirt above the beating of his heart, that she was in a storm of love. Every throb of his blood responded to her, but as he held her close to him with all the strength that he could muster he controlled himself, feeling that she was like some small lonely bird in his hands—the nightingale, perhaps, that they had released—and that he must keep her safe from all harm, must watch over her and guard her.

Her cheek resting against his, she murmured, "I have wanted you so to-day—oh, terribly! It was all I could do not to go to the office to see whether you were still there. Yes, I felt this morning that you had disappeared. Just as you came here that night. You don't belong to us really—not to mother, nor me, nor the town, nor any of us. You'll go one night just as you came. I know you will. I know you will."

He held her closer and closer, her body in his hands as though it were his body. But he felt a swift strange apprehension born through her words. Was it so? Did he not belong here? Was this place, this love, this work a dream, and was there some other life waiting for him that would catch him back and awaken him to reality?

No, his love for her was real enough. He knew it: it went far beyond the desire of body for body, far beyond these embraces that were only the feeble sign of its presence, deep into some dark under-world of longing.

"We can never separate, you and I," he spoke to the pale shadow of the sky, the dark curtain of the tree above their heads. "If we were to quarrel, to separate, never meet in the flesh again, I would still hold you, you will never be free of me."

"But I don't want it like that," she answered. "Oh, Johnnie, I want us to be married—soon, soon, soon. You aren't mine until then; but when we are sleeping together, and when I can look up and see you sleeping there beside me and know that the whole of you is mine, that you aren't a ghost—"

"And when we have children," he broke in upon her gently.

"No, I'll be jealous of them. They'll take you from me, part of you. I'll be jealous of anybody, anything—"

She drew herself away from him, resting her elbow on the grass, looking up at him.

"Where were you to-night before you came home? You were later than usual. I know. You went in to see those Longstaffes."

Her voice that had been soft was now sharp, a little shrill, with a common Glebeshire tang in it.

"Yes," he said quietly, "I looked in there for a moment."

She drew farther away from him.

"I knew it. You're always going in there. What can you see in those people?"

He made no answer. She waited, then went on, her voice more shrill. "I know what you see in them. It's that girl, that girl that ought never to have shown her face in this town, bringing back her baby and all. I—"

She broke off, aware perhaps of the speed with which they were travelling away from their happiness of a few moments before. She plucked at the grass.

He drew her back to him. Her body was at first stiff, then yielded, and with a sigh she buried her face in his coat.

"Maude, Maude," he answered her gently, "you must trust me more than that. You must know what my love for you are. There can be nothing but trust when two people love one another as we. Tom Longstaffe were my first friend, outside your house, in all this place. He were the first to hold out his hand and take mine. I don't hope you're jealous of Tom Longstaffe—" he laughed.

"No, not of him," she murmured, "but of the girl—"

"Then, there is the boy," he went on, "the small boy. He is a fine little boy, strong and brave, and until you give me some I must have some children somewhere near. Always I had to have, in Copenhagen, Stockholm, everywhere."

"But you'd give them up if I asked you?" she said quickly.

"Give them up?" he asked. "How do you mean?"

"If I said that I wouldn't marry you unless you gave them up—"

"Ah, but you wouldn't," he answered her. "You couldn't. It wouldn't be you. Another woman, yes. But I couldn't love another woman while you live."

"But if I asked you to give her up?"

"Give her up? Miss Longstaffe? Yes, if I loved her. I would see then that I must choose between you and her. But I don't love her. I shall never love her. You don't understand, Maude, how my love is for you. It is everything—all my body, soul, spirit. While you live there will never be another woman. I have waited for you all my life and now I have you. But I must be free too. Not free to love other women, but to have my friends and my life. And you must be free too, to have *your* life."

She realised that. He was just. She believed in what he said—now. But later? She leaned up, drew his head down to her. So they stayed for a while, then quietly walked down the darkening fields towards the town.

CHAPTER II

THE FIRST LECTURE

THREE days later Maude went for a week to the little village of Rafiel to stay with an aunt who was expected to leave money.

Johanson wrote her five letters, and these are extracts:

MY DEAREST BELUVEDEST DARLING—I am escaped the dull wether its been since you left by a lot of work but I am thinking so much of you and I hav had no word from you onely that line with lov, I don't hope you're angry with me?

I am beginning to wok to-morrow for the lecture and every one are so nice about it onely old Miss Eldred with complains over my not giveing her more to do because I am always thinking of myself. Well, I'm not are I, darling? It shall be fine for the lecture, first I shal talk about thery and such things, not much talking you know becaus my english is bad and then there will be five of us—me, Walter Pearce, Harry Pearce, Franklin and my young Trennent boy and we shall do all the exercises and the pyramyd and everything. Then I shal talk some more and it will be all over—one hour and a haf I think. I shal look forward darling til your coming and seeing me mak my ecercises properly wich you never hav yet. I think of you allways morning afternoon evening and I hop we shall spend a nice time together when you return. I do love you so—I do—I love you for ever and ever and ever. A great hug from your devoted luver,

HJALMAR.

. . . Last night I could not sleep. It aren't like me at all not to sleep but I wanted you so badly my darling. I walked down and up my little room and thought of you and how you would be sleeping and then of all the great towns in the world and not one haveing any one so luvley as you and I sent you such heeps of lov that I think you should have waked in your sleep and known what I were thinking.

The work are moveing finely. The two Pearce boys are proud I have asked them and I have nau aranged everything for my perfermence, I feel something like a Cirkus darling like a cammul or ellifant you understand how I would feel dont you but Cannon Ronder says it shall do all the people good and I'm sure I hop so. I am nau ending this but shal write again to-morrow and I thought your letter should hav been longer but it was very sweet what it said and I lov you more with every breth I breath.—Your adoring luver,

HJALMAR.

. . . I were so tired yesterday with all the work for the lecture and all the audinary work to that I com home an hour erly. I read a book Miss Midgeley have given me, very fine, *Anna Karenina*, by a Russian about marriage happy and unhappy. I dont hope you shal be like Anna darling onely when I am returning to wok when we are married you must not be dul without me as she were without her husband that is the way for married people to be unhappy with one

another. There is another man in the book Levin his name is and although he is
a Russian that dossent matter because he is like a brother to me. I feel like he
does about everything. Your mother have a cold and Judy sulks she wont spik to
any one and we doessent know what is the matter.

Fletch is asking me about the new buildings I should hav will I hav them
and I said yes allthow I must borrow money from him but I must have more
room nau dont you think so darling? Your mother is a wunderfull woman. I luv
her allmost like you not quiet but neerly. She is so quite but allways the same
and we understand one anuther wunderfull. You must forgiv my spelling dearest
onely english is not written as it is spokken is it. Your muther dossent want me
to tak the money from Fletch but what shall I do? I must have more room and
there is no other place will do like these rooms in Market Street and I must hav
them from Fletch if I get them. What do you say darling? In your letter you say
you count the minites till you see me again and so I do you. I am onely hoping
we shal be married in two or three munths I cant waite longer for you and these
engagements are cruel are not they when two people luv one another like you
and me. O darling com home, com home I ake and ake for you to hav you in
my arms and mak you happy with kisses and heer your voice and see your
eyes—Darling, darling if I could writ to you in Swedish language I would say so
mutch but with this spelling it caches me up. I luv you so more every
minit.—Your luving luver,

HJALMAR.

. . . and the day after to-morrow you shall be home again. It seems to mutch
to beleeve. I am coming to the station although I should not because of my
wok. That goes splendidly and every one seems keen at the lecture. In anuther
day or more there will be notices in the tawn about it and then they will buy
tikets or I hop so. Would not it be terrible darling if no one bought tikets and
onely a few friends came but I dont hope that and Cannon Ronder says that
every one are comming. I had a dream of you last night singing in my garden
not a garden you know of but one I dream of and allways the same garden. You
was never in it befor but last night you were there singing in a tree and I could
not see you but you sang that you were allways there now and would never leave
me and that made me terrible happy. You told me once that dreams were
foolish but somtimes I am not certin which are dreams and which are real. You
are perhaps a dream what is truely you I mean. . . . Com quick, I want you. I
want you I must kiss you soon. . . .

She returned, looking so lovely that he did not know why every one in the
street did not stand transfixed by her beauty. But they did not; only old Looney
sat motionless watching the sea draw its crystal line up on the shore beneath the
shaggy rock.

Notices were posted.

A LECTURE
ENTITLED
PHYSICAL FITNESS AND ITS

RELATION TO HUMAN HAPPINESS,
WITH DEMONSTRATIONS,
WILL BE GIVEN
BY
HJALMAR JOHANSON,
GYMNASTIC PROFESSOR
(Stockholm, Gothenburg, Copenhagen),
ON
Wednesday, May 22nd, 1907,
IN THE
TOWN HALL, POLCHESTER.
Chairman—CANON RONDER.

———————

Doors Open 7.30.
Carriages 9.30.

They were posted liberally. It was impossible to avoid Johanson's name. He felt shy like a girl. He walked up the side streets home.

Then four things occurred, all small things and all, for their consequences, important.

First, he met Mrs. Bond in the street. She looked like a flower, so dainty and fresh and dewy she was. She smiled—the smile that has made people happy from Timgad to Beersheba. It made Johanson happy; he was happy already because it was a fine day and the tickets were selling so well for his lecture. He looked down at her, and she looked up at him. She did not like men who were too tall; that was something that she had against him from the first.

"Oh, Mr. Johnson, I am so glad to see you. I am coming to your lecture, you know. I am looking forward to it so much."

"Yes," he said. "It shall be very interesting."

"I'm sure it will be," she answered. (What a conceited man! she thought.) "And so good for all of us. And oh, Mr. Johnson, my boy Horace tells me that he is in your gymnastic class at school, and he is enjoying it so much. I do hope he is good at his work and improving."

Johanson should have been warned, but it was a beautiful day and every one was smiling. Then he had never been a cautious man. He hated the Bond boy; of all the boys in the class that was the boy the most hated by him. The Bond boy was mean and false and treacherous, trying always himself to avoid work and to fasten it upon others. Yes, he hated the Bond boy, so, looking down upon the smiling mother, he answered, "No, he doesn't work. I'm sorry to say it, but he's the most lazy boy in the class. He's not keen at his work at all and he's too fat, much too fat for his years, mite in the face too." And, having said this, he looked at Mrs. Bond with the same friendliness as though he had said nothing at all to wound her maternal heart. And she smiled back at him with all the courtesy of a thousand European civilisations.

"Oh dear, I'm sorry to hear that. I must speak to him. He didn't give me that impression; he seemed to be enjoying his work so much. All my three boys are coming to your lecture and I'm sure it will do them so much good. We *are* so looking forward. . . . Good-bye. Good-bye—"

And that same afternoon she began her work, declaring at Mrs. Ryle's, "I met that nice gymnastic man in the High Street this afternoon, and I do like him so much. It's quite untrue that he's getting swollen-headed, as people say, and the rest. People are so unfair. Of course a foreigner has a different code of morals altogether from ourselves. Nevertheless to say, as people do . . ."

The second thing that occurred was an impulse. He had an amazing unexpected impulse to strangle Canon Ronder. He went, as always, twice a week, to massage Ronder in his house. This deed was executed in his bedroom. He did not like the Canon's bedroom because it was, to his feeling, too effeminate. The curtains were of old rose brocade, there was a piece of African silk on the bed, a copy (a fine one) of Botticelli's "Primavera" over the mantelpiece, a dressing-gown of dark brown silk over the back of the chair. The Canon, during the massage, wore pyjamas of white silk. There were flowers in the room, rose-coloured tulips, and on the floor a thick purple-tinted Persian carpet. Too much silk, too many colours, not enough windows open.

When the Canon lay on his bed (the African silk removed from it), his pyjama jacket open, his skin was so fat and so smooth and so white that Johanson felt, looking at him, a strange kind of impropriety. He had not a hair on his chest, and without his round spectacles his eyes were strange, cynical, sarcastic, sensual. "He didn't ought to be a clergyman" had been Johanson's first thought when he saw him naked, without his spectacles, stretched upon his bed.

However, he had been to see him now on so many occasions that he had lost some of his uneasiness, almost all of it. Then to-day, unexpectedly, it came back to him and in great force.

"Turn over, please," and Ronder slowly, like some animal rolling in a pool, turned over.

All this while Ronder, lying on his back, had been talking and talking well. He had stared at the ceiling and from it had extracted the true purpose of his discourse, which was as follows: that by this time he and Johanson were friends—was it not so? The town in general recognised this, and it was felt by everybody that he and Johanson were working together for some common purpose, and that purpose was the advancement of Polchester.

Now, each had his own gifts, Ronder his and Johanson his. Johanson knew so much that no one else in the town knew, but Ronder was older, had more knowledge of the world and had more knowledge especially of Polchester, its citizens, its classes and divisions, its true needs. This lecture that was coming might be taken as the first public step forward made by Ronder and Johanson together. Would Johanson then be guided a little by Ronder? This town was a queer one, odd in its prejudices, superstitions, sudden resentments. One false step might ruin everything.

Now—and Ronder, gazing at the snow-white ceiling, hoped that Johanson would remember that he had not anywhere in the world a better friend—would Johanson mind a little plain speaking? He, Ronder, had heard one or two things. This was, like all small towns, a terrible place for gossip, and Ronder had heard that Johanson had been expressing in public his horrified surprise at the state of things in Seatown. Of course, Seatown was not perfect. Something had already been done and there were plans for the future—well, Johanson might trust the Cathedral body to see to the future. And was it really quite Johanson's place to meddle in this matter? Wasn't he interfering a little in the province of others? Did he understand sufficiently as yet English conditions? He had heard that some hysterical women in Seatown had been proclaiming Johanson as a kind of miracle-worker. That was a dangerous mood if it went too far. Those people down in Seatown had foreign blood in their veins—foreign blood, dangerous when roused. And then another thing. Ronder did hope that Johanson did not mind this friendly word. But was Johanson wise to make such close friends just now of the Longstaffes? Excellent fellow, Tom Longstaffe. One of the best clergymen in the whole diocese. But Johanson, being a foreigner, did not in all probability quite realise what English people felt about Miss Longstaffe's behaviour. Poor girl! Ronder, who was a man of the world, could see clearly enough the extenuation for her fault. But a fault it was, a fault against God and the social laws of our country, and she had been, beyond doubt, ill-advised to return with her child to the place where it had occurred. He did not blame her; it was natural enough that she should wish to be with her father, but Johanson must remember that he was now beginning a splendid work that might mean the happiness and well-being of many thousands of human beings, and that he had but recently engaged himself to a charming girl in the town, and that people *would* talk. . . .

It was at this moment that Johanson said, "Turn over, please."

After Ronder turned over he had but little opportunity for further advice. Johanson gave him that evening an excellent massage. His white flesh crimsoned. His stout legs were bent backwards, his thighs twisted, his arms stretched. Once or twice he uttered little cries, he panted, he writhed. Once he half rose in protest.

At the end he sat up, breathing very heavily. "Oh, dear me!" he cried. "You did give me a pummelling!"

Johanson laughed. His round, boyish countenance expressed nothing but happy friendliness.

"If I hurt you—" he began. He stopped and then added reflectively, "It won't last long."

"You didn't mind what I said, did you?" asked Ronder, feeling for his spectacles.

"Not at all. Not at all," laughed Johanson.

The third incident was brief.

One evening returning homewards, he ran into the Longstaffes to tell them some agreeable news about the lecture's prospects. The door was open. No one was in the hall. He called. There was no answer. He crossed into the study and, knocking, entered.

Little Tom Longstaffe, his face puckered with distress, was standing there. Mary Longstaffe, turning to leave the room, almost ran into Johanson. She was crying.

He had seen her always strong, absolutely controlled, like a man rather than a woman. This was a new figure revealed to him. She brushed past him without speaking and left the room.

"Why, Tom, what's this?" he cried. Then, as Longstaffe looked at him in a kind of bewilderment as though he had not recognised him, he went on quickly, "I'm sorry. I should not have come in. I'll come to-morrow."

"No," Longstaffe said, smiling through his trouble. "It's all right. We're a bit upset. Only a letter a beastly woman's sent me about Mary. I was a fool to press her for her reasons for giving the church up. One ought always to leave people alone. But she was one of the best workers we had—"

"About Mary?" Johanson asked. "What about Mary?"

"Oh, the usual thing. That until Mary leaves the place she must give up coming to the church. That I ought to understand the scandal it's making, and so on and so on. I didn't mean Mary to see it, of course, but she opened it by mistake. And now she says that she must go back to London, she and Billy, and the trouble is that now I don't think I can get on without them. Having had them here these weeks makes it so hard. And yet there's my work. . . ."

Johanson breathed deep. "That's what this town is," he said slowly. "After all these years they can so persecute you. . . ."

"It's right," Tom interrupted, "from their point of view. I saw it, of course, from the very beginning. It's no animus against Mary, but the thing she stands for. Forgive her and you have to forgive so much. And they have children, girls of their own."

Johanson was silent, thinking steadily.

"But not the cruelty," he said slowly. "Not the persecution. And how can they judge? With their own faults. . . . Who is good enough? It's blindness, dead blindness."

He looked so deeply distressed that Tom went up to him, drew his arm through his and so stood close to him.

"Don't you worry about our troubles," he said. "We'll see the way through them."

"But I must worry," Johanson answered. "You're my friend."

"Yes," Tom answered, laughing. "But friendship doesn't involve such burdens."

"It involves every burden," Johanson answered. "It were as though it happens to me myself. I am you, you am I."

"Well, the sentiment's all right even though the grammar's a bit mixed," said Tom. "It's something having you for a friend. Yes, it *is* something."

Johanson turned away slowly.

"I must go to Mary," Tom said. "Come in to-morrow."

Johanson walked away, thinking deeply. For the first time he had forgotten that Maude was waiting for him.

The fourth incident was a dialogue, and it stepped, one spring evening, out of the great West door of the Cathedral.

The shining stretch of grass was deserted. Perfect peace rested there. No human soul to be seen until Ambrose Wistons pushed back the leather flap of the door and emerged. A moment later Johanson followed him.

For a second Johanson hesitated. It had been dark in the Cathedral, a changing shadow of purple dusk. He had been standing, as he loved to stand, before the Brytte Monument, feeling that odd companionship with the young artist who preceded him. Surely something there? Something stirring in the heart of the grey stone seeking for his affection, wondering impatiently, perhaps, why contact was not achieved more easily? Was it only fancy bred of his love of the beauty of the brass and stone? or was it that he had a friend here who was struggling to tell him something that he should know? As the dusk fell closer about him and he turned away, as he always did, with a sigh for something baffled, bewildered, frustrated, was it only fancy that the ghost of a sigh came to him across the evening air? At least, leaving the great church, he was aware in his very heart of the personality of that young artist taken away so early and yet lingering so long. One beautiful conception, one fine thought, one gracious kindliness—how interminably long these things lasted, irritating all the cynical souls, exasperating those who would see life truly as it is, encouraging the sentimentalists in their false and cowardly dreams! Life as it is! How difficult! If it would only stand still for one moment to allow one to survey it properly. "Now, life! Stand still, can't you? How can I photograph you if you are always moving?" Life as it isn't! Some hope there. Daily bread for the poets at least.

But Johanson was not troubled. He took all the fish that came into his net, threw back the small ones into the water again and consumed the others. Cruel? If the position had been reversed he would not have grudged the fish their meal.

Now, coming into the proper clear-minded air, he saw Wistons. He had spoken to him only once since that conversation of theirs, and that had been for a moment in Orange Street, courteous, friendly, but with no contact. The man had warned him that there could be no friendship with him, but it was not friendship that Johanson needed. He admired this man as he admired no one else in Polchester, coldly, perhaps impersonally, but with a certainty of his courage and his passion for truth. He must speak to him even though he were snubbed.

"Sir." He came up with him. Wistons stopped abruptly. "I beg pardon, but it were such a lovely evening." He paused, fingering his hat which he had taken off like an awkward boy.

Wistons turned and held out his hand. "I'm very glad to see you, Mr. Johanson. I didn't know you were in the Cathedral."

They walked slowly together across the Green.

"I hope you'll forgive me," Johanson said, "but I couldn't help speak to you. I think often of the talk we had. It helped me so much and I thought I should tell you that."

"It helped me too," Wistons answered gravely. "How are you getting along? I see you're giving a lecture. That's good. I'm glad."

"You think it's good?" Johanson said eagerly. "I feared you might feel it impertinent of me after being here so little a time—"

"No, no. How could I? The more people that you can interest in such things as bodily fitness and healthy exercise the better."

"But it don't stop at that," Johanson went on still more eagerly. "The body's so mixed with the rest. I'm beginning to think of so many things, Mr. Wistons, that maybe isn't my business at all, and yet if I stay with what *is* my business I'm not comfortable. I'd wish not to think of the other things, but they won't lie down."

Wistons turned to him almost angrily. "Why do you come to me?" he asked. "When I can't help myself, how can I help others?"

They had stopped and stood looking at one another.

"Because," Johanson answered, "more than any other in this town you care for the truth. Many questions are coming to me now, Mr. Wistons, that never come to me before. Every day there are more. They won't leave me alone. I wouldn't speak to you now, but what you said the other day when we talked gave me encouragement."

Wistons looked at him for a long time without speaking. Then he said abruptly, "Will you come out to my house one evening, after this lecture, and have supper with me?"

"Yes, sir, I will."

"That's good. I'll write to you."

"Thank you, sir. I'll be glad of it. Good night."

"Good night."

And now it was the night of the lecture. Already by seven o'clock there was a little crowd outside the Town Hall doors, for the most part small inquisitive boys who climbed about the steps, made faces at the statue of Sir Samuel Bowerman, M.P., to the right of the door, and whistled and shouted until Perry, the policeman, a splendid figure, advanced and rebuked them. Then, his back turned, they triumphantly resumed.

It was the right kind of evening for the lecture, fine and dry, but not too warm. We had not, in those pre-war years, had so many lectures in Polchester that we could regard this one indifferently. And this was an unusual lecture. We had had nothing like it since Signor Della Rosa, the Strong Man, in '92. So, by seven-thirty, there was a thick stream pouring through the doors into the vestibule. Here you bought your tickets. The unreserved tickets were the ones that sold. It was understood that the "Quality" had bought all the reserved seats weeks ago, and then when Tommy Probyn, a tall, haggard man, the owner of the "Curio" shop near the Cathedral, who was superintending the ticket selling, announced that this was not so, but that there were three whole rows of reserved seats still for sale at only a shilling more than the front unreserved, there was the trouble of sitting with the "Quality," perhaps cheek by jowl with Mrs. Combermere herself! No, happier in the balcony (front three rows, 1s. 6d., fourth and fifth rows, 1s., sixth and seventh, 6d.). The sixth and seventh rows were very quickly filled, and by the rowdy element. But the rowdies were to-night good-tempered; from the very first you could tell that their strange cries, fragments of song and violent whistling were all tuned to love and admiration. To-night at least they had come to praise Caesar not to bury him.

In the two front rows of the balcony and in the middle part of the hall were the decent people of the town. In the very front row of the balcony were Mr. Cassidy with his family (Mrs. Cassidy, three girls and one boy) and Mr. Mildmay with *his* family (Mrs. Mildmay, ancient mother of Mrs. Mildmay, two girls, one boy); and Cassidy and Mildmay, being founders, instigators, leaders of the tradesman's gymnastic circle, felt that had it not been for them Johanson would not exist. They, therefore, with great dignity and benevolence prepared to enjoy their evening.

Some trouble was caused by Mr. Shortt who arrived, having on his arm a very ancient female in rusty black and a bonnet with bugles, and enquired of Mr. Probyn for his two reserved tickets; when given them he complained loudly because his seats were not in the front row. He held up a tumultuous crowd of fellow-citizens while he put his case; it seemed that both he and the lady in bugles had been already celebrating the famous event. It appeared that the front row was reserved for members of the Cathedral body, and as soon as Mr. Shortt discovered this his voice was raised in very violent complaint indeed. Who were the Cathedral body? What had they done for Mr. Johanson or indeed for any one in this town that they should be given the front seats? Had not he, Mr. Shortt, been Johanson's first friend in this place? Had not Mr. Johanson sent especially for him to help him in his Italian art and reproduction of ancient masterpieces? And had he not helped him? Had not he drawn some of the most beautiful . . .

At this moment the voice of Mr. Perry, the policeman, could be heard from somewhere in the back of the crowd making enquiries as to who was obstructing. . . . Mr. Shortt's voice fell into murmur; his arm was violently pulled by the old lady; he accepted the seats offered to him.

The next excitement for everybody was the arrival of Mortimer Shandon the Mayor. It was known that Mr. Shandon always considered very seriously before he allowed the sunshine of his presence to break out over any gathering. He took his duties as Mayor with extreme seriousness. He was a large, heavy, solemn man and was as clay, I am sorry to mention, in the hands of one or two of his Town Councillors; Aaron Sharpe, Jim Curtis and Ben Eagle may be named in this connection. He sailed up the middle aisle, the black wings of his fine frock coat floating behind him and his pale white-haired wife trying as ever to catch up with him.

In his party to-night were Aaron Sharpe (thin, intellectual, high-domed forehead) and Reuben Fletch. He nodded graciously to favoured ones as he passed on his way. But scarcely had the sensation of his arrival ruffled the waters of expectation than a greater breeze arose. Who could this be but the Dowager-Countess herself, and with her young Lord St. Leath and still younger Lady St. Leath.

Like a splendid white cockatoo the Dowager pecked her way to the front. Here was excitement indeed! How long was it since she had last attended any town ceremony? *And* with her daughter-in-law too! Was it true that they were for ever quarrelling? No matter. She was a sweet little thing, young Lady St. Leath. How pretty she looked in her dress of pale blue silk, and how proud Johnny St. Leath seemed to be of her! It wasn't her fault that her brother, etc. etc. etc. She was a good sort, she was. No false pride about her! Our Town can praise nobly when it pleases.

And then, as though they had all been waiting for the Countess, in came the Quality. There was Mrs. Bentinck-Major and there Julia Preston, there old Mrs. Combermere with her walking-stick and there Ellen Stiles, sitting by all perverse fortune next to Mrs. Bond and her three boys! And there the Canons Foster and Martin, Bentinck-Major and Rogers, Ryle and Ellis. So eager was the public interest in these public figures that scarcely any attention was paid to Mrs. Penethen and her two daughters Maude and Judy as they quietly found their way into their seats in the middle of the room. And Maude was looking very pretty too. She deserved *some* attention.

Notice was, however, taken of the entrance of Tom Longstaffe and his daughter. Some cheek bringing his daughter out in public with him like that! Wonder she didn't bring her child with her! Great big woman! Ought to have known better. Didn't look as though she minded either. All of which added to the general sense of pleasurable excitement very greatly. Another figure, quite unnoticed, was Samuel Hogg who stood, near the door, smiling in his genial way upon everybody.

It struck eight o'clock, and, a moment later, Canon Ronder appeared on the platform. How did he always work his miracle? How did he contrive, so easily and with such ready grace, to throw his spell over them all? In a moment of time he had the hall in his hands. A smile, a little joke, an intimate allusion to something known only among the townspeople, his voice cultured but not superior, and the whole appearance of him so smart, so bright, so kindly! No one in our town could approach him at *this* game! No, and perhaps not in the whole world, thought his old aunt sitting in the second row and watching him with eyes loving but also cynical.

In five minutes he made the whole room feel that it was all his doing that Johanson was there at all, and that it was the very best thing for Polchester that Johanson *was* there. It was as though he, Ronder, had gone out into the highways and hedges of the world and had found, after infinite trouble, the very thing that Polchester was needing. No one else in Polchester had known—only Ronder. And he loved Polchester so dearly that no trouble was too great for him did the town benefit from his labours. And here, as many of them knew already, but as all of them would know after to-night, was the best thing that Polchester had ever had.

He stepped aside, looked towards the door and then, as Johanson came in, waved his hand. His face was one happy beaming smile.

The Hall broke into a roar of applause. It clapped again and again. It cheered. The rowdies in the gallery stamped their approval. A hush fell. Johanson stepped to the front of the platform.

He was dressed in a singlet, white cotton trousers and white shoes. His face, neck, shoulders, arms, were a dark red-brown. He stood simply and quietly and, with a shy smile, explained that, as many of them knew, he was not a very great speaker of English. So he would speak slowly and he hoped clearly, but if any one in the back of the hall could not hear, would he please call out and say so.

And then some one cried from the gallery, "Aye, Harmer John, we will"—at which every one laughed.

He explained then, slowly at first and afterwards with greater confidence, what it was that he had come there that evening to do. Some of the things that he said have become now such commonplaces to every one throughout the world that it would be very uninteresting to recapitulate them here. But at that time in our town it was all new to us and had even a spice of adventure, daring and almost impropriety in it. Johanson had on his right hand a blackboard and over this he threw some charts. First, a chart of the interior of the human body and a chart so decent and proper that it was quite impossible to tell whether it were male or female. Nevertheless this public exposure of the human mechanism was something of a shock to one or two of our ladies. Then he showed us muscles and nerves and arteries, all very clearly and in a language that a child could understand—did, in fact, understand, because Mrs. Bond's youngest boy was heard to declare that "there was nothing new in all that stuff. He knew it all by heart."

Then, putting aside his charts, Johanson explained that five minutes a day, in the morning, before the open window would work marvellous results. He showed what harm obesity could do to the heart and enumerated the muscles that with most of us are never exercised at all. Old stuff this! Yes, but not for us. We seemed to be that night in the very vanguard of human progress. What if, for an instant, a blinding vision of a new world flashed before us? Before all of us—Ellen Stiles and old Shandon, Jim Curtis and Mrs. Mildmay, poor, dear Ryle and ancient Alice Ronder—a new world of giants and heroes, goddesses and angels? The vision would pass and soon enough. We were not so mad as to hold it and thus threaten our daily security. But, fleeing, it left something in its train.

Having explained some very simple exercises with diagrams, he paused.

"And now," he said, looking up at the ropes and rings that had been slung from the ceiling, "myself and one or two friends shall try and show you by exposition what I mean."

He bowed. Frantic applause. He retired to the back of the stage. He bowed again. A little pause, and his companions entered—Walter Pearce, Harry Pearce, Franklin and the Trenant boy. At the sight of these well-known faces the Hall broke into renewed applause. These were our own, our very own. Every one knew Walter and Harry, had known them from birth, and their father, grandfathers and great-grandfathers before them. Walter (working now in the Post Office) was a short, thick-set youth with a round, brown face, and of great strength. Harry was tall and slim, paler, more graceful than his brother. Robin Franklin was a young giant in the coal business; of young Trenant, having been earlier introduced in this chronicle, it is only necessary to say that this was the proudest moment of his life.

They were all dressed like their master. First they went through a drill of the exercises of which Johanson had been speaking. I was not present on this now famous evening, but I have been told by more than one surviving member of that audience that at once every eye was fastened on Johanson. How is one to peer, at this distance of time, through the mists of legend and fable that surround his figure? Had he some miraculous gift of grace and beauty of movement, something quite beyond his natural strength and fitness? Would he, if one could see him now, rouse in one that same sense of excitement and battle and mystery? Himself, his character, his thoughts, the conflict that he raised in our town, the picture seems to rise clearly enough before me. No one simpler, more straightforward, more honest; those qualities come clearly enough from every statement of every observer. But this physical effect . . . of that there are a thousand different reports. One saw this, another that, and always perhaps they saw some aspect of themselves, hostile or friendly. He antagonised, he attracted because of the response that he roused. No one, through all this strange time, no one from Looney to Wistons was indifferent to him; love, hatred, confidence, scorn, the reaction always came. To-night, of course, there was no hatred and when, at the last, the young men swung through the rings and formed a pyramid on his support, the rhythm and the grace were so perfect that every one in the hall jumped up and applauded. His friends vanished and he stood once more alone on the platform. He stood there for a moment hesitating.

He did not look glad nor triumphant, but puzzled and distressed. He wanted to say something. The words came to his mouth and he forced them back. The pause was long enough to be awkward and make every one uncomfortable. Mrs. Bond said afterwards that "really she did not know where to look."

Then quite abruptly he broke out, "Thank everybody for their kindness," and with a sharp little bow turned and vanished. Thunderous applause followed. There were repeated shouts from the gallery: "Harmer John! Harmer John! Harmer John!"

He did not appear. The floor broke up into excited little groups and, in the first enthusiasm for a remarkable experience, social difficulties were forgotten. Something true and something beautiful had been created there before their opening eyes, as though it were a bud bursting into flower or a fountain unexpectedly revealed, and they were triumphant and also a little sad as though unforeseen truth had jostled settled conviction. Mrs. Bond talked to Mrs. Tape of "The Cathedral Arms" with charming friendliness. Young Lady St. Leath, her eyes lit with pleasure and happiness, talked with the Precentor and little Bentinck-Major. "But it was beautiful! beautiful!" she could be heard crying. Every one lingered as though they expected something more to occur. The room slowly cleared. Two old women appeared with brushes. Perry could be seen, monumental, waiting for emptiness and silence. Where was Johanson?

Would he not come round and join them there? They wanted to congratulate him. Vaguely Mrs. Penethen, who knew him now, felt that something was wrong. At the end his eyes had been fighting something or somebody. She with her two daughters waited in the vestibule of the hall. He had promised to escort them home. But when they were in the house again he was not there.

He came in very late, and only Mrs. Penethen was up, reading. She was going to speak to him, but when she saw his face she only said "Good night," and when she heard his door close blew out the lamp and went up herself to bed.

CHAPTER III

FROM GABRIELLE MIDGELEY'S DIARY—II

So many things interfere. For instance, I was getting on with my work nicely last night, properly set, house all quiet about me, my drop of whisky beside me and my head as busy as Mrs. Jellaby's, when what must I do but leave the whole thing and work for two hours or more at this diary? This entirely useless diary, because no one will ever set eyes on it save myself, and although it clears my brain, I suppose, of some tiresome stuff, more tiresome stuff rushes in so quickly to fill up the empty spaces that I am not, I fancy, very much benefited.

The truth is, I'm an old, brooding woman, and real life will keep breaking in upon my attempted inventions. Not that I think this book of mine to be bad: I would never have so nearly finished it if I thought that. It's a nice, nasty, cynical, bitter production, and I'm properly proud of it. It will make so many people uncomfortable.

But unfortunately the more cynical I am on paper, the more sentimental does my daily life appear to be. That's perhaps true of all cynical writers, and conversely I never knew a crueller, more selfish or harder-hearted man than Stewart Frost, the author of all those mystical sentimental Innisfree kind of books that fluttered the '90 dovecotes.

I can look at myself quite honestly, of course, and say that I am sentimental in one direction only, but then that direction has, like the lean kine in the Testament, swallowed up all the others. This Johanson? What am I to do with him? Am I in love with him? No, that I can honestly say, I am not. Not that a woman of my age might not be in love with a man of his if she wished. It has happened often enough. But I know, by this time, what love feels like, and I am not in love.

Nor have I the maternal feelings for him that Ma Penethen is experiencing. I have no maternal feelings for anybody, not one soul in this world. I never wanted a child from any man and I'm happy to say I've never had one. No, I don't yearn over Johanson as a mother at all. I've wanted to smack him often enough, but that's been out of sheer irritation and exasperation.

I think friendship's the thing that I feel, a well-wishing-God-be-with-you kind of friendship. Very much what one man feels for another, I suppose. I like his brain although it's only half awake and only a quarter educated. I like his heart still better. That he has, and let us be quite unsentimentally clear about it, the best, truest, soundest, honestest, warmest heart of any human creature I have yet encountered. And then I suppose there is just enough sex in the thing for me to appreciate his strength and good looks. But honestly they count very little. I don't want him to kiss me and put his arm around me, and often I feel him much too big for my little room. No, it's friendship, and when you see a friend heading straight for disaster, you want to do something about it, don't you? And yet is it disaster he's heading for? Is it not the most brilliant success?

The principal fact just now is that he came back from his undoubted triumph at the Town Hall a most unhappy man. I didn't go to the lecture. I hate lectures anyway, and I suffer such agonies when my friends make fools of themselves in public (as they most of them in the old days used to) that I long ago resolved to spare my feelings. My precious feelings would not, I think, have been damaged on this occasion.

He had a most unquestioned success. The Town has been talking of nothing else since, and every one is longing for the next one. But the man himself is unhappy and dissatisfied as I have never seen him before. He came up to my room yesterday evening after supper and stood there fingering the things on my table in a restless way that he has, which always drives me crazy.

So I told him to stop it and asked him straight out what was the matter. Oh, he couldn't say. He roved restlessly about the room. He was dissatisfied. Ashamed with himself. Ashamed with himself? Good Heavens, why? Something he'd done—or rather something he'd not done. He'd been a coward. A coward? (That really surprised me.) How?

Oh, he'd liked the applause the other night and so he'd left out the principal thing he'd meant to say lest he should make them angry. That was cowardice of the worst sort.

Oh, I see! (I was very bitter here.) He'd wanted to preach to them, to make them better. Well, if he wished for my opinion. . . . No, he broke in upon me, I knew that it wasn't that. He didn't want to preach to anybody. But what had he done? Nothing but glorify himself. He had wanted to show them his idea of what life might be, and instead he had pushed his body about like an actress. All the applause had been for himself because he was strong and knew his work. That wasn't what he wanted. That was the wrong direction. He didn't want them to think of himself at all, but of making their town beautiful and not to be cruel to unfortunate people. . . . Preaching, preaching, preaching! I broke in. I hate preaching. Leave people alone. Don't try to make them better.

But he *wanted* to leave them alone. Couldn't I see that? But he must put in front of them his idea—his idea, so easy, so happy, if only a few would see it. But all he was doing now was to glorify *himself*. . . . And there was Maude, angry because he wouldn't give another demonstration next week, angry because he wasn't proud of himself. Ah! Garibaldi, who went back to the fields when the king came with his army, Levin, who was so humble and so happy with humble men, what would they have said if they had seen him the other evening, strutting about, pushing out his chest, performing like a dancing bear. . . .

But next time he'd show them. Next lecture they should realise what a filthy place Seatown was. . . .

He was more childish than I had ever seen him, child though he always was. He wasn't far from tears, I believe. His anger with himself was the motive of it all. He hadn't realised what a cheap thing a public performance like that would be.

And he hadn't his earlier confidence in his dear beloved Polchester any longer. He'd lost it. Of course, no one but the naïvest of the naïve would ever have had it. It wasn't Polchester's fault that he fancied it perfect. God defend us anyway from our idealistic friends! But he isn't blaming Polchester—he only wants to make it see what a heaven-sent place it might be. And how to make it see that without preaching to it?

The foolish part of it is that I believe he's infected me with his idea. Me! who am on the point of finishing a novel that for bitterness and irony will give points to the bitter Maisie South herself!

But when he talks to you, laugh at him though you may, there is something in it. Three people, four people, five people . . . find them and start your little crusade. Get them to find five more people and those five five more again. How many people must really see that the brewery beyond the Town Hall is hideous, that Seatown is a disgrace, that cruelty at tea-parties is a crime as bad as child-beating, that the detracting view of any one at most is only half the view, that beauty grows and grows with what it feeds on. One blue plate means one Persian rug, one Persian rug means one good water-colour, one good water-colour means a new wall-paper, one new wall-paper means a new view from the window. . . . And why are we all standing still doing nothing, letting a tiny minority do all the work?

And it is so fine after this string of platitudes to snuggle down into my chair, pile up the fire and not care a twopenny damn if every soul in this world suffers the torments of hell.

And what do I really care? Do I want to save the world or improve it? Not, in my heart, one little bit. But I do care for the man and I want him to be happy.

But his way would be easy and inevitable enough if it weren't for his love of Maude. He'd just go the path of all fanatical Quixotes. Preach a bit in the market-place, be kicked out of the town (they can be a bit rough at times, my dear fellow-townsmen), stumble on somewhere else, preach again, kicked out again, and so go on to a dreary old age, dragging a few other fanatics with him.

But he's not all fanatic; that's the trouble. And he knows it. He's admirably practical at his own job, and if he'll only settle down here now, go on with his work, fall in with the Ronders and the rest, shut his eyes to Paradise, he'll make a very nice little income for his dear little Maude and the results of their devotion. He will have his work, and she the civic honours and respect that she longs for. I'll do him the justice, however, to say that if he didn't love her as he does there'd be no struggle at all. He does love her with all the passion, sincerity and worship that a physically vigorous man who has never been in love before can feel. He adores her. He's not quite so blind to her though as he was. There are things in her that worry him. She's not so perfect as he first thought her, but he loves her all the more for that. She needs protecting, advising, encouraging. He wants to be her mother, her father, her brother, her sister, her friend, her lover, her child and her comrade all in one. Lord! why didn't any one ever love me like that? I'm worth a thousand Maudes and always was. Just because I haven't yellow hair. The fools men are!

Which brings me to Maude. She rushed in this morning. None of that hanging about looking at me out of the corner of her eye that she used to have! She doesn't know me any better than she did nor love me any better either, she's still afraid of me, but this affair has really shaken her right out of her selfish little body. She does love him in her own shallow way and will even continue to love him after all the intimacies of matrimony if he'll only follow success, make money, get a position, keep his fine friends.

But what's he after now? She simply can't understand it. She rushed at me as though I were her only hope. "You, Miss Midgeley! You understand him! You have more influence with him than any one else! Talk to him! Find out what's the matter with him! Is he crazy? Here he's just been and had the most wonderful success. Every one's talking about him. Every one's praising him. And he thinks it's a failure. What's the matter with him? Isn't this what he wanted? Oh, Miss Midgeley, talk to him, talk to him!"

Dislike her as I do, I couldn't but be sorry for the poor child. She was so helplessly bewildered. She was so proud of him. I suppose she had never enjoyed a night in all her little life as she did the other evening when she sat there and heard every one from the Cockatoo Countess downwards praising her man. *Her* man! HER man! It must have seemed like the reward of all her life to her. And now it's all gone wrong. It's like finding your milk's all sour or that you've had your purse stolen. And, I repeat, she does love him in her own way. She does want to understand him. "Tell me, Miss Midgeley, why he's like this? What's disappointed him when it was all so splendid?"

And what, pray, is the use of my telling her anything? How is she ever going to understand that he isn't thinking of himself in this at all, or wouldn't be if he weren't in love with her, and that he hadn't realised, until this public performance showed him, that no one here cares about the thing he truly has at heart. He's bothered by a dream, but what are dreams to Maude unless they are dreams of his arms around her and his lips upon hers? But I did try to tell her something, and the result was even worse than I had expected.

I tried to show him to her a little as I saw him and, in trying, I said something about his being a "stranger"—not only a foreigner, but also some one, in his capacity for dreaming and worrying about impossible unrealisable hopes, who would never be entirely at home in a world which to commonplace people like Maude and myself was always straightforward enough.

I could have said nothing more unfortunate. If terror is too big a word, fright will do—and that was what came into Maude's eyes. She knew that—she knew it a great deal better than I could. It was his queerness—that was what she couldn't stand. He talked about his dreams as though they were real: some place that he went to in his sleep, a nasty place all empty and cold and full of trees and statues. It was as real to him as Polchester was; well, she called that "spooky" and she wasn't going to stand it. After their marriage she'd put a stop to it. It was indigestion as likely as not, but whatever it was she was not going to stand it. Dreams were all nonsense, as every one knew.

And it was just this dreaming that was standing in the way of his getting on, as every one could see, and that horrid Longstaffe woman, who should be ashamed to show her face instead of flaunting about as she was doing, was just the one to encourage him.

Now Maude was truly launched and revealed herself as the little mean, selfish, cruel, greedy, vulgar, jealous egoist half of her is. But only half of her. I'll do her that justice; and a justice I wouldn't have done her half a year ago, because she at an instant dropped Mary Longstaffe and her grievances and became something very genuine, touching, and human. She spoke of her love for him. She did love him, oh yes, she really did! "I know you don't like me, Miss Midgeley—you never have and I don't blame you in a way. Of course you think I'm not fit to clean his boots. Oh! I know I've been a bit spoilt and made to think a lot of myself. Loving him so has sort of made me see that—and then I get tearing jealous when I could do anything—I'm so mad. And then he's so irritating, not seeing which way his bread's buttered, and how's he going to keep me after we're married and children perhaps, if he hasn't got a good job and made friends with the principal people. And they won't be his friends, Miss Midgeley, if he goes preaching to them about what they ought to do and how they ought to pull the town down and all the rest of it. Such nonsense! As though he could know anything about it, being a stranger and only here a few months. What is he, after all, but a gymnastic instructor? He's got to keep his place, Miss Midgeley, hasn't he, like anybody else?

"But, oh dear, I do love him! I do terribly. I just want us both to be happy in a nice little house and every one liking him. Because he is lovely! he is indeed. No one knows how good he is!"

Thus Maude *loquitur*. Something touching about the creature. And, oh dear, how pretty she looked as she stood there! It isn't only her hair, although that's beautiful enough. It's the daintiness of her, the perfect colouring, her lovely skin, the absolute proportion of her little body, the animal grace of her movements, her helplessness as though, if you deserted her, nothing could save her from destruction. And yet any one less helpless than Maude I have never known!

I did my best with her. What I tried to show her was that she must stick to him whatever happened, even though he got whipped out of the town without a rag to his back. That he was worth that and ever so much more. But I could see that the very thought of disgrace and unpopularity terrified her. That, I am convinced, she'll never stand, and if that's the way he's going he'll lose her. Lose her! Why not? She'll cheapen everything he believes in. I've noticed in life that when two humans live together, one of fine material and the other of base, there's never any doubt of which way the issue goes. The baser metal always wins. There's something bed-rock in complacent selfishness which nothing can wear away. Yes, but on the other hand she's malleable. She does see in a sort of way that this is the chance of a lifetime, that she'll never get anything like it again, and that if she does let jealousy and meanness and selfishness break in, she'll be doing something she'll regret for ever. She sees that subjectively; it pokes its head up and reminds her every once and again. But of course her nature will be too strong for her and the only question that truly remains is as to whether *his* nature will be too strong for *him*. Will he give up his dreams and lie down in Maude's bed never to rise from it again? That's the point. There's the struggle and we'll see what we'll see. . . .

. . . Such a tempest of rain and wind to-night like that night when Johanson first came to us. He hasn't been in my mind the last two days (the book has absorbed me—all my old excitement returned for a wonder), but this morning when that strange girl Judy came to dust my room she brought him back to mind again. And that is a queer girl too—impossible to believe that she's Maude's sister, as dark as the other's fair, as dry as the other's talkative, industrious as the other's idle, as thoughtful as the other's thoughtless. Thoughtful! yes, but about what? I think she likes me in a kind of way. At any rate thinks I have brains. I make her talk when I can.

I began this morning: "Well, Judy, what did *you* think of the fine lecture the other evening?"

"What did I think?" She turned round fully upon me as though I had challenged. "Oh, it was all right."

"All right? Most people had much more praise for it than that," I answered, going on with my work.

"As to what they did," Judy continued, "I don't see there was much in that. Why, the acrobats at the Fair in the summer do more than they did."

"Yes, but the acrobats do things that no one else can do. The point of Mr. Johanson's lecture was that he was showing people things that they all could do if they liked, and be ever so much the better for it."

Judy smiled, one of her grim smiles. "I'd like to see mother and Mr. Hogg and Mrs. Cassidy doing those exercises he showed us."

There was silence for a little. Then Judy turned, looking up from her work, to me and said, "Don't you think, Miss Midgeley, it was a pity his showing himself off like that? Seemed to cheapen him somehow."

So she had felt that, felt what he did, felt it, maybe, because he did. I could be sure that she was the sole creature in the whole of Polchester who had realised it.

"I wasn't there," I answered quietly. "I don't go to lectures. But many excellent people have given lectures. It's quite a decent thing to do, I believe. Going to them—that's another matter."

"Yes, Miss Midgeley." She said nothing for a little, then began again: "But it's different showing off as he did. It's silly of me, I know, but I couldn't help wishing he wouldn't. So many strangers there, not knowing him as we do. He's too good for that."

"So you think he's a fine man, Judy?" I asked her.

"Yes, he is," she answered quite gravely. "Don't you think he is? He's kind and generous and quiet. I like quiet men."

"Quiet? No, I hadn't thought of him as that He's so cheerful. Sometimes too noisy for my taste."

"But quiet inside, Miss Midgeley. Not always changing every minute. You know where you are with him."

I saw in a flash that she loved him—loved him truly, deeply, steadily as none of the rest of us in this house do. I had perceived this, of course, long before. I have set it down, I fancy, in this very diary. But I had not before perceived its strength. His love for Maude—Judy's love for him—real love. Her mother has that same steady strength, but she is beyond physical love now, and the maternal is of another star, not a less lovely one, but another.

And if Judy had had yellow hair?

She came to the table close to me, her thin pale plain face all lit with the determination of her thought. "Miss Midgeley," she said, "you've travelled, you've lived in London, you've seen the world. How would he be outside this little town? We have so few strangers here. We can't compare him. But you've seen all sorts. Would he be just ordinary in London? I suppose there are lots of men who can do the things he does, many as kind, plenty cleverer. Would he not be noticed in London?"

"He'd be noticed by some people," I answered her. "Perhaps not by very many. There's not much time in London to notice things."

She nodded her head. "If I knew him in London," she said, "perhaps he'd need me more," and, a moment later, she left the room.

Sitting here half dreaming, staring into my little fire, I have a vision. Johanson and I are given leave to do what we will. Together with eager hands we pull this place down. House after house goes toppling. How we tear up the bricks, scattering them over our shoulders! How we work, the sweat pouring into our eyes, panting with our eagerness!

The place is empty, naked, void. A voice, shouting from the skies, roars: "Now! Create!"

CHAPTER IV

LIFE AND DEATH OF A CRISIS

FOUR days after the lecture Johanson received this note:

> PYBUS ST. ANTHONY.
>
> DEAR MR. JOHANSON—You will perhaps remember that you promised me that you would come and have some supper with me one evening? Would next Wednesday suit you? There is a convenient train that leaves Polchester at 6.30, reaching here at 7. The Rectory is easy to find, up the village street and to the left at the top of the hill.
>
> I am looking forward to seeing you.—Yours truly,
>
> AMBROSE WISTONS.

He was surprised at his own pleasure at receiving this letter. He had but just been through three of the most disturbed and uneasy days of his life. His discomfort had been so sharply acute that he had been utterly unlike himself, silent, morose, preoccupied. And preoccupied with what? He did not know. With something that stole like a dark cloud from the thin horizon towards him.

But Wistons would resolve his trouble. He knew at once as he saw that handwriting on that page that it would be so. The cloud retreated. He was himself again. Then he was aware of Maude.

They had taken their evening walk, and now were under their dark embosoming tree, upon whose thick texture the stars were like silver buttons.

He kissed her as though he had found her again after a long absence. She surrendered herself at first with that light sigh of abandonment, as though this were the one moment for which she lived, that he had come so especially to connect with her. Then she seemed to recollect. She drew away from him, sitting back against the broad wall of the tree, looking at him critically.

"You *have* been queer these last few days," she said.

"Have I?" he said. He was lying full length on the grass. As she looked her gaze altered, more intense, flooded with an intensity of longing and passion and desire, a strange intensity for Maude's light fickle eyes that were not meant to hold so much. She bent forward and kissed him, first his mouth and then his eyes. Afterwards, with a queer humility that he had never seen in her before, she took his hand and kissed it.

"I love you so much, and sometimes you're so queer and such a stranger. What are you thinking of when your eyes are so far away? You aren't seeing me at all. It's your silly old dreams. I *hate* your dreams. They are what make you so queer."

He laughed again. "Why should you hate my dreams when you are part of them?"

"I'm not part of them. I want to be part of them."

"You're part of everything that I am. You can't not be whatever I am."

"I'm not yet. You haven't got me yet. Perhaps I'll marry some one else."
She sprang up and stood, light-footed, fairy-shaped against the giant tree.
"I'm free. I'm not any one's yet."

He leaned forward and caught her, held her between his hands, then drew her down to him.

"You are mine. You are mine. You are mine. Don't pretend. You know it. My heart is in your body and yours in mine. Come more close, more close. Now are you mine? Have I caught you for always . . . for ever?"

No one ever came that way. The silence was absolute, save that once and again the leaves of the tree gave a little shiver of exquisite comfort.

It was time to go. They rose and moved slowly down the field. She was supremely happy. She felt her power. It seemed to her that she could do anything with him that she pleased. She scurried in her brain to find something. She knew that he did not care for dancing. He had never yet taken her to a dance, so she said:

"I want you to do something."

"What is it?"

"Promise me before I tell you."

"Certainly not. That never for anybody."

"Oh, you must. It isn't something you'll mind."

"Then tell me what it is."

"Promise me first."

"Maude, don't be so childish. Tell me what you want."

He knew that she was pouting, and he could feel her hand stiffen against his arm.

"Yes, you're so fine with your words. You say you'll do anything for me, but then when I ask you a little thing—"

"I shouldn't promise God Almighty anything without knowing it first. That takes my freedom."

She was reassured. He still loved her best, better than any one in the world. God couldn't get more from him than she could.

She pressed tightly the muscles of his arm again: "I want you to take me to a dance."

He laughed aloud. They were just entering the quiet and deserted street.

"Oh, is that all? Why, of course, I will."

"But you don't like dances." Her triumph seemed too easy.

"No, but I'd do more than that if it gave you pleasure. When is this dance?"

"It's next Wednesday. It's the Bible Class of St. John's."

"Why, of course—" He stopped. "Oh no, I can't. I'm terrible sorry. I have an engagement that night."

"You can change it."

"No, I can't. It's important."

"More important than me." She drew her arm away, tossed her head, walked faster, gaining a little on him.

He could change it, but he knew with an instant surprise that he did not intend to. He had a reverence for Wistons that made it seem an impertinence to bother him. He was obstinate too. He felt that swift resentment at the interference of women in men's affairs that every man born into this world has felt at one time or another—and often felt with the woman he loves the most.

Her whole body was shaking with anger, and he knew that their first real quarrel was upon them. He was desperately sorry; he wanted to take her in his arms, stroke her hair and tell her how sorry he was, but he would not change that engagement.

"You needn't hide who the engagement's with," she said. "I know well enough. You needn't lie to me about it." Because he never lied about anything, it gave her especial pleasure to say that. She could the more admire his marvellous honesty, set up like an altar in the middle of the jungle of hatred that she was feeling.

"You know that I never lie," he answered quietly. "It is with Mr. Wistons, the engagement. I am to go to supper there."

"I don't believe you," she retorted. "You are going to that woman." She had never ventured so far as this, she had never loved him so much, and she had never felt such a delicious excitement.

Jealousy was a human emotion that he had never known. He could never have jealousy of another human being, because he believed so intensely in liberty. If you loved another human being, how could you take their freedom from them? They gave you as much as they could, and you took that and treasured it. But the rest—if you took it by threat and extortion and tyranny, how shameful you must be.

But although he did not understand jealousy he did, because he loved her so much, understand Maude. He caught up with her.

"Darling, don't be angry. I shall take you to one dance after another, but Mr. Wistons is the man I have most reverence for in the world. He's not my friend like Longstaffe, and if he were my friend I would ask him to change the engagement, but we are not on such terms. He is very good to give me an evening. I promised him to go when he asked me. Now I have written and said I should go that evening. I don't hope you shall be angry and make us both so unhappy."

She turned on him a face under the lamp, cold, hard, gleaming like a cut and sharpened stone.

"Yes, you have plenty of words. You can talk a lot, but when it comes to doing something! You're selfish, that's what you are. You never think of any one but yourself. And you're so stupid. You're so simple. You don't care what people say about you or what they think. You're engaged to me, but you go to that woman's house every day, although she's had a baby when she wasn't married, and you don't think of *me* and what people will say—"

"Of what people will say?" he answered. "What does it matter what people say if you haven't done wrong yourself? And they will say anyway. Were you a saint from heaven, come down to earth, they should talk all the same."

"Yes, you mayn't care, but what about me? Am I not to mind?"

They were close to their door. He stopped her, put his arms about her.

"Maude, darling, we must each of us have some freedom, and we must trust one another. The Longstaffes are my friends; I can't be unkind to them or disloyal. You have friends I don't like, Hogg, for an example. But you must have your freedom too. Only while we trust one another we can have our freedom. If the trust goes, then the freedom goes with it, but if the trust goes, then we are no more together. If we don't trust we don't love."

She turned from his embrace.

"Will you give that woman up? Will you promise never to see her again?" Her voice shook, quivering with the intensity of her feeling.

"But, Maude dear, I can't. Her father's my true friend. I love him and would never give him up for anybody."

"I'm not speaking of him. I'm speaking of her."

"But he loves her. I couldn't give her up without leaving him too."

"Then you won't?"

"Give up my friend? No. Never."

"Then it's over. Do you see?" With a trembling hand she opened the door. "I don't love you. I hate you. It's all over, I tell you."

The door was banged. He stood there, his heart aching for love of her; he had never before felt so tenderly about her. But his purpose did not change and he knew that it would not.

Next day they were reconciled. It had been their first quarrel and it was over, but everything was not quite as it had been. Her power over him had been questioned; she would not rest now until she had completely asserted it. To assert your power completely over another human being is to condemn two souls to permanent imprisonment.

He felt the change in their relation, and it was with a heavy heart that he set off for Pybus St. Anthony. He was experiencing that loneliness belonging to lovers who are too confident. We are so close together that not God Himself can separate us—one body, soul and spirit. Then, in a moment of time, a word, a phrase pokes up its ugly face and there is no relationship at all—strangers in a strange place.

As he walked down the long Polchester platform to find the little local train, lonely by itself like a poor relation, his love for Maude constricted his heart, hurting him physically. She seemed to accompany him down the platform, treading lightly at his side, and saying to him again and again: "Am I not worth everything? Is there anything of more value than me? Surrender yourself. Will you give me up for a shadow?"

As he climbed into the stuffy, tight little compartment he knew that the crisis of all his life had climbed in with him. He had, in fact, never known any crisis before. Life had been direct. First there had been his mother to protect, and he had protected her; then there had been his father to fight, and he had fought him; then there had been his living to earn, and he had earned it; then there had been his work to love, and he had loved it. It was when the other loves had come to him that the struggle had begun, love of beauty, love for his friend and love for a woman.

As he sat there and saw the little fields, brilliantly lit by the evening sun, the hedges like wet lines of paint, the cottages so characteristic of Glebeshire in their isolated defiant pastures, his heart ached as though he were saying farewell to it all. And yet he could formulate nothing. His problem was a wood in front of him, into whose heart he had not yet penetrated. He knew that Wistons would help him.

He was the only traveller to alight at Pybus St. Anthony. The little village was dead and bright like a picked bone as he walked up the sunny hill. Maude was still with him, walking beside him and saying, "Am I not of more value . . . ?"

He turned to the left at the top of the hill, walked down a little by-road; he opened a white gate sorely in need of paint, pushed up a weed-stained drive and saw the Rectory, bare, four-square, unadorned, impersonal. When the old Glebeshire servant answered his ring and he stood in the hall he felt as though nothing had been done to this house for ever and ever. And it did not care that anything should be done. If help were offered it would refuse it. The pictures would fall from the walls, the fresh wall-paper wither, the stair-rods trip the unwary. Everywhere was the proud spirit of resistance. The old servant ushered Johanson into Wistons' study. It was exactly as he had anticipated it—absolutely spare, distempered white, a table, a crucifix, a photograph of Leonardo's "Last Supper," a wall of grimy and dishevelled books.

Wistons looked pleased to see his visitor. For the first time in their acquaintance there was something warm in his greeting. They talked a little, trivially, and very soon went into the other room for supper.

Wistons did not apologise for the food which was bad—poorly cooked turbot, cold beef and hard potatoes that clung sullenly to their jackets, apple tart with pastry of lead. Wistons did not apologise, and Johanson did not consider it. He ate heartily and happily. His mind had cleared. His depression had retreated like a defeated enemy. They achieved during the meal that relationship that was to last to the end. It was not so personal as friendship; it was rather the frank intimacy of two human beings who recognise in one another those two great qualities, reality and honesty. Whatever the future might bring they would always meet with interest and, cataloguing in their minds the true human beings they had known, they would remember one another.

After supper they went out into the little garden. The moon was a sickle of apricot, the scent of the flowers lay thickly on the evening air, peace flowed like a river down the hill. They sat on two old shabby garden chairs and Johanson faced his problem.

"I must settle it now," he said, leaning forward, and staring at the sky that flowed above the sharp wall of the garden like a stream of pale lemon-coloured water. Tiny clouds of gold moved on a faint wind. Wistons, a true observer of men, studied his face as he talked. Although it had in the curve of the mouth and the determination of the chin a man's character, its roundness, the simplicity of the blue directness of the eyes, the buoyancy of the brow, had still the happy unclouded kindliness of the boy who has not yet learnt to distrust.

The brows drew together in perplexity as a boy's might. Wistons knew that the man was face to face with the first real trouble of his life. "I must settle it now, but what is it I must settle? Sometimes I fancy that I am inventing all my trouble, making it up like a story. Perhaps you shall tell me that, sir, when I have finished, but I don't think you shall. When I first came it was all simple. I was lucky and got my work quickly and made friends. No man ever was helped so fast in a foreign town. Shouldn't I then be satisfied? Here I had my work that I could do, and I was not lonely, and then I fell in love and was loved too. Should I not have been happy, sir? But I was. I have always been happy. But from the first there were something more. There was two things. First, I don't hope you shall think me foolish. There has always been a place I dream of in my sleep. I saw it first as a little boy when my father had beaten me and I slept because I was tired. It were always the same place, a house, empty but for a few things, very clean and shining with sun. Long stairs with the sun gleaming on them, open doors and mirrors with green trees reflected, running water. I myself placed some things there, a statue of Donatello, the Leonardo "Virgin of the Rocks." There was always birds singing, water running, trees and a line of hills. It is so real to me I could tell you of the marks on the walls, the hollow in the hill and the thin white road out of my window. I were very happy there. Secondly, there were the Cathedral. You know the Brytte Monument and the young man who made it? I seem to have known him and spoken to him. And when I were with him I had ideas that I couldn't control—my own work, the gymnastics and the rest, was unimportant and didn't matter. I wanted what he too had wanted, to make a beautiful place with beautiful people. Just one place, or one street even, or one house. But that were not my business. My business were clear—to do my work and mind my own affairs.

"Then when I fell in love everything was lost in that. I had never been in love before. I loved her the moment I saw her, but for some time I did not know that she loved me, and then when she said that she did, oh, sir, wasn't I happy? For a time I seemed to have everything. I sang all day, and every one else was singing too. My work grew and grew; every one was more kind and more kind. All was made clear and straight for me. Perhaps I were too happy. I had suspicions of being too comfortable. I don't know what it were, but I began to dream again and then to watch the people around me. I saw that some of them were for using me, not badly, you know, sir, but for their own purpose, not caring for me and my work for what was good in it, but only for what helped what *they* wanted me to do. Do I make it clear?"

"Perfectly," said Wistons.

"Then there came two things. I have a friend. His daughter came home. She had once been unhappy and unfortunate here. You know, of course, sir, who I mean. People were cruel to her. I had not thought they would be so narrow or so self-righteous. Perhaps I am not to blame them, but they are hurting her because they like to hurt, not because they are shocked by what she did. It makes them feel better to make her feel worse.

"And then there were Seatown. I went down one afternoon. Oh, sir, it is terrible, the dirt, the walls tumbling, the windows broken, the smell, the rags. In such a town as this, so beautiful, so old, so happy, to have such!

"It's only a little place, one street, fifty houses. One day would pull it down. I was made unhappy by that. You told me once I couldn't build before I pulled down. Perhaps that is true. But what right had I to say anything? It were not my business. I am a stranger. And deep in my heart I don't wish to change people. I am not confident enough of my own goodness to teach others. But if we were all at it together, not because we were better than others, but because we all saw the same thing to do and set about to do it!

"Then the lecture came. It were a success, you know. I was happy for most of it, seeing my friends there pleased in front of me, but at the last, when I came to make a speech, I were in a moment ashamed. What was I doing standing there glorifying myself? This wasn't the work I intended. I wanted to make a speech speaking of Seatown, and all working together for one beautiful place that the world might see and so make more beautiful places. But I was frightened. I knew I should make some angry, should lose some friends and most of all disappoint my girl. I was afraid. It was the most shameful moment of my life and I went from the lecture and hid myself.

"After that everything was clear. Certain in the town made me see that it were not my business to say anything were wrong with the town or the people in the town. One important gentleman told it me quite plainly, and that I must give up the daughter of my friend if I would go on to be a success here. Then my girl—she is Miss Maude Penethen, sir, and I lodge with her mother—she is young, and she wants me to be the greatest success the town has ever seen. That she must have—success for me, you understand, not for herself. She wants everybody to like me, you see.

"With every hour from the lecture I see more clearly I must make a choice. I must be quiet about Seatown, I must not see my friend's daughter, I must do what certain gentlemen and ladies of the town tell me, and then I shall be a true success here. I shall marry and have money and build a big business, later perhaps in Drymouth and then in London. I know I can because I have that practical gift. But if I try to change anything, be myself, and keep my integrity and freedom, I am ruined here, and so it will be everywhere. Always the same in every place. And perhaps I shall do nothing in the end. Just be a failure, you see.

But if I work here at my gymnastics I *must* do good. And Miss Penethen she won't love me if I'm not as she thinks moral, if I am friends with people who she thinks are wicked. She must be happy and see me happy too. I understand her so well. She is young and beautiful, and she is proud of me. If she's no longer proud she don't love me. So I must do what every one tells me or I lose my work, my girl and my friends. And for what do I lose them? For a dream, an idea. And why should I meddle with other people? But how can I live and not be honest? How can I live and not be honest?"

He ended with that despairing cry.

He had poured out his words tempestuously, but Wistons had understood him.

"This question of honesty," Wistons said at last, "aren't you making too much of it? It is not, I think, of such overwhelming importance these days. Your trouble comes down to very little if you look it in the face. To get on, to make a good job out of the material world, to put money by, to live on twenty-four hours a day according to a sharp materialistic pattern, to study success as an art—all of that is the point in these days when God has been proved a liar and all religions a sham. Where's your trouble? Stay here quietly, do what you're told for a year or two, give up ridiculous dreaming, get power and position and then, when you're really strong in the place, pull down Seatown if you like."

"You!" said Johanson. "You to advise that!"

"Well, why not? What do we think of honesty when, to take only a small example, at this very moment one of the principal dignitaries of my church is neglecting his ecclesiastical duties (for which by the way he is quite decently paid) in order to earn easy money by writing sensational articles in the daily press? The thing is as old as the world. You wish to give up your home, your job, your love, because one or two old houses are falling into ruin, and a lady of your acquaintance has not been sufficiently called on. Folly!"

Johanson answered.

"Why are you so bitter about life? Has every one always disappointed you? Have no one been true or honest?"

"I am not bitter," Wistons answered. "I was putting a point of view to you that many very good people hold, and with much justice, I daresay. When I was a young man I had a friend who came up from the provinces to London. He was a painter. For some while he made very little progress. He was a hard-headed, clever fellow with no nonsense about him, but he had, rather to his own surprise, a very warm heart. He thought that this got in the way of his success, so he did what he could to cool it. Great fame came to him in a night. That was the critical moment of his life. He might have been contented with that—it was enough to content any man. He might have sat down, thought less of himself and his career, learnt to love his wife, who was charming. But he chose the other. He wanted more success and more money and more and more and more. He got rid of his wife, who was, I daresay, tiresome from the successful point of view. He got fatter and fatter and ever more deeply concentrated upon himself. He is, I admit, a very happy man."

"You think he's done wisely?" Johanson asked.

"Yes. He's concentrated upon certainties. He has possessions that he can finger, a stomach that needs an ever-widening waistcoat, motor cars and a fine sum at the Bank. He is laughed at and sneered at, but he comforts himself with the thought that those who laugh at him are the jealous, unsuccessful ones. He has touched on certainties. And what are the other things? The spiritual life? What man or woman alive to-day but has doubts of its existence? God, Christ, the Saints? Does not book after book seek to prove them fairy-tales? This death—has it not a tangible stink of corruption about it that is never out of our nostrils? Art, friendship, love, are they not for ever fading and failing? What are we but a little gas and water, formed for an instant, blown back into æther a moment later? Why think of others who think only of themselves? Why pray vainly to a God who is not there? Why study the life and words of a Christ whose every movement is riddled with modern suspicion? Why cheat ourselves with all this illusion? No, let us clutch our certainties. You are a fool, Johanson; you are giving up something for nothing—for nothing at all save certain defeat. What can you do in this place with your reforms? You are a foreigner. I told you before and I tell you again that they will not let you take one single step against their will. And why should they? This is their town, they have built it on certain moralities, certain social laws. Those moralities and those laws make them safe. They have to protect their wives, their children, their earthly property, their heavenly souls. You come from outside and attack them. Why should they not defend themselves?"

"I will not attack them," Johanson answered fiercely. "I told you I would not wish that. I have no right, as you say, and no desire. But I must be honest. I must not be something that I am not. I would say to them, 'I think in this way and in this, but that are only myself.' I must not lie about myself."

"Yes," answered Wistons, "but you are against them, and the things you want may seem to a few others desirable, and so a little group will grow, and that group will not be contented, as you are, with simply stating their ideas. They will want to put them into practice. Then hostilities begin whether you wish it or no."

"It is more simple than you suppose," Johanson said in a little while. "I have no doubt that it is right to do. I must not agree to what I know to be wrong, I am not to interfere with others, but my own integrity is to be protected at every cost. At almost every cost. Here is the struggle, you see. I love that girl, Mr. Wistons, with heart and soul and body. If I for a moment look over the wall and see myself without her it is terrible, standing alone in the world. Once that were possible. I did not mind to be alone, but now that I have been close to her, to be alone will be a terror. I love her body, but much more I want her for my companion, some one who knows my troubles and I knows hers, some one I can always talk with, some one who is true whatever else may happen, some one who knows me and loves me although they knows me. Some one half me and I half them. She is not very wise, perhaps, she is young. She can't think of two things at once, and she must have some things or she is angry; and she values some things falsely. We shall quarrel—perhaps often—but my heart shall be hers and hers mine. I love her so that if I can't have her I can never be intimate with any one again."

They sat in silence. After a long time Johanson said, almost timidly, "What am I to do, Mr. Wistons? What am I to do? I can't lose her."

"And must you lose her," Wistons asked gently, "if things go badly with you in the town? Doesn't she care for you more than that?"

"She is very young," Johanson answered, "and she is jealous. She loves me, I am sure, but she has been spoilt. She wants her way. I know that if we were married a year or more I could control her, but now, if I don't promise not to see my friend's daughter, I'm afraid her jealousy shall, at some moment, separate us."

"Then go on for a year with your work," said Wistons, "be married, keep quiet for a while about Seatown. That will come right if you wait. There are others besides yourself who are moving in that."

"And give up my friend?" Johanson asked.

"Oh, you can be diplomatic about that. Go there a little less, not see the daughter privately. . . ."

"But they are my friends," Johanson broke in. "Do you think at once they would not see that I was as the rest of the town? 'Yes,' I say to them, 'I love my girl, and she doesn't like that I come here. So we meet in secret, you understand?' Oh yes, *they* understand! Only a little flush in the face, a little dropping of the eyes, but Tom Longstaffe's heart is hurt for ever and I have been false to my word. No, no—No, no, no!"

"Then," said Wistons quietly, "you must persuade the lady you love, explain to her. If she loves you—"

"If she did not love me," Johanson broke in, "I could, perhaps. But she are jealous because she love me. Jealousy is so strong that the one who has it cannot reason. They can only cry out like they have been wounded. It is not themselves, but a disease in their stomach like a cancer. And when it is cured they wonder they have had it. . . ." He sat there, his hands clasped tightly together. In a voice full of pain he said at last: "Oh, Mr. Wistons, show me how to keep her, and yet be honest, show me how."

"There is no way to show you. This is something you must fight out with your own soul as I have had to fight it out and many another man. Your real life is at stake now."

"You believe, then, in a real life?" Johanson said urgently. "My dreams aren't all mist, my desires not all untrue, there is something—?"

"I believe," said Wistons, "that if God Himself came flaming before us here in this poor garden and commanded us to put away our superstitions, to bury our beliefs, to abandon our little shreds of ideals, to think only of the material

160

life because there was none other, to know that Christ Jesus was a sham and a fake, to practise selfishness and gain and worldly success, to put heaven away from our eyes and to pray no more, I believe that behind this thunder there would be a still small voice comforting us and bidding us still believe—

"If the spirit of man is a delusion and a joke, then it is a joke of so much greater power, glory, hope and comfort than any serious word that I will go to my grave feeding it, caring for it, giving it all I have.

"I know how loose words are," Wistons went on quietly after a little while. "What have I said that means anything or that can't mean anything you like to make it? But what I know is that there is more in life than anything that men can do or say, that there is an immortal spirit whose history, whose struggles, whose victories and defeats give the whole meaning to this life which is only one short paragraph in the book of that greater life. These are our fleshly conditions and we must obey them, but through them, always, we must be waiting, listening, for ever at attention to catch the movement of that other life. Your honour, your courage, your self-sacrifice, your gentleness, kindliness, if you lose these things you had as well be a sheep's carcass hanging in any butcher's. That I *know* to be true." Then he added, "There's a storm coming. I've felt the thunder over the hill a long time back. The breeze has gone."

He came over to Johanson and put his hand on his shoulder. "Come into the house and drink some bad coffee."

Johanson stood up.

"No, thank you. I think I'll be off. I'm going to walk back and I'll not be caught by the storm."

Wistons answered, "Very well. I won't keep you." He added slowly, "I've not been much help to you. It's my fate never to help the people I want to, but I doubt in this whether any one could help you much. It's your own fight."

"Yes, it's my own fight." Johanson shook himself like a dog coming out of water. "But you have helped me. Immense. I don't know which way it will be, but whatever way it is I shall never forget what you have said."

Wistons nodded his head.

"All right, then. Come up again some time. I shall always like to see you. I wish you luck."

They shook hands and Johanson strode away.

The sky blackened, the stars vanished, and a little underground breeze rustled along the ground like a creature whispering news; a distant mutter grumbled behind the hill.

The way back to Polchester was straight enough, but as he left the little village and pressed to the top of a bare and desolate hill he felt as though he were entering strange and hostile country. As is so often the case with the inland Glebeshire country, thick and wooded valleys give place with swift precipitancy to plains as bare as a knuckle-bone. On these plains there is little life, never a tree to be seen, only a bare cottage or two clinging, with feet stubbornly implanted, to the hostile and ungracious soil. It was on such a desolate plain that Johanson now found himself.

But he was not conscious of the scene nor of the coming storm. As he left Pybus behind him, so, too, Wistons faded. It was true that Wistons had helped him, but rather by listening than by his own words. Those words had been, it seemed to Johanson, a little melodramatic, a little sentimental. They might mean anything or nothing. This spirit of man, what was it? This after-life—was it of any use to consider that when one had so much ado to carry through the present one? Johanson had never, in that sense, been a religious man. All his impulses, both spiritual and temporal, drove him towards the creation of something in this world. That seemed to him to be his whole business. He prayed sometimes to God; he thought, as every man must do, of the consequences of physical death, but he did not *live* for any after-life. His business seemed to be all with this one.

Clergymen, he had often thought, took it too readily for granted that men's constant preoccupation must be with the life of the spirit. They slipped into phrases that were too easy to be interesting. He knew that Wistons was different from other men in that his constant preoccupation was with the spiritual life, and that his angry, starved, lonely, discomforted soul had no other hope but the hope beyond the grave. Wistons was no humbug and no loose thinker either, but for that very reason he could not understand Johanson's aching love for Maude. There was all his trouble, all his problem this night. He was going to lose her, he was going to lose her!

He saw her with marvellous clarity as he strode across the plain. True and deep love is not blind: it sees defects and weakness with an intensity that is part of its agony. He knew that she was spoilt and shallow, ignorant and vain, that she would not be able to endure the tests of unpopularity and poverty and hostility, that her code of morality was harsh, limited, stupid, that her view of the world was provincial and ignorant, but he saw also beneath all this most truly that she was a child capable of infinite tenderness and goodness, were she only loved long enough and wisely enough. Give him one year and he would change her so that her own mother would not know her! He would make himself so necessary to her that when at the last test came, she would endure anything rather than leave him.

But now—seeing her only for a short period of the day, not sharing with her those loving hours of the night that bind human souls together as no other power can do—the least trouble, a flash of jealousy, a refusal on his part to go her way in some social matter, and she would be off riding ferociously on the wind of her outraged vanity.

He knew that it was not only Mary Longstaffe that would be the trouble. Unless he bowed his head to the Ronders and the Bonds, unless he smiled on Hogg and his wretched Seatown, unless he permitted himself humbly to be patronised by the Cassidys and Carlyons of the town, unless he surrendered for many a year his dream of beautiful buildings and a place worthy of that

Cathedral, unless all this were so, his whole position would change, his business would droop, it might be that real hostility would break upon him. He had at least one enemy in Hogg, who was only waiting for his moment.

And then he would lose Maude. You might fancy that she was worth but little if she were so easily lost. But she was as yet but half created. Every lover has the thought that he is creating the one he loves, not in his own image, but in something far more beautiful and divine. He would not have loved Maude so dearly had she not needed his tender care. Love is only half love if it is not half maternal.

He felt the first warm drops of rain upon his face. The little breeze had gone and the air was so close that he seemed to be packed within an iron cage. The thunder cracked across the plain, a God snapping his giant fingers. The cold, pale face of the lightning swerved like a turning mirror across the earth, and he saw a white world, bare, chill and dead. Then the thunder burst, cracking again and again inside his brain, as it seemed. The rain descended like whips and the ground hissed like snakes.

In that instant it seemed that he saw Maude, lovely, untouched by the storm, her hair uncovered, her arms out to him. He caught her to him, stumbling to the ground, and murmured as he caressed her cheek:

"Darling, darling . . . it's all over. Stay with me. I give up everything for you. What is anything else worth if I haven't you? Come closer. Come closer. Love me terribly. Yes, yes. I will do that and that and that. I will do anything, everything. Only stay with me, love me. I will shelter you. Come here under my coat. No one shall touch, no one shall hurt you. Yes, yes, I will do all you tell me. No, I have given up my dreams. They worried you, so I threw them away. . . . Love me, love me, love me. Put your hand there on my heart. Here, I will lay my head between your breasts—so. Now close my eyes as you kiss them. Slowly, slowly. Don't sigh, darling. No trouble shall ever come to you again. Only let me lie here. Draw down my head and kiss my eyes again. Come closer, closer so that the rain does not touch you. Now let your heart beat with the beating of mine. So. Both of us together. Now we are one body and one flesh. No one can separate us. Have no fear. Have no fear. . . ."

The lightning flared across his eyes. He was on his knees alone and the plain was like the plain of the moon in its desolation. Maude was not. He had betrayed himself for her, and the reward was not enough. He knew, absolutely, that it was not enough. Maude had come to him, had crept into his very spirit, but the betrayal of himself that had invited her had changed her into dust.

He struggled to his feet. The rain was coming down in a joyful flood, dancing in the plenitude of its power. He was soaked with it so that he became part of it. The thunder was remote; the lightning palely trembled on a far horizon. He stretched his arms, raised his head to heaven.

He knew that his crisis was finished and for ever. Not for God himself could he betray the Godhead in himself, far less for man.

It was as though a thief had come in the night and tried to steal, as he slept, the only treasure that he had, and he had woken in time.

He had realised Maude utterly, possessed her completely, and it had not been enough. Nor would anything else be enough to compensate for the loss of his immortal part.

He gazed about him bewildered, like a man who had been sleeping. He pressed the back of his hand, washed with the rain, against his eyes. The crisis had been so swift. He did not know how long he had been on his knees. It was truly as though Maude had been there. He had possessed her, had triumphed with joy, and then had known that desolation of betrayal and dismay at his unexpected loss. All this, it might be, in a second of time. He did not know. It had been like a revelation, and his whole life was settled by it.

As the rain washed his face he felt the strength rise within him like a flood. It was so wonderful to see his purpose so clearly. Yes, he would love Maude no less, he would keep all the love in the world that he was permitted to keep, but he had been given his scale of values, values mortal and immortal.

He walked on triumphantly, through the rain.

CHAPTER V

SUMMER NIGHT

I HAVE remarked elsewhere in other chronicles of our town on the strange progress of rumour. Polchester was less confined and provincial in 1906 than it had been in 1897, but it was closer to that earlier town than to the modern city that Carstairs Bellows and the rest afterwards made of it.

The town life was still very largely a family affair. Servants, related through centuries of Glebeshire ancestry, still carried gossip from door to door, and from the filthiest Seatown slum to the quiet splendour of the Bishop's library at Carpledon the chain ran link by link from house to house.

The gossip was seldom of evil intent. People will see a puppy, kettle tied to tail, chased by small boys, and will shrink with horror at the sight; returning then to their tea, they will happily chatter away the life and happiness of two human beings who have never harmed them. Sight is everything: for most of us what we do not see we do not feel.

Our Town had seen Harmer John and, foreigner though he was, had loved him. It had taken him to its heart and, of course, expected him to be sufficiently grateful for that honour. He had begun to show his gratitude quite properly by giving the place a new hobby, by declaring his devotion to its beauty, by engaging himself to a native and by providing a novel and charming entertainment. All this was well: for a mere foreigner very well indeed. He must now carry on that good beginning by devoting himself to the town's interest, transforming himself into a true citizen—difficult work for a foreigner, of course, and only to be achieved by his complete surrender to the town's wishes.

A week or two after the lecture it began to be whispered that this same surrender was neither so swift nor so desirable as it should be. Some one said that some one else had said that some one had heard Harmer John say. . . . Some one said that Harmer John was having trouble with his girl, and some one added to that that his girl thought that he was spending too much of his time with another lady.

Here, indeed, you touched upon one of the tenderest spots in Polchester morality. Once publicly engaged, you were engaged. To walk out casually with a lady to see whether you liked her, that was a wise precaution against too precipitate matrimony, but, engaged before the world, proclaimed at a dinner, danced upon and sung over, after that, there you were and there you must stay.

Of course, one knew what foreigners were: dangerous in sexual matters as no Englishman could ever be. Did one not know what Paris stood for, and although Harmer John came from the North somewhere, as far from Polchester as Paris was, nevertheless, once out of England the danger was the same. And if Harmer John once played fast and loose with a Polchester girl . . . !

Then, Rumour continued, there was this Seatown affair. What had happened in Seatown? No one precisely knew. He had gone down there and laid his hand on a sick child's forehead and the child had instantly recovered. Since then certain women in the town were always bringing him children with colds and coughs and headaches, and he cured them just by looking at them.

Witchcraft? Well, this was a modern world and we know that witchcraft is nonsense—nevertheless these foreigners learn funny tricks in these foreign places. Every one knew that you cured colds with quinine, not by looking the patient in the eyes. That was hypnotism or mesmerism, the kind of thing practised once at the annual Fair in our town by a foreign gentleman in a shiny tall hat and a soiled white shirt, chased ultimately away by the policeman. In any case what had Harmer John to do with Seatown? Why was he down there so often? Some of the roughest men in the place had been heard to suggest that if he came meddling with their women they'd have something to say. . . .

There was also the case of Mary Longstaffe. Rumour had something to murmur about that. It had, of course, been hard on the girl that her lover should have died before he could marry her, and had she only stayed away from our town nobody would have interfered. She would have been pleasantly and easily forgotten. Had she wished even to pay a short visit to her father, so forgiving is our town and so conscious of human weakness that it might, for a brief period, have turned aside and looked the other way. But to come back and live, bringing with her the child of her sin! There was obstinacy, pride and rebellion! Why, it was as though Polchester were nothing at all, a mere paltry village to be insulted quite casually by anybody! No, no, thank God, our town had its pride. It had also its moral code. The sons of our Archdeacons might run away with the daughters of our citizens, but at least they had the grace to run away and stay away. Mary Longstaffe's presence in our town was a perpetual menace to our good name and proper pride. Once an evil liver always an evil liver. Didn't every one know that? The pleasures of the flesh once tasted were too pleasant not to taste again!

And here she was at her old tricks, detaching a man from his girl—and alas, it seemed, if all that Rumour said was true, that he was only too ready to be detached.

Nevertheless, at this present time our town had no intention of being unkind to Harmer John: it had its eye upon him merely, and entirely, of course, for his good.

It was not very long before many people noticed a change in the man. It was not that he was less pleasant or friendly, but rather that he was sterner and something more preoccupied in his thoughts.

But the true change in him was made manifest to Ronder earlier than to any one else in the town. The massage was finished and Johanson was about to leave the bedroom when Ronder, with that charming friendly smile of his warranted to put dragons at their ease, said, "And now, my dear fellow, what about the next lecture?"

Johanson, putting his things away in a small bag, said, "Oh, I don't know."

"You don't know?" Ronder shook his head with the greatest friendliness. "Come, that won't do. We are all expecting it, people are demanding it. Besides," he drew near to Johanson and put his hand on his shoulder, "it is necessary for the town. You are now a factor in the town's progress, remember. You are no longer a private citizen."

"Am I not?" Johanson straightened himself. "I shall have my liberty though, Canon Ronder."

It was then that Ronder felt the change in the man. It had been his happiness that, all his life, he could deal with human souls as though he played a game of chess. He was aloof from them, vastly indulgent to them, feeling no surprise at their weaknesses and folly, liking them, often helping them and never pitying them. But this playing of them one against the other had become such a passion with him that he now often played his game simply for the love of playing it and without any definite purpose.

So, of late, he had been aware that at times he seemed to beat the air; people eluded him as once they had not done; his touch was no longer so sure. Many persons in the town, from Ambrose Wistons down to Samuel Hogg, seemed now to bear with them a faint air of hostility. He had been sometimes suspicious of late that people laughed at him. Did he lose his power over others he lost everything in life save his private self-indulgences, and he was still alive enough to see whither they might lead him, had they rein.

But here in Johanson was a man whom he felt that he completely controlled. What made it pleasanter was that he liked the fellow. He liked his physical size and strength and health and good humour and naïveté and honesty. He appreciated good qualities in others immensely; they added to his sense of his own well-being.

This man, a foreigner, knowing little of the world and with an infinite and touching belief in the honesty of others, was ideal for his purpose. He had never hitherto doubted but that he could mould him exactly to his shape and pattern.

Now, in one flash of perception, he doubted. There was something in Johanson's eye, voice, the squaring of his shoulders, that caused Ronder to wonder whether after all he had known the man at all. And the thought that was to be common in the next weeks to many of his fellow-citizens came to him. After all, with these foreigners, you never can tell!

"Your liberty, my dear fellow! Why, who is threatening that?"

Johanson smiled, "Nobody."

"That's all right, then," said Ronder. "We must see about a date. If I am to take the chair for you again, as I should very much like to do, it won't be so easy to find a free date within the next month or two. It's extraordinary how things pile up! We should have it before the weather gets too warm and before the children's holidays start. Let me see!" He stood in his handsome dressing-gown and furred bedroom slippers delicately considering.

"I'm in no hurry, sir," said Johanson, taking his bag and turning towards the door. "My mind's not clear yet about what I shall say. It shall be necessary to go a little farther than the last time."

Again that new note in the man's voice!

Ronder did not intend to stand any nonsense; it would be as well to put down that furred bedroom slipper here and now!

"Come, come," he said. "What do you mean by that? If I'm to take the chair for you I must know what you intend to say. You're not going to plunge into controversial matters, I hope."

Johanson turned from the door smiling with all his accustomed warm friendliness.

"Canon Ronder, you've been very kind to me for a long way back. I would like to do always as you would wish me, but I must be myself. I can't be another. I see life as I see it, and I see this town as I see it. I can't see it another way."

"Now, my dear friend," Ronder came up to Johanson, placed his hands on his shoulders, and the two faces were so close to one another that Johanson could see the little curling hairs in Render's ears and the tiny red veins (and later they would be purple) that ran down on either side of his nostrils, "we are friends, are we not?"

"Yes, sir," said Johanson, moving his big shoulders ever so slightly.

"And have been friends ever since we first met, I think. We both love this town, and we have both of us certain gifts that we can place at her service. Now there are things that you know that I do not, and there are things that I know, knowledge of the world a little, perhaps, that you have not yet learned. You have not, I am afraid, taken our little talk of the other day to heart as I should have wished. I am not asking you—as indeed how could I?—to cease your friendship with any one here, only to be a little more discreet, a trifle less public—"

"You speak of Miss Longstaffe?" Johanson moved away from Ronder's touch.

"Oh, why mention names? My good fellow, you won't take this amiss, I know. It is only because you are a stranger here—"

"But I like it better to mention names," Johanson interrupted. He paused a moment, then continued: "Canon Ronder, you are a clever man. You understand the world. Do you not realise that if some one have a friend whom they know to be good it is when all the world try to part them that they stick the closest? Tom Longstaffe was and is and ever shall be my friend. His daughter I hardly know. I like her, yes, but all women is rather shadowy to me just now because I love one woman so much. But Miss Longstaffe is a good woman, I think, and courageous and honest, and she have a dear little boy. Do you think I would give up my friends because they are abused by people? Why, no! You would not yourself!"

"But no one is asking you to give them up," Ronder answered impatiently. (Lord! how tiresomely simple the fellow was!) "Surely you can be as friendly as you like with them without being for ever seen with them in public? That's all I ask. A little discretion. Your friends here want people to look up to you, to admire you. If you are to do good work in the town you must show every one that you put some value on morality and decent living. You are entering on a public career. It is not as though you were a nobody. Many eyes are upon you."

"It is not true," Johanson answered slowly, "that I am seen often with Miss Longstaffe in public, but speaking to me this way, Canon Ronder, will assist me to be so. I am not a boy. I have my pride like another man. Were you the best friend I have in the world, Canon Ronder, you should not dictate to me my loyalties. Good afternoon." And before Ronder could shape his next indignant sentence Johanson was away.

But he could not be preoccupied with Ronder, nor with any gossip that there might be in the town. His one thought was for Maude. In some way he must persuade her sufficiently of his love of her and of her absolute need for him, so that, whatever troubles might come, she would not be able to leave him. Give him only time! Give him only time! Could he only make her understand that he not only did not love Mary Longstaffe, but that she was hardly more than an acquaintance, and if then after that he might show her that she, Maude, was the first, last and only love of his life! But with it all he was not very clever. He had had but little experience with women, his honesty (a quality not universally practised by lovers) was for ever in his way, and he did not know that Maude, like most women, lived on little assurances and demonstrations.

He could, perhaps, during those important weeks, have chained her to him for ever, had he been a little less single-minded, a little more subtle. But he was not subtle; he was not clever at perceiving the things that people wanted him to be, do or say.

And yet he was wise enough to understand the real spirit that Maude had; he understood it better than any one, including her mother.

He understood it better than any one ever would again. The divine spark in Maude at this moment was a small quivering flame, but it was alight. He could have fanned it into a fire that would have made her a noble woman.

Poor Maude! She also had had no experience of love. She did not know what this strange confusion of feeling—of jealousy, selfishness, unselfishness, physical desire, maternal tenderness, passionate surrender, autocratic domination, weariness and excitement might be. For the first time in her trivial vain little life she encountered love, and it was not love exactly as she had thought it would be; it was love with difficulty, love that needed great qualities of unselfishness and charity and patience. Those qualities had not as yet grown in her to sufficient stature.

She was in a thousand moods a day. Before he came home from his work she sat up in her room listening for the sound of his step. Her heart beat thickly, her cheeks were hot, her throat dry. She loved him so terribly that all she wanted was to stay quietly beside him and feel him to be there. When he came she would be so good. She would not say one word that would irritate him. She would not mention the name of that horrid woman. . . . She would not tell him the gossip that she had heard in the town, that he had quarrelled with Canon Ronder or that the men in Seatown were going to duck him in the Pol.

These things had disturbed her terribly; she watched his popularity rise and fall with the breathless anxiety of a farmer watching his weather-glass. But she would not say a word. She would only tell him that she loved him and loved him and loved him. And then when she had been with him two minutes out it all came—all of it. How some one had said that he had spent all the day in Mary Longstaffe's room; how some one else had said that he and Mary Longstaffe were planning to run away together; how again she had heard that if he were not careful and kept his tongue quiet he would lose all his clients; how this, how that—out it all came in an angry tempestuous flood, ending always with, "And you don't love me. I know you don't. Otherwise you wouldn't behave so."

When first she had said that, it had delighted her to see the look of astonished pain and surprise in his eyes as though he were truly amazed that any one for a moment of time could doubt his love. But she had now said the same thing so often that it was impatience rather than pain that his eyes showed.

"Tell me how much you love me," she demanded. "More than you ever thought you could love anybody? More than every one in the world together? More than—"

At first he answered her with passionate assertions, but now the demand was so frequent that he refused to answer.

"If you can't see," he said, "I shan't tell you. It is an insult to ask me so often. You must know without for ever asking." And one day when his arms were around her and his cheek against hers she was entirely reassured and felt that she could snap her beautiful fingers at all the Mary Longstaffes in creation, but by the following day she was all uneasy again and the reassurance was demanded once more.

His love for her was so clear to himself and so patent, it seemed to him, to all the world that he did not know how to make it clearer. He sought Mrs. Penethen in his trouble.

That wise woman had made hitherto no comment. She never offered advice, she never asked questions. Only when something must be done she said so; so far as the household affairs were concerned it was always Judy who did it.

It may be expected, however, that she had her private anxieties. Her attitude to Johanson was still very much what it had been on the night of his first appearance. She had felt a mother to him then: she would feel a mother to him to the last. But she had passed, in other years, through such deeps of emotion, sorrow and self-control that she would be always an observer rather than a participator. She knew his trouble, though, before he came to her.

They took a little walk together to the Cathedral and then round to the green paths under the grey walls. Between the trees, heavy now with the bright green leaves of the new summer, the waters of the Pol flashed and sparkled in broken segments and squares and circles. Once and again the Cathedral chimes came softly down to them like the very voice of the summer trees.

Mrs. Penethen always dressed in the same fashion when she went out—a black or a purple bonnet, a dark cloak that fell in straight folds like a knight's mantle, a white collar and white cuffs to her black dress. She seemed like the foundress of some mysterious order.

"You may have to take her away," she said, looking at him with her soft gentle eyes so unlike the sternness of her figure.

"Take her away?" he repeated, startled.

"Yes, it may be the only thing. Here she must be the wife of Somebody, that is her great determination. If things go badly with you here it will hurt her dreadfully. In another place she won't mind so much because she won't hear so much."

"You think things are going to go badly with me here, then?" he asked.

She stood still looking at a splash of river intensely blue between the curve of the leaves.

"I don't know. But you're too strong to be beaten into the shape they want, and it will take you years to beat *them* into anything. Do you know that you can't change people?"

"Oh, you can," he answered eagerly, thinking of Maude, "if you care enough."

She shook her bonnet.

"No, you cannot. I never changed my husband. He learnt to keep some things out of my way and I learnt not to bother him with questions. That's the most married people ever learn." She went on after a moment: "I was in service when I was a young girl. My mistress was determined to cure her husband of taking snuff. She died, poor thing, in the effort."

"But Maude is so young. If I have her only long enough with me I can make her see and feel in her very soul that I love her." He stopped for a moment, took off his hat and felt the sun on his head. "It's that—that she can think I don't love her—it's that that beats me. What should I do, Mrs. Penethen? Tell me what I should do?"

"I'll tell you what you should have done," she answered with energy, "only, of course, it's too late now. It's Judy you should have married."

"Judy!" he cried. "Judy! Why, she hates me!"

"No, she does not," Mrs. Penethen answered. "She loves you and has always done. And, much more than that, she understands you. She knows what you want. She saw that that lecture was tomfoolery. She'd like to see you fight the Town and beat it. She'd back you in anything. She's the only one in all this place who knows you. And she always has."

He felt a sort of provoked irritation. He did not want to think of Judy, that dark frowning girl who never laughed and watched him ironically. Besides, he did not believe a word of it.

"Misfortunately," he answered drily, "it's Maude who I love, and love her so that no other woman can be even thought of. Can't you persuade her of that, Mrs. Penethen? Can't you make her see that she have so much reason to be jealous of the moon as any other woman?"

"Jealousy isn't reasonable," answered Mrs. Penethen; "any one will tell you that. I was jealous once of my husband and a girl in a grocer's. She was ugly and stupid, but I hated her. I'd have poisoned her sugar and flour for her if I could. I never knew whether I had reason or not. Jealousy's a thing to make you ashamed of yourself if anything ever was, but it's a thing you're to be pitied for too. Maude's jealous. Can't you see that woman less than you do?"

"I don't see her very often," he said, "but her father's my best friend. The people here all cut her. Wouldn't you stand up for your friend?"

"But if you have to choose between her and Maude?"

"Choose!" he burst out. "But that's ridiculous. I don't hope that you too think that I am in love with her!"

"No, I do not. But just now, things being as they are, I think you're a little too honest about it. Why tell Maude when you've been there? There's no need. I heard you two or three days ago saying you'd just come from there."

"But why shouldn't I say when there's nothing in it?"

"Bless the man!" She shook her head ironically. "Don't you know anything about women? They'll put up with anything if it isn't set right in front of their faces. All they want is the permission to cheat themselves. They don't bless a man for too much honesty, I can tell you."

He stared about him in a kind of dismay. "I don't understand it," he said. "It should all be so straight with me and Maude. I love her, heart, soul and body. So I have always done. I will give up anything to her, everything I have—"

"Except what you think to be right," said Mrs. Penethen.

"Yes," he answered. "I'm not worth Maude's having if I lose that."

"I don't think women care much," Mrs. Penethen said. "What they want is to have a man, all of him, head to toe. Most women, I believe, would rather have a man of poor character and have all of him than a man of good character and only a bit of him. I don't know. It's hard to say. But what I'm afraid of with Maude is that she'll get into one of her tantrums and fly off and find herself engaged to somebody else before her head's clear, and then still be too proud to come back to you again."

He stopped and stood there in the sunlight bareheaded. She saw that he was dreadfully troubled.

"Oh, Mrs. Penethen," he said, "I mustn't lose her. I mustn't. Life without her would be such pain. Oh, help me not to lose her! You're her mother. Tell her. Advise her."

All her heart went out to him. She put her hand on his shoulder.

"For just now," she said, "I'll advise you. Don't at this time see the other lady too much and don't tell Maude when you have seen her. And don't get into trouble with the people here before you've married Maude. You've only got to wait until October. When you're married, if you have trouble she'll have to share it whether she likes it or not. And that will be good for her too."

She looked up whimsically into his face out of her soft grey eyes.

"All the same," she said, shaking her bonnet at him, "it's Judy you ought to have married."

A summer night came. The old phantasmal fires belonging to the soil here before bricks and mortar were thought of had their brief hour of resurrection, in a flaming sky. Loge, at some unseen Wotan's bidding, hemmed in the Cathedral with a wall of fire, and the woods caught the blaze and the Pol was stained with scarlet. It sank, and a pale wash of silver white flooded the scene.

As dusk passed into early night and the stars stamped the sky, summer became vocal. It was the first real summer night of the year, and a faint film of silver light hung like gauze about the quiet streets. Scents of flowers and trees and hedgerows penetrated everywhere. Mrs. Dunning, the widow who kept the "Blue Boar," that stuffy little hostelry at the south end of the market, smelt them and opened the sitting-room window and leaned out and looked at the stairs. Samuel Hogg, watching with smiling face Fletch play Cassidy the grocer at billiards, smelt them and went into the doorway of the Y.M.C.A. building and sniffed contemptuously the air. Mrs. Combermere, finishing a pleasant and solitary little dinner in her house in the Precincts, a book about dog breeding propped up against the water-jug in front of her, smelt them and told her little servant-maid that she should be out with her young man that evening—a night for lovers. Miss Ronder, finishing *her* meal opposite her nephew the Canon, smelt them and, looking cynically across the table at his eager intent to get the very best out of his Angel on Horseback, thought of carnations, her favourite flower, masses of them, dark crimson and wine-purple. Wistons, sitting alone in his tangled little garden at Pybus, was bathed in the flowers, in the soil of the hill, in the water of the running stream. He was thinking of Christ, watching for Him, as he often did, to come in through the garden gate and quietly, peacefully to sit down at his side. So they would sit, the two of them, in the little garden, friends who needed no words.

Johanson smelt them. He stood in his bedroom, his head through the open window, looking up at the fiery stars. Fiery they were to-night, some of them so restless as though they were intolerably excited, and the steady ones shining with an extra gleam. Maude had gone to supper with those tiresome dull people the Boultewoods. He couldn't abide them, mother, son and daughter. He felt strangely as though they menaced him in some way. They! Those flat-faced cows! He was in an ill temper to-night, knowing that Maude had gone out to supper with them only to irritate him. She had asked him to take her to the house (it was at the south end of the town), and then when he had eagerly agreed she had laughingly told him that young Boultewood was coming to fetch her, and that he could accompany the two of them if he liked. She was always teasing him in this way now, and behind the light superficiality of it there was something serious and restless and angry.

Oh, why could she not be quiet and trust him and see that he loved her? Why must she be for ever probing him and defying him and relenting, scolding him and forgiving, vehemently accusing him and then passionately repenting?

As he looked out and swam up to the quivering silver of the stars he longed for tranquillity. Everything was rocking to a crisis. On such a night he could not stay within doors. He took his hat and walked out.

He thought he would go round towards the south of the town and perhaps he might meet her walking back. She would not be eager to stay very late; the family bored her quite as sharply as they bored him; she had gone there only to provoke him and would soon have enough of it.

On the south side of Polchester overhanging Seatown there is a little public garden. In 1907 it was a very small and overgrown little piece with a tiny battered rococo temple, and some stairs and rain-washed garden seats. Now, as every one knows, the efforts of Cassidy and others have changed it into a fine public park, and once again, after more than a hundred years, the streets beneath it have become fashionable. From it you can no longer look over and down to the small cluster of Seatown lights, for Seatown is no more.

But to-night Johanson looked down. The one Seatown street showed its straight line of scattered lights, and behind that line the others lay coiled like the eyes of watching animals nested lazily in the warm night. The place had a stranger fascination for him than anything else, save the Cathedral, in Polchester. He knew that in some fashion it was here that his destiny would reach its crisis. In some fashion, too, that little bunch of dirty houses would be his test, and he fancied that as he looked down those eyes looked up, lazily, contemptuously, but with some shadow of apprehension.

He turned away; it was not with Seatown that he was occupied to-night, but with Maude—always and for ever with Maude.

He turned, saw first the little temple black against the milk-white sky with stars hanging to its roof like birds, and then, close at his side and quite unconscious of him, Mary Longstaffe.

His first sense when he realised that she had not seen him was to slip away. Here was danger, the course against which even Mrs. Penethen had warned him. Then, ashamed of his even momentary hesitation, he went up to her.

"Miss Longstaffe! All alone?" he said.

He saw her face in the starlit haze. She had been thinking sad thoughts. Her broad strong figure, the fine brave carriage of her head belied the almost childish distress in her eyes. She covered her melancholy with a smile as she turned to him, giving him her hand.

"Yes," she said. "It was so lovely a night that I couldn't stay indoors. Father has gone to some meeting and isn't to be back till eleven. Then we shall share our family cocoa."

They walked up and down the little garden path together, and at once, as it always was with them, they reached a basis of frank comradeship that Johanson knew with no other woman in the world.

"I have been a little sad to-night," she said. "Anything very beautiful has something sad in it, of course, because it is unattainable, I suppose—beauty. It slips away from you so quickly. And then on a night like this the time when I was happy here comes back so sharply. Of course I have my lover still. He never leaves me.

"But sometimes, however sure one is of that, one aches for something tangible, the pressure of his hand again, the touch of his sleeve."

"How do you mean," he asked, "that he never leaves you?"

"I'm not a sentimental woman," she answered. "I've lived in London now for years, working like a man. I'm no spiritualist. I couldn't even swear to you that I am sure of a future life. But I mean that literally Lance never leaves me. I think that perhaps when I die we shall be separated, but until then he is as much with me as he was before he had that accident. More, because then it was often difficult for us to be together. Why," she said, turning to him, "do you think I could ever stand it with all these cats here behaving to me as they do if he wasn't at my side all the time?"

"What do you mean? That you can see him—definitely?"

"Of course. More definitely than when he was alive. We do everything together. Oh, but what is it?" She turned to him almost passionately. "Do I cheat myself? Of course I don't see him, nor hear his voice, but most of the time he does seem to be there. Only there are the intervals. There was one this evening. I dread them so much. At those times I feel that it is all a sham. There is no Lance. Billy is all that remains of him."

They walked a little while and then she said, "I'm so glad I saw you to-night. You were just the person. But we mustn't meet very much just now, and you must come to our house less often. I've been talking to father about it."

"I must? Why?" Johanson asked.

"Because it's doing you harm. We are marked people at present. You've got your business to build up, and it would be really serious for you if your reputation were damaged by knowing us. I shan't be here for so very long, I suppose. I can stand it, but when father loses his congregation through me it is time I went away again. It's hard. I have only father and Billy and Lance. I don't want to interfere with any one. Only to be left alone with my three. But they won't permit it. And next time I go father will go too, leave the work of his life. I ought never to have come—and yet, I don't know, father and I have had some wonderful days. So," she said, staring down at the Seatown lights, "you won't come to our house very much just now—will you, please?"

He laughed. "A fine friend I'd be, Miss Longstaffe, loving your father and your son, and being a friend of your own, and giving you all up for the town's gossip. Would you think that of me now?"

"But it's serious," she went on. "There's another reason. Don't think I don't hear everything. I do. There's the lady you're engaged to. She doesn't like your knowing me. Forgive me if I'm poking my nose in where it oughtn't to be, but you mustn't make *her* unhappy—"

He was silent a moment before he answered. "No, I mustn't. But I've had all this out with myself. I can't give my friends up for nobody. I can arrange that those who don't like one another don't meet, or be tactful, you know, about speaking of them, but where my heart is there I must be loyal. Maude shall have that. She must, if we are to be happy."

His face seemed to her sterner and older than she had ever seen it, as he now looked at her. "You know, Miss Longstaffe, that shoe shall very soon be on the other leg. It will be whether you and Tom care know me, not me you. I shall in a little time be the most unpopular man in Polchester. . . ." He shrugged his shoulders. "It shall be new to me, that experience. Men have always liked me, and I like to be liked. But soon they'll drive me out of this town if they can—"

"Why? What are you going to do?" she asked.

"Do? Nothing! That's just it. I won't be under their orders. If they ask me whether their town is beautiful I shall say, 'Yes, it is beautiful, but your slum is filthy.' If they ask me, 'Are we not fine people?' I shall say, 'Yes, but you can be finer and me too.' If they say I must lick Ronder's shoes, I shall not. I am a foreigner. Very quickly, in a night, a foreigner is a suspicious person. First I was good because I were pleased with everything and had no opinions. So it might have gone for a long while. But I saw Seatown and the way they treated you. And they wanted me to be a sort of clown and turn somersaults for them. But I shall make one beautiful thing, somewhere, some place in the town, and then they'll kick me out. I know it."

"Yes, I see that," she said. "You must be yourself. We are alike in that. Well, here's luck."

She held out her hand and he took it.

"Don't forget that you're not to get into trouble because of us. That would make us very unhappy."

They walked out of the little garden and turned up the street towards the market-place.

At the corner he paused. "Forgive me," he said, "I shall wait here. Maude—Miss Penethen, you know—I'm engaged to, she's been taking supper with some friends here, and she would be returning just about now."

As he spoke two figures emerged from a side street. He saw, instantly, with a sense that this was fate, and prearranged by an interfering Heaven, that these were Maude and young Boultewood. There was nothing to be done. Young Boultewood was laughing in that idiotic way of his like a braying ass. Maude was quiet, walking swiftly. "Perhaps she is hurrying back to me." He had an instinct to push Mary Longstaffe into a doorway. Anything to prevent the meeting. But he did not move. His companion, who did not, of course, know Maude by sight, went on: "Well, then, I'll wish you good night. I'm so glad that we met like that. It was the greatest piece of luck—"

Maude saw him. Her eyes shone. She was about to stop. Then she saw Mary Longstaffe whom, by sight, she knew well enough. Her face sharpened. She looked at him, raised her head defiantly and walked quickly on.

CHAPTER VI

THE QUARREL

H<small>E</small> caught as though from a long way off the words repeated: "Well, I must say good night—"

He dragged himself back. "Oh, no, Miss Longstaffe. I'll see you to your door. It's almost my way home, you know."

She talked perhaps, and perhaps he answered her. He saw men as trees walking, and the clouds, frustrated by a cloudless sky, rolled baffled at his feet. He could think only: "I must see her to-night. I must explain to her. I can't go through the night without having seen her."

But when he reached the house it was dark and silent. He held the candle high in the kitchen, but its quavering light showed no figures, and from all the place there came no sound. He went up to bed and lay there through the warm night, struggling with his distress. As always, his window was open and his blind up, but the stars could not help him. No one from outside could help him. Maude and he must fight this out alone.

He went, as lovers always do, round and round in a circle. If he would give up Mary Longstaffe, mind his business and do what he was told by his superiors, Maude would love him. If he didn't she wouldn't, and if she didn't. . . . Could he endure it?

That was the question that leapt at him out of the starlight. Life without Maude. He had faced that question at Pybus and answered it, but now it was presented to him more immediately. Life without Maude. Life without Maude. And if he did what he was told. . . .

After a little troubled sleep in the morning he got up and went out. It was eight o'clock. They were washing their door-steps and opening the shops. Old Looney was walking to his accustomed market-place seat. He smiled, greatly pleased, when he saw Johanson. The sea had been very quiet down in the caves all night, just lapping up against the rock. But to-day bad weather was threatened. One must look out. The line of foam over there was angry. It couldn't be held back for ever. That wasn't in nature. And when the undertide had force enough—why, then you'd see something! Looney chuckled. He hadn't sat there watching all this time for nothing. He wasn't going to miss it when the day came.

Johanson stayed at his work, but when the last stout client had departed, with merely a nod to old Billy, he hurried away.

He found Judy alone in the kitchen. She stared at him defiantly; her sleeves were turned up and her brown arms rested on the table as she looked at him. But he had no time to waste on Judy.

"Where's Maude?" he said.

"In her room," Judy answered. Then quickly and almost under her breath, as though she were ashamed, she went on: "Look here, don't see her to-day. She's cross to-day and liking to be. She's patting herself on the back because she's got a grievance. Leave her a day or two and she'll come round."

But he hadn't even answered her. He was up the stairs and knocking on Maude's door. "Maude! Maude!"

There was no reply. He waited, then he knocked again. "Maude! Maude! It's me—Johnnie."

At last her voice, cold and sharp, came to him: "Well?"

"Please speak to me for a moment. I beg you."

The door opened and she stood there. "Yes—what is it?"

"Will you not give me ten minutes in the box-room?"

The box-room was a small place on the floor above, round the corner from Mr. Fletch's bedroom—strange, odd-cornered, with some dusty bookshelves holding dustier magazines, two old chairs, a table and a cupboard piled with forgotten relics. Mrs. Penethen's house was not well suited to lovers. There were two sitting-rooms, but Miss Midgeley had one and Mrs. Penethen herself the other. But the lovers were never interrupted in the box-room. From its curious slanting window you could see out over the roofs of Polchester to the green country beyond, almost to the edge of the plain that dropped down to the sea. They had come to look on it as their own.

She looked at him sternly.

"Very well," she said.

They went up together without a word. She stood in front of the slanting window, the grey clouds rolling behind her as though she had evoked them to assist her grandeur. For she was grand. She was fully conscious that to-day she had the power, the whip was in her hand. She was pleased that there was going to be a scene. As with most women when they are in love the thought of reconciliation after bitter words was intoxicating. She was already playing her part in that second consoling drama before the first ruthless one had begun. But beneath this was a torturing love for him, a determined obstinacy and a raging jealousy.

He spoke humbly, looking up at her in the way that she liked best with eyes that adored her. "Please, Maude, whatever we say we mustn't be angry, either of us. Do you see that? Don't you agree? No? For us to be angry would be terrible, because we love one another. We can talk quietly like friends, can't we? You see, I didn't know she'd be there, Miss Longstaffe, I mean. I knew you wouldn't like it, our being together. But we met by chance."

"I don't care," she answered, "who you meet. You can be with who you like for all I care."

"No. No. Of course it matters. Everything matters that gives you pain." He came to her and put his hand on her sleeve. She drew away sharply. He pulled himself up, standing close to her, looking with love into her face, but no more attempting to touch her. "Maude, listen. Let us be married soon. Very soon.

Next week perhaps. All our troubles come from this, that we are not together enough, only a little of every day, but when we are married then we shall know—"

"Married!" she broke in sharply. "A nice time we should have if we were married, and a pretty sort of husband you'd make if you went on as you've begun. No, thank you. When I have a husband he shall be some one I can trust."

"Not that!" he said, flushing. "Not that, Maude! Say what you please, but I am honest with you. I don't hope you'll deny that. You *must* not. Other things I've been wrong about. I've been stupid, sometimes I don't understand, I'm a foreigner—"

She caught up that word. "Yes, that's it. You're a foreigner. I don't understand you nor does any one else. You come here and every one's kind to you, and then you begin to criticise everything just as though you'd been here all your life. You know better than anybody, you do. You take advantage of every one's kindness."

She had worked herself up now finely, and he saw her, in a flash of understanding, almost exactly as she was. Drawn up against the window, her lovely hair and eyes, the perfect proportion of her body under her thin summer frock, the pouting movement of her lips, her little hands clenched, her young breast heaving, she looked the child that she partly was. He saw the child, he adored it, worshipped it, but he saw beneath the child something ancient and permanent, obstinacy, jealousy, hurt pride. She was already a woman in her more dangerous attributes. Oh! if he could but catch the fleeting child and hold it in his arms and keep it and make it secure! But there was the danger also of his own obstinacy and anger. She could rouse him and irritate him more easily than any one else in the world, because he loved her more.

"Maude, darling," he said quietly. "We are fighting air. What are we quarrelling about? About nothing at all. Because you saw me with Miss Longstaffe. I've told you that were an accident."

"You're not to see her again."

"How do you mean—not see her again?"

"Not see her again—not go near to her, have nothing to do with her."

He moved his body impatiently.

"We've had all that out before. I can't give up my friends unless they are false or do you harm intentionally. Can't you see that, Maude? I don't ask you to give up the Boultewoods, although I don't like them. What will we be, both of us, when we are married, if we give up all our freedom? We shall be slaves, the one of the other."

"Oh yes," she retorted furiously. "That's right. It doesn't seem funny to you to compare my friends, who are decent, respectable people, with that woman who's a—"

"Stop that!" He caught her wrist. His face stared into hers, and it was a new face for her to consider, cold and resolved. The boy's half-naïve, half-humorous twist had gone from it. Let me introduce to you, Miss Penethen, Mr. Hjalmar Johanson from Copenhagen. Yes, some one quite new. She realised it. She was excited and frightened.

"Oh, you're hurting!"

He caught her other wrist and held that too.

"You shall drive me away from you if you talk like that, Maude. . . . Let's have done with this foolishness. We love one another. What is all this quarrelling over? We will give in to each other always when we can, but there are some things we must not ask the other to surrender. Now kiss me and have done with this."

She broke into passionate crying, crumpled up into his arms, had her scene of reconciliation that she had desired, but beneath their demonstrations of love two other persons, darkly habited, crouching low in their caves, muttered—

He had, at the same time, other troubles. He paid the first instalment on the new rooms to Fletch, and was entitled now to enter upon them when he pleased; he went and looked at them. They were fine rooms, desolate, with torn wall-paper and straw-scattered floors. They were fine rooms, and he knew what he could do with them, but he was conscious that he had taken them too soon.

Business was falling rather than rising. Of course one must expect that the summer would be a slack time; it was difficult in the warm weather to expect people to care about physical exercises. But the preparations for the autumn season were not progressing as he wished. He had gained during the last month no new clients in the town, and enquiries, in answer to his leaflets, had come in very slackly from the country.

But worse than any of this was some odd change in himself. He was not working and thinking and planning with his old enthusiasm. It was as though he had lost much of his interest in himself and had transferred it to something outside himself. He stared at his Donatello and Leonardo photographs as though he would drag their souls from them. He stood in front of the Brytte Monument in the Cathedral, studying every line and vein of the beautiful marble as though he had himself worked at it, and again and again he seemed to feel some one at his side, some eyes upon him, some hand softly on his shoulder. In these early summer days Polchester was very beautiful, and he would stand in the streets gazing up at the roofs as they cut the field of deep sky or down upon the flags at his feet like another Looney! To make something beautiful, to form something in the town that would flow like water in a flagon into his empty spirit. Be practical, man, and go back to your job! He stood at the window of his office and looked hungrily out into the market-place. One day he did a mad thing. It was early evening, and the market-place was a pool of dim blue water under the crags of the houses. At the foot of the Market Cross some one had left from the last day's market some debris, pieces of wood, loose paper. He went down, walked hurriedly from the door, then, trying to seem casual, walked over to the Cross, kicked, still, as it were, casually, the paper and boards away, cleared the foot of the Cross, rubbed his hand caressingly against the stone, then slowly went back to the office. Only Looney, sitting on his bench, observed him.

Thirdly, he felt an altered attitude in the town. He had burnt his boats with Ronder of course. The weather was too warm, the Canon thought, for massage just at present. Then when Cassidy one afternoon spoke proudly of Polchester, saying that it was a perfect town, no town like it in England, Johanson pulled him up sharply. "Lord, man! Don't you see how beautiful it *might* be! How can you be contented? Don't you see. . . ."

But Cassidy didn't see and went away with an aggrieved expression.

Nor was he, Johanson, as amiable and light-hearted with every one as he had once been. He was haunted always now by a desire that they did not share, and so he was a little separated from them. Sometimes he had an impulse to start to work with his own hands at some street corner, to clear dust from here, to chip off with a hammer some ugliness there. He saw himself possessed with divine power, raising in the space of a night at the top of Orange Street a statue. Such a statue! A figure more human than the Donatello "David," more significant and urgent than the "Winged Victory!"

All the Polcastrians to wake one morning to find it there! And then how they would start to rebuild their city; first, all the windows and doors in Orange Street would be cleaned and shining, then down with the brewery at the market turning, then to limbo with the Town Hall, now for widening the High Street, that great sweep up to the Cathedral broad and shining with trees on every side, then . . .

Laughing, he would come out of his dream. He was almost home. And walking back he had cut every one. They would notice and speak of it. No matter, when they saw his statue!

The next phase of his struggle with Maude was desolate and desperate. Her determination to dominate him was subconsciously resisted by him with an intensity that he did not himself recognise. He loved her, but he would not surrender his free soul: she endeavoured to capture it with every device that she knew.

He was in some ways casual; call it, if you will, dreamy or phlegmatic. One morning he left the house and she was not well; she was in bed; she sent a message to him to come back early that evening. So he would have done, but a piece of work took him to the outskirts of the town, a ferocious thunderstorm further delayed him, he accepted an invitation to dine where he was, and he did not return to his lodging until after eleven.

All the evening he was thinking of her. He knew that she would understand, as he would have understood had she been kept somewhere. But, of course, she did not understand; her anger seemed to him to be selfish, but what it truly was was feminine. He had not realised that her femininity (very young and naïve and urgent) demanded altogether different proofs from his masculinity. What seemed to him overwhelming evidence of his love was to her nothing;

something that was to him ludicrously trivial was to her everything. Then he had his masculine life. He liked to be with men, to be jolly, to have men's careless friendliness around him; it was easy, natural, unburdened with atmosphere. But she felt that if he were not with her then he ought to be lonely and to be missing her, and when he came and showed her very frankly that he had been happy away from her she was enraged. She was selfish, yes, and greedy and rapacious, but all this was because she was not sure of him. Had he been one of her own country people, a native of Polchester, she would have known instinctively how to deal with him, but Johanson was always just out of her reach, as he was out of the reach perhaps of every one in our town.

So that she was in a perpetual state of irritation, nervousness and longing. He was so often not demonstrative at the times and in the manner that she wished. He would be thinking of his work, or perhaps of nothing at all; or he would be eager to talk about something and would not be caring at that moment to make love to her. But she wanted to be made love to eternally; she could never have enough of it. She would invent for herself the way that he would behave, the things that he would say, how he would look, and then when he did not behave and speak and look as she had invented, it was as though he had wilfully deceived her.

And behind these things there was her jealousy, and there was the ever-growing fear that in the town he was a failure. People said that he was swollen-headed after the success of his lecture, a bit above himself. He waxed impatient with his pupils and scolded them about their stomachs and double chins. Canon Ronder shook his head over him, and every Cathedral lady in the town questioned his open friendship with the immoral Miss Longstaffe.

He had been heard to say that had he the power he would pull half of Polchester down. He consorted with the lowest kind of women in Seatown; it was suspected that he would leave the town without paying his bills.

All these things and many more were agony to Maude, to whom Respectability, Popularity and Conventionality were the three corner-stones of the building of life. She was a snob through fear and selfishness. Her snobbery was only skin-deep. Had she married Johanson and gone away with him he would soon have snatched it from her, but, at present, she cared terribly about Public Opinion, and Public Opinion was changing about her lover.

It seemed so little a time since his success. The night of the lecture had been the turning-point; everything had gone wrong since that night.

So they turned, like the figures in the Tower in Strindberg's play, round and round upon one another.

Moments of real comprehension and perfect mutual love wheeled upon them like flashes from a lighthouse upon a darkening sea. But the days passed. Their relations became more and more restless. Maude was now a perpetual image of irritation. He was for ever doing wrong, not coming when he should, not speaking enough, speaking too much, never loving her enough, ruining his future and therefore hers, above all not surrendering to her the Longstaffes.

The catastrophe, at such a time, at such a place, was inevitable.

It had its origin, as catastrophes between lovers so often do, in tiny things, but those tiny things were small symbols of fundamental differences.

Johanson had bought Maude a little present, an old French silver box; he had found it in a small shabby shop behind the market-place. It was curiously worked with Cupids and wreaths of roses.

He had bought it for her because things had been going so wrong between them during the last days. He could not understand it. Some one must be supplying her with false information, because on every evening of his return she had some new story against him that, during the day, she had collected—stories of his carelessness, his unpopularity, his stupidity. There was some enemy at his back.

Moreover, the incessant scenes were wearying him. They were interspersed with reconciliations, and every reconciliation seemed final, as though there could never be a quarrel again, and then two hours later there would be accusations, recriminations, miseries again. Every quarrel in one fashion or another attacked his devotion to the Longstaffes—they beat up, one after another, like waves against the rock of his loyalty. But here neither his love nor his pity for her made him yield an inch: he had an obstinacy about certain things that was as hard as it was dumb. His love for her through all this trouble did not alter at all. He realised that her anger with him came from her love for him, but at moments now a sort of despair of their future together came over him and then, on the other side, the desolation of his life without her. . . .

He gave her her present. She was in her room and standing at her door. He caught her to him and kissed her hair, her eyes, her mouth. As he did so some strange terror invaded him. He saw at once the old dissatisfaction in her face. There was going to be a scene. He was tired, the day had been difficult and the air hot and thundery. To-night there must not be a scene. He could not endure it.

She thanked him perfunctorily for the present, barely looked at it, went in and laid it on her table. Then she returned, and leaning against her door, her hand on her hip, regarded him ironically. Her eyes, though, were not ironical. They pleaded with him as though they said: "Don't mind the rest of me. I love you, but I'm lost. I'm always saying and doing things I don't mean and don't want to say and do."

"Is it true that you said that to Mrs. Bond?" she asked.

"Mrs. Bond?" he repeated, bewildered. "What Mrs. Bond?"

"*What* Mrs. Bond?" she answered. "How many Mrs. Bonds are there in the town? One's enough, I should think."

"Well, what about her?" he asked gently.

"What about her? Oh, nothing. Only I wanted to know whether it's true that you told her to her face that her boy was hopeless."

"Hopeless? No, I don't think I told her that."

"Well, whatever you told her you've ruined yourself in that direction. She only happens to be the most important person in the town, that's all."

"I'm sorry," he answered, still very gently. "But what's made you bring all this up to-night?"

"I only thought you'd like to know. It's important, isn't it, if you make enemies of all the chief people in the place?"

"Maude, Maude!" He went up to her and put his arms around her. "Aren't you tired of all this? Why can't we be happy together? What's come over you lately? We were so happy, and we ought to be happy still."

"Oh yes, of course, it's all my fault," she broke out, drawing away from him. "It's never anything you've done. We're supposed to be going to be married, aren't we, and all the same I've got to stand by and see you ruin everything without protesting. If you think I am, you're wrong."

"I don't hope I *am* ruining everything," he answered her slowly. "But if I are can't you tell me of it in a friendly way? Let's be friends, Maude, whatever happens, and not for ever this anger as though you hated me."

"Sometimes I think I do hate you," she answered quickly. "You're so *stupid* and so *conceited*. You don't see what every one else sees, that you'll just have to leave the town if you go on like this, telling every one what they ought to do. Well, I'm not going to leave the town, I can tell you, so if you leave the town you leave me."

And all the time her eyes besought him: "Don't believe this. I don't mean it. Take me out of this. Help me to escape."

Very distant thunder rolled, as though some one were moving furniture there in the empty depths of the Cathedral.

"Now," he said sharply, feeling as though the thunder were rolling in his own head, "you've got to tell me, Maude, who's putting you up to all this. Who tells you every day things against me? There's some one behind this—"

"Oh," she answered scornfully. "If it's hearing of all the stupid things you do you needn't think it's any special person. One's only got to listen for a moment to any one."

"I didn't know," he answered quietly, "that my affairs were of so great importance to every one. You must exaggerate in that, Maude. But it's your friend Mr. Hogg who tells you these things. I know it quite well."

"If you know it, why do you ask me?" Maude answered. "At any rate he's fond of me and doesn't want to see me give myself away for nothing."

Hogg, as he had long known, was his real enemy in the place. Any mention of him roused some cold, deliberate anger in his heart, the worst and most dangerous element in him.

"We have indeed gone far from one another," he said sternly. "If you can listen every day to lies from a man like that about me, how can we trust one another? What has *happened* to you, Maude? How *can* you be disloyal, you . . . ?"

"Yes," she answered furiously. "You can put my bad man against your bad woman. You can leave me for hours because you want to be with a woman who's disgraced herself, and has the cheek to come back here and stare every one in the face. That's what you do and then you dare to talk to me!"

He caught her, held her for a moment rigid in his hands, then shook her, crying to her: "You stop that! You stop that! You drive me crazy! You've no decency! You want a good beating, that's what you want."

He let her go; she stumbled, caught at the door, ran back into her room, banging the door behind her. But a moment later it had opened again and she appeared there quivering, shaking with passion. They were both so angry that they did not see one another, but only images of themselves distorted.

She screamed at him: "You brute! You've beaten . . . You've beaten . . . hurt . . . I'm done with you, you cad. You're a foreigner. You don't belong here. You don't belong here. We all hate you here! You'd kill me one day. Yes, you would. And then you'd be hung. Yes, for killing me. You cowardly brute! No Englishman. . . . No Englishman. . . . It's not safe with you. I'll never be alone with you again. You're not safe. No Englishman. . . ."

She rushed past him down the stairs. He followed her.

He saw in a confused mist the old kitchen, Mrs. Penethen, Judy, Miss Midgeley and Fletch. And he saw Maude in the midst of them crying out.

He watched the ring of startled faces, the eyes amazed, the heavy motionless bodies. He heard her voice, shrill, sharp like a parrot's screech.

"He hit me! Mother, he hit me! Don't let him touch me!"

Then he saw her, the mist clearing, the kitchen clock and the china plates jumping at him, make a movement, snatch something from her hand, and throw it furiously (and awkwardly as women throw). He knew it was the ring (the funny old silver one) that he had given her.

"I'm done with him! I'll never speak to him again! You're all witness. He beat me. . . . I'm done with him."

She rushed past him back up the stairs.

He stood there for a moment looking at the stupid faces. Then he went and got his hat from the wall and without saying a word to any one went out.

CHAPTER VII

GABRIELLE MIDGELEY'S DIARY—III

OLD women. Old women. Old women. Some one has written an article about them in the *Spectator*. How old they are. How nice they are. Nicer than old men. That is what swiftly I am becoming—nicer than some nasty old man. I am running into old age like an express train. I haven't a minute to wait. No station to change at. Nor is it true to say, as approaching-old-age women always say, "I feel as young as I did at twenty." I don't. Sometimes I feel nine hundred and ninety-nine and a half. I feel so to-night.

They are playing billiards in the Cathedral. One can hear the click of the balls. But where do the Cathedral noises come from? Ghosts? Brandon and the Black Bishop amusing one another? I am so old that I can afford to believe in fairy-tales.

The life has gone from this house so completely that one can listen to the Cathedral noises as easily as one pleases. When Johanson left this house, for two of us—for Judy and myself—everything went with him. I shall change my lodging, I fancy—or leave the town altogether. Sentiment? Not entirely. He *had* a life, spiritual as well as physical, that gave zest to my old withered turnip of a soul. And the love of the two of them held such promise. I could have beaten them both after that wretched scene. Why could he not have stayed? Next day she would have been another creature. He might have excused her youth and vanity and silliness. But I must be fair to him. I think he did. Before he moved his things to his new lodgings he came here to say good-bye. He meant to win her still. To be away for a week and then to return. She had been too sure of him, he thought, and now she would miss him. I'm not too certain. I begged him not to leave her. She has bad friends here who egg on her vanity all the time. When he is there he can beat the lot of them, but when he is away she sees him as something foreign and queer—and somebody who has insulted her. That's her word. She came and talked such nonsense to me on *that* theme that at last I drove her out of my room. I told her a few home truths first, though.

I told her that she was giving up, for a miserable petty jealousy, one of the finest, most generous and noble human beings that ever descended from a monkey. Sentimental? I was sentimental all right. As I talked I saw a kind of heroic figure, one of the Donatello statues he's so fond of, and as unlike the real Harmer John as may be. Never mind. She listened to me. She even cried a little. Yes, and she even said that she would never love any one again. And she went further than that. She said that love made her uncomfortable and that he had such funny ideas. It was better not to love a foreigner, perhaps. Foreigner. Foreigner. Foreigner. I could have smacked her. When his heart was as warm and true and honest as this Johanson's, what was she bothering about his foreign blood for? There were plenty of Englishmen, yes, and Polcastrians too, who had more foreign hearts than he had. Yes, that was all right—of course he was a good man and kind too—but she was frightened of him all the same. His *ideas*. Now there was a thing. What was he doing here making himself so unpopular? It might be silly of her, but really she couldn't be the wife of an unpopular man. And he didn't care whom he offended—he didn't really. Mrs. Bond or Canon Ronder, it was all the same. I broke in upon her there. How *dared* she talk of loving him? Love? Did she call that love? Why, she didn't know what love was. She interrupted me then. Oh yes, she knew what love was very well. And she loved him. And she would never love anybody else. She was sure of that. But she thought that perhaps she wasn't meant to feel that kind of love. There was something unnatural about it. She wasn't a very grand person. She never would be. She knew her faults well enough. She'd only make him unhappy, always disapproving of the things that he wanted to do. She would never understand him. She ought to marry some one much more commonplace and ordinary, but no one would ever again make her feel as Johanson had made her feel. And she was glad. She didn't want to feel that way.

She wouldn't see him any more because if she saw him, even for a minute, it would all begin again. She did hope that she wouldn't see him in the town.

Queer girl. But then there was something in what she said. She looked so pretty as she stood there. And so tiresome. And a little vulgar. She's quite right—she isn't good enough for him—but without her—what will he do without her? What will he do in that lonely lodging? I have to wax myself to my chair or I'd be running off to see after him. Mrs. Penethen's been often. But she has a right. I'll take him some books one day, pay my proper polite little call.

Judy's the third of us. Yesterday she coolly asked me what we intended to do about it. What we intended to do about what? Why, Mr. Johanson. Did we know that he was in that wretched lodging all alone with no one to see to him? Did no one care what happened to him? It wasn't her business, but she hated to see people so false. Pretending to be a friend of some one and then deserting them when their luck was out. Oh, she named no names. But all the town was the same. Taking him up one minute and dropping him the next. She as good as said that I was as bad as the rest. She positively looked as if she hated the sight of me, and then stalked out of the room with her head in the air.

The next thing that happened to me was a meeting with that dear, lovable creature, Mrs. Bond. And where? Of all places in the world—the Circulating Library. My old flame, old Professor Henning. Professor of what? Of languages, and now, penniless, eaten up by his white beard, stamp-collecting in his dirty little lodging, starving his body and increasingly liberating his soul. Never mind about him, but, as this Diary knows, I like him. I like the way his eyes flame out of his beard and his long white hands, so clean, so thin and so aristocratic. The Circulating Library is always our rendezvous.

We can sit there in its hinder end keeping company with Godwin and Barham and Miss Ferrier and Jane Porter without too much consciousness of our advancing years. Dust and bookworms and one or two bright ideas—because really the Professor and I are very witty together. We laugh consummately. Or rather I laugh and he crumbles in his beard.

Miss Leeson, the librarian, is a nice young thing. *So* young. Clean and shining like a new penny. She is kind and considerate to the aged too, and eats sugared almonds out of a little paper bag, and we hear from our corner her teeth crunching and her sighs over the Corelli that she is investigating. I like the place, the sun (when it shines) making Jacob's ladders out of the curtain of dust and the spiders spinning webs over the faces of dear, dead authors. And I slip a bun into the Professor's pocket.

Two days ago I was discreetly waiting and listening to Miss Leeson's gay little tinkle, the door opened and there was my dear Mrs. Bond. Why do I detest that woman so thoroughly, and especially in that she is always so polite to me? And why is she polite? I am nothing. I am less than nothing. I am less than that again. And yet she is polite. Because, of course, she intends to get something out of me. But what? She regards me perhaps as some one just a little international. Because of my London life and because I have published books. She hopes, maybe, that one day I shall put her into one. I shall, and she won't recognise herself. That will be her tragedy. When she greets me, she always looks me over, as though she were wondering whether she could possibly endure for another minute acquaintance with a creature whose appearance is so quaint as mine. She pulls herself together. You can see her valiantly determining that she won't be put off. No, she won't be. But why won't she be? Why make the struggle? Most mysterious.

She is always so smartly dressed and yet not beautifully. Too much. Too little. And her face is too soft. Without bones. And too pink. The curls above her white forehead are too black and too hard. They gleam like metal. But how friendly she is! She held my hand in both of hers, while her eyes, surveying my odd costume and my strawberry features, revealed their accustomed struggle. Her nobility won, and so, accepting one, she launched into her stream.

Where was I living now? I always tell her and she always forgets. Why, of course, in those same rooms. And then—why, surely yes—was she not right? That was the very place where Mr. Johanson had lodged. *And* was lodging no longer.

Too sad. Such a pity. Such a nice man and such a disaster. What was sad and what was a pity and what was a disaster? Why, Mr. Johanson. She understood him, she fancied, better than most people here. Because he was not English. She had seen so much of the world. She had been surprised that a man of high character, as she understood him to be, should have given up the girl to whom he was engaged—and a nice, pretty girl too—for—well, one must not believe everything but some one else apparently was involved. One only heard half the truth about these things, and, for her part, she defended Mr. Johanson wherever she went, but he had apparently been very rude to Canon Ronder, which was, people felt, ungrateful of him when the Canon had done so much for him. But she *liked* him. She didn't want to see him go to pieces. That nice, pretty girl would have been so good for him? Why had he left her?

A question at last. I can remain impassive for ever. A sort of deadness. She felt it. It made her uncomfortable and so she asked her question. I answered it. I told her in the sweetest way possible that she was a liar. Oh! she didn't know that I was telling her that, of course. She thought that I was paying her compliments. She *knew*, of course, that I knew. And living in the same house. She had always felt just what I felt, that he was one of the *honestest* men—one of the *truest* ... and when people said these things. Yes, there was something boyish about him. So attractive. And when people said these things. ... For instance they said ... I stopped her there. I didn't want to know what they said. No, naturally. But opinion had changed. They had all liked him so at first. He had become all in a moment so independent—as though he knew better than anybody else. She liked that strength of character. But, of course, for a foreigner to judge everybody! The English character was something all to itself, was it not? And could a foreigner ... ? That was the question.

And on that question we left it. She stared at me as though she was wondering most truly *why* I existed and then passed on to the bright Miss Leeson to secure the book that was being kept for some one else, but would be yielded to her simply because of her autocratic power.

She leaves devastating ruin behind her. One knows the people—men and women—who do that. One cannot listen to them for five minutes, and they at their sweetest, without sniffing death and destruction. How and why do they do it? Is it a kind of jealousy of the human race or a sense of their own unworthiness that impels them to pull down others to their own level? In the old London days there was Forrest the novelist, son of a clergyman too—how smilingly he hated his fellow humans, how eagerly he sniffed out mean motives, how greedily he listened to detractions! And dear Mabel Barmes with her biting tongue, her clever newspaper criticism and her over-written novels, how her eyes would shine and her sallow cheeks faintly flush when some one came up for condemnation! Why do they like it? Where's their fun?

Anyway, I know that Mrs. Bond, curse her, made me on this occasion profoundly miserable. Foolish of me. Didn't I realise her by this time and understand her false and mean little soul? Nevertheless, the sense of her power depressed me. My poor Harmer John—so helpless against her! I might encourage myself by remembering that in the end, his character against hers, she's snuffed out like a candle! But, in the meantime, the things that she can do!

Enter my dear old Professor. We retired quietly to our spiders and philosophical discussions. Considering the Infinite extinguishes the Bonds, but how few souls have time enough!

And so I've paid my visit. With my books under my arm I climbed the stairs and found the room. He's at the top of that house that hangs over the descent to Seatown and swings there in the wind like a weather-cock. He has two rooms, and the sitting-room is all cuckoo-clock, plush divan, wool mats,

flowers and fruit under glass. Amidst these relics of a happier age I found him sitting, his coat off, elbows planted on the table, looking out between the geraniums at a sky that was as green as a primrose leaf. He might have been in Daddy Wordsworth's little boat:
"Away we go—and what care we
For treasons, tumults and for wars?
We are as calm in our delight
As is the crescent moon so bright
Among the scattered stars.

Up goes my little Boat so bright.
Through many a breathless field of light,
Through many a long blue field of ether,
Leaving ten thousand stars beneath her;
Up goes my Boat among the stars."
Yes, he was as remote and as tranquil I would have said; but at the sound of my coming in he turned and I saw, by the flush on his cheek, that he was hoping for some news from me, that he thought that I wouldn't have come if I . . .

And then, he had that particular courtesy and tenderness that is so peculiarly his. Old-fashioned, I fancy. I am a plain, bitter-tongued old woman, attractive to no one, but he always treats me as though I were Queen of the Andes. He brought me one of those chairs with warm, adhesive seats, and took away my shabby ulster, and seemed so happy to see me—almost as happy as I was to see him. He looked different. Older. I asked him why he hadn't come back to us and when he was coming. He sighed and then said that he had meant to return at the end of the first week, and that then Mrs. Penethen had been to see him and told him that Maude was so strange that she thought that he had better wait a little. He had been to the house and had tried to see Maude and had failed. Could I tell him anything or advise him, perhaps? His unhappiness came through then and I saw, in a flash, that he had been having a desperate time. I don't know why, but I got in the break of his voice, as he asked his question, a sense of his love for her far stronger than anything that I had had before. "I am very bad without her, Miss Midgeley," he said. "I have temptations to go to her and do everything she asks, give up my friends, all . . . but we wouldn't be happy that way. I know it. But I am very bad without her. The nights are so long. I miss her terrible."

I told him of my talk with her and I advised him not to wait any longer, but to insist on seeing her. She wasn't in a state to be left alone. There were others influencing her. She loved him, I was sure; or at least she was as near to it as her nature, timorous, selfish and vain, permitted her. I tried to say something then about her being unworthy of him, that he would find some one else. . . . He broke in upon me there and poured out to me his picture of her. How touching, and, at the end, how true! He saw her just as she was, but he saw her also as she would be if he cared for her enough! That is true of Maude. She's beguiling in her possibilities. He gave me proof after proof of her subconscious longing to be taken by him and held against the enemy like some fortress. But how was he to take her without surrendering his own fortress first?

Ridiculous similes. We had just talked like two friends up there in that high little room with the sky turning to crystal and the geraniums smelling woollier and woollier. My first friend for years. He is both boy and man, so that I am, with him, both mother and friend. Mother! I, the most sterile of women! Yes, he has taken from me a little of my sterility and I will bless him for that to my death. He has the divine gift of tenderness and compassion. Nothing is mean to him nor ignoble. If he hates, it is some poison in the nature not the poisoned soul that he detests.

And he is so unconscious in his goodness and kindliness of heart, that one wonders why no one has ever drawn his attention to those qualities!

He seemed to me as I talked to him to be a little dazed. He told me quite frankly that his experience of unpopularity was new to him and bewildered him. It was so short a time for the change. It bewildered him but did not frighten him. His mind seemed to be set on some new purpose, and this new purpose would make him happy later on. Not his work. I asked him about his classes and the rest, and he scarcely seemed to care. He meant to be busy, he said, about something that had nothing to do with himself; he meant to get himself right out of it.

Oneself. Oneself. Wouldn't it be fun to be rid of oneself or at least to be so completely occupied with something else that oneself never occurred to one? But the room was dark. One couldn't see the geraniums any longer. I left him urging him not to leave Maude alone for long. There were Boultewoods and Hoggs and all sorts waiting for their chance. . . .

I snivelled a little going down the stairs. He seemed to me so *very* lonely.

He has seen Maude. No success. She insisted on her mother being there. She wouldn't say anything except that she thought they would never do for one another. Quite polite. Trying to be a lady. Her mother longing to whip her. Harmer John very patient, eating her up with his eyes. Then quietly he went away. . . .

CHAPTER VIII

SEATOWN FANTASY

JOHANSON'S position was now extremely precarious. When he had arrived in our town he had saved a few hundred pounds, but he had put them into his business. His expenses had, after the initial outlay, been slight and the business good, but then came the time when he developed his advertising in the country, purchased new instruments for his exercises and paid Fletch the advance for the new rooms. He had never been very wise about money, but spent what came to him as it came. He had always been generous to the point of folly, but after his engagement to Maude he tried to realise that he had new responsibilities and must save. But this business of saving seemed to him to have something mean about it. There were so many in the town who were hard-hit. He himself had been so fortunate. He owed them something for his luck.

But he had not thought of the difference that the summer would make. He lost one client after another; finally he decided to close his place until the beginning of September. Billy and son went on a discontented holiday.

It was strange to find himself idle, and this coincided with his quarrel with Maude and departure from Mrs. Penethen's. He sat up in his high room, looked out at the clouds, and waited.

He had not long to wait. What came to him was Seatown.

A very hot August that year. And before Seatown, plus the hot August, came to him, he was compelled to face something very new and strange, a surprising and menacing loneliness. Menacing because it seemed to promise in the future something even worse than its present performance. He had never been lonely before. Even in the worst days of his childhood there had been people about. Now it was as though, by some mysterious device, a wall of cotton-wool had been let down between himself and Polchester. There was silence on every side of him, and only blank faces turned his way.

His landlady, Mrs. Prespin, had the blankest face of any. That was because she was preoccupied with her mother, a very, very ancient lady, over a hundred or so they say, and so bitter and melancholy that, as the maid of all work darkly muttered, "She'd be 'appier dead." She was, however, not only alive, but also her daughter Mrs. Prespin's whole existence. Where Mr. Prespin was no one knew nor cared, and had not the ancient Mrs. Mathias existed, Mrs. Prespin might have looked about her and asked herself whether it was wise to admit into her beautiful rooms so dangerous a foreigner as Mr. Johanson.

But when he, after climbing the stairs, having remembered his earlier vision of this house, enquired for rooms, Mrs. Prespin was so deeply occupied in heating milk for her mother that she could but answer, "Yes, that rooms were there," without once looking at her prospective lodger. Mrs. Prespin squinted and found it difficult to look at anybody; she was white and long, with a high bony horselike head, but her devotion to her mother made her almost beautiful. The surprising thing about old Mrs. Mathias was that, in spite of her hundred years, she was not bed-ridden, but would make sudden dramatic appearances, her withered head wrapped up in a red shawl, her feet in clinging, grey, tapping slippers, would push herself half through a door, look in with her red-rimmed eyes, move her toothless gums, and disappear again.

So that Mrs. Mathias and Mrs. Prespin were not, by any means, what Mrs. Penethen and Miss Midgeley had been. They were, in fact, exactly nothing at all.

He increased, too, his loneliness by that sensitiveness that all men who are suffering under unpopularity feel.

He did not go to the Longstaffes as he had formerly done, because he thought that Tom might not wish his name to be connected any longer with Mary's. He had, innocently, made scandal enough in that direction. But he missed Tom Longstaffe terribly.

It was, of course, not seeing Maude that, during these first weeks, drove him almost to madness. Yes, to madness; for he would walk his bedroom floor for hours at night struggling to forget and only more hopelessly remembering, and he would pierce the hurrying clouds with his gaze fixing her there in their woolly folds, seeing her eyes, her hair, hearing her voice laughing beyond the sun.

Was she also thus missing him? Strangely, although again and again he had spoken of their love for one another, he had never been sure of hers—he was not sure now. She would miss the happy times but would lazily congratulate herself on her escape from the difficult ones. But there were things that she *must* remember—evening half-hours beneath their sheltering tree, embraces, whispered desires, loving confidences, things that she *must* . . .

And then the long white face of Mrs. Prespin: "Well, mother's a bit better to-day, thank you, Mr. Johnson. Yes, she just went off for an hour or two, which is a thing to be thankful for at her age. Mother always says: 'If I get an hour or two these days I'm thankful,' but she really is a bit better than yesterday, thank you. The heat affects her, of course, but she's wonderful, considering, I do think. It's just the pain in the back that troubles her, but, as I always tell her, you must expect something when, you're over a hundred."

You must indeed, and what ancient Mrs. Mathias expected nobody knows, but the tip-tap of her slippers about the floor was like mice skipping behind the wainscot—some company after all for a lonely man.

From his windows he could see the whole of the town—below him Seatown, the river, the fields rising to the wooded hills; on the other side (screwing your neck round the window) the narrow street winding up to the market-place, a glimpse of the High Street, and then the Cathedral towers striding above the roofs across the sky.

Directly below him was the street, hesitating an instant before its downward plunge. Just in front of the house it widened, having no buildings opposite but only a thick wall, leaning on which visitors, idlers and philosophers might gaze down over the rock to the waters of the Pol, the Seatown huddled encampment, and the farther country.

To the right of this wall Johanson noticed on his second or third day a deserted patch of grass, some grey stone and a forlorn tree that huddled into the wall's corner. It was the desolation of this tree that first caught Johanson's attention, the way that with a sort of desperate despair it clutched the wall with its arms and protested in waves of exasperation against every wind. Then, going out into the hot August light, the patch of shade beneath the tree was inviting. He walked across the street to investigate. He found an old broken seat worn with rain and washed free of paint, cracked and bird-soiled. The grass was thick and tangled; to the right of the tree, and almost hidden by the overhanging wall, was something else, some old deserted monument of grey stone.

He did not stay then to investigate it further, but strangely enough that night when he was lying in bed he thought of it. He had been lying there restlessly, turning over and over, his heart aching for Maude. His heart beat wildly: he seemed to be on the edge of some foolish action, as though he might dress and go out and beat on the door of Mrs. Penethen's house. He did not know what he might not do. The night was so hot, he had had now a fortnight of this loneliness and longings; his nerves were stretched to their limit.

It seemed so impossible that only a month ago they had been so close and so intimate, and that now they were separated by this wall of misunderstanding.

When he had talked to her the other day he had seen on her set and determined face the presence of some obstinate resolve. Although her mother had been there he had got up suddenly, gone across to her, put his arms around her and said: "Maude, Maude, come back to me." He had felt her body tremble, and for a moment her hand had fluttered on to his; nevertheless, she had said in a small remote voice: "Will you promise never to see the Longstaffes again, then?"

After that it was hopeless. There was a blind resolved obstinacy there that had behind it some subconscious reasoning. Mrs. Penethen tried to do what she could. There was nothing to be done. Maude would only return on her own conditions, and they were conditions to which Johanson would never agree.

But to-night the heat seemed to strangle his brain. His body was damp with sweat. He jumped up, flung off his pyjamas, and walked naked about the room. It was then in the depth of his loneliness and unhappiness that he thought of the tree, the grey stone, the wall. He went to the open window and looked out to the splendid night fiery with stars. The Cathedral clock struck half-past three. The town slept like a dead man; the blue haze that enwrapped it quivered with the coming dawn, and there, pale like the skeleton of a tree, was that for which he was looking. It seemed friendly to him, to be as lonely as he.

He put on some clothes, went quietly down the creaking stairs, lifted the chain of the house door, and stepped out into the beautiful night, soft with southern softness, quiet and still with the silence of mysterious preparation.

He crossed the road, bent over the seat, felt its poor neglected roughness with his hand, and then, stepping into the rough tangled grass, looked at the grey stone. In the dim veiled light he could see but little; with his hand he pulled away some weeds and then some clinging ivy.

Kneeling down, he found that here was something round and smooth; very dimly he could discern carved figures. Pulling away more of the ivy, he saw at last that this was a deserted fountain filled with earth, and, on the earth a broken figure, the upper half of a Satyr holding a wine cup. He took out the Satyr's head and arm and held them against the sky, then, carefully he replaced them upon the soil that filled the circle of the fountain. His hand rested for a moment on the grey stone; then mysteriously comforted, he returned softly to his room.

To those who know Polchester now in these chilly post-war days it will seem incredible that so recently as 1907 we should have possessed anything as medieval as the old Seatown. The modern river-side street with its neat line of workmen's cottages and gardens, its border of young trees and its low wall of pearl-grey stone, is altogether admirable. To quote the *Polchester Courier* for March 10, 1924: "We have here something of which we may be proud—modern and yet beautiful; practical and yet dignified; modest and yet artistic. The pretty gardens rich with lovely flowers, the fine asphalted road, the raised walk that gives the visitor an opportunity of surveying the beauties of Nature in a practical and commodious manner, the cottages themselves with their pale stone, their dignified outlines, their perfect sanitation—these are things, we repeat, of which the Polchester citizen may well be proud."

And the Polchester citizen *is* proud. I am proud. We are all proud. It is only a pity, perhaps, that we had not the opportunity of being proud a little earlier. The Polchester that Johanson found was divided into three very distinct camps—there were the citizens, the rebels, and the ruffians, and all these three parties were huddled together within an area of a mile or so.

The citizens, who considered themselves the chief of the Polchester kingdom, consisted of four or five old families who had been among the earliest settlers in Glebeshire. These families worked honestly in the town, for the most part at net-making, and kept themselves entirely apart from the other Seatown population.

The rebels were the loafers, and numbered the most here. They were the scavengers, the idlers, the wasters, drifting in from the sea, the country farms, other towns such as Drymouth and Buquay. There were some foreigners among them, but for the most part they were pasty-faced, lean-shanked and furtive-eyed, and lived by mean theft and petty larceny.

The ruffians were the dashing ones, the romantics, the buccaneers. They were less in number than the rebels, but infinitely more energetic and dominating. They were gypsies in origin; and dirty vagabonds though they were, their rich brown colouring, large black eyes, jet black hair, told a story. It would need a George Borrow to investigate sufficiently their beginning, but on some old day some caravan had stumbled into Polchester streets, had rested for the night, and permanently remained. The ruffians were the enemies of all civilised society. They nourished in those happy days before the word Bolshevism was known, nor had even the most learned among them heard the blessed and holy name of Karl Marx; they followed perhaps rather the pattern of Robin Hood and the late beloved Turpin, save that they had no grace of charity or humour.

They had no saving grace of any kind, being cruel, mean, treacherous, superstitious, disloyal, avaricious, morally debased, and of a physical filthiness. But they had romantic names—Romilly, Carne, Santin, Escarpia, Froment. Johanson had already encountered one of them, Bloody Bill Romilly, a creature six foot four in height and black-bearded.

On Harmer John's first visit to Seatown, as I have recorded, he stumbled by accident into the room of a woman who had a sick child. He sat beside this child, stroked its forehead, talked a little to the mother, and went away. But the child at once improved and soon was out of danger. There may have been some virtue in the touch of Johanson's hand—there are all around us people who have a gift of this kind—but I should imagine that there was a much stronger virtue in Johanson's heart. He always loved children so passionately that it would be strange indeed if they did not feel something pass from him to them.

The mother, who was the beaten and down-trodden wife of one of the ruffians—a sandy-haired blackguard known as the Sandpiper—lost no time in proclaiming the miracle. It was not odd that it should have seemed like a miracle to her. A stranger comes into her place from nowhere, speaks with an odd accent, is taller and bigger than any one she has ever seen, sits down beside her sick child and cures it, and vanishes. Was it not natural that she should speak of it?

Nor did he become less of a miracle when he appeared again. He came on several occasions, bringing little gifts for the child with him.

He would sit there and talk for an hour perhaps, and mostly with the child Emily Maud, who of course adored him. The mother did not talk but sat there with her eternal sewing-machine—like the woman in Hood's poem, she made shirts—and watched them.

The Sandpiper arrived once, stared for a long time without saying anything, and went out again. Women sometimes came to the door and stood there looking. One day a woman asked him whether he would come and look at her little boy. The doctor could do nothing with him. Johanson went and found an attic so filthy that the child was almost invisible.

When discovered he seemed to be suffering from little but vermin and bad food; he was a boy like a blackberry, with a merry eye. He, with a mangy dog, attached himself to Johanson, would watch for him at the corner of the street, and even on one occasion ventured as far as Johanson's lodging. His name was Husky, an allusion to a queer throaty voice that he had, and his dog was called Charlie.

When the news of this second marvellous cure spread about the excitement was immense. His town nickname, Harmer John, caught the Seatown fancy, and it was to be heard everywhere. Ladies in various stages of undress waited for him on stairs, at doors, down the street, and begged him in hoarse voices to cure colds, coughs, toothaches, asthma, rheumatism, internal pains of every kind, and many quite unmentionable Seatown complaints. He tried to explain to them that he could cure nothing, and that the first thing for them to do was to sluice their floors with water, open the windows, and drink less. Of course they would not listen. He made at once enemies to the death of the two local witches, Mother Harper and old Mrs. Clay.

Mother Harper was long and thin, with grey wispy hair and protruding teeth; old Mrs. Clay was bent so double that she did not look like a human at all, and she walked leaning on a stick just as a witch should.

He also made an enemy of the local doctor, Rufus, a fat, drunken, man, white-haired and purple-nosed.

When he found that his visits were causing a disturbance, that the children and dogs clung to his heels, the women collected about him and the men leaned against the wall and scowled at him (he was not popular with the Seatown men; they hated him from the first) he came no more. For several weeks Seatown did not see him, and his only connection with it was the mysterious appearance of young Husky and Charlie at his heels in various parts of the town hitherto unblessed by his presence. Then came the trouble with Maude, and he took up his lodging at the Seatown gates.

From that moment Seatown haunted him. He no longer cared for the consequences; do something for that abandoned place he must. It was unfortunate that by the time he began his regular visits to Seatown his glory in the upper town had begun to fade. Although the Seatown inhabitants cared defiantly less than nothing for the opinion of the outside world, they were snobs like the rest of us. Every one in Seatown very soon knew that Harmer John had treated his girl wrong, that the clergy thought badly of him, and that he had said that he wished to pull Seatown to pieces. Half the place hated him then, and the other half looked on him as a magician who was to be justified only by successful miracles.

A few, the mother of Emily Maud and one or two others, worshipped him; certain children and dogs followed him devotedly wherever he went. The others, instructed by their elders, shouted at him and called after him abusively.

There was a nice young clergyman, Grahame, whose especial spiritual province Seatown was, and Johanson might have found him a fine ally had he not unfortunately gone just now to Buquay on his August holiday. It need scarcely be suggested that he was badly in want of it.

Johanson was discovering in himself new elements. He had always been obstinate, but something was in him now that was more than obstinacy—something hard and almost remorseless. So far as Seatown went he could no longer say that he did not wish to change people's opinions. He did not care whose feelings he hurt, how many enemies he made, if he could alter the Seatown conditions. The filth, the smells, the broken windows, the overcrowding, the incredible immorality consequent on that overcrowding, the degradation and despair—the complacency of the Upper Town about these things stirred a deep and unchanging anger.

There is nothing in our English life, perhaps, more amazing to the visiting foreigner than the close juxtaposition in towns both big and small of absolute poverty and degradation and comfort and security. Very much has been done during the last twenty years to improve the housing conditions of our towns, but in 1907 Polchester was not the only place in England with a Seatown. Only in Glebeshire there has always been a strain of foreign blood in the people that gives them something alien, picturesque, if you like, and also dangerous.

Seatown had a sharp and brilliant colour like some exotic flower.

Our Town Councillors and aristocracy were not easy about the Seatown conditions—the trouble in 1902 had showed that—but once begin to change things and you stirred up a whole world of responsibilities, slanders, accusations and denials. Anything better just now than a public scandal—and just now was always.

Hogg and others, whose business it was to see that Seatown remained medieval (there were many things and persons in the present Seatown very useful to Hogg) knew that once scandal burst consequences might be disastrous for them, were very active in helping the Upper Town to forget the Lower, and the Upper Town was not unreluctant.

Then comes this abominable foreigner. . . .

The Sandpiper was one of the first to express publicly his dislike of "this bloody foreigner." Having one day knocked his wife's face in because she upset his beer, and being confronted by Johanson while he was resting from his gentle exercise, Johanson kicked him out of the room and tumbled him down the smelly stairs.

From this moment he, so far as Johanson was concerned, physically disappeared. It was as though when he landed on the bottom stairs he vanished through the ancient boards into the bosom of Mother Earth—physically disappeared, but not spiritually. That was, as Johanson now discovered, the very oddest thing about Seatown—that it was impossible to put your finger directly upon any one, but that you walked as though in some place of ghosts. It was as though the mists that gathered about the Pol, morning and evening, enveloped so much more than their own slow waters and low-hanging fields.

Hogg, for instance, was never to be seen there, and yet his presence was ever to be felt. He did not once during these weeks encounter Johanson, and yet Johanson was never free of his presence.

Johanson had thought at first that he would bring together one or two of the principal Seatown residents and form with them a little band of reformers—but the clergyman was away, the doctor hated him, and—there was no one else.

There was literally no one else! Try and put your finger on any one and he at once disappeared! Only idle women, children, lounging loafers, foul-mouthed buccaneers, and dogs remained. Young Husky remained and Charlie and Emily Maud—and Bloody Bill Romilly.

This last, as Johanson soon perceived, was deputed his principal harasser. Romilly's large black-bearded lumping body was soon at every quarter. The Sandpiper and others were doubtless not far away, but they did not appear.

Johanson believed always in grasping his nettle, and he at once followed Romilly to his lair. That was not so grim a place as you might have imagined, but rather a tumble-down cottage on the edge of the country above the mill. Romilly was resting, lying on a pile of straw and sacking when Johanson invaded him. His great body stretched its full length, his tangled beard, his small and puzzled eyes and, oddly enough, rather fine and delicate hands, made a queer picture in the tumbled and thick-smelling cottage.

He did not raise himself when he saw Johanson, but asked him what he wanted.

"I want less of your company," Johanson said.

Romilly laughed, and then explained that he could bloody well go where he bloody well pleased, and what the hell was a bloody foreigner doing down in Seatown anyway.

Johanson explained that Seatown was free to all the world, to himself and to others. He would come there when he pleased and, he repeated, he would like less of Romilly's company.

Romilly slowly rose from his straw and, stretching his arms and yawning, asked Johanson what he intended to do about it. The two men stood facing one another. They were much of a size; Romilly's open shirt showed a chest with black hair like a bear's.

Romilly surveyed him curiously and still with that puzzled look in his eye, animal and a little pathetic.

"Will you fight?" he asked at last.

"Now?" asked Johanson.

"No. To-morrow night at the 'Sucking Pig.'"

"Yes. If you fight fair," Johanson answered after a moment's thought. Romilly would fight fair. There was something in the man's slow gaze that promised it.

"Now get out," said Romilly.

Johanson woke at five the next day. He went to his window and looked out at the lovely summer morning and the town as quiet as a sleeping child. Layers of sun were stretched above it, awnings of faintly washed colour, and the Cathedral towers were of bright gold.

He bathed himself, dressed, and very softly went down the stairs. He had a jack-knife and a little hammer and chisel. The street shone in the sun with the freshness that Nature gives to things before human beings have meddled with them. A little breeze rollicked down the hill. There was no human being to be seen.

He walked over to the seat and the tree. He knelt down on the grass before the stone fountain and worked there with his hammer and chisel for an hour or so. Then, as the first comers began to pass down the street and the Cathedral bells chimed seven, he returned to his room.

The "Sucking Pig" was an inn a mile out of the town on the border of the desolate strip of moor known as Humpathumb (and of that same place there is a story to be told one day). In 1907 it was kept by an old blackguard called Coffen. It was burnt to the ground in 1910.

On that fine summer night its central room was crowded. Johanson, surveying it, felt a strange throb of satisfaction. At last there was a hope that he would come to close grips with his enemy. For weeks past everything had eluded him; he had been fighting shadows. Now at last there was Bill Romilly's dark face and hairy chest to batter at. He felt as though here at last was his first opportunity to knock down a bit of Seatown. Everything in his other life, even Maude, was distant and misty to him to-night. He knew what the results of this thing must be in the Upper Town. "A drunken brawl. Fighting in a low pub. Oh, quite gone to pieces, my dear . . ." He cared not at all. To-night was his first step on his real road.

As he looked about him he wondered what kind of a fighter he would turn out to be. He hadn't been in a real fight since he was a lad, but he was in splendid condition, which Romilly most certainly was not.

It happened as it had been arranged. They were lounging about, drinking. Romilly pushed Johanson's arm, muttered something; Johanson replied, Romilly knocked his glass of beer out of his hand. Instantly from all over the room there were cries of "A Fight! A Fight!" The crowd scattered and then ranged itself back against the bar and the three walls. A short, squat, broken-nosed fellow touched Johanson on the arm: "I'll be behind yer," he said. The centre of the floor was clear, and about it in the strange mingled light of the summer evening that was fading into ivory beyond the windows, and the harsh light of the jerking, hissing gas, the faces pressed. Everything was irregular: here eyes swollen and protruding, there a beaked nose, here strange caps and shawls, there a whole face thrown up into sharp relief like a dead upturned face in its motionless intensity, and behind these a restless, ceaseless murmur and shuffling of bodies like the lapping of sea on the rocks.

Two chairs were set in the empty space. The two men stripped to the waist, buckling their trousers about them according to time-honoured tradition. A long thin man with a face like a skull stepped forward and announced that these two gentlemen having had a difference of opinion they intended to settle it here and now with their fists as gentlemen should. That Mr. Ben Hawser would referee. This last was received with murmurs of approval. Johanson noticed, as he sat there, that there was no louder sound. It was more like a dream than reality. Seatown still maintained its odd quality of being yet beyond touch. Those odd sinister faces, the queer half light beyond the inner circle, the dark background like the outskirts of an undiscovered wood, the tall thin fanatical body thrown into bold relief near the window of old Mother Harper, the witch, the pursuing murmur as though persons unseen were always on the move behind him, this was all in its outer aspect unreal, unlike any life that he knew, but in his inner soul it was part of an intense reality; as a sinner may feel, perhaps, when at length he comes to grips with that sin for which all his life he had been searching.

They made a strange contrast as they stood up facing one another; Johanson's body so white, without a hair on his chest, Romilly covered with a thick black felt on his shoulders, arms, breast. They were men much of a size, and Romilly had not so much fat on him as you might have expected from a man who must be out of condition. As they stood there Seatown obviously considered that it had not for a long time had the opportunity of beholding two mightier men. The faces dipped and bobbed, the hissing murmur of the water dragging back over the sand rose and fell, and a flood of orange spread fan-wise over the reed-misted, water-logged moor beyond the open window.

There were to be no pauses, no breathers, no rounds. Simply one man was to knock the other out of sight. Seatown sighed once again its satisfaction. This was the way to deal with the stranger within its gates.

Mr. Hawser murmured something and the fight began. It was at once very plain that neither man was a trained fighter. Romilly had fought most of his battles (and they had been many) in liquor, but to-night he was serious sober. Both men were cautious, circling round one another, their eyes intent, as though wire stretched from face to face holding them.

Johanson hit out and lightly grazed Romilly's cheek. Romilly breathed hard, gazed at Johanson with that same dumb look of enquiry that was so especially his, then got one in on Johanson's right breast, which flushed a dull red. Johanson returned and caught Romilly hard on the left shoulder, breaking the skin.

Johanson was aware then that this man wanted to kill him, and that every man and woman in that place wanted to kill him.

He had intruded; he had stirred up their nest and they would get rid of him. But sure as he was of this, he was also sure that to-night the fight would be fair. Seatown had some traditions, this of fair fight on such an occasion was one. But on a later occasion . . .

He felt arising in himself an eager burning longing to smash Romilly's nose flat. He bore Romilly no kind of grudge, but his big black lumbering body was a kind of insult. The thing was so large and clumsy, and yet so elusive. Anger was rising in him, not at all against Romilly, but against anything as ugly as Romilly's body. There should not be in the world anything as ugly as that, and it was Johanson's duty to break it up. But it was strangely difficult to touch. Johanson knew that he must conserve his strength, and that every unnecessary step that he took he must pay for, but when he seemed to have that black heaving mass at his mercy suddenly it wasn't there.

The circle of his horizon narrowed. He had at first seen the whole room with the bar, the shining tumblers, the wall with the old dirty coloured print, the pressed circle of faces, the open window with the evening like a glass picture. Now it narrowed and narrowed, first to the shining floor below him, to the queer ugly face of his supporter, to the chairs opposite him; then that closed in and he saw only Romilly, Romilly with his sweating forehead, his black beard with beads of perspiration on it, his heavy breasts and a roll of his fat hanging over his tightened trousers. Then it narrowed again and he saw only a square of flesh, first here, now there, something that he must get into contact with.

He had not a great idea of self-defence. He knew that Romilly had caught him first here then there. He dimly expected that at some moment there would arrive a swinging blow that would pitch him down into darkness, and this expectation gave him a sense of urgency, as though he had not much time and must get his blow in first.

He did get his blow in. Romilly's face seemed to leap at him, and his own fist crashed out and met it. He felt the contact of bone with bone. Romilly's face was red through the black, a flush of blood that covered the whole sky, so that for an instant Johanson could not see anything but that. Romilly lurched and tottered, but then was as strong as ever again: in a moment he was back and crashed as it were with his whole body into Johanson's forehead.

The floor rose in a great curve, as though worked by an engine, and stood over Johanson. Some voice somewhere said: "If you don't hold on to this thread you'll fall into the very bowels of the earth and never appear again. Your life depends on holding this." A tiny white thread, its end tipped with silver, was held out to him, and he held on to it with every force—moral, spiritual, physical—that he possessed. The floor was still hanging above him, and he, standing on the edge of it, almost slipped into that eternity of blackness quivering with stars that waited for him. But he did not slip, and when Romilly returned with a hand extended that need give but the slightest push to tumble him over he managed to evade that hand and, sick, blinded, tottering, kept his feet. Slowly the world returned. He felt about him an air of surprise that he should still be there. The pain in his head was awful, but the rest of his body was strong enough. Vigour was flowing back into him and, turning, he saw Romilly quite clearly, blood trickling through his hair and the big body shaking uncertainly.

That vision was his salvation. He saw Romilly only for an instant before blood trickling from his forehead bruise blinded him, but that instant was enough. With every atom of the vigour of all his past and present life behind it, his arm shot out, his fist crashed into Romilly just under the chin, and Romilly fell and where he fell he lay and where he lay there he stayed, stretched his length like a dead man.

Johanson stood staring. The murmur around him was still low and ceaseless—like bees now buzzing in the bracken. Yes, he stood and stared, not thinking of anything save that he had hit Seatown at last. And Seatown also knew it. The faces did not change, the bodies scarcely moved. The gas hissed and fretted, there was no light now beyond the window and so still was it that a stream in a field could be heard jumping down the hill, hurrying to the Pol.

Johanson was sitting on his chair, a towel over his shoulders. No one congratulated him, but his second bathed his forehead with a sponge. Romilly had been dragged to a chair and men were bending over him. But Johanson did not care about Romilly. He was watching with a curious, almost somnolent, gaze the faces in the room. They stared at him abstractedly, unmalevolently, but with a definite purpose in their gaze.

They would let him alone to-night, but they would finish him off later. Time enough. Time enough. He was almost asleep there in his chair. How his forehead ached! What a headache he would have to-morrow!

Then, slowly rising, he moved off. Quite silently they all made way for him.

CHAPTER IX

THE LAST LECTURE

Aɴᴅ here I must, I am afraid, bring myself into it. I have reached the moment when I had my one and only glimpse of Johanson. I was, myself, present at that famous last lecture.

I was at the end of my first year at Cambridge and had come to stay for a week or two with some relations in Polchester. I had been brought up in Polchester and every stone in it was familiar to me: on my very first evening I heard of Johanson.

The way that his story came to me was, I think, instructive: he was described to me, quite simply, as a foreign ruffian. I was asked to imagine to myself a man who had come from some dangerous place abroad with definitely sinister designs upon our simple-hearted town. He had in the first place "wheedled" himself into people's sympathies by a tale of ill-luck and hardship, he had been boarded and cared for by one of the "kindest women in the town" (my informant was at least correct there), had started a gymnasium and interested some of the "foremost clergy" in his efforts, had managed to engage himself to the daughter, "a most beautiful girl," of his landlady and then—THEN—what had he not done that was shameful and base? He had betrayed apparently every one, leaving his fiancée for the company of a most immoral woman, had come out in his true colours advocating the pulling down of most of the town, had insulted those of the clergy who had been so good to him, had played some charlatan tricks with the women of the place, pretending to cure their children of all sorts of diseases, and had finally been fighting in some low pub in the slums among a drunken crowd of the town's worst citizens. And, after all this, he had actually the impertinence to announce another lecture; notices were posted all over the town.

It must be remembered that this was the first I had ever heard of the man. I did not know of the existence of most of those who were afterwards to give me all the full and elaborate information upon which this history has been built—Judy, Mrs. Penethen, Miss Midgeley, Maude herself, Ronder, Tom Longstaffe, Mary and the rest. I knew nothing of life, of course. I saw him that evening as the foreign ruffian described to me by my aunt.

This was exactly the fashion in which almost every one in our town was at that moment seeing him. That last fight down in Seatown had given the final touch to Legend No. III.—the legend of the foreign ruffian.

I wonder myself that his new landlady when she saw him with one eye closed and a bruise on his forehead bigger than a duck's egg did not at once beg him to seek rooms elsewhere. But, she afterwards confessed, "She had taken a sort of liking to him!" She didn't know how. She didn't know why. There it was.

She was sort of sorry for him. And then, of course, all her attention was given to her mother.

For himself I know that at this moment he was considering not at all what the town was thinking about him. He was occupied, as Tom Longstaffe discovered, with two things and two things only, and these two things warred the one against the other.

One was his idea, which grew in him with ever-increasing force, that somehow he *must* get rid of himself. If he could do that and do it completely, then the most wonderful discoveries awaited him. He would see and feel and be surrounded by such beauty as he had never even begun to imagine.

I fancy that now his old dream of his empty house with its shining purity, its view and its murmuring trees was always with him. It was in some way *here* that his discovery would come to him.

But on the other hand there was his other preoccupation, and that was Maude. He thought of her morning, noon, and night. How was he to rid himself *of* himself when he loved her so much? It was he who loved her, he, Harmer John, he, Hjalmar Johanson, he, not an abstraction, not a spirit, but he himself with his bones and blood and beating heart!

It was not only that he wanted her so badly, but that he was afraid that she was so unhappy. He was, himself, suffering so terribly because of his separation from her that he could not but believe that she was suffering too. I don't know, and no one will ever know, how often at night he went and stood outside that house and went quietly away again. Mrs. Penethen came to him when she could. She promised to tell him instantly when there seemed a chance. But the chance never came. I suppose that it was Maude's fright that held her back. She saw him in an atmosphere of danger and terror and distress and she wanted her safe little life of comfort and assurance and that her own free will should do what it pleased. What lover is there who has not sometimes, at the very highest moment of his love, felt terror at the increasing surrender of his own self-will? I imagine that Maude had never seen Johanson as he really was, but had loved him for the very strangeness that frightened her. She had perhaps—and who will ever know?—many and many a moment during this time when she longed to run and surrender everything to him. But she wanted her own way, and there was something in him—some independence—that she would never be able to conquer, and the stories in the town grew and grew (you may be sure that they were all brought to her ears) and people flattered her and encouraged her in her selfishness, and she was very young and very ignorant—and so she missed the chance of her life.

If she had, at this time, once been alone with him for an hour he would, I think, have won her back again. But would it even then have lasted? I fancy not. There were certain things to which he must have held, and those things would have terrified and antagonised her to the end.

Had he been a cleverer, more sophisticated, man many things would have been different. But he was not, as every one must have seen by this time, a clever man at all.

The ideas that he was discovering for himself were not new. They were as old as the oldest hills. Nor was he subtle-minded, nor was he very quick at perceiving what others were thinking. He could only see one or two things at a time, and those things that he saw he clung to. So he went on his inevitable way, but before he reached the climax of his last lecture a queer thing occurred.

At the beginning of September he reopened his office. Nobody came. He sat there day after day, sent out his circulars, did a little correspondence with people in the country, and waited. All his regular classes—the School, the tradesmen, the Young Men's Christian Association—these had all lapsed. He put an advertisement in the local Polchester paper, and one or two people came to see him, but his enemies and detractors warned them, I suppose, and they did not come again. Two of his most active enemies at this time were old Miss Eldred and the miserable Shortt. They went about everywhere loudly complaining. To listen to them you would think that Johanson had robbed them of every penny they possessed.

He was not, I imagine, at all surprised or disappointed that he was thus abandoned. His mind was now fixed upon something quite other than teaching physical exercises to Polchester citizens. One thing, however, worried him, and that was old Billy Trenant. That old man was a perfect nuisance. It would be pleasant to draw a picture of the man's touching fidelity, the faithful servant (another Caleb Balderstone) remaining when every one else deserted his master. And he did remain. Let that at least stand to his credit. He remained from some real dim sense of loyalty—but he remained complaining, grumbling, abusing, criticising. As with every true Glebeshire peasant there was a note of patronage in his attitude to all other humans, be they kings or paupers. He had patronised Johanson even at the height of his admiration for him. Now he admired himself immensely for remaining, and let Johanson know it. His Glebeshire pride must have suffered a horrid blow when all that splendid erection tumbled to the ground. Deep down he must have felt for his master, and it would seem from his after account of his devotion that he had always loved him and loved him to the last. But he showed his love, like many another, in grumblings, complaints and mutterings. He would not allow his son to come to the office any longer, and indeed there was no work for the boy. There was no work for the old man either, and, of course, no pay. He stayed there in the outer room cursing.

The lecture was to be in a week's time. There was every kind of rumour about it, and there was no doubt but that the place would be full. Johanson had taken this time a big room at the back of the Public Library, often used for local "Penny Readings," Missionary meetings and so on. This time there would be no chairman.

Then the surprising thing occurred. Johanson had a visitor, and the visitor was Canon Ronder.

I have received two accounts of this interview, one from Ronder himself and one that Johanson gave to Longstaffe. It seems that Ronder, on this occasion, obeyed one of the sincerest and truest instincts of his life. For once he did not stop to consider whether this were a wise step or one calculated to help his schemes. He came simply because in his heart he was fond of the man and thought that he was rushing to his destruction. He may have had, too, some guilty sense that he was responsible for him, he may have felt a deep discomfort about Seatown, and, most probable of all, he may have had some startling vision of the rapidity with which he himself was changing. On that morning at least it was not only Johanson's descent of which he was aware.

Johanson was greatly surprised to see him. He had for the moment quite forgotten Ronder's existence. He was pleased to see him, though. He never at that time or any other bore the slightest grudge against any human being. Hogg he hated, but impersonally, as he hated disease, meanness, and evil-speaking.

His forehead was still bruised, his eye yet discoloured, but he showed no embarrassment when Ronder came in, greeted him as warmly as he had ever done. Their relations were, however, now altered. They were equals, and that sense of power and command that Ronder had felt at the last meeting was now increased.

"I have come," Ronder said, "to ask whether you would care for me to be chairman again at your approaching lecture."

It was a fine thing for Ronder to do, and Johanson knew at once that it was so. Johanson saw by that time clearly enough into Ronder's character; he knew how much his social prestige meant to him, how he had worked unceasingly for many years to obtain his present command in the town, how deeply precious to him was his power over his fellow human beings.

"That's good of you," he said, smiling into Ronder's face. "It shan't be like the last lecture, you know."

"That's all right," Ronder said hurriedly. "I don't ask you anything about it. It's better perhaps that I shouldn't know what you mean to say. But I'm delighted to take the chair if you wish me."

"There's likely to be a row, you know," Johanson went on.

"Yes," said Ronder. "There may be."

"I'm not a popular man any longer."

"Not so popular as you were," said Ronder.

"I don't hope," said Johanson, still smiling, "that I should be as mean as to drag you into one of my rows."

"That's all right," Ronder repeated firmly. "If you want me I'm at your service."

"That's fine," Johanson said, his eyes smiling. "I shall never forget that you offered. I thank you. But this time I shall be alone."

Ronder said: "You'd better have some one with you, you know. After all it may help matters." He got up from his chair, hesitated, then went on: "I don't understand you. You're like no man I've ever met before. You seem to *want* to make trouble, and yet, knowing you, I would have said you were one who wanted to live at peace with his fellow-men."

"I do want to live at peace with them," said Johanson.

"Well, then—"

"But not if, to do so, I must be dishonest."

"We've had all this out before," Ronder said rather quickly. "I know you've got some idea in your head that won't let you rest, but couldn't you have given that idea a better chance if you'd gone on as you were going at first, if you'd established yourself and won all men's regard—wouldn't they then have listened to you more readily?"

"I don't know," said Johanson simply. "I had to think as I thought, and then say what I thought. Men are finer than I and cleverer and know the world, but I don't understand. No, I don't understand two things. Men don't seem to care about Life, nor they don't seem to care about Beauty."

"About Life?" Ronder asked.

"What Life's for. What Life means. They are always asking to be happy, but they don't care about Beauty. How can any man be happy when he doesn't care for Beauty?" Then he put his hand on Ronder's sleek, rounded shoulder. "Don't you worry yourself about me, see? I find my own way. I must, but I'm pretty glad you came to me as you did. I think that was fine."

Ronder's heart, in spite of the fatty degeneration of the last years, was filled with alarm and distress about the perils into which this poor, foreign devil was so blindly rushing. He had heard, I suppose, a good deal during these last weeks; he knew something of the Seatown gentry, of Hogg and his friends. His concern was the most genuine human feeling that he had known for many a day. Johanson offered more than one man a chance at that time.

"Don't you see," he began, pacing the little room in his agitation, "that it serves no purpose at all to raise such hostility? Upon my word, I don't know how you've done it. The things I hear are absurd, of course. But Seatown—" He stopped at the name, having his own none too comfortable thoughts in that connection.

"Was it wise," he went on more quietly, "to interfere there about matters in which you could not possibly have any real concern?"

"Concern!" Johanson broke in. "Concern! Do you know, Canon Ronder, what that place is? But you can't know. Come down with me any afternoon and I shall show you—like beasts . . . like beasts . . ." His voice broke. "In my own country," he went on more quietly, "there are horrible places—in Copenhagen and Christiania too. But these are big industrial towns; there is problems that belongs to our time, difficult, gigantic problems I know nothing of. But here in this little town, so small, so beautiful, that there should be such a place! One day's work would take it all away. Can't you see that? Can you have your breakfast and your dinner in quiet when at your door there are the four families in one room, men, women and children sleeping in one bed, humans like pigs, sorrow and hunger and cruelty . . . and no one cares? Oh! you English, what is it with you? You are so moral and you look unblushing on such immorality, you are so kind and you watch patiently such cruelty, you are so religious and you listen without caring to such blasphemy, you are so wise with all you have learnt from your old civilisation and you permit such stupidity. . . ." He came up to Ronder, took him by the shoulders, shook him. "I don't understand. Why do not men care more to make the world beautiful for others? How *can* they be so indifferent?"

"It's true what I prophesied," Ronder said. "I said the time would come when you would want to change men. It *has* come. You're just like all the others."

"Yes, it *has* come," Johanson cried, "I *can't* be quiet. I can't. And if there are so many others, where are they? because I would join them and work with them. Two or three of us—what we could do! I'm so alone in this. No one cares. Every one goes on as if everything was all right. And I'm not clever. I don't know anything. I've never learnt anything. . . ."

Then he laughed, looking a boy again as he used to look. "Of all men the worst is the one who would teach others when he don't know anything himself. I'm just such a one."

That was true. Ronder felt it. Of all the types of man presented to him the one that he hated most was the noble Propagandist, the He-Man, the Splendid Saviour of Men who dealt in vague words and, thumping his tub, gathered in the shekels of the sentimentalist. Johanson, by all the rules, was becoming such a one. But his ignorance saved him—his ignorance and his honesty. Ronder was sentimental when his brain allowed him to be. He was sentimental now. He felt as though Johanson were a small son of his who was going to a boarding-school for the first time. He always liked children if they were not impertinent to him.

He renewed his offer of taking the chair. Johanson refused it. Then Ronder, ashamed of himself both because he had done so much and had not done more, hurried away.

Johanson sat on alone in his little room, forgetting Ronder, forgetting the lecture, forgetting Seatown; longing, longing, longing for Maude.

These empty hours without work were not good for his strength of control.

Every one knows how swiftly in a small provincial town alarm can raise its head. I remember when I was a small boy in Polchester that a housemaid had her throat cut, and the story rose that Jack the Ripper, weary of London as a background for his crimes, had chosen our little town for a week or two. There was no basis for this tale, but every night for weeks young men went out after dusk with sticks to search for the monster. All the kitchen-maids of Polchester cowered beside their kitchen fires, and all the teeth of all the old women chattered. . . .

So it was now with Harmer John. In the days that preceded the lecture there was no story about him too fantastic to be believed. He was the emissary of a secret society, a hireling of a foreign nation sent with dynamite in his pocket to blow up the Cathedral; he had been seen o' nights talking at street corners with sinister characters; some early riser had seen him creep out of his house at four in the morning, look up and down the street, then cross over to a tree and hide himself there; men and women recalled how in those earlier days of his popularity he had wormed himself into their secrets and extracted their confidences. He was a leading member of a secret society of Jews and his real name was Moses Aaronson. And so on, and so on. . . .

Myself, being at that undergraduate stage of my education when nothing was holy to me, and cynicism my only wear, of course discarded all these stories and laughed openly at my aunt, who was one of the principal purveyors of them. My aunt, a gaunt and bony woman, as superstitious as she was kind-hearted, declared to me: "Why, one of his principal friends, they say, is the chief lunatic of the town, an old man who has been crazy ever since I can remember!" This seemed to me a real argument in favour of his innocence, but to herself it was final proof of his wickedness.

I was interested; there was not much in the Polchester of those days to amuse an idle undergraduate. I looked about me trying to see the fellow. I even went down to Seatown, his favourite haunt, I was told.

But the nearest I got to him was old Looney, whom I discovered watching the tide in the market-place.

I looked at the old man but did not speak to him. I felt a kind of shyness.

There was some talk that the police intended to prohibit the lecture, but that, I imagine, would not at all have suited the plans of Hogg and the rest.

Excitement about it was intense. Every kind of catastrophe was expected. My aunt implored me not to go. I would not have missed it for all the aunts in Christendom. When the evening arrived I found a companion in young Jeremy Cole, older than myself by two years and just finished with Oxford. He was a good, stout fellow, with no nonsense about him. He had spent only a little of this vacation in Polchester, but had picked up quite another version of the story. He knew Longstaffe. Longstaffe had told him that this was a man in a million. But I was sceptical. "One of these Hyde Park orators," I said. "I know them!"

Cole was not a man of many words. "There's no nonsense about Longstaffe," he said. "If he likes a fellow there's something in it."

We set off for the Library together. Our tickets were for reserved seats, but we congratulated ourselves on being twenty minutes before time when we saw the mob that pressed about the Library door. It was evident at a glance that we were going to enjoy a disturbed evening. There were men and boys hanging about there who had certainly come for no other purpose than to make a row.

There were actually three whole live Polchester policemen at the door. Three, and in the same place at the same time. I had not seen so many Polchester police since the '97 Jubilee.

The crowd was at present good-natured. We had not very great trouble in passing through the doors (Cole is a thick-set, stocky fellow, as an Oxford Rugby half needs to be), and then we streamed up the stone staircase with all the Polcastrians. I noticed at once that the crowd was not very respectable, many more men than women, and men of the kind who shout to one another as they go and whistle loudly through sheer vacancy of spirits. It was the kind of crowd you may see any day at a League football match.

I had heard that his first lecture had been honoured by the presence of the Cathedral "Quality." Perhaps to-night they would come in later, because their seats would be reserved, but it was, I think, as I felt these men jostling past me up the stairs that I was conscious of my first twinge of sympathy towards this man Johanson. I felt in the air about me that "crowd" savagery that springs often from nowhere at all, something for which no individual is responsible, but to whose power every individual yields.

Cole felt the same. "There's not going to be much lecture, I fancy," I heard him mutter as we were pushed forward.

However, when we passed the doors into the hall we found everything quiet and decorous enough. The hall was nearly filled. Our seats were towards the back under a narrow overhanging balcony and not far from the door, as I noticed to my relief. If there was a bad row we might want to get away quickly.

Nothing could look more proper. It was one of those commonplace, square, flat-faced rooms with white distempered walls, bad paintings of certain plain and elderly gentlemen, round white gas globes and an empty stage with two chairs, a small table, and a jug of water.

As we seated ourselves I wondered whether there would be room for everybody. The place was already three-quarters filled, and still they were pouring in. We were all pushed very closely together, and Jeremy Cole had to put his arm around the back of my chair to hold on securely.

As the hands of the smug-faced clock turned towards eight o'clock the room seemed to be absolutely packed, and there was a thick gathering of men and boys around the door. Two mild and elderly men who were showing people into their places went constantly to the door and called out that there was no more room inside, but still people pressed forward, and there was a great deal of protesting and noise and laughter.

I saw, as I looked about me, that the impression that I had had coming up the stairs was a true one; not only were the "Upper Ten" not present, the better townspeople were not there either. It was in truth a pretty ruffianly gathering. The majority of those in the room had certainly not paid for their tickets; whether some one else had paid for them was another question.

I remember that as I looked about me two faces detached themselves from the crowd, one familiar and one not. The familiar one was that of Samuel Hogg, and indeed he was standing quite close to me, leaning against one of the grey mottled pillars of the balcony. I fancy that I got the impression as I looked at his fat body and flushed red face that he surveyed the scene as though it were all his handiwork—an air of pride, that is, and self-congratulation, he was smiling pleasantly, and looked most amiable. But he was very quiet, apparently rather far away in his thoughts and not wishing to disturb anybody. He was dressed in a very decent suit of dark blue.

The other face—unfamiliar—was that of a girl. She was sitting some way up the room on the outside of her row, and leaning outwards as though she wished every one to see her. She did not, however, give the impression of showing off but rather of defiance. She was dark and slight, plainly dressed, not pretty but noticeable because of the challenging, fierce, hostile way she looked about her, as though she were saying: "You thought I wouldn't come, but here I am and I don't care who knows it."

One other thing. Just after eight o'clock had struck I heard some one—a man—behind me say: "His girl—you know, Maude Penethen—just gone and fixed herself with young Boultewood. That'll make him pretty mad. Wonder if he knows it."

His companion said something and he answered: "Can't imagine. He's a rotter, that young Boultewood. Always was and always will be."

Soon after the strokes of the clock had died away a door at the back of the stage opened and Johanson came in. There was a demonstration as soon as he appeared, but not a very violent one, some clapping, some booing and hissing. He seemed to pay no attention to that, but came forward quietly to the front of the platform and stood there waiting until it had ceased.

He was a fine man to look at, finer than I had expected. With his breadth and height he had also a magnificent carriage that would have made him noticeable anywhere. But the thing that struck me most strongly was his perfect control. Men give away a great deal of their real personality in that first moment of their appearance on the platform, and you could not doubt when you looked at this man but that there was something very honest and noble about him. At least so it seemed to me.

Then his face was agreeable, simple, direct and, what I had not expected, rather humorous. A boy's sense of fun perhaps, although to-night there was something in his gaze as he looked out over the room indignant and surprised. He stood very well, his hands quietly at his side. He was dressed in a dark suit and wore a black tie.

The demonstration had quickly died down and, as a newspaper man would have written, you could hear a pin drop.

I liked his voice too when he began to speak. There was a marked foreign accent and he used certain words, noticeably prepositions and adverbs, wrongly, but he spoke remarkable English for a foreigner who had been in our country for so short a time, and his voice was strong and carried admirably. I liked the simple way he spoke, without any ostentation and as though he had forgotten himself entirely.

I was prejudiced then at once in the man's favour, but when it came to the things that he said, that was quite another matter.

You must remember that I was at that stage in my young life when I was entirely disillusioned, and thought that I knew everything. Because I was deeply sentimental at heart I was terrified of any point of view that could, even faintly, be called sentimental. In religion I had flung "the Churches" behind me, and if pressed would perhaps have confessed to some very superior sort of Buddhism. I had picked up at Cambridge a jargon of old-world weariness. There were beginning to be heard very faintly at that time the whisperings of the creed that those two clever gentlemen Freud and Jung were afterwards to make so popular—namely, that nothing was anybody's fault, that you were what you were. Also the first signs of that universal pessimism and realism that the war made so inevitable. I was a young jackass, and entirely pleased with myself.

Jeremy Cole was otherwise, having given most of his attention while at Oxford to football and birds. I liked him, but wished him cleverer. When he astonished us all later I couldn't understand it—but I understand it now.

After three minutes my condescending pity for Johanson knew no bounds. It was exactly as though a child of six were expounding life to us; at the end of a quarter of an hour I was surprised to find myself still listening, and I decided that it must be the man's obvious sincerity that held me. At the end of half an hour (when the crash came) I was on the man's side, let him talk what nonsense he pleased.

He had begun, diffidently and with rather a charming shyness, by saying that this lecture was a sequel to one that he had given some while before. In that other he had spoken entirely about care of the body, and had shown them some simple means by which the body could be kept strong and healthy. But that, as he had told them then, was only the beginning of living rightly. He must apologise when he was himself ignorant and inexperienced for making statements that probably to many in the room had been obvious long ago. But he thought that it was always interesting if one man should tell, honestly, to others the things that he had found to be true. He was not trying to force his ideas upon any one, but there might be some who thought as he did, and, if there were, he would be glad to meet them.

He explained then how all his life he had been concerned with physical culture, but that it was only after he came to this town that he discovered that this physical culture was unimportant compared to the other things that it led to.

He had, like other men, often wondered about life, what it meant, what it led to, why human beings were alive at all. The religions that he had encountered had not satisfied him, and he was perpetually dissatisfied with himself because he was so selfish, and only cared for the things that brought himself happiness.

Then he made his first discovery—that this pursuit of selfish happiness was no good, no practical as well as no moral good. Why, one day he asked himself, was he always so preoccupied about making himself happy and so intent upon himself that he was missing all the time the beauty that was on every side of him? If he thought more of the beauty that was outside himself then he would think less of the dissatisfaction in himself. He then gradually saw that this beauty went farther than the beauty of material physical things. It was fine to have a beautiful body, to have it in splendid trim, to feel healthy and strong. That was the first duty of beauty, to keep your body fit. Beyond that was the beauty of all outside things—the beauty of Nature, the beauty of pictures and of music, the beauty of furniture and of houses and of streets. That was the second duty of beauty. But beyond and extending these was the third beauty—the beauty of conduct, of unselfishness, loving-kindness, fidelity and courtesy. And this third world of beauty led to God.

He found then that all the trouble in the world came from two things, from selfishness and fear, and that as soon as one became interested in something, however small, outside oneself, one became less anxious for one's own safety, less eager to challenge others. There might come a time, he thought, when we would be, all of us, so busy with the creation of beauty, whether of beautiful things or of beautiful deeds, that our concern for our own safety would be forgotten altogether.

Our health, our daily bread, these things would be found to be much more simply obtained when we were not always concerned about them. The conduct of life rested, it might be, on certain very simple things like fidelity to our word and thoughtfulness for others. If we made only one beautiful thing, not for ourselves, but because we would pay our debt to beauty, we had done something with our lives.

So far he had gone, and you may imagine what I felt. The triteness, the sentimentality, the cheapness of it! How many millions of times had the world not been greeted with little books, little orations, little sermons proclaiming just such a creed! How many good and stupid women, how many humbugging charlatans, how many idiotic cranks, how many sentimental priests and pastors, had not, in the history of this old, grey, disillusioned world, proclaimed just such platitudes! I looked around me expecting to find in others the exasperation that I was feeling in myself. I did not find it. They were listening. The row that Cole and I had confidently expected was not yet upon us. There they all were, staring in front of them, with wide-open eyes, cow-like, complacent. I had the sense that they were not listening very much but were rather, in some way, mesmerised. Mesmerised by the voice, perhaps, or by the quiet attitude of the man.

This led me to consider more closely the speaker. I had to confess to myself that I liked him. He might be talking sentimental nonsense, but at least he was in utter earnest, speaking only because these things seemed to him to be the most important in the world, and they would not let him be quiet. I listened to him with less intolerance, expecting no longer to hear anything but tiresome platitude, but expecting to find in the man himself a personality that was, far more than I had supposed, worthy of my august attention.

He went on to say that he knew that one answer that would be made to him was that he knew nothing about the social conditions of modern life, that it was very easy to talk about beauty, but that when you had no money and a family to provide for there was not a great deal of time left in which to think about extras. That when you were hungry or saw those you loved hungry, you thought about your stomach, not about beauty. To that he answered that there were very many, even in this little town of Polchester, whose conditions were easy enough to allow them to create beauty in the lives of those who were less fortunate. The creation of beauty could go on in any place. Something was for ever being created every moment of the day. Creation was always at work, and if it was not beauty that was being created then it was ugliness. Every word of slander or unkindness about another was creating more ugliness, every hypocritical condemnation of some one for a fault when we were in our own private lives, as we all well knew, so guilty, was an act of ugliness.

Every insanitary room, every house insecure to the wind and rain that we allowed to stand, was a work of ugliness.

He had come to Polchester, loving it at his first sight of it, feeling that here was his home. What had he found here?

He paused. A stir, like a little wind, ran through the room. What had he found? He had found hypocrisy, evil-speaking, slander, malice, and the worst slum in Europe.

I caught my breath at that. I knew that the moment had arrived. I looked again hurriedly about me and I saw still, in most faces, that same staring gaze as of a crowd mesmerised.

But a voice, detached, like a stone flung through the ceiling, cracked the silence.

"Yah! You and yer beauty. What about yer mistress up to St. Paul's?"

The silence, although cracked, held. Johanson's voice came back clearly and without a falter:

"My love for this town—"

They were the last words we heard. Chaos was upon us. Look back as earnestly as I may it is chaos that I see. I can remember that shouting and screaming of voices, fragmentary sentences: "Go back to your own bloody country! We don't want you. Oo are you preaching at? Oo crawled in at the Rec'try winder? Oo kissed two girls at once? What about yer own dirty be'aviour?" And this rhyme:
Harmer John! Harmer John!
Went to bed with his trousies on;
Kissed the girls and made 'em cry;
Maudie, Mary, pudding and pie!
But it was not possible to hear anything distinctly. The more respectable part of the audience, seeing that riot was truly upon them at last, fled for the doors. The less respectable, in a shouting, bellowing mob, pushed for the platform.

Things—vegetables, rotten eggs, bad fish—were hurtling through the air; men and boys were scrambling down from the balcony, sliding the pillars.

Cole caught my arm.

"Come on," he said. "They'll do him in if some one doesn't stop them."

I looked across the room and saw that he was standing quietly and without any alarm on the middle of the platform. Men, shouting and waving their arms, were scrambling up towards him. As, tumbling over chairs, we reached the front of the hall some heavy fellow made a lurch at him. He moved back, still without any sign of alarm, towards the wall, and as Cole and I clambered on to the stage, we saw him struggling there, several men and boys striking at him and dragging at his knees.

I forget then exactly what occurred. We rushed forward, and soon there was a glorious mêlée. Cole was no mild antagonist, and I think that the mob very soon retreated. But I know that my dominant impression was of Johanson, his collar and shirt torn open, being extremely quiet and doing little more than keep his assailants back. I had the notion that with one thrust of his arm he could have scattered them all to the Hebrides.

In any case, in another moment we found ourselves, the three of us, tumbling towards the door at the back of the stage and then, surprisingly, alone, breathless, in the cool current of air that a dark passage provided.

We could not see very clearly, but I fancied that he smiled and said:

"Thank you. I don't hope you're damaged at all."

He shook our hands, I think. Then, very quietly, was gone.

BOOK III

HOW HE LEFT US
<hr size=2 width="100%" align=center>

CHAPTER I

ALONE

MRS. BOND was out early one morning. Awaking pleasantly after the healthiest of sleeps, she had seen, as it were in a vision, that the sleeves of the new dress would never do. They would *never* do. And how could it be that she had *not* seen that last night. She had considered the sleeves while undressing and they had seemed to her exactly the thing. And now this morning ... Miss Nightingale, the little dressmaker just below St. Paul's Church, was both cheap and obliging, so obliging, indeed, that she encouraged Mrs. Bond to bully her, and positively enjoyed being trampled upon.

Cheap and obliging, yes, but so hardworking that before you knew where you were those sleeves would be finished, and then what a business of altering and altering. Sleeves were important in 1907.

So there was nothing for it but to hurry through breakfast and go down and stop her. So tiresome, but it was Mrs. Bond's duty to Polchester that she should be properly dressed, and for her duty she would do anything.

It was a lovely September morning and Mrs. Bond, having enjoyed a pleasant chatty time during the last week or two and having most amiably been as kind as possible to half a dozen reputations, was in excellent spirits. The sun shone upon everything, and Mrs. Bond could not help but think that she was rather like the sun beaming upon Polchester with the rays of her happiness and talent, and what Polchester would do without her Mrs. Bond, modest though she was, found it impossible to imagine. Miss Nightingale also found it impossible to imagine, and said so, which was noble of her, considering how little Mrs. Bond paid her, and how much work she demanded of her.

She scolded her now about the sleeves, and explained to her that she would never to be able to retain the custom of the best people in Polchester unless she kept her eyes open, and Miss Nightingale, although this alteration in the sleeves was precisely the one that a week ago she had recommended, entirely agreed with her.

After this had been most satisfactorily settled, and Miss Nightingale, who had sat up all night to finish a dress in time, had sighed and smiled and sighed, and then sat down to the sleeves, Mrs. Bond greeted, as one sovereign another, the sun again.

Slowly she took her way up the hill. One did not hurry on so lovely a morning. It was then that she saw a strange sight. Positively shining in the sun was a seat, and this seat was newly painted a dazzling white. So new was the paint that tied to the corner of the seat was a notice "WET PAINT" written in a large and sprawling hand.

Mrs. Bond had never noticed this seat before (and, indeed, she was not often in this low part of the town). Nor would she have noticed it now had it not been for the sun. From no spirit of vulgar curiosity, but rather because she was in a way Polchester's guardian and must be aware of everything, she crossed the street and examined the seat. Then she saw something truly astonishing!

Behind the seat and under the shadow of a spreading tree was a little fountain, the prettiest little fountain ever!

Surely it was new. Mrs. Bond had never seen it before, she had never before noticed this corner with its charming view over the lower town, the river and the fields. Avoiding very carefully the fresh paint, she bent forward. Here was a beautiful thing! With her continental taste she could most truly appreciate it. A little improper, perhaps (the Satyr wore no fig leaf) but here too her continental taste helped her. The delicate symmetry of its gentle curves, the running groups of figures (gods and goddesses, Bacchus and his crew, Paris and the apple, what were they?), the carving of vine leaves and fruits and flowers, how delicious and classical! And how nobly it stood, raising its central figure so daintily and with such dignity! Then, peering more closely, she saw a date. 1735. 1735! All those years and she had never seen it until now. Nor any one else. No one had ever spoken about it.

She stayed for a moment, losing, for the briefest instant, her consciousness of herself, Louisa Bond, her consciousness of her position, her wit and talent, her kindliness and good-humour.

With a little breath of a sigh she moved away. Here was something for her to speak about! She was the first, positively the first! And with that up swept her consciousness again. She was her normal self, thank God, once more.

On that same morning Johanson spent half an hour with Reuben Fletch in his office. Very quiet there. Very friendly and very cold.

Johanson was there in that neat, stern and unaccommodating room exactly half an hour. He was very uncomfortable. He always hated to ask for anything, and especially did he hate to ask Fletch for anything.

And yet he must. He must ask whether the payment of the next instalment for the new rooms might be postponed for a little. Or possibly they might be let to some one else. The business that he was doing just at this moment did not quite justify him . . .

How he hated it! And yet Fletch was, as he had always been to him, very kind, speaking in his low voice, smiling often, conveying no hint that he had ever heard that Johanson was a failure, or was conscious at all of the terrible scandal of the recent lecture.

But no one in Polchester was able to make Johanson feel so absolutely that he was both a foreigner and a fool. He was both these things—he knew it well. But he did not want Fletch to tell him.

Fletch, smiling a little sadly, shook his head.

"You see, Mr. Johanson" (he was one of the people in Polchester who knew Johanson's name exactly), "those rooms are an awkward size. A little difficult. And, of course, you are liable. No getting away from that, I am afraid. I fancied that you were a little precipitate, but I didn't like to say anything. It was not my place. We all make mistakes, of course."

Silence followed. Fletch never said anything when there was nothing to say. Johanson stood in the middle of the room without moving. Yes, he was a fool. He saw it in Fletch's eyes, and he saw it also in the eyes of the young clerk who entered at that moment.

"Well, you shall let me know if anything—"

"Why, of course I'll let you know, Mr. Johanson."

"Good-day."

"Good-day, Mr. Johanson."

Later it was a wet afternoon, wet with a thin driving rain. Autumn had come in and you knew that in the woods the trees were shaking their heads and shivering, aware that they were soon to lose their leaves. The lamps were blurred and people were not visible, only umbrellas.

As he entered his room, closing his door behind him, he was aware, as though it were personified for him by the actual presence of a dark and silent stranger, that the worst and most terrible hour of his life was with him.

He had known few bad hours although things had often not gone well with him, and it was because of this, perhaps, that he had kept until now so much of the boy's temperament. But on this dark and shivery afternoon in this desolate room he was a boy no longer.

There are states of the soul—dark, lonely, suspicious states—that no boy can know. Johanson was aware that such a state stood now behind his chair. He sat down at the table, took some papers that had to do with his business, set them before him and tried to study them. He knew that he must once again close his office and this time perhaps permanently, but that did not touch him. He knew that beyond the rain-starred window the little fountain was standing, but that did not touch him. He knew that below the fountain was Seatown, miserable enough on this wet evening, the place that had of late become with him an obsession, but that did not touch him.

He saw none of these things. He saw only himself facing him at the other end of the table. He saw himself as a fool and as a failure, a complete and total failure.

He was not as a rule a man who thought about himself, and all the events of the last months had been driving him towards one end and one end only, that he should forget himself altogether and lose himself in other greater things.

But now he saw only himself, himself Hjalmar Johanson, the fool, the foreigner, the failure.

This was the first thing that hurt him, that he felt himself now a foreigner in this little town that had seemed only a few short months ago to be his true home. He had loved it from the moment that he had entered it, and it had seemed at once to respond to his love. It had something so beautiful, so touching and so personal about it that it had appeared to him as though it must have been meant for him. Now it had abruptly been taken away from him. It was not only because the people here who had before been so friendly were now so hostile. He had known, on that day when he had visited Wistons, that the choice that he had made then would estrange them from him. The scandal of the last lecture had not distressed him; he had felt after it triumph because he had been honest with himself and had tried to say what he thought was true.

No, it was the town itself that had withdrawn: the streets were foreign now, the houses frowned on him, and the stones of the market-place were hard to his feet. What right had he, the town might say, to come here, a foreigner, and patronise it with his notions, his ignorant childish notions.

He told Longstaffe afterwards that he fancied that the rain as it lashed the window was carrying the message of the town's scorn and dislike to his ears.

Then, behind the town, he saw Maude. Now he lowered his head and groaned aloud. He could see how foolish, yes, and how ignorant and how selfish he had been. He had talked to her so much of liberty and that they must both be free. But what freedom had he allowed her? Had he not resented every friendship that she had made? Had he not driven her into the arms of the Boultewoods and Hogg and the rest? Could he not have found some way easier for her than his insistence on her obedience and acquiescence in his ideas? When they had been engaged for only a few weeks he had begun to tell her what she must do and what she must not do. Was that his sense of liberty? And his selfishness! He had thought of her, yes, but only that she might be with him and that he might see her and hear her laugh and watch her smile!

Just before entering the hall on the night of his lecture some man near the door (he had not seen his face) had come up to him and whispered: "Your Miss Penethen's engaged to young Boultewood." All through the evening those words had whispered and whispered. Young Boultewood! A miserable ne'er-do-well with whom she could never be happy.

Stung with this thought, he paced his room, walking fast, his head down. Oh! he must persuade her! He must show her! He must do something!

He sat down again and quickly wrote to her. (This letter was found afterwards in the drawer of this same table.)

DEAR MAUDE—You shal not want to here of me but I beg you becaus we was friends before and hav butiful memorys to read this littel letter. I am not spelling this very wel becaus I am writing it fas becaus of my feelings but I do beg you just to read it and think of what I say.

I hav been told that you hav engaged yourself to mary young Mr. Boultewood and I think that perhaps you hav done this becaus you are angry with me and not becaus you luv him. Dear Maude I don't hope you shal do this when you don't luv him truely. Place me right out of youre mind and don't say I shal do this becaus I hate anuther man but only do it if you luv him. Perhaps I am wrong and you do luv him then Maude I have no rite to say a word but if it is becaus you hate me don't do it Maude don't do it. You hav all your life to come and I am not important enuff for you to spoil your life becaus of me. Think not of me but of yourself Maude.

But when he had finished this letter he felt in a greater despair than before. What influence could he have over her now? What influence could he hope to have? He had no right, and when she read this letter she would only be angry and more obstinate than before in her purpose.

He had lost her, but he thought that he could bear that, if he had not also the belief that he had ruined her.

And for what? For the prosecution of some vague, empty ideal that would be childish to any other man than he. Why could he not have waited quietly in the town, doing his honest work, winning the approval of all good men, minding his own affairs? Why must he resent so intensely that Ronder and others, men older than he, and wise in the ways of this country, should show him what he should do, and should order his steps a little? Was it not the last arrogance for him to resent their advice and think that he knew better than they? His evening with Wistons, that had seemed to him at the time to involve a genuine struggle of the soul, now, in retrospect, appeared to be only the struggle of his self-will and conceit for liberty.

His continual assertion of his friendship for the Longstaffes appeared to him now a mockery. What had come of that? What had he done but to involve them, in further and more public scandal? Why, he had not seen them during the last weeks. It was true that he had kept away from them after the fight in Seatown, and the fiasco of the lecture, out of a kind of delicacy, and they had stayed away from him, he supposed, for something of the same reason, but how ironical that he should have wrecked all his life with Maude for the sake of people whom he never saw!

And Tom Longstaffe! Tom whom he loved more than any one in the world after Maude (and more deeply than Maude in certain spiritual ways), Tom who was more than a brother, who had seemed part of himself, who had shared his heart with him, had not come near him. And why should he? Was not Tom's first duty to his daughter and Billy? His daughter had been involved already enough with this foreigner! That was how Tom must look at him in spite of all the devotion that they had, most truly, felt the one for the other. It was not possible, it might be, to have a real friendship between men of different nationalities. Their points of view must differ so deeply. And then Tom had his religion. But it had seemed for a time as though he and Tom had had their hands upon the very souls of one another.

Now, strangely, it was the thought of Tom Longstaffe and not of Maude that drove the sharpest agony into his spirit. It was dark now, but he did not care nor heed. He walked swiftly up and down the room thinking only of Tom, of their first meeting in the mist outside the Cathedral, of the first real talk they had had when they had smashed through their shyness, of the day when they had walked up to the football match together, of the afternoon of Mary's return, of fun with Billy and of evenings alone in Tom's study when they had said very little but had felt their love for one another like a tight wire holding them together. That had been friendship real enough and true enough while it lasted, but it had not lasted because Johanson had not been worthy of it, because he had been thinking only of himself and of his ideas and wants and ambitions. What feeling had he really given to Tom, how much had he really considered Tom's work and Tom's religious ideals and Tom's love for his daughter?

He sat down at the table again, weighed down with self-reproach and loneliness. He was truly alone; nothing now remained—his ideals, his dream, his work, his love, his friendship, everything was gone for him.

I do not know how long he sat on there in the dark, the rain always driving against the window and his only company, but at last the worst temptation of all came to him.

He seemed to be no longer himself. Another soul sat darkly in his body, and to this soul came the thought of putting an end to everything. With that thought came a sense of great relief, as of a crisis achieved and a question answered.

He got up and lit two candles. Then he crossed to the old worn sofa that was against the wall, and under the sofa was his old, shabby, black bag. He dragged this out and like a man who is moving in a dream felt deep in it and, under shirts and collars, found an old revolver that he had had with him ever since the old Stockholm days.

He took it out and fingered it under the candlelight. There was one shot in it. He sat down at the table, drew the candles towards him, placed the revolver between them and leaned his head on his hands, staring in front of him.

He did not think any longer. He seemed to be already dead and the room smelt strangely empty. Several times he picked up the revolver and looked at it and laid it down again. A slight movement was all that was needed. It seemed to him that he was sinking through the earth, and that when he reached a certain depth he would crash with a bump, and that with that bump all would be over.

He was looking at the revolver so intently that he did not hear the opening of the door.

Some one sat at the table beside him, but he did not look to see who it was.

He and the stranger sat together without speaking.

The stranger put out his hand and took the revolver.

The stranger was Tom Longstaffe.

His first feeling was one of irritation, and also of unreality and melodrama. Some one had come in and prevented him just as they always came in in plays and stories—in what is called "the nick of time."

His next sensation was one of extreme weariness. He could just have laid his head on his arms there where he sat and dropped off to sleep. But at last he said: "Well, Tom."

"Well, Johnnie. I thought I'd come and see how you were getting along."

He had not put the revolver away, but had laid it on the table on the side of him away from Johanson.

Johanson looked up and felt a sharp warm comfort at seeing Tom Longstaffe sitting there just as he used to be in his black coat and with his brown, rough face and kindly wrinkled eyes. He was touched oddly by the rough, brown hands with the stumpy fingers laid out there on the table. He was dragging himself up, up, up from that deep place beneath the ground where he had been and it took a long time.

They were silent for a little, then Longstaffe said:

"I tell you what. Do you know what time it is? It's supper time. I'm hungry. Have you got anything to eat?"

That "I tell you what" was so like the old Tom that it pulled Johanson up a long way from under the ground. He was almost all the way up now.

"I don't know," Johanson said slowly, "I hadn't thought about eating."

"Well, I had," Longstaffe said, laughing, "and I'm hungry, I can tell you. I had a service at seven, and I came straight down."

"If you're hungry—" Johanson said, rising. He moved about the room at first blindly, as though he did not know where he would go next. Longstaffe did not watch him, but went on talking, talking about anything. Little foolish nothings. What somebody had said about the weather, what the church looked like now there was the new reredos. Then he began about Billy, and soon there was more than enough for him to say. Billy had done so many amusing things. Billy was like a piece of quicksilver; why, do you know what Billy only the other day . . .

Slowly Johanson, stumbling about the room in the candlelight, came right to the surface. He did not hear what Longstaffe was saying, but it was comforting to hear his funny jumping voice again. Oh! yes, it was! He realised the room now and knew what he must do. He must give Longstaffe some food. He laid the cloth on the table, got out the cheese and the bread and the butter, lit the fire and put the kettle on. He had a tin of corned beef. He opened it.

Turning to Longstaffe, he said:

"What time is it?"

"Half-past nine."

Half-past nine! And he had been in that room ever since four o'clock.

"It's a long time, Tom," he said at last. "We haven't seen one another. I've missed our meeting."

Longstaffe looked him directly in the eyes. "We thought you'd had enough trouble through knowing our family. We thought you'd be up to see us when you wanted to see us. I've waited and waited for you to come. I couldn't wait any longer."

Johanson said nothing to that. The kettle was boiling, so the tea was made and they sat down to the table. Johanson ate very little, but Longstaffe ate a great deal. He seemed truly hungry. He went on talking, too, gaily about the things he had been doing, the people he had been seeing, about Mary and Billy.

Then, without warning, Johanson broke out:

"Tom, if you shouldn't have come to-night . . . It's been terrible. I've been seeing myself as I truly am. Yes, as I truly am. I have been thinking myself fine and honest and I'm not, Tom, I'm bad—truly bad. What have I been here but selfish and thinking only of my ways, and what I should do here? And I have been telling every one what they should do. Canon Ronder, he's been so good to me, and what did I do? I went to him telling him he was all wrong and I were all right. I don't hope you know, Tom, all the things I've said to people. That Mrs. Bond, she isn't much, but what right had I to tell her her boy was no good. She loves her boy, don't she, the same way as I love you, Tom? What should I do when some one comes and tells me you're no good? I've just been stuck up on myself and the fine things I'll do for this town, and what's it all come to? A foreigner knowing nothing—that's what I am. I'm ashamed. I have no right . . ."

"No," said Tom quietly, lighting his pipe. "You were all right. You had an idea. You weren't pushing your theories for yourself, but because of your idea. Your idea wouldn't let you alone. And your idea is fine. Perhaps you're a little simple yet, Johnnie. You came to this town thinking it was all Paradise and it wasn't. No place on earth is. If any place on earth was we'd all go to it, and we aren't ready for Paradise just yet. And you're a little simple about people too. They are more mixed than you think them, not bad altogether, nor good altogether, but a bit of both. You've rushed in too quickly, maybe, wanting to put everything right at once. But I don't know. If you waited you'd lose the force of your idea perhaps and become just like the rest of us. It's hard to say. I've been angry myself the way they've treated Mary, but why should I be? We all have to protect ourselves. We none of us are safe. Life's dangerous all the time. And so we hit out at one another all the time, loving one another really maybe."

But Johanson would say no more. They sat opposite to one another, one on either side of the fire-place, and Tom talked. Johanson looked at him with an odd, hungry look, as though he could not have enough of his plain face and his wrinkled eyes.

Tom talked and talked. The fire died. The room was cold. He got up at last, knocking out his pipe.

Johanson rose also, still not taking his eyes from Longstaffe's face. "Good night, then," he said. "It's been kind of you coming."

Holding his hand, Longstaffe hesitated. His face flushed. He looked up to Johanson, who towered above him.

"I tell you what," he said, "do you know—if you don't mind—I'd like to stop here to-night."

"Stop here?"

"Yes. Sleep here."

"But where will you sleep?"

"On that sofa. It's just the length. Have you got a blanket and a pair of pyjamas?"

"Oh! yes. Of course." Then Johanson added, with a sigh, "Oh! I'd like you to stop!"

"I'll look funny in your pyjamas!" They both laughed.

Johanson found the pyjamas and the blanket.

When Johanson was almost undressed Longstaffe said: "Aren't you going to do your exercises? You always do, don't you?"

"Yes," said Johanson, "I forgot." Stripped, under the candlelight, he did his exercises.

Longstaffe, sitting on the sofa, his legs lost in Johanson's pyjamas, watched with eager admiration.

"I say, you're fitter than ever! Wonderful! I wish I could keep my body like that!"

Johanson paused, pleased.

"Am I truly all right still? Not fat?"

"Fat! I should think not! Not an ounce of fat anywhere. Touch your toes again. That's something like!"

"Ever seen me do this?" Johanson raised himself on his toes, raised his arms, his body stiff as though of shining metal. "I can stay like that for ever so long."

The candles guttered, throwing fantastic shadows.

Soon Johanson was in bed and Longstaffe on his sofa, the room dark.

"I say, Tom." Johanson's voice came. "I was terrible lonely to-day. I'm glad you came. Oh! I'm glad you came!"

"You won't be lonely any more, will you?"

"No, I shan't be."

"Good night, old man."

"Good night, Tom."

CHAPTER II

THE WATCHERS

I SUPPOSE that any boy who has been living, during his early and impressionable years, in a Cathedral town acquires two things—a sense of romance and a sense of the past, and these two things are only one and the same thing for some people. M. Proust will tell you what a historical church can do for an imaginative child.

But I am not at all sure that for young Polcastrians the spirit of the town was not more potent than the spirit of the church. That Rock to which the town clung with all its toes, that mysterious country flowing ever away to yet more mysterious seas, that rich and ancient blood that is the fine inheritance of the Glebeshire native, those fights of armoured men up and down the paths of the rocky hill, the beacon flaring from the higher peak, the lights streaming from the Cathedral doors as they opened to admit that sombre procession of silent monks and priests—these things were not of yesterday but of to-day, yes, and to-morrow, too.

Many a time I have heard a Glebeshire man tell his tale truthfully and soberly enough, and then be accused of melodrama by his hearers. "Such things," they murmur, "don't occur in Cathedral towns." But it is not the event that is melodramatic (and that is a poor word for a fine thing), but the Glebeshire man's vision of it. He can no more not see it in a romantic way, poor fellow, than help breathing. Your modern realism is of no use to him. Why, of how ordinary a kind was the decline and fall of poor Brandon in our town. How many times in one day's paper will you see just such a collapse recorded, but for all of us, happening against such a background as our Cathedral, it seemed to involve the contest of immortal forces. "There's more in our town than meets the mortal eye," I heard old Cassidy murmur once, and many of us would agree with him.

I have noticed often enough with most of us who belong to Polchester and Glebeshire that time seems to have no boundaries—past, present, and future scarcely exist for some of us, and confused and dreamy we sometimes are. Young Cole, who is built, physically at any rate, on a stocky pattern, has told me that when he was a tiny fellow he saw the Black Bishop in the Cathedral. He has no doubt of it at all, nor does it surprise him that it should have been so. There are no ghosts with us. Physical death does not divide. Like us or no, that is the way we are.

It was so now in all the town's chatter about Harmer John. Every one was watching to see what would happen, but not only were we—Ronder, Mrs. Bond, old Ryle, anybody you please—the watchers, there were others, thousands and thousands of them, who were spectators too.

I was very conscious of this when one day I went to take a cup of tea with an old lady who had been often kind to me, one of the leading characters in our town, Mrs. Combermere. She was, of course, not so very old, but to a boy of my age, who had heard of her as a powerful figure in his very earliest days, she seemed as old as time. She was one of the principal figures in our town, a downright, masculine lady, a widow who lived with her dogs and her Tory ideas, and thought both the dogs and the ideas the best of their kind.

She had inhabited the same little house in the Precincts for I do not know how many years, and she thought that the best of its kind also.

She was very faithful to old friends and did not care, as a rule, for newcomers. Mrs. Bond, for instance, she abominated. I could be pretty sure of my company, and, entering the little old-fashioned candle-lit room, I found that my expectations were justified. Her house was never very tidy, and many things that seemed to my modern eyes unnecessary accumulated, but I expect that she was about her possessions as she was about her friends. When she had acquired them she liked to keep them. Herself seemed to occupy most of the space. She was square and solid, and had dressed in the same fashion ever since any one could remember. She wore stiff, white collars, short skirts, a shining, black belt at her waist, and her dark hair was brushed straight back from her forehead. She had not even now a single grey hair, and she smoked large, fat cigarettes and had been doing so for twenty years.

I expected to find Ellen Stiles, Miss Dobell and old Doctor Puddifoot, and those were precisely the people I did find. Old Doctor Puddifoot had brought into the world many of my generation; now he must be getting on for eighty, and had retired from practice, living only for golf and port. Ellen Stiles was the Mrs. Bond of an earlier generation, and yet that is an unkind description because in *her* gossip malice had never been intended. She liked to see the proud pulled down from their high places, but also she liked to see the lowly exalted, and often in her day had assisted in exalting them. But her day now was over. She was simply an untidy, forlorn and shabby old maid.

When I had been given my chair and my cup of tea the conversation that I had interrupted continued as though I did not exist. Young people were not unduly flattered in the Polchester of 1907.

Nevertheless, I was unexpectedly called upon. "But you were there," Mrs. Combermere cried, turning round upon me sharply as though I had committed a crime. "Tell us about it."

"Tell you about what?" I asked.

"The terrible lecture and Harmer John. I hear that you and the Cole boy saved him from being torn to pieces."

I answered lamely enough. For some queer reason I didn't want to speak about it. Why? I don't know. I wasn't ashamed of myself, and I wasn't ashamed of Harmer John either. But I didn't want to talk about it.

"What did he say? What made every one so angry? Was it all arranged from the beginning?"

"Of course it was all arranged," Ellen Stiles broke in. "That horrible Samuel Hogg. He bought all the tickets and packed the place. That poor man! I think it's a shame the way the town's treated him."

"You would!" Mrs. Combermere answered. "You're as sentimental as ever you were, Ellen, and so you'll be to the end. The point is that the man proposed pulling the town down, and certain people didn't welcome the idea."

"No," I said, "that wasn't quite the fact. What he'd said—" I paused. What *had* he said? I wasn't sure. I broke out: "He's a jolly fine man!"

Strangely enough they agreed to that, and Mrs. Combermere came out in her strange, grumpy voice: "Of course he's a fine man—but he's a foreigner and a simpleton. He should have known that English people have no imagination."

Puddifoot, who had been lying back, stomach protruding, eyes half-closed, in his chair, muttered:

"Went to his first lecture. Finest man to look at I've ever seen. Why couldn't he stick to that instead of wanting to interfere with everybody?"

But Mrs. Combermere returned to me again. "But you—you've told us nothing. Come on. Speak up. Fine man, yes—but what more?"

I was held by the stupidest inhibition. I blushed and stammered like a baby. At last I got out something; I hadn't thought that he'd said anything to offend anybody, but that of course they were all waiting to be offended; they had come there intending to make a row. He talked for a long time, though, before they interrupted—

"Well, what did he say during that time?" Mrs. Combermere broke in impatiently. "That's exactly what I want to get at and nobody can tell me."

I couldn't tell her either. He certainly hadn't said anything that was very new, only that beauty was of three kinds, the brain, the heart and the soul, and that we ought to be creating it instead of always thinking of ourselves. And that we worried too much whether we were happy or no and so missed the beauty that was all around us. That our bodies ought to be beautiful and our surroundings ought to be beautiful and our lives ought to be beautiful and . . . and . . . as the platitudes came stammering out of me I felt increasingly foolish. I ended: "Oh! it wasn't what he said. He spoke like a baby, all the old things, and it was exactly as though they were so startlingly new to him that they must be new to every one else too. I laughed at him at first, but you couldn't help liking him and then—when they went for him—the odds were too damned unfair!"

"I do think," said Ellen Stiles, nodding her head, "that it's most true what he said. We ought to think more of others, certainly, and—"

"Oh! shut up, Ellen!" Mrs. Combermere interrupted most rudely. "The infant here is right. There isn't anything in what he says—anything new at least. The point is that he believes it, that he's got an idea that's more to him than his happiness or personal safety. That's what's affected us all. That's why we're all frightened of him, because he's making us all uncomfortable, because we *know* we're wrong and slack and self-satisfied and greedy. Don't I know it about myself? Didn't I start life with fine ideas, and where are they all gone to? Don't

I know that if I got up to-morrow morning with the resolve to think less of myself and more of other people, determined to grumble less, to help to rid the town of the slums, to give my two maids better bedrooms, to go up to London once a year to see a picture gallery and hear some music (I used to care for those things once), don't I *know* that I could do all these things and that life would be better worth living if I did? But I'm set, hard and fast, and the very thought of that man going round disturbing the place is irritating! Ever read *The Heir of Redclyffe*, Ellen?"

"When I was a girl," said Miss Stiles, "and cried myself sick over somebody's deathbed."

"It's that sort of priggish, moral, uplifting effect this man's having on all of us. But he isn't a prig, so far as I can see. He doesn't want to make a soul in the town better. He's just got a notion, and his notion won't let him rest. After all, there *is* something in it. If only a few of us stopped quarrelling and backbiting and seeing only the mean side of our neighbours and—No, it's no good." She stamped with both feet on the ground. "I'm too old to change either myself or other people."

"What's this," old Puddifoot drawled out, "that Mrs. Bond's got hold of? About a fountain or something there behind St. Paul's. Been there for years, and he dug it up and stuck it together. Pretty thing, she tells me. Funny idea for a man to have. He's a bit cracked, of course. Trained his body too hard and gone in the top story."

"Yes, that's very English of you, Charles," said Mrs. Combermere, "because a man finds something beautiful and troubles about it you say he's mad. I must go down and have a look at the thing. And where is the man now, anyway? They say he's living in Seatown and is likely to be murdered at any minute."

"I don't know where he's living," said Ellen Stiles eagerly, "but I do know that the police are talking of asking him to leave the town lest there should be any disturbance. The Seatown people are just furious with him for saying that their houses ought to be pulled down, although they are really in a shocking state, I believe, and you'd have thought they'd be grateful to him for bothering. But not at all. They can't say anything bad enough about him, and I'm sure there's going to be trouble, and then what a scandal there'll be!"

"It's most peculiar," said Mrs. Combermere slowly. "There have been plenty of foreigners in this town before, but I can't remember anybody who has affected everybody in the way this man has done. The truth is he's managed to put his finger on one or two things that nobody's quite comfortable about. It's all very well to say that we're proud of this place and there's nothing the matter with it, but as a matter of fact we all know that there's plenty the matter with it, only we're all too lazy or too frightened to bother."

"All the same," said Ellen Stiles, changing her side now that Polchester was down and Harmer John was up, "I don't quite see why *he* should come and tell us all our business. What does he know about us or England? Why should he push Mary Longstaffe in our faces? Why should he be so rude to Canon

Ronder and Mrs. Bond and the others? Why, he said the most dreadful things to Mrs. Bond about her boys!"

"Not half as dreadful as I'd say if you gave me a chance," Mrs. Combermere interrupted. "Of course he says rude things. If you have an idea in your head that won't let you alone, you feel that there isn't a moment to be lost. You *have* to speak about it to everybody and you haven't time to think whether you're rude or no. I had an idea once about giving dogs garlic in their food and I couldn't rest for a minute. I had to tell every one. Besides, who cares whether old Ronder's feelings are hurt—greedy, self-centred tub of a man. Why—!"

At that moment, I remember, the maid announced Canon Ronder. There was, of course, not the slightest sign of confusion written anywhere on Mrs. Combermere. She did not greet Ronder very warmly. He knew her well enough by now and did not, I suppose, expect any great cordiality. I think that it was during this summer that he began to deteriorate. You may connect it with Johanson or not, as you please. Movements, men, circumstances, come strangely together in life, and our sins, our merits, our braveries and our indifferences seem to wait as though with predetermined knowledge for the moment of their fulfilment.

You can suggest, if you like, that Johanson was Ronder's chance deliberately offered to him, and he missed it. Or you can shrug your shoulders and deny that the two men had any real contact. I only know that it was just at this time that Ronder's deterioration became obvious to everybody. He was losing touch with himself, some one said. And some one else said that he liked his food better than his prayers. He was certainly lazy now and began to be less neat in his dress and careless about his sermons. He was also less amiable than he used to be, they said, and you never knew where you were with him. He didn't know, I fancy, where he was with himself.

On this very afternoon I noticed, I remember, that he seemed uncomfortable. It may have been that he knew that we had been talking about him before he came in.

The conversation flagged and died. Then Ellen Stiles, getting up to go, remarked:

"I shall go down and see that little fountain. It's a pretty idea, I think. I expect there are all sorts of things in this town that no one knows about."

"Fountain? What fountain?" asked Ronder, peering up through his glasses.

"Oh! didn't you know?" Ellen Stiles was quite stirred. "Mrs. Bond says that this man Johanson, whom everybody's talking about, found an old fountain somewhere, dug it up, cleaned it and stuck it together. It's very pretty, they say."

The effect of this on Ronder was odd.

He sprang to his feet, nearly upsetting his cup of tea.

"We've had enough of that man," he cried, "disturbing the town and all law and order. He's got to go, and the sooner the better. I spoke to Griffiths about it yesterday. He's nothing but a charlatan of the worst kind. There seemed to be something genuine in him at first, but he's nothing more than a vulgar tub-thumper. He refused all my advice, wouldn't listen to my warnings, wouldn't listen to anybody, and now, if some one doesn't get him out of the place, there'll be some disastrous riot. But I won't be held responsible. No, I won't! His blood will be on his own head. He was warned often enough."

"But no one will dream of holding you responsible. What have you to do with it?" Mrs. Combermere asked sharply.

Canon Ronder didn't answer. He sat down again. Very odd he looked, flushed and bewildered. So odd that I thought that the only decent thing was to leave, and leave I did.

I went out into the dusky town in a curious mind. When I was a child I read a book that had a very odd effect upon me—Mrs. Oliphant's *A Beleaguered City*. It is, I think, as forgotten to-day as all the other books by that fine and plucky lady. I cannot myself very clearly recall it, but as I recollect it had for its theme the invasion of a certain town by the spirits of the departed. These returning citizens crowded the streets, pressed in upon the doors, peered from the windows and invaded the churches, with what dramatic effect or to fulfil what purpose I cannot remember.

Now as I came out of Mrs. Combermere's door into the deserted Precincts that old book drove itself upon my mind. I doubtless then, being in the early twenties and not very far from my childhood, remembered the story clearly enough. It may have been responsible for my mood, but, however that may be, I remember that I stood upon Mrs. Combermere's threshold hesitating. It was one of those September evenings when autumn mists seem to be on some secret purpose, as though they shrouded the earth with their vapours that they might the better, undisturbed, go about their purpose of preparing the way for winter. The long stretch of the Cathedral Green was faintly grey, the row of old houses on the Precincts' further side showed here a gable, there a rough chimney, here a square of shrouded light, here a roof faintly glimmering under the prophecy of an early moon.

The Cathedral itself towered up gigantic above the pattern of grey shadow. It was dark like ebony and the buttresses went flying off into the mist as though they were the limbs of some gigantic beast straining muscles in some urgent progress.

When I walked on to the path that bordered the Green I felt as though I were pressed in upon by a crowd of figures. I was not conscious of any movement save my own, but, to my romantic imagination, it was as though a thickly packed crowd of persons was waiting there for some coming event. Emerging from the small heated room of Mrs. Combermere's tea-party, I should have felt chilled and drawn my overcoat closer about me, but rather, as I remember it at this flight of time, I was conscious that the atmosphere was warm and close and thick. To persons of a clear and ordered and realistic brain such impressions are, of course, mere folly, but to many of us they do occur, and I should be failing in my purpose if I did not record what I felt.

I crossed the Green, and it seemed to me that I was truly elbowing my way as I went. I was not frightened or anxious either, and it was as though I were asking myself, without any astonishment, for what all these people were waiting.

When I reached the Cathedral door I was surprised to discover that the Cathedral was not closed, and, pushing aside the heavy curtain flap, I found that there were still lights in the choir and that the organist was practising. I remembered that within the next ten days there was to be a performance of the *Elijah* in the Cathedral. Doubtless a practice for this had but just ended.

No one, however, seemed to be in the great church but myself and the organist. My steps echoed brazenly as I walked up the nave. I had no very definite purpose in my mind. I liked the beauty of the dim lights, the faint patterns of the carving, the great height of the soaring roof, the round strength of the unfaltering pillars. Then I realised that I was not alone. Some one came out of the shadows towards me, and, with a sharp shock of recognition, I realised that the some one was Johanson.

I had, of course, never before met him face to face. You could not call that hurried encounter with him on the night of the lecture a meeting. I was never to meet him face to face again. I wouldn't like to say how much of this book has been built up on this same meeting, brief though it was.

My first impulse was to move on, and then something compelled me to speak to him.

"I beg your pardon," I said. I stopped and he stopped.

"You are Mr. Johanson, aren't you?"

He said "Yes" and smiled.

"I haven't any right to speak to you," I went on. "But I just want to say," I stammered a little, "that I did most awfully admire your lecture the other night. I—I was there, you know," I ended lamely.

He looked at me and then he actually recognized me, amazing when you think of the confusion and disturbance of that evening. "Why, of course, you were there," he said. "You came and helped me, did you not? It was a rough ending." He held out his hand. "I am most glad to see you again. It is fine that I have a chance of thanking you for your assistance."

My chief impression as he spoke to me was that all the people who had spoken to me about him, or, in my presence, had talked of him, had known nothing whatever of him as he really was. I fancy that he affected every one he met differently, and that every one thought that their impression of him, hostile or friendly as it might be, was the only true one. He was, of course, much taller than I, and seemed very large in that dim light. But what I chiefly felt was the jolly friendliness of his smile and the extreme courtesy of his manner. When you are just at the beginning of life and pretending to be brazenly certain about everything in it, you are tremendously at the mercy of the attention paid to you by your elders. And that attention has to be just right! If there is any patronage then you don't forgive it in a hurry. But there was no patronage in Johanson.

"I don't hope that you had any harm from that evening," he said most earnestly. "They were rather rough, weren't they? They didn't like, you see, my telling them what they ought to be doing. And they were quite right. We none of us like it, naturally enough. I should, perhaps, wait a bit. But that doesn't matter here," he went on. "I wasn't expecting the doors would be open to-night. I came in half an hour ago and they were practising for the *Elijah*, and I sat down and listened. Splendid singing! I had my entertainment all for nothing!"

Then, shyly, but as though he were really interested, he asked me about myself—did I live in Polchester, and had I always lived there, and didn't I think it was a beautiful town, and was I going to be long here? I answered his questions eagerly, telling him that I was in my first year at Cambridge, that I liked it very much, that I had been born abroad but had come to Polchester as a child of six and had lived there, off and on, ever since, but that my parents lived now in London and that I had been staying here for a fortnight with my aunt.

It was extraordinary with what swiftness I felt that I knew him. I was a shy youth in those days, very much wrapped up in myself, very suspicious of strangers and especially of foreigners, but I would have told him gladly anything. I felt no difference in our ages except that perhaps he seemed rather younger than myself, but he was so kind and so friendly that he made it very easy for me.

We walked about a little, he showing me first one thing and then another that pleased him, always rather diffidently, as though, of course, I must know so much more about this place than he. Then we crossed over to the Brytte Monument.

We could not see it very clearly in the dim light, but I found at once that here was the very enthusiasm of his heart. He went on talking about it as though he himself had created it. He knew every faintest mark in it, all the little figures, the flower and fruit pieces, the ins and outs of the patterns and designs.

"But what do you think?" he broke out, seizing my arm in his excitement. "What do you think I found? Down near where I have my lodging I found a little broken fountain all under the earth with the weeds on it. I put it together and cleaned it and cleaned the seat near it and made it all proper. It's truly a beautiful piece. But this is the wonderful thing! It has a date on it—1735—and I'm quite sure it was made by the same young man who made this monument. Yes, I'm sure. It's his work, absolutely. No one could work his way. He was a genius, you understand. Entirely a genius. You've read about him? Oh, you must read about him! And I don't hope you'll think me silly, but from the first time I saw this monument I thought I knew the young man and that he knew me and he was wanting me to do something. What was he wanting me to do? Why, to find his fountain. He knew it was there all broken and dirty and he sent me to find it. Is that silly to you? Oh, but it isn't silly! Why shouldn't it be? You must come and look at the little fountain. You'd like it. Will you promise me to come?"

Of course I promised. I would have promised him something a great deal more difficult.

He would have stood there, perhaps, talking all night about his young genius, but the organ had ceased, some one had turned out the lights. The old Verger came to us telling us that he was about to close the Cathedral.

We went out into the Precincts and through the mists the moon was faintly shining.

He looked at me, as we said good-bye, as though we had been friends all our lives.

"You will promise me to come?" he said again.

"Rather!" I answered. "Of course I will."

He gave my hand a great grip, nodded, smiling at me, and strode off into the mist.

CHAPTER III

PENETHEN INTERLUDE

T HAT agony of absolute loneliness was never to return to Johanson again. There was at least one human being in the world now who believed in him and loved him.

But those hours changed him. Every one who saw him and spoke to him after that night is agreed that there was something new in him—if they cared for him, it was something more gentle and understanding; if they hated him, it was something more arrogant and aloof. "He's playing the bloody aristocrat," some one told Hogg.

I imagine that what was to worry him now most urgently was the business of paying his way. He was almost penniless. He would in two months' time have to find a very considerable sum of money.

There were no prospects of any kind for him in Polchester, and leave Polchester he would not.

Destiny, however, was to settle this question for him in its own fashion. Meanwhile the obsession of Seatown increased with him rather than diminished. Although he saw but few people and bared his soul at this time to no one but Tom Longstaffe, he must have been aware that the climax of his lecture disturbance had raised questions far beyond his own personal fate. Many a Polcastrian had had for a long time an uneasy conscience about Seatown, and especially about one aspect of the question that I have not yet mentioned.

I don't know how many public-houses there were in Seatown at this time, but I fancy that roughly one was provided for every thirty inhabitants of that district. At eight o'clock in the morning you would find the houses all crowded, and at eleven at night out they would all tumble, crowds of the most wretched drink-sodden creatures this country could show. Here I may quote, perhaps, a more eloquent writer than myself: "In the streets you will see groups of the most utterly drink-degraded wretches it is possible to find anywhere in the kingdom. Men with soulless, bloated faces and watery eyes, dressed like tramps, standing idle with their hands in their pockets. But there is not a penny there, or they would not be standing in the mud and rain; and as for doing any work, they are past that. Here that rare spectacle, a man without a shirt, has met my sight, not once nor twice but several times, the naked flesh showing through the rents of a ragged jacket buttoned or pinned up to the neck. These loathly objects are strangely incongruous at that spot, under those great towers, in sight of the green, open, healthy downs. . . ."

Under those great towers! Yes, something incongruous indeed! Johanson did not find any of these "objects" loathly. His heart ached for them, and once seen by him they could not be forgotten for a moment. Always they hung there, a dark shifting tapestry, in the back of his mind. But what could he do?

Unaided, hated as he now was, feared as he became, he could do nothing. Unaided, no. But, as I have said, he was aware that in the background other faces were now stirring. It was not for him, as for so many figures in popular romances or plays, to lead with uplifted hand a fine movement of revolt. His hope was to wait, to hang on, to stay until by constant reiteration of the Seatown scandal he could force others to act with him. All his passionate desire now was that he should be able to stay in the place.

He would hang on to that indifferent Rock with all the force, spiritual and physical, that he had.

It needed courage. It was not easy to move about the streets always under hostile eyes. He had outraged all the peaceful and law-abiding conventions of the town by the disturbance that he had made. The one desire of every one, save one or two, was that he should go. "Throw him out and forget him!" Even the tiny affair of the fountain was against him. What right had he to go meddling about with our statues and works of art? Granted that the fountain was a pretty thing, why could he not have left it to some one else, some Polcastrian, to discover? Nevertheless, no one interfered with it. Many people went to see it, and in one week's number of *The Polchester News* these three questions among others appeared in the "Do you know" column:
Do you know

That Seatown streets after eight o'clock at night are a scandal to which decent Polcastrians are able to be blind no longer?

That it is time some of our Church dignitaries ceased to frequent tea-parties and employed their valuable time among the poor of our city?

That the recent discovery of a valuable work of art in our city is causing some of us to wonder what the Town Council are thinking about it, and whether they've got some more of the same covered up with street rubbish which they are too lazy to clear away?

Beautiful days came with the beginning of October. The fountain looked fine in the sun.

Then one morning Johanson's landlady came and asked him whether he would mind finding other rooms. He was not surprised. He had been expecting this. But he was sorry for her nervousness. She was so anxious not to hurt his feelings. She wouldn't have bothered him for the world but people were telling her that there might be some trouble in the house and she couldn't have any trouble because of mother. She didn't mind for herself, really she didn't, but if there was any trouble and mother heard of it, it might finish her, and then . . . She fingered her apron. Of course he would go. He would go at once. Oh! no, at the end of the month if he didn't mind. To give him plenty of time to find somewhere else. . . . She didn't wish to inconvenience him.

And that same morning he had another visitor—Mrs. Penethen.

At the sight of her standing there in the doorway so quietly in her long black cloak, at the first glimpse of that kind and austere countenance, his conscience rebuked him that even in his loneliest moments he had fancied that he was without a friend. Hers had been the first hand that had touched his in that town, and from the beginning until now she had been the same to him, loyal, honest, faithful. Not a week had passed since he had left her lodging but she had been to see him. He knew that all men might revile and abuse him, but that she would not flinch from him. And yet even in that first warm welcoming glimpse of her he was aware that although she stood beside him, she also stood apart from him—and not only from him but also from every other human being in the world. She was, and had been for many a year, lonely, as he could be but rarely, and, although she perplexed him in much, he understood this, that there was something in that odd English blood of hers that he would never understand. These English! Queer, apart people! but even at their worst more honest than any others that he had ever known.

She came in quietly, as she always did, and sat down beside him. He had been struggling with his poor finances, striving as many another to make them better than they were, and he had in front of him a paper covered with figures.

She settled herself comfortably, and then looking at him with that grave motherly look that he knew so well, said: "How are you?"

"Very well, indeed."

"I'm glad of it," she answered him.

He wasn't one to waste time when he was eager about anything and he began at once:

"Tell me about Maude, please. Is she happy—with that young man?"

She told me afterwards that it was always the hardest thing for her when he began to speak of Maude. His eyes were so anxious and distressed and so *childish*, urging her, as children do with their elders, to tell him something good even though it were not true. And yet, of course, it was the truth that he wanted.

"Happy? Is Maude ever happy? She doesn't know what she wants and she never will. And she wants more than ever she's going to get. All the ha'pence and none of the kicks."

"But that fellow—he's not good enough for her. He can't make her happy. Perhaps I couldn't, of course. But he can't. I know he can't. But she should be happy—she'd be so fine when she was happy. She needs happiness."

"What's all this about happiness?" Mrs. Penethen said sharply. "There's too much talk about happiness in this world, it seems to me. Happiness! Happiness! Happiness! All of them wanting happiness! That's what most of them are so unhappy for. Why, you don't think it's the first thing yourself."

"No, I don't," he answered slowly. "Not for myself. But for her it should be."

"Well, it isn't her I've come to talk about," Mrs. Penethen then answered firmly. "It's something more important. I've come to ask you to go away."

"Go away!" he repeated.

"Yes," she answered hurriedly. "I mean it. Oh! it's for your good I'm asking. You know what I think of you, you know how much I'd have done for you if I could have had my way. But just for a while, until things are quieter. It isn't safe for you, truly not. I know what I'm saying."

She says that he drew away from her then as though she had become, in a moment, some one he couldn't trust. "I didn't think you'd want that," he said at last. "You're my friend. Surely I thought so. I don't hope you think I've done anything bad to run away about."

"Run away! No," she answered impatiently. "But for a time you can't do anything here. They're angry about the lecture and things you've said, or if they're not angry, all of them, it's Hogg and some others who are telling them they ought to be. What do you know about how they feel here? What have you ever known since first you came here? Why, if I'd had any idea of what it was going to let you in for, your being in this town, and the way they would treat you, I'd have bundled you off that first wet night you came to my door. Indeed, it's often enough I reproach myself for not having managed things better. But how was I to tell that all this would come of it, and all the more when everything went happily at first."

He must have seen then, I fancy, that something very real and urgent disturbed her, driving her from her accustomed equanimity, and that whatever her reason might be, her only motive was her concern for himself.

He smiled and took one of her hands in his.

"What is it," he asked, "that's worrying you so badly? Are they meaning to shoot me or what?"

"I can't do other than beg you to go," she answered. "I'm your oldest friend in this town, aren't I now, and I'm old enough to be your mother and I'm fond of you as I've never been fond of a man since my poor husband died. There's a thing for an old woman like me to say! But just because of that and because I've always been honest with you from the beginning, you can believe me when I say that it's right you should go. They mean to make you go whether you wish it or not. And only for a time, mind. I'm not saying for long. Just for a while, otherwise—Oh! they'll be sitting on you one of these nights, some of those Seatown roughs, and they're a mad lot down there, especially when they've been drinking. Why should you mind to go? There's no shame in it!"

"Is this anything to do with Maude?" he asked her.

"Maude! No!"

"Then I'm not going." He got up and began to walk the room. "Of course I'm not going. Where should I go to? Do you think I don't love this town, although they've been unfriendly just of late? and there's Maude. Though she don't love me any more, I must see after her a bit—in the background, don't you see?"

"Maude! Maude!" Mrs. Penethen broke in. "I'm sick of Maude, although she is my own daughter. What's she got to do with this? Mind what I say. It's serious. There are those working against you who've been against you from the first. Why give them the chance they're wanting? Ah! go! Please go!"

She stood in front of him, stopping him.

"If it's money you're needing—" she began.

He put his arms around her and kissed her. Then he led her towards the door.

"I'm staying," he said. "Yes, as long as I'm alive, I'm staying."

She saw something in his face that told her that all appeal was hopeless. Something, she said afterwards, that was not himself but something stronger than he.

He was like a man doomed. All her way home she could think of nothing but that melodramatic phrase "a man doomed," and then broke into that old irritation that she had known in connection with him from the very first. "He's stupid. Stupider than any man should be."

She sat all that evening worrying in her head at desperate schemes that would get him away from the town. But he was never to know that it was Maude who had been her chief informant, Maude who had urged her to go and see him, Maude who was sitting at that moment of her mother's visit in the Boultewood's parlour thinking her fiancé a contemptible ass, longing to see once more that strange man with whom her life had been for a moment connected, longing and hoping too most passionately that, for her safety and comfort, she would never set eyes on him again.

But she was to set eyes on him.

Two days after Mrs. Penethen's visit to him, on a fine autumnal afternoon, he walked up to the thick lane that runs above the villas over the top of the town high above Orange Street. This was a favourite walk of his. Above the lane, with only a step or two, you reached downland, and from a high point there, on a clear day, you could discover the sea. Where the lane allowed gates to intercept its high hedges you had a splendid view, the green fields sloping to the town, and from the very heart of the roofs the Cathedral rose like a gigantic ship tugging at its moorings, seeking to float away into the sea of sky. Seen from here the town was the town that he loved, all beauty and peace. It did not seem so difficult, when he saw it thus, to recover his old first vision of it and some of his old faith in it. And when the world was so still about him, only faint stirrings in the hedgerows, the distant roll of some cart, the cry of a child from a near-by farm, he seemed to himself to be approaching that moment when, if only he had sufficiently rid himself of his own desires and his own fears and if only the world outside were quiet enough, he would catch that whisper that would explain everything. From his earliest childhood he had had some expectation of the kind, so that as a little boy he would drag at his mother's hand in the street and force her to pause and then, hearing only the noise of the traffic in his ears, would move impatiently forward again. Lately, in all the trouble of his personal life the possibility of that whisper had seemed irretrievably remote; for many a month he had not dreamed his old dream. But now, again, after that terrible day in his room when Longstaffe had come, he had recovered his earlier self-possession.

He was at peace, as he had not been since the first days of his engagement to Maude.

So he was walking along the lane, rejoicing in the crystal stillness of the air, watching a leaf, amber coloured, twirl and turn and twirl again, so human in its movement that he could almost hear it sigh as it abandoned itself to submission.

He told Longstaffe afterwards that he would never, until he died, forget that leaf. It seemed to have some special message for him. He watched it as it lay, finally, lifeless on the ground. Then, looking up, he saw Maude Penethen walking slowly, quite alone, in front of him.

What the surprise of that must have been! It might seem that it would be impossible to be for so long in the same small town and not to meet, but it was true, nevertheless, that he had not seen her since that day at her mother's house when he had had that last interview with her.

He could not believe now that this was she, but he knew the blue coat and the hat with the blue feather, and then every movement told him. There was something in her walk that seemed dejected and lonely and went straight to his heart.

He did not know what to do. He stood still, staring. Only they two alone in all the world! Should he turn back? No, he was not strong enough for that. The sight of her, although it was only her back that he saw, made him so hungry for the sound of her voice and the light in her eyes that he could no more leave her than the castaway could escape from the ship that is in sight to save him. But perhaps she would think that he had followed her and was to take advantage now of her loneliness? He could not think clearly though. His heart was hammering, his eyes were clouded. Another moment and he had said in a voice strangled by his feeling: "Maude, Maude. Please, I must speak with you."

He told Longstaffe afterwards that he knew, at the moment that she turned round and realised him, how completely and utterly he had lost her. She was terrified—no other word for it. Terrified as though he had been some tramp who, alone there far from any possibility of human assistance, would offer her violence. And whether it was of him, or of her love for him, that she was terrified, no one will ever know. Certainly Maude Penethen, or rather Mrs. Boultewood, of "Ivanhoe" Villa, will never say.

I suppose that, during all those months, she had been thinking of him unceasingly, and as the reports of his various misdemeanours reached her ears she must have been in a strange confusion of thanking her stars that she was not married to him and longing for his embraces.

At least that is how I see her. Many people after the event expressed wonder that he should have cared for her. But, having the heart that he had, the mixture of her fear of him and her longing for him touched him everywhere. She was, too, her mother's daughter, lonely and apart against her will. She would regret him to the day of her death. She gave Boultewood no easy time, I fancy.

But she clung to safety and the things that she knew. Safety and the good report of the world.

When she saw him she looked desperately about her and then said: "Don't. Don't. I don't want to speak to you."

"We must speak," he answered gravely, recovering his self-control. "It isn't right that we shouldn't. I shan't hurt you or say anything wrong. You know I've never hurt you, have I? I only want your happiness—no one wants it so much as me."

She told her mother later, when haughtily she gave her version of the meeting, that if he hadn't looked so unhappy she wouldn't have stayed with him. But I fancy that that was her romantic gloss on the situation. I don't imagine that he was unhappy at all or sentimental. His love for her was so settled a thing in his heart that after the first shock of the unexpected encounter he quite quietly set about the business that the opportunity of the meeting gave him—to see whether there were any way in which he could help her.

For myself I believe that she fell under his spell again immediately, and that if he had thrown his arms around her she would at the moment have done anything he asked her. He had not lost her the less absolutely for that. Later all the old fear would have returned and returned only the more strongly.

But, of course, he did not fling his arms around her. He did not even touch her hand, as she was very careful afterwards to tell her mother.

He told Longstaffe that it was surprising how quickly they fell into their old way, talking quietly, he asking her questions and she giving him answers that at least if they were not true were what she wanted him to believe. His one eager desire was not to frighten her and for a while he did not.

"Maude, allow me just for these minutes to think that I have a right to ask you about yourself. Are you happy and comfortable?"

"Of course I'm happy and comfortable," she answered him. "Why shouldn't I be?" That in the old sharp way. Then more softly: "I'm glad we've met after all this way, because there's something I've always been wanting to tell you. I didn't treat you rightly when you were with us. I didn't, indeed. I was just hateful. But you weren't like any one I'd ever seen before and perhaps if we'd married at once and gone away out of this place ... But I don't know—" She looked at him then almost appealingly as she went on, and how, for the next days, he was to remember the look! "I'm not much of a girl. I'm not, truly. You're lucky to be rid of me. I've been spoilt. That's what it is, I expect. And I don't want to change either. You're the only one who could have changed me, but I'd have fought you for trying to. We'd never be happy together. And there's another thing. You made me think of all sorts of ideas I didn't want to think of. You wouldn't leave me alone, would you? You said you wanted us both to be free, but you wouldn't be contented until I did and thought what you wanted me to."

That was penetrating of her. "It might be I'd have learnt too," he answered her. "I've learnt something since I came away from you, Maude. Oh! I've wanted you so. You don't know how I've wanted you."

The temptation then to take her in his arms was terrible. He had to stop where he was and think of her. If he thought of her enough, her helplessness and easily roused fear of him, the temptation weakened, but if he saw her only in a mist of all his longing—

He stood, gazing over the break in the hedge and the green of the sloping field swung up to the blue autumn sky, and the thin veil of smoke above the town enveloped him in its spidery haze.

She stood quietly beside him. It might have been his moment. Who can tell? He conquered it and walked on, not looking at her.

"Let's not talk of the past," he said. "I was wrong, but I was very ignorant. You were the first woman I'd ever loved, and you shall be the last. Also it isn't easy for a foreigner to love an English woman. You mistook sometimes the things I said, and I was so eager to have you always and I was jealous—"

She felt, I think, that she had just escaped a great danger, and she began hurriedly: "And now aren't you going to leave Polchester for a while? I know you haven't meant anything by what you've done here, but what you say is true, I expect, that you are a foreigner and don't understand the way people feel here. English people are funny. They don't want to be told what they ought to do. They're angry with you, some of them. Won't you go away for a little until it's all quiet again?"

He shook his head, smiling. "No, I won't go away. Don't you see why I can't? Don't you see that the two things in the world I love, the two things I think the most beautiful, are here, Polchester and you. I don't hope you think I'm rude to say that to you when you're engaged to be married now to another man, but I don't mean it in any way that can offend you. I know, of course, that it's better for us not to see one another. I shan't try to meet you. Indeed I shan't. But the time may be when you'd want a bit of help. I don't," he went on laughing, "seem just now anybody to help another very much, but it shan't always be. I have friends here, and I am young and strong. You may want me one day, and it would be terrible that I wasn't here. And then I can't leave Polchester. It isn't what I think when I first came here, but perhaps it's something better. No, I can't go away, Maude, thank you very much."

Once more he had, I believe, a chance. What could she think, contrasting that oaf Boultewood with the man beside her? If she was happy, what was she doing walking all alone up there by herself that day, she who hated to be alone? But it was well for him that she didn't give him his chance. There was a better destiny waiting for him than anything that Maude could offer him.

She continued to try to persuade him to go, but felt as her mother had felt before her, that there was some stronger resistance there than she could conquer.

They had come to the point where the broad road up from Polchester met the lane. He stopped in front of her, looking at her, as though it would be the last time that he would ever see her.

"Remember then," he said, "that though you can't love me you're the only love of my heart. There won't be ever another. All that's good in me, Maude, is yours. If it may be one day you're lonely or unhappy, it shall be, perhaps, a comfort to think that there's some one who loves you and can't ever change. It's a happiness to me that I've been able to say to you: 'If all the world comes to tell you that I've gone away and left you, it won't be true.' But I don't want anything of you, Maude. I don't want anything of any man, and, I think, that's surely the way to be happy. Don't you think of me, if you think at all, as unhappy. I've had my unhappy times, but I'm a happy man. And I'll be happy serving you, even, though you don't know I'm doing it."

She was frightened then. Something in his look, in the way he held himself, brought back her old fear. She told her mother, "He didn't look human, somehow. The thing that's foreign in him came out and frightened me."

She expected, perhaps, that he would kiss her, but he didn't move even to touch her hand. She nodded, tried to smile in an easy fashion, then started quickly down the hill.

He stayed there looking after her.

CHAPTER IV

OCTOBER 7: ON THE HILL

I BELIEVE that that meeting with Maude raised him to the height of all imaginable happiness. It may seem strange that it could be so, but it restored to him, I fancy, the one possession whose loss it had been hardest for him to bear—his right to care for her. He had, for months, lost all touch with her; now, although he might not see her, he would know that she was conscious of him, that she knew that he was there, and that if unhappiness or trouble came to her it would be to thought of him that she would turn.

Johanson was human, a great deal more human than many, and whether that altruistic condition of feeling would have contented him for long, who can say? It may have been one of his "lucks" that that particular test was not to be offered to him.

In any case the boy that was still in him helped him to react with extraordinary swiftness from one mood to another. He was now as happy as he had been in his first Polchester days. He rushed in at once to tell Longstaffe all about it. He gave him the minutest account of his meeting with her, every detail. He was filled to the brim with new plans. What was he going to do? Well, the next thing was that he intended to live down there in the very heart of Seatown. Yes, he did. That was the only way to do anything. He wasn't going to missionise them or improve their minds or anything of the sort. He was going to know them, and they were going to know him. He thought he could earn enough teaching a few some exercises, a little boxing, maybe. Or he would *make* things. He was quick with his hands and could make a wooden box as well as any one. It wouldn't cost him much to live down there—that was one certain thing.

I think it was then, for the first time, that Tom Longstaffe became seriously alarmed. In spite of everything that had happened Johanson seemed to have no time realisation of the way that those men hated him. If Seatown had become an obsession to *him, he* had certainly become an obsession to them, and it was that most dangerous of emotions, ignorant crowd hatred fanned by Hogg or another to a sort of fanaticism. Johanson was "the bloody foreigner" to them, and they "were going to bleeding well chuck him out"—and here was he planning happily to live in their midst.

Longstaffe tried to show him some of this, but he didn't care that day. He had seen Maude again, he was to be allowed to look after her, he was to begin his work again, honestly now in the way that he wanted it.

He was lonely no longer, workless no longer, homeless no longer. Then his dream came back to him again.

One night, physically tired out with a walk that he had taken all day with Longstaffe across the Downs towards the sea, he fell at once on tumbling into bed into heavy sleep.

He had poured everything out to Longstaffe, telling him many things for which this narrative is the richer. They had been, both of them, so happy together that there had come a moment when, standing on a shoulder of the moor and looking out to the thin purple scarf of the sea, it had seemed to them possible to go on—and never to come back. A moment's dazzling illusion of eternal happiness, swinging through air into space, with no duty, no foreboding, no regret to burden them. Then, laughing, they had turned back. It was in many ways the happiest and fullest day of their lives. Longstaffe at least was never to know such a day again.

And now, closing happily his eyes, he swung at once into the place from which for so many months he had been excluded. For it was like that, as though he were returning to his own place after a long absence abroad. He was walking up the long smooth path. A cool pale light was in the air. The white house stood open and waiting for him. The flowers, the trees, the stream that tumbled over the stones between the lawns all greeted him without wonder or surprise, but with an infinite quiet pleasure.

He moved with an incredible freedom and ease. The house when he reached it was shining with light. It was empty of everything and yet strangely filled. There again were the gleaming stairs and beyond them the long still gallery. Looking out from a window of the gallery, he smiled with joy when he saw once more the line of plum-coloured hills, the dark texture of the trees framing them, the sun sparkling behind the darkness, when he heard the singing of the birds and, coming up to him from below, the chatter of the stream.

Oh! but he was glad to see it again! He was home now. He could rest and think and listen. And soon—he knew it as though he had been informed of it—a message would come to him there. He would be told what to do.

His part was to wait there listening for the message. . . .

Next morning he woke to find the sun pouring into his room. While dressing he discovered this written on a grubby piece of paper and pushed under his door:

IF YOU DONT LEEVE THIS TOWN SOON
YOU WILL BE THRONE OUT.

He smiled at that. He felt strong enough to-day for anything.

He spent the morning writing part of a fairy-story for Billy. He couldn't write English. But that didn't matter. It was plain enough for the child to understand just as though he were talking.

This thing had begun a long while ago. He had told Billy stories when they were out walking together, and he had discovered, very much to his own surprise, that he was crammed with stories. He didn't know where they came from. Perhaps his mother had told them to him, or told him pieces, and he himself had added the rest.

Once he began there seemed to be no reason why he should stop. The Swedish forest, the long seashores, the islands beyond Stockholm, these were soon peopled with a moving, stirring world of dwarfs with peaked red caps, kings stirring with their jewelled sceptres their piles of glittering treasure, the wood-cutters' huts and the wolves that threatened the wood-cutter's little daughter, the dark silent pools on whose lonely banks princes, turned by evil magicians into frogs, croaked for some one to come and deliver them—no, there was no end to them, and Johanson was as deeply excited by them as was Billy. Then Billy wanted an old one over again, and Johanson couldn't remember, so there came the order that they must be written down. That was what Johanson was now laboriously doing. He was in the middle of the best one: "The King's Daughter and the Humpbacked Prince."

After his frugal midday meal he thought because it was so lovely a day that he would go and see whether Tom or Billy or Mary would come for a walk.

The whole town was glittering with light as in one of his own fairy-stories. Passing through the market-place he saw old Looney sitting there. He was asleep, his head fallen forward on his chest. The warm sun was too much for him. For the first time for many a day he had ceased to watch. Who knew but that fate, malicious a little, would choose that very moment to produce the crisis for which Looney had so long been waiting?

Coming up to the house he saw Billy on the lawn trying to stand on his head. He could manage it almost, he cried to Johanson, telling him to stop and watch, if his legs wouldn't be so wobbly. He commanded Johanson to hold his legs; then everything was fine. He could see the tree all upside down, and the smoke from the chimney was like a flag. Then he began to choke and Johanson turned him over.

Tom Longstaffe came out on to the lawn.

"Mary and Billy were going up to Parmiter's Field," he said. "Why not go up with them?" Parmiter's Field is a famous spot in our country, because from there you can have one of the finest views in all Glebeshire.

"I had come to ask for a walk," Johanson answered, picking Billy up and holding him in the air with one straightened arm. And that was the way that Longstaffe would always afterwards see him, his legs stiff, his head thrown back, he laughing and the sun broken into fragments by the dark tree circling round him.

Mary came out, and the three started off. By the gate Johanson turned back.

"Good-bye, Tom," he cried.

"Good-bye."

"See you soon."

"Come in to-morrow evening and we'll have a talk."

"Yes, I will."

Longstaffe stood there looking after them. He had a funny impulse, he told me afterwards, to call Johanson back for a moment. He had something. . . . No, he had not. . . . He went back reluctantly into his study. He sat there for a long time staring over his pipe at the thought of his friend.

They went gaily up the hill. The day was so beautiful that every one was happy. A little nondescript dog, who had no home and no family, looking about for something exciting to do, went with them. He was a funny little dog with a head too large for his body, and although during the short span of his days he had had nothing but kicks and abuse, nevertheless, he was still confident in life and expected it at any moment to do him some wonderful turn.

Johanson was always very much at his ease with Mary. She was so quiet and so sensible that he could tell her everything. They never reached a greater intimacy than that, and they never would, perhaps because she was so sensible. The one passionate experience of her life was behind her, and she would never have another. Even her love for her child was not passionate. She was writing a book, she told Johanson, a book about certain famous women, Mary Wollstonecraft, Harriet Martineau, Emily Brontë and some others. That was the first of that series of works by which afterwards she made her name.

She told him about the book, and he told her about anything that came into his mind, and at last about the dream that he had had the night before. Dreams, she told him frankly, she didn't believe in. Well, but if during many years the same dream returned to you again and again? Something to do with your digestion, she fancied. And Johanson laughed, tossing his head. "You won't believe in anything, Mary, unless it is sensibly explained, will you?" And she agreed, gravely, that she thought that everything had its sensible explanation.

Soon they reached the moors, and their feet were treading the springy turf. Whereas the wet, windy autumn days are full of melancholy and the spirit of distraction, the warm days when the sun beats down upon a world almost breathless in its sense of suspense are full of reassurance and comfort. All that full summer is gone, but now we can confidently hope because we feel that at the very instant of death new seeds are being sown, new colours are being born, new life is pushing forward. Standing on these moors on such a still, sunlit day as this, time stands motionless. All the past—the life of the Saxon, Dane, Roman, Briton—is continuous with ours, and because the pageantry of summer is withdrawn we can see the more plainly things that those vanished glories had hidden.

From Parmiter's Field on such a day as this you could draw within your arms a vast sweep of hill and valley, black bunches of wood, isolated farms gleaming white through their trees, streams of silver thread, and best of all the slow, rounded shoulders of the Downs. Polchester flamed beneath the sun, windows sparkling like eyes, the Pol bending it in and the Cathedral crowning it.

They threw themselves down upon the warm, dry turf, and the small dog growled like a kettle and rushed at imaginary enemies, and then abandoning himself flung himself down against the warm hollow of Johanson's thigh and lay there panting, his tongue out, his shaggy eyes sparkling with pleasure.

Now was the time for the story to be continued. No other thing would keep Billy still. Johanson turned over, lying full length on his stomach, his head propped between his hands, staring at the vast curtain of sky and seeing, over the brow of the moor, the Polchester roofs, the Cathedral crouched like a man, and the rising fields.

"When the dwarf came to the wood it was nearly dark. He couldn't see very clearly because, as you may remember, he had only one eye and he wasn't brave either. 'I don't hope you think I'm frightened,' he called out just to comfort himself. Somebody laughed. He couldn't see nobody, although he turned to the left and the right and everyway, but somebody was laughing—"

"I know," shouted Billy, too badly excited to be silent. "It was the woodcutter's daughter."

"Hush, Billy," said Mary. "You mustn't spoil the story."

"It were *not* the woodcutter's daughter," said Johanson. "He looked everywhere about him and he said out loud, 'Who's that laughing?' 'Wouldn't you like to know?' said a voice above him, and looking up he knew that some one was in a tree, but yet he could not see who that somebody was. And then—right at his feet—something dropped, and he could see although it was almost dark that it was a beautiful pearl, the loveliest and the roundest pearl any one had ever seen, all white and shining.

" 'Pick it up,' said the voice, and although he had the rheumatism very badly, he bent down to pick it up, and when he had it in his hand it was just an ugly bit of nasty coal. Then he was so angry he stamped with his foot in his rage, and the voice laughed again and said, 'If you're as angry as that you'll never find the golden key,' which was what he had come into the wood to discover, you shall remember. 'I'm just wasting my time,' he said, and he was going off when another beautiful pearl fell at his feet. He was so greedy that although he had the rheumatism and was in a hurry to be gone, he had to stoop down and pick it up. But when that was in his hand that was a piece of coal too, and this time he was so angry that he took off his fine red cap and threw it on the ground and stamped on it.

" 'You'll never find the golden key if you get so angry,' said the voice again—"

And so the story went on. No movement in all the world. They must have seemed like painted figures there against the rim of the moor and the great scoop of blue sky from whose texture the colour slowly drained, leaving it even paler as though to prepare for the ardent glories of the sunset.

"There, then, that's enough," Johanson said. "The story's finished for to-day."

"Oh, no," Billy cried. "It isn't finished. I want—"

But Johanson didn't answer. It seemed to Mary Longstaffe that he had been gradually losing knowledge of what he was saying. The words had tumbled from him drowsily, almost as though he were falling asleep, and yet his eyes were wide open and staring.

Billy asked no more, but played with the dog, who had wakened and was biting at anything he could see.

"Mary," he said, not turning to her, but still staring before him. (She said afterwards that his whole body as he lay there had the tenseness of expectation, so that she herself looked out to the horizon wondering what it was that he saw.) "Isn't it a funny thing that I shall have been here in this place all this time and done nothing except put together a little broken bit of carving?"

"You don't know what you may have done," Mary answered sententiously. (I can hear her saying it. Mary was always a little sententious.) "Nobody knows the result of their own work. You may have influenced many more people than you know. You have, I'm sure."

He did not seem to have heard her. "It's an odd thing," he said. "To-day I'm right back to when I were a boy. There seems to be no time between. I come clattering up the stairs, you know, and I look out of the window half-way up the stairs and there's all the roofs covered with snow, and a blue star shining, and I say with a thump of the heart, 'It's beautiful,' and I'm sad because it's beautiful. And I run a bit up the stairs and then run back to see it once more in case the star should be away. But there it still is and it's like as though I take it in my pocket and keep it there.

"And then I run upstairs, and there's father washing his head because he's been drinking too much, and mother's crying, and for the first time I'm not afraid of him. For the first time, yes, because of the star in my pocket. . . .

"Strange! Strange! I have it all round me here—the clock with the face of the moon and the old picture of the skating in the snow and the cage with the yellow canary—and father splashing the water about the floor, looking through the towel like a beast at me. Mary, what does life mean? What is driving us for ever to do other than we want, never to be easy and quiet?"

"God is driving us," she answered.

"God! God!" he replied. "This word! It is so easy and it means nothing. But Beauty! That's a word now that means something, and I know to-day that I've come at last to the way to have beauty, to touch it as I touched that star.

"To-day I want nothing for myself and I fear nothing for myself. I have lost myself. I am empty of myself. Always before I wanted something for me. Me, Hjalmar Johanson. But now I will begin to love beauty away from myself and to make things for others. And perhaps after all this beauty is the same as your God, Mary. I know it is the same as love. It is part of the woman I love and the place I love and the work I love. But it isn't for me any more. It's for something greater than myself. I can die to-night and it goes on, I go on, we all go on for ever, and all things are more beautiful and more beautiful until at last all is beauty."

It was something like this that he talked, and I suspect, although she never confessed it, that to Mary it all seemed very childish. She had read so much and had so good a brain that Johanson was always to her like an ignorant, uneducated boy. She didn't like him the less for that, but she liked him for other qualities, his loyalty, courage, honesty, not for his intellect.

I suspect, too, although this also she never admitted, that she gave him then a nice concise pocket philosophy of her ideas about life (the sort of things that wise men publish—"How to live wisely," in fifty pages of neat tidy print), but I don't imagine that he listened to her. He liked her, too, for all sorts of things, for her honesty, courage and loyalty, but not for her intellect.

But she remembers that he said at last, "I'm so happy to-day, happier than ever before. I have people to love and work to do and I fear nothing, I want nothing. How lovely the world is and how quiet and how still. Just the time to listen for a message from somewhere. I can feel the earth under me and the sky above me and my body's fit and my brain's clear. I'm hungry and thirsty, the sky's full of colour, the trees are turning brown, I hate no one. I have friends and a woman I love. . . . I'll build a town one day, Mary, that shall be the most beautiful town ever seen, with white towers and streets of fine stone, fountains and a great hall, gardens of every flower and woods to shelter when it's hot, and squares for processions, and every man shall have his own place free for himself and work that he may enjoy and time to see beautiful things, and no one shall be afraid of anything, and there shall be the finest bands playing you ever heard!"

But it was turning chilly, and Mary was afraid lest Billy should catch a cold. So she got up and brushed the soil from her dress and said she thought they must be going.

Johanson wanted to stay a while, so, Billy waving his hand a great many times, they left him. Only the little dog for some mysterious reason stayed with Johanson.

He remained there a long time. I hope that he had a magnificent sunset. No one can remember what the sunset was like that day.

The only witness was poor old Mr. Shortt, who told some one afterwards that he was taking a walk up there, and saw some one standing gazing at the sunset.

When he saw that the "some one" was Johanson he meant to speak to him. He had had every grievance against Johanson during the last months and had complained bitterly of him everywhere. But he was a miserable old man and couldn't afford grievances when there was a chance of making a penny or two. So he advanced towards him, apparently intending to speak to him. But for some reason or other he didn't. He couldn't himself explain it. The man was busy with his own thoughts—"just as though," Mr. Shortt said, "he were speaking to some one." And then with a desire, I suppose, to show his audience that he was still capable of the most gentlemanly feelings: "He was wrapt in his own thoughts and looked so pleased about something that naturally I wouldn't interrupt him."

So he went away and left Johanson standing there.

CHAPTER V

OCTOBER 7: LIFE AND DEATH

H E came down into the town in the dusk with the little dog at his heels. Several people saw him—young Walter Pearce, Aaron Sharpe, Mildmay.

Mildmay, who had too genial a digestion and, as auctioneer, too general a profession to quarrel with anybody, spoke to him.

"Why, Mr. Johanson," he said, "you look as though some one had left you a fortune."

Johanson, laughing, answered him something and swung on. It must have been nearly dark when he reached his lodging. Running upstairs, he was met outside his door by his landlady.

"Mr. Johanson," she said, agitated as usual, "the boy would wait." She, too, noticed and afterwards recorded that "he looked as happy as anything."

"Boy! What boy?" he asked.

"The one that's been here before. He's in your room and brought 'is dog with 'im too."

Johanson knew then that it must be Husky, and sure enough it was he, standing in the dusk holding on to his mongrel.

He smiled his confiding smile and explained that he had come there because of his aunt—"she was terrible bad and wouldn't see no one but Mr. Johnson." This old woman, a drunken old thief and responsible at an earlier time for the most villainous, disorderly house in Polchester, had been from the first one of Johanson's fiercest opponents. Husky lived sometimes with her, sometimes with a sick mother and sometimes with himself, but his old aunt coloured his conversation more than any other human. She was the only creature alive whom he feared, and apparently because he feared cared for in a sort of way. It was perhaps admiration rather than affection. She was the wickedest, filthiest, hardest-swearing member of his circle and so stood for something.

Johanson must have doubted when he heard that she wanted him. It wasn't in him to suspect tricks or plots, but he must have doubted. But Husky wouldn't lead him into trouble. Then Husky advised him not to go. He had told his aunt that he would deliver the message, and now, having delivered it, in his queer, broken voice he gave it as his opinion that he'd better go back and just tell his aunt that he couldn't find Mr. Johnson. Why, Johanson asked him, wasn't his aunt really ill? Oh yes, she was terrible bad. Dying, the doctor said. And she had a sort of idea that Mr. Johnson could keep her alive. Doctors were no bloody good. At least that was her opinion. But she was sick all right. Terrible sick.

Johanson must have been reluctant to go. He had had so good a day and he wanted to sit in his room and think about it. At least that's apparently what he said to Husky, that he wanted to stay in his room and think about something.

That stuck in Husky's mind because it seemed to him so very odd a thing for any one to want to do. He never wanted to stop and think about anything. However, Husky was relieved. He didn't mind his old aunt dying, and he had his own private reasons for thinking it better that his friend, Mr. Johnson, shouldn't go down there to-night. So he jerked the piece of string that attached the mongrel to his person and prepared to depart.

Then Johanson changed his mind. No, he would go. If the old woman were really ill, and asked for him, he must go. Did she die, and he not going, he would reproach himself. In an hour he would be back.

A funny mood then invaded young Husky. He didn't want his friend to go. There were a lot down there who might do Mr. Johnson some damage. They had been talking about it for weeks. He could go down in the morning. After all his aunt might not die to-night. She had been ill for days and nights. This was just a fancy she'd taken into her head to see Mr. Johnson. He'd just go back and tell her that Mr. Johnson had been out and he'd left a message.

But now Johanson had made up his mind. He was going, and that was all there was about it. He saw, perhaps, a change of mind in the Seatown populace. If this old creature turned to him, who also might not turn?

Husky kicked the dog to ease his feelings a little, and led the way down the stairs.

From the moment of his leaving his rooms to the witness of Rufus the doctor nothing is very clear. Something happened on the way down, because Johanson didn't reach the foul apartment of Husky's aunt until nearly eight o'clock. That is, they took close upon an hour to go from Johanson's rooms to the farther end of Seatown. Husky can explain very little. He says that Mr. Johnson stopped to speak to somebody and that he couldn't see "who the bloke was."

I believe that somebody—Romilly perhaps?—did his utmost to prevent Johanson from going on. I have tried in every way possible to discover who that somebody was, but at this distance of time accuracy is difficult. Longstaffe, Ronder, Mrs. Penethen, Mary, Miss Midgeley, even Maude Boultewood have an astonishingly clear picture of all their contacts with him, but when you pass from the witness of these four or five people you pass into the world of legend, and legend, often enough, of a curiously flamboyant and sentimental kind.

We shall never know, I suppose, who had that half-hour's talk with Johanson. It must have been urgent or Johanson would not have stayed. I like, as I have said, to think that it was Romilly. Sentimental? Well, people of Romilly's natural animal order are what more sophisticated beings call sentimental. They are not afraid of making fools of themselves. They simply don't think about it.

Dropping down into that old Seatown at night was an adventurous affair. There were very few lights and many holes and stumbling-places. Very little life to be seen until the crowd tumbled, reluctantly, out of the public-houses.

On this particular evening there was a wonderful sky of burning, flaming stars and a thin slip of an orange moon. Seatown, silent and starlit, had its beauty. The river, owing to a recent fortnight of rain, was running high, almost to the top of the river wall.

Dr. Rufus died after a severe bout of delirium tremens in 1912, but he told Longstaffe something of the events of that evening. His was not a very glorious part in the business, and he alluded huskily to the necessity of his visiting another patient when his retirement from the scene asked for explanation. But I don't know that one can blame him exactly. He had always hated Johanson, and it would have been a little melodramatic of him to offer his very useless carcass . . . But it might, after all, have been better than the delirium tremens.

He was there, standing over Husky's aunt, when Johanson and Husky came in. Three old women (Mrs. Clay and Mother Harper were two of them), like the "Macbeth" witches, attended Mrs. Furkins' (such was the name of Husky's aunt) departure. For light there were two candles whose flame blew in the breeze that came in through the broken window-pane. It was good that the pane was broken, because the smell in the room was, apparently, appalling.

Rufus, in spite of himself, admired Johanson for coming. He was, I suppose, as drunk as usual, but not too drunk to notice a good deal of what passed. He said afterwards that if Johanson hadn't been always so damned interfering he would have admired him. Johanson, he confessed, was the sort of man that he might himself have been if everything hadn't been against him. But everything had been against him from the first: he didn't care who knew it.

Mrs. Furkins was stout and red even in the hour of her death, and was in complete possession of her faculties. The three witches stood at the foot of the miserable bed and looked at her gloomily.

They told her it was lucky for her that she was dying without pain and drew lively pictures of other and much more painful deathbeds.

Old Mrs. Furkins was in terror, abject, gasping, tortured terror. Terror of death. She believed in hell fire and no reassurances on the part of Rufus could comfort her. Only one man could reassure her about death, and that was "Armerjohn." Once, and over again, she repeated his nickname, as though it were a talisman against death. "Armerjohn, Armerjohn, Armerjohn . . ."

Some woman apparently had died in Seatown a few weeks earlier and Johanson had been with her. Something he had said had reassured her. Mrs. Furkins had heard of this. She was not terrified because of her sins. Her sins didn't bother her. After all there were many worse. She could give plenty of instances. But this hell with its perpetual burning, its little red devils with pincers, its shrieks and groans and agonies, and all for ever—for ever and ever.

Somewhere, from her far, far distant childhood this picture of hell, after years of dismissal, had peered up at her again. For a week now she had seen nothing else. Only Armerjohn could reassure her.

The old women at the foot of the bed (fuddled with drink) were themselves alarmed. Long while since they had thought of hell. But it was well known that just before you kicked the bucket you saw things clearly, and if Carrie Furkins was destined for hell then were they also. They expected, then, the arrival of Johanson with a good deal of interest. They were eager to see what he would do.

What he did was to go over to the bed of the old woman, draw a rickety chair and sit down beside her. He paid no attention to Rufus. After Hogg, he abominated Rufus more than any one in the town. Nor did he greet the three witches. Carrie Furkins gulped with relief when she saw him. Gasping she explained to him that she knew that she was about to die, and was going to hell, and that the idea that she had of hell was giving her no end of a fright. She didn't want no parson's business about her sins and praying for mercy and the rest of it. She wasn't going to pray for mercy to any one. But she understood that he knew more about hell than any one else in the place, perhaps because he was a foreigner. He had given a lot of comfort to Mary Armstrong some weeks back when she was worrying about the same thing. Would he tell her what he had told Mary Armstrong?

The room listened attentively. Even Rufus thought that he might hear something to his advantage. Johanson looked at Mrs. Furkins kindly and told her, as simply as though he were speaking to Billy Longstaffe, what were his ideas of the matter. He told her that whatever she'd done (and he was sure that she had done a lot of things that she'd better not have done) that no hell was eternal, that everything was always changing and that he believed that Mrs. Furkins would find that physical death made very little difference to her condition. She would have to mend her ways after she was dead and set about being a little more useful and a little less harmful to others. There would probably be people to help her, and she would have to work a lot harder than she had hitherto done.

On the other hand she would be stronger and would be rid of all the mess that drink had for so many years been making of her. He might be wrong about other things, but there would be no fire and no pincers. That he could promise her.

Mrs. Furkins raised herself in her bed and smiled triumphantly at the three witches. What had she told them? This feller knew more than all the rest of Polchester together, parsons and all. She sank back on her grubby pillow with a mutter of relief and, then and there, passed away.

It was now the turn of Rufus and the old women. Johanson found the smell of the room overpowering. He moved to the door, opened it, and, to his amazement, found the rickety staircase crowded with figures. They had not, I suppose, come into the room of the dying woman because they were held back by some sort of superstition. They were waiting for him outside.

While he stood there peering into the dusk, Rufus slipped out beside him and vanished down the stairs.

His first thought must have been that they were all going to some function on the upper floor. Young Husky, to whom some of these details are due, says that he stood back as though expecting them to pass.

Then some woman's voice shouted: "There 'e is, the bloody furriner," and some one raised a lantern. In this flickering light Husky recognised one or two faces that meant trouble.

He whispered: "I'd go back inside, guvnor, for a bit, I would," and was, I've no doubt, considerably tempted to go back himself, but the thought of the corpse, maybe, kept him where he was. Then one of the witches came to the door and screeched out: "She's gone. Carrie Furkins' gone!" and then some man from the stairs shouted back:

"Then 'e's murdered 'er, that's what 'e's done. Throw 'im into the river."

So far young Husky is clear. After that there is much confusion. It must have been at the sound of those cries that Johanson realised at last that he was in the hands of his enemies and that his enemies intended mischief.

From what he said to Longstaffe I believe that, until this moment, he fancied that that fight of his had won him favour with the Seatown ruffians. And so it might have done had it not been for Hogg and others, who had for months been working behind his back. But I believe that it was honestly now for the first time that he realised that these men really hated him and meant to hurt him if they could.

He stood without moving at the turn of the stairs and spoke to them. He asked them what the matter was, what they had against him.

At that there was a kind of rush up the stairs at him. Men pushed from below, there was a great deal of shouting, men's and women's voices confused. The lantern vanished and everything was dim and half seen.

Several men made for him at once. He tried to hold them off from him, but one of them fell backwards down the stairs and dragged Johanson with him. At that the brutal mob-instinct was roused, and tumbling, cursing, hitting out blindly, shouting, they were all pell-mell together.

There was a sort of struggle in the passage and then they were out through the door into the street. Here, under the starlight and the moon, everything was clearer and there are several witnesses to what followed.

He was seen to rise from his knees and with a great lift of his shoulders and arms thrust several men from him. For a moment he stood clear, and if then he had turned and run I have no doubt but that he could have escaped. He was pretty sorely hurt by then. One cheek was bleeding severely, his coat and waistcoat were gone and his shirt was nearly off his back. He was angry now, breathing hard, his head back and his eyes, one woman said, "all fiery." In any case he was in a rage and he caught one man who went for him a blow that landed him gasping up against the wall. Then they were on him again, four, five, six of them. The struggle was quite silent now, only muttering and curses. Slowly he sank down, disappeared, then was up again, was raised for a moment above them all. His face was now bleeding in many places. Then some one threw a stone, which hit him on the side of the head. Once more they were all around him; they were moving him to the river wall. He seemed to be struggling very feebly. In the dim light it was all shadowy, not men but ghosts of men and all working in silence.

They were raising him slowly, and just as his body touched the top of the wall he made another struggle but weakly, his head moving aimlessly from side to side as though he did not know what he was doing. The narrator of this part of the struggle could see then that he was almost naked, but his trousers were all about his feet, so that he was trussed in them helplessly.

He was above the wall, men striking at his body, some figure leaping up at him like a maniac and trying to tear at his hair.

For an instant of time he appeared in the starlight as though he were standing on the river wall.

His knees were bent but otherwise he seemed to be standing there quite naked and gigantic: this observer said that he was clear in the starlight for a moment, his arms moving, his bare chest heaving, his thighs rising as though against a gigantic weight. He raised his hand, he cried something, and there must have been something triumphant in his cry because afterwards it was said by several that he shouted victoriously as though he had beaten the lot.

Then he vanished back into the rushing stream of water.

A woman burst out screaming, and the shadows vanished like smoke.

CHAPTER VI

MISS MIDGELEY REVISITS . . .

I HAVE been asked to give, with what circumstantial detail I can, an account of a day spent by me in Polchester in the month of October 1913.

I am very glad indeed to do this, just as I have been only too glad to offer certain extracts from my journals.

Well, to begin my little narrative. Late in the month of September of that year, 1913, I went down to Drymouth to stay there with a woman friend. I had been working all through the summer in London at a book for whose progress the use of the British Museum was essential. Any one who has been compelled to use that reading-room through the summer months, day after day, will sympathise with the condition of fatigue and brain-exhaustion in which by the middle of September I found myself.

When, therefore, this chance of a holiday in the south of England presented itself I eagerly snatched at it. I had left Polchester shortly after Johanson's death in 1907 and I had never returned. One of my intentions now was to make a journey over to Polchester one day from Drymouth and see how the old place looked.

This intention was doubly strengthened when I read one morning the following in *The Western Morning News*:

A POLCHESTER CELEBRATION

On October 7 will be formally opened by the Mayor of Polchester the new street of houses facing the Pol.

This street is to be known as Riverside Street, and it promises to be one of the finest streets in Glebeshire, bordered, as it is, by the waters of the Pol and faced by a beautiful bank of rising fields and woods.

For many Polcastrians October 7 will be a significant day. Formerly the site now occupied by the new street was covered with one of the worst slums in Great Britain, long felt by the citizens of Polchester to be a scandal utterly unworthy of this Cathedral city's great traditions.

Many efforts were made to rid the town of this eyesore, but no effective steps were taken until a shameful riot on October 7, 1907, opened the eyes of every one to the urgency of the matter. It is felt, therefore, that the civic ceremony could not take place more fittingly than on October 7, just six years after the original disturbance.

The civic ceremony, which will take place at ten-thirty in the morning, will be followed by a service at the Cathedral, at which it is hoped that all the Cathedral dignitaries will be present. This will be succeeded by a luncheon in the Town Hall.

After the formal opening of the new street by the Mayor, a tablet to the memory of a foreign resident of the town who lost his life in the riot of 1907 will be unveiled.

Here was exciting news for me! Then Harmer John had come into his own at last!

My friend saw that I was moved beyond my usual habit and enquired the reason. I may say that it is not often that anything in this amazingly unoriginal world can excite me. I told her no more than that on October 6 I would pay a visit to Polchester, returning by evening train on October 7. She offered to accompany me, and I told her I would see her to Paradise first. No, this little trip I must accomplish alone.

It was at first my idea that I would sleep that night of October 6 under the roof of my old friend Mrs. Penethen, with whom at irregular intervals during these years I had corresponded. But, considering the matter further, I decided that "The Three Feathers" should have the honour of offering me a bed. Old friends not seen in the flesh for six years are apt to be unexpectedly difficult. You try to pick up the old threads and behold! they were snapped long ago!

Nor am I now, in my selfish old age, very easy for anybody, nor, what is more, do I wish to be. I have spent years of my life in trying to be pleasant to unagreeable people and I cannot see, on looking back, that the results at all justified the efforts.

No, I could see Mrs. Penethen and myself sitting one on either side of that vast kitchen fire-place staring at one another and twisting our brains for suitable subjects of conversation. Horrible. The indifferent silence of "The Three Feathers" infinitely preferable.

On the afternoon of October 6 I packed my little bag and took my place in the slow train that through the long hours would, unless for some mysterious reason it changed its dull mind, drag its length across the flats of north Glebeshire.

My last flatterer! Is it unnatural that I should cherish his memory? How many times during these years in London, when life has seemed so dry and sterile, have I longed for him to burst in with his enthusiasm, his eagerness, his hope! Just to see him sit down at the table and deliver to me his latest idea, and then to see him wait for my reply, so eagerly, so confidently, so certain that it must be true what I say; and, in face of that eagerness and confidence, how often did I examine my little stock and feel almost shy of producing such shabby goods. But not shabby to him! Nothing was shabby to him. Bad or good, yes, but everything radiant with a bright, fresh colour, as though the sun had risen on this old world for the first time yesterday.

It was raining at Polchester when, at last, my train consented to arrive. Safe in "The Three Feathers" I was quite excited to see once again in the hotel lounge the wall-paper with the yellow chrysanthemums, the copy of Frith's "Railway Station" and the large, red vases with the everlastings. The same waiter, too, with the thin, pale face, the red nose and the stammer—and then from some mysterious, magical distance the sounding through all the fortresses of wall-paper of the Cathedral chimes, so that I could see as I bent over the flickering fire the tall High Street shining under the lamps in the rain, the dark dignity of the Arden Gate, the heavy mass of the Cathedral walls. I had a book with me, I remember, that was just the thing for my mood, Zack's *On Trial*, a magical thing, the kind of book that I should have liked to write had I genius, throbbing in every page with just that same passion for creating beauty that was also Harmer John's. And as I went up to bed and heard the rain hissing on the panes and saw the stuffed birds under their glass, and caught the faint click of the billiard balls from the floor below me, I seemed, for a moment, to revive the thirst for life that old age, disappointment in my fellow human beings, and the reading-room of the British Museum had almost robbed me of.

In the morning the weather was lovely, a blue sky without stain and a nice smell made of burning autumn leaves below my window, rashers of bacon coming up to meet me in the hall and the naked shiveriness of the oil-cloth on the stairs.

I was told by my friend the waiter that every one would be at the opening, and that I must go early if I wanted a good place, so at ten o'clock down the hill I went.

Most of the town went with me, and, as it seemed to me, a gayer, happier crowd than it would have been in the old days. It was, perhaps, the brightness of the day. In any case the old town was very much alive.

And so I reached the new street. And what did I think of it? Well, it was hideously ugly, so ugly that, at my first sight of it, had I been younger and more open to illusions I should have turned my head aside and cried. Heavens! This was what my Harmer John had made, he with his dream of avenues and statues and noble buildings with fountains playing! Yes, hideous—but I am sure, after all, a vast improvement on that terrible old Seatown slum. No slum here any more. The neat, sober houses each dressed in that dull, grey stone that is my especial detestation, each with his two windows decorated with nice overhanging slate eyebrows, each with his grey ears pricking up to heaven so neatly in their appropriate places. Oh! the ugliness of that street! But there was a fine, smooth road in front of the little houses, a mild, grey stone wall and the river Pol beyond—that last, at least, as it had ever been.

All so clean, so neat and comfortable. Every little house with its bath (h. and c.) and its excellent sanitary arrangement, a little garden back and front to every house. No slums any more and no old inhabitants of the slums either. Whither had they all fled, those ghosts of the sinister past? Hiding in the caves of the sea and the hollows of the Glebeshire valleys? Or all reformed with clean faces and clean collars, forming part of this handsome crowd that pressed in on every side?

No time for more speculation. On a platform in front of us (we were all packed together at the street end), behind a table covered with a red cloth, stood the dignitaries of the town. I recognised some of them. Why, cheery

Mildmay, the auctioneer, was mayor, and very happy in his handsome robes he looked, and there, on either side of him, a little aged but only a little, were Mortimer Shandon and Ben Eagle, Cassidy, gigantic Carlyon and Massing of the Post Office. No sign anywhere of my old friend Mr. Hogg.

Some of the Cathedral folk also. Pretty Lady St. Leath with her stout, amiable husband, Mrs. Sampson, Mrs. Ryle and, of course, my adored Mrs. Bond. How amusing to see them all again! To see them still here, leading apparently the same lives, busied in the same interests, while I had been lost in that London turmoil, forgetting their very existence.

Whether it was in some fashion like coming home again, I don't know, but they appeared to me a kindly-faced, generous-minded little group—I liked to fancy—so sentimental was I at the moment—that some of this was Harmer John's doing.

So sentimental was I that I thought quite highly of old Mildmay's speech. I don't remember now a word of what he said, but I can see him still in my eye all flushed and cheerful, taking every bit of the work upon himself, quite complacent about everything. So were we all. Myself was complacent. I stamped the ground with my umbrella, shouted "Hear! Hear!" with the rest, and congratulated myself most warmly for this fine improvement in our dear old town.

The sun was now shining fully upon the row of self-conscious houses, and that was an excellent thing, because we could not see them without hurting our eyes, and so did not look at them, and so were able to shout "Hear! Hear!" more convincingly than ever.

Then it was all over, and, in a great surging mass, we moved up the street.

I was lucky in this, that having been on the outskirts of the first ceremony I was one of the earliest to move up the street for the second.

This second ceremony was, of course, the unveiling of the tablet to Harmer John. There we all stood in the broad space just in front of the house where, during the last months of his life, he had lived, staring at that beautiful view that he had so greatly loved.

Staring also at his fountain. There it was, I very close to it, kept from it only by some railings, looking so brave and handsome and noble in the sun, the dark, friendly tree standing over it, the old grey wall behind it. And on the grey wall was a little brass tablet, covered at present by a white cloth. By this time I was, let me at once confess it, very considerably excited—excited as I had never been in all the last six years. And how delightfully was my excitement increased when I found that Lady St. Leath was to perform here the ceremony!

She came, smiling so prettily, into the enclosure, stood under the tree, and then facing so, blushing a little, made a speech. It was a very small one, but most honest and sincere. What she said was that she had scarcely known Hjalmar Johanson, and that she regretted now, as many others do, that she had not. She said that he was a real lover of their town, and that his only thought had been to serve it, but that, by many people, he had not been understood.

They were all ashamed now of their mistake, and because they were ashamed they had subscribed together (and she would like to say that subscriptions had come in from all parts of the town) and put up this tablet. She pulled a string and the simple record stood there:

HJALMAR JOHANSON,
FRIEND OF THIS TOWN,
DIED OCTOBER VII. MCMVII.

Every one clapped and Mr. Cassidy made a sentimental speech, to which I did not listen.

Every one moved up the hill to the Cathedral service. I stayed there a while quietly by myself.

I went later to pay my call on my old friend Mrs. Penethen. I found her alone, in the old kitchen, and very much the same as six years before I had left her. She was surprised, of course, to see me, and pleased, I think—pleased if I did not stay too long.

I sat down and we talked very happily together for an hour or so.

She had not gone down to the ceremony, she said. I gathered that she found this new Johanson legend pretty absurd. They were as false now about him, she implied, as they had been before when they threw stones at him. She said, however, very little about him—one interesting thing, though, in connection with Maude. I asked, of course, very soon about that young woman. Mrs. Penethen replied drily that she was as well as could be expected. Was she happy? No, she was not, and never would be. But she ruled her husband, I gathered, with complete severity. Mrs. Penethen also told me that after her marriage she had fought a ferocious battle with the mother-in-law, fought it and won. Mrs. Boultewood, senior, had retired to Buquay, where she sat in a lodging-house and counted her money.

Had Maude, I ventured to enquire, quite forgotten Johanson? Forgotten him? No. Indeed, she had not. She had the maddest idea: she thought that he was not dead.

"Not dead!" I cried. "But that's lunacy." Yes, it was lunacy, Mrs. Penethen agreed, but lunacy or no that was Maude's idea.

Absurd beyond anything, I continued, because if ever in the world any one lived who would show himself and return to those he loved it was Johanson.

Mrs. Penethen agreed entirely. It was all silly foolishness, but many besides Maude had the same idea—ignorant people, of course. There were stories. He had been seen in the woods above Orange Street, on Parmiter's Field, he had haunted the disappearing ruins of the old Seatown. "Always laughing, always jolly, they say he is. I wouldn't think," continued Mrs. Penethen, "anything at all about it if it didn't disturb Maude so. But the girl's always thinking about it, expecting him to turn up one day."

No, the body had never been found. That was why his death could not be brought home to any individual. The scandal, however, had been terrific (as I could myself remember) and Hogg had been forced to leave the place. No one had intended, of course, that the attack on Johanson should go as far as it did, but that was the way of these things. You couldn't tell where they would end.

Canon Ronder's reputation, Mrs. Penethen told me, had suffered greatly in the affair. He had done nothing wrong exactly, but that he should have mixed at all in such company was considered very damaging. He took now a less prominent part in the town's life. He had grown extremely stout. There was talk of his retiring to a country living.

So passed a very pleasant hour. We had, each of us, our memories, and these we mutually respected. She was relieved, I think, when having invited me to share her midday meal I refused, saying that I had some sandwiches with me, and on this lovely day intended to sun myself on the hill. So we parted with friendly feelings and guilty of no indiscretions afterwards to be regretted.

And going down the street whom should I encounter but Judy Penethen? Aged greatly, growing strangely like her mother, dark, reserved, kindly. It was hard for me, as I stood there exchanging commonplaces with her, to believe in that day when she had stood there in my room telling me that she loved Johanson.

It had been so, nevertheless, and although she did not mention him, yet, strangely, in her quiet demeanour, I felt a deep, deep reserved force still of passionate feeling. Of the four women in that house who each in her own way cared for that man, Judy had been the one who truly loved him, who would always love him, I did not doubt, for the remainder of her repressed, reserved life.

It was her slim, stern figure that, more than any other I have in these later days remembered.

Nevertheless, once up in the woods above the town, sitting on a bank under a canopy of gold and amber leaves, feeling the sun beat warm upon me, I soon forgot Judy.

I forgot everything and every one save Harmer John! I thought of him with eager longing. Could I but see him for a moment again and tell him that, through all these years, I had not forgotten him!

Was he perchance somewhere about his beloved town on this day when every one was praising him? or, like Arnold's gipsy:
At some lone homestead in the Cumner hills,
Where at her open door the housewife darns,
Thou hast been seen, or hanging on a gate
To watch the threshers in the mossy barns.
Children, who early range these slopes and late
For cresses from the rills,
Have known thee eyeing, all an April day,
The springing pastures and the feeding kine;
And marked thee, when the stars come out and shine,
Through the long dewy grass move slow away.

I repeated the beloved words to myself, nibbling also at my sandwiches. The blue intensity of the sky and the thick gold of the autumn wood, the still crystal air and the beauty of the so familiar poetry, brought me an exquisite mood of silence and tranquillity.

I sat there, without moving, as it were in a state of happy trance. Then—was it sleep, was it fancy, how shall I ever know and who will there be ever to tell me?—did the leaves part, the branches spring aside and a face, so familiar, so gay, glance through at me! Did I, for a moment of time, see him head to foot, strong and happy as he used to be, there between the branches smiling at me with all his old humour and friendliness?

I called out "Harmer John! Harmer John!"

Of course there was no answer. The sun was in my eyes. I had been asleep perhaps, or my desire for him had created him for an instant before my eyes.

And yet I feel, to this very day, as though I had seen him once more. I seem to remember that his face was older, thinner, stiffer than it used to be, that the sleeve of his coat was brown and ragged. How should I know these things?

I brushed the crumbs from my dress, burned the paper that had held my sandwiches (How I detest the untidy, messy ways of the modern generation!) and set off on the path down to Polchester.

THE END

Made in the USA
Las Vegas, NV
23 September 2024

95674312R00148